Essential
Statistics

Essential
Statistics
for
Public Managers and
Policy Analysts

Third Edition

Evan M. Berman, Ph.D.

XiaoHu Wang, Ph.D.

Los Angeles | London | New Delhi
Singapore | Washington DC

Los Angeles | London | New Delhi
Singapore | Washington DC

For information:

CQ Press
An Imprint of SAGE Publications, Inc.
2455 Teller Road
Thousand Oaks, California 91320
E-mail: order@sagepub.com

SAGE Publications Ltd.
1 Oliver's Yard
55 City Road
London, EC1Y 1SP
United Kingdom

SAGE Publications India Pvt. Ltd.
B 1/I 1 Mohan Cooperative Industrial Area
Mathura Road, New Delhi 110 044
India

SAGE Publications Asia-Pacific Pte. Ltd.
33 Pekin Street #02-01
Far East Square
Singapore 048763

Acquisitions Editor: Charisse Kiino
Production Editor: Elizabeth Kline
Copy Editor: Amy Marks
Typesetter: C&M Digitals (P) Ltd
Proofreader: Barbara Johnson
Indexer: Jean Casalegno
Cover Designer: Visualization
Marketing Manager: Chris O'Brien

Printed in the United States of America

Library of Congress Cataloging-in-Publication Data

Berman, Evan M.

Essential statistics for public managers and policy analysts/
Evan M. Berman, XiaoHu Wang. — 3rd ed.

p. cm.

ISBN 978-1-60871-677-7 (alk. paper)

1. Public administration—Statistical methods. 2. Policy sciences—
Statistical methods. I. Wang, XiaoHu, 1962- II. Title.

HA29.B425 2012
519.5—dc23   2011040925

This book is printed on acid-free paper.

12 13 14 15 16 10 9 8 7 6 5 4 3 2

CONTENTS

Section IV: Inferential Statistics

Chapter 10
HYPOTHESIS TESTING WITH CHI-SQUARE

Chapter 11
MEASURES OF ASSOCIATION

Chapter 12
THE T-TEST

Tables, Figures, and Boxes

TABLES

FIGURES

"IN GREATER DEPTH . . . " BOXES

PREFACE

This third edition of *Essential Statistics for Public Managers and Policy Analysts* continues the positive features of the previous editions: brevity, straightforward instruction, and hands-on application. Professors who teach statistics know well the challenge of balancing teaching of statistical concepts with practical applications that students value and the development of data analysis skills. This third edition, like the previous ones, continues to provide professors with a flexible approach that helps them find the right balance. It is designed both for courses that cover statistics in a separate, single term, as well as those that combine statistics with research methods over two semesters. Professors can pick and choose from material in ways that help them construct and teach the course that is best for them. Professors can bring in their own material, too. We hope that instructors who have used past editions will find that this revision improves on, but does not alter, the strengths at the core of this approach. *Essential Statistics* continues to offer a conceptual understanding of statistics that can be applied readily to the real-life challenges of public administrators and policy analysts. Key ideas are presented in a concise manner which has now helped make Essential Statistics one of the leading texts for the course.

This third edition has benefited greatly from user feedback, which has led to the following improvements:

- This edition introduces a coauthor, XiaoHu Wang, who is well-known in the field and who brings a wealth of experience and applications in the area of performance management, budgeting, and finance. Many students desire these applications, and his skills nicely complement Evan Berman's, providing an even more rounded approach.
- Chapter 9 ("Getting Results") is new. It offers readers further guidance on doing basic, descriptive analysis. This also helps students and professors to get more from spreadsheet applications.

- Chapter 13 is new, now discussing ANOVA as a separate topic. Professors can freely choose the extent to which they want to cover this topic.
- Material on performance management was added throughout Section III, extending and applying the previous focus on performance measurement. Numerous minor improvements were made, for example, in the discussions of key concepts and applications such as standard deviation, and we added a few more concepts, as well.
- We strengthened the design features of this package that give it flexibility. The textbook remains useful as a standalone textbook, independent of the workbook exercises. Similarly, the workbook continues to be usable regardless of one's commitment to any software package.

The conceptual and hands-on approach followed in *Essential Statistics* is increasingly popular among students and professors alike. The success of this book confirms that people want a practical approach to doing and using analysis. The increasing availability of user-friendly and affordable statistical software has ended much of the rationale for doing hand calculations. On all but rare occasions, the text restricts hand calculations to situations in which they strengthen and enhance students' understanding of basic statistical concepts. The text presents the assumptions, purposes, and applications of statistics, illustrated by real-world examples and numerous tables, charts, and graphs. Learning objectives start off each chapter, and key terms are set bold italic in the text and listed at the end of chapters for quick and easy review. Because students have limited time and demand a high degree of practical application, this book quickly gets to the point and shows them multiple applications they will need on the job. It also includes several "In Greater Depth . . ." features and "Getting Started" and "Key Point" boxes that quickly point students in useful directions.

This book is for both one- and two-semester courses. If the program requirement is for a separate course on statistics, the instructor may want to exclude some of the new material on research methods. Yet those early chapters may serve as a handy refresher for students. If the program requirement combines quantitative methods with research methods, then the section on research methods will likely be a welcome feature. Such courses may skip some of the later chapters in the book that address advanced topics on inferential statistics. The additional datasets and exercises help strengthen both types of courses.

Finally, globalization and internationalization mean that U.S. professors sometimes go abroad. Since the last edition, Evan moved from Louisiana State University to National Chengchi University—Taiwan's top social sciences university. XiaoHu recently moved from the University of Central Florida to the City University of Hong Kong—one of Asia-Pacific's premier research programs in public administration. Statistics and public administration are not limited to the United States, of course. Yet, U.S. professors and students should rest assured that we are firmly committed to meeting their needs and requirements, including for NASPAA accreditation (even as sales of this book are increasingly growing outside the United States, too).

A UNIQUE LEARNING PACKAGE

This textbook is part of a unique resource set consisting of several valuable teaching tools. Developed in tandem with one another, each piece has been crafted as part of a larger learning package to enhance and reinforce lessons learned in the classroom.

Exercising Essential Statistics

The accompanying workbook complements the textbook. Its aim is to strengthen students' learning and extend their ability to apply the material from the text, offering them opportunities to practice through carefully crafted exercises. This third edition of *Exercising Essential Statistics* contains even more exercises for students to work through, with an average of twenty-eight per chapter. Corresponding directly to the core text, workbook chapters cover the same learning objectives and consist of four parts that facilitate learning, testing, and application. The first part, "Q & A," identifies key learning points in a question-and-answer format to help students test their comprehension. The second part, "Critical Thinking," contains open-ended questions designed to stimulate students' thinking and deepen their insight. The questions carry the material one step further and are excellent for in-class teaching, discussion sections, and homework assignments. The third part, "Data-Based Exercises," includes computer-based applications that use the datasets provided on the CD-ROM included with the workbook. These exercises will help students get comfortable working with data. The fourth section, "Further Readings," lists other books, resources, and examples for anyone interested in further research. Workbook pages are perforated and three-hole punched so that students can easily turn in work for credit and later save them for reference.

The datasets reflect students' and professors' preferences for real-life data that shed light on important problems and issues that arise when working with data. The datasets cover experiences of the public and nonprofit sectors. They are based on employee and citizen surveys as well as environmental, welfare, and public safety data. This third edition includes new datasets, such as quality-of-life indicators for cities and data relevant to nonprofit organizations. In a few instances, plausible hypothetical data are used. The sets include both cross-sectional and time series data. They contain complete documentation, including survey instruments, which many readers will find useful. Data are provided in Excel, SPSS, Stata, SAS, and SYSTAT formats so that students can access these sets with a range of software programs. Recognizing the widespread use of Excel and PASW/SPSS, the workbook includes chapters on Excel and using SPSS. The last chapter of the workbook provides documentation for the datasets on the CD-ROM.

The workbook and datasets span a wide range of areas and are designed to support integration with other areas of study in master's degree programs in public policy and in public administration. The workbook covers many examples from human resources management, organizational behavior, budgeting, and public policy. The problems are written with those students in mind who have not yet taken these courses. In addition, the datasets are quite extensive, enabling professors to develop additional applications in the areas they choose to emphasize.

Instructor's Resources

A complete suite of instructor's resources—created by the authors—are available to adopters. Homework assignments, test questions, PowerPoint lecture slides, sample syllabi, and a solutions manual to the workbook's exercises will help lessen class prep time and assist with teaching. To access these resources, please go to http://college.cqpress.com/sites/berman/ to register and download materials.

ACKNOWLEDGMENTS

As always, numerous people contributed to this project. We would like to thank Charisse Kiino, publisher, for her unwavering support for this project; no author could wish for more support or a better technical team. Amy Marks provided some of the very best editing an author could have, and Elizabeth Kline did a superb job with production. The authors also thank numerous assistants who helped in various ways, as well as the academic reviewers who generously pointed out improvement opportunities: Joel Elvery, Cleveland State University; Gerry Gianakis, Suffolk University; Ray Gonzales, University of Southern California; Jack Huddleston, University of Wisconsin, Madison; David Ivers, Eastern Michigan University; Matthew Jones, Portland State University; Naim Kapucu, University of Central Florida; and Yahong Zhang, Rutgers University, Newark. Despite all the help that we received, the authors reluctantly accept that any remaining errors are ours alone. In addition, we give special thanks to the faculty and administrators at our universities, past and present, as well as numerous practitioners with whom we have worked over the years. We remain impressed by their professionalism and commitment to public administration. Evan Berman continues to be indebted to Professors Jonathan West and Bill Werther (both of the University of Miami) for enriching his early career in more ways than can be enumerated here, and he also thanks Chung-Yuang Jan of NCCU (Taiwan) for enormous support and encouragement in recent years. Both Evan and XiaoHu are greatly endebted to their spouses, Dira and Yan, for support and much more. Finally, we want to thank hundreds and hundreds of former students who indirectly contributed to this book through their feedback. They have never been shy in expressing themselves.

Evan M. Berman, evanmberman@gmail.com
XiaoHu Wang

Statistics Roadmap

Starting Point

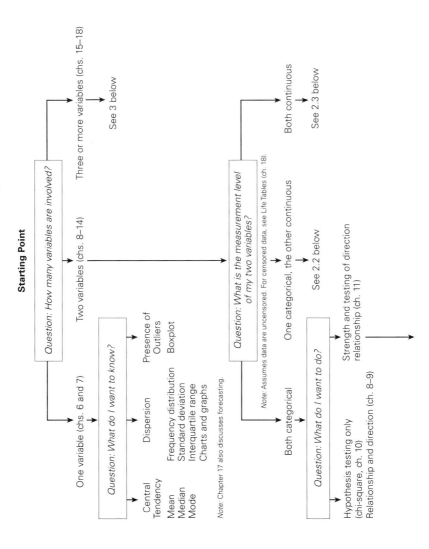

Question: How many variables are involved?

One variable (chs. 6 and 7)

Two variables (chs. 8–14)

Three or more variables (chs. 15–18)

Question: What do I want to know?

Central Tendency	Dispersion	Presence of Outliers
Mean	Frequency distribution	Boxplot
Median	Standard deviation	
Mode	Interquartile range	
	Charts and graphs	

Note: Chapter 17 also discusses forecasting.

Question: What is the measurement level of my two variables?

Both categorical

One categorical, the other continuous

Both continuous

Note: Assumes data are uncensored. For censored data, see Life Tables (ch. 18).

Question: What do I want to do?

Hypothesis testing only (chi-square, ch. 10)

Relationship and direction (ch. 8–9)

Strength and testing of direction relationship (ch. 11)

See 2.2 below

See 2.3 below

See 3 below

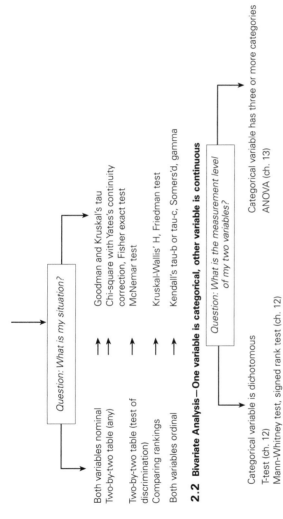

Question: What is my situation?

Both variables nominal
Two-by-two table (any) → Goodman and Kruskal's tau
→ Chi-square with Yates's continuity correction, Fisher exact test

Two-by-two table (test of discrimination) → McNemar test

Comparing rankings → Kruskal-Wallis' H, Friedman test

Both variables ordinal → Kendall's tau-b or tau-c, Somers'd, gamma

2.2 Bivariate Analysis—One variable is categorical, other variable is continuous

Question: What is the measurement level of my two variables?

Categorical variable is dichotomous
T-test (ch. 12)
Mann-Whitney test, signed rank test (ch. 12)

Categorical variable has three or more categories
ANOVA (ch. 13)

2.3 Bivariate Analysis—Both variables are continuous

Question: What is the measurement level of my two variables?

Both variables are continuous (not rankings)
Pearson's correlation coefficient
Simple regression (ch. 14)

Both variables represent rankings
Spearman's rank correlation coefficient (ch. 14)

3. Multivariate Analysis (ch. 15—18)

Question: What is my situation?

One continuous dependent variable
Multiple regression (ch. 15)

One dichotomous dependent variable
Logistic regression (ch. 16)

Time series data
Time series regression
Forecasting (ch. 17)

More than one dependent variable
Path analysis, SEM, MANOVA (ch. 18)

Introduction

For many professionals and students, past experiences with statistics often have been less than fully satisfying—perhaps nightmares best forgotten. This is both unfortunate and increasingly unnecessary. This book, now in its third edition, is guided by the underlying philosophy that statistics is an enterprise that is both practical and increasingly easy. Modern advances in computers and software have reduced the importance of hand calculations, allowing students to work readily with real-life applications. Conceptual understanding and application are central to statistics, not arithmetic and cumbersome calculations!

For public managers and analysts, this book shows how to apply the principles and practices of statistics to problems of public management and policy analysis. Whether through program evaluation; policy analysis; performance measurement or management; or program client, citizen, or employee surveys, statistics offers public managers and policy analysts ample opportunities for "speaking truth to power."[1] In doing so, these professionals inform public discourse and add value to democratic processes at all levels of government. Data and analysis can also make programs more effective and efficient, reaching more people and serving them better. The ability to analyze data will enhance students' skills and help further their careers.

This book is part of a set that consists of

- A textbook: *Essential Statistics for Public Managers and Policy Analysts*
- A workbook: *Exercising Essential Statistics,* which includes
  - Exercises with applications in public management and policy analysis
  - A CD with datasets and presentations in various formats

The textbook can be used apart from the workbook (it stands alone), and the workbook, while assuming the use of a statistical software package for analysis, is not committed to any particular software. All these materials include features that make it easier to understand statistics and to benefit from its application. The textbook is written in an accessible, direct, and economical style. A flow-chart located in the front of the book, called the "Statistics Roadmap," is a quick reference tool that will help guide readers to choose the correct statistical method for their research. From there, eighteen chapters build upon each other, taking the reader from the very fundamentals of research design all the way through advanced statistics. Each chapter begins with a list of learning objec-tives—the skills and concepts students can expect to know when they have fin-ished reading. Key terms are shown in bold italic and are listed at the end of each chapter for easy reference.

The workbook extends conceptual understanding through application of statistics principles, drawing on the practical problems of managers. Chapters 1 through 21 of the workbook correspond to the equivalent chap-ters in the textbook and are organized in five parts: "Q & A" reinforces key learning points and assists in test preparation; "Critical Thinking" stimulates insight into statistics principles; "Data-Based Exercises" emphasizes hands-on skill-building and additional applications; and "Suggested Readings" recommends books for further study in areas of interest. The workbook is an integral part of this set and is recommended.

The datasets on the CD are based largely on real-life data and include employee and citizen surveys. They also cover topics of environmental, welfare, and public safety interest and are relevant to all levels of govern-ment. Chapter 21 of the workbook contains complete documentation for the datasets, including survey instruments that can be tailored to students' own situations. Data are provided in Excel and PASW/SPSS and other formats for use in other software packages. The workbook also includes a tutorial for using SPSS and advanced Excel features. The CD has some useful bonus material, too, such as examples of reports.

The workbook, together with these datasets, teaches students how to apply statistics to practical problems in the real world. Students will also discover the principles that allow them to go beyond these examples to specific problems they encounter in the workplace. After using this learning package, readers will see not only how practical and easy statistics can be but also how the effective use of statistics can help them.

We'd like to hear from you. The textbook, the workbook, and the CD reflect decades of feedback from other professionals and students. Don't be shy. Let us know what features you like and what should be improved upon. Now, let's get started!

Evan M. Berman (evanmberman@gmail.com)
XiaoHu Wang

Note

1. This phrase is borrowed from the classic work of Aaron Wildavsky, *Speaking Truth to Power* (Boston: Little, Brown, 1979).

Why Statistics for Public Managers and Analysts?

CHAPTER OBJECTIVES

After reading this chapter, you should be able to

- Appreciate the importance of using data in public management and policy analysis
- Identify levels of competency and proficiency in data analysis
- Describe strategies for increasing proficiency in data analysis
- Understand the importance of ethical principles in data analysis

ROLE OF DATA IN PUBLIC MANAGEMENT

Why research? Why statistics? The ethos of public management is to "go out and make a difference," not to sit behind a desk and crunch numbers. Public managers often join agencies because they seek to serve and help their communities and country. Not surprisingly, some managers are puzzled by the suggestion of engaging in research and statistics: research appears boring in comparison with developing and implementing new programs, and statistics seems, well, impossibly challenging with little payoff in sight.

In fact, analytical techniques involving research and statistics are increasingly in demand. Many decisions that public and nonprofit managers make involve data and analysis, one way or another. Consider the following common **uses of analysis and data**:

First, data and objective analysis often are used to *describe and analyze problems*, such as the magnitude of environmental disasters (for example, oil spills), the extent of social and public health problems (such as homelessness or the AIDS epidemic), the extent of lawlessness, the level of economic prosperity or stagnation, or the impact of weather-related problems such as brought on by hurricanes and snowstorms. For example, it matters whether the illiteracy rate among 12 year olds is 3 percent or 30 percent, or somewhere in between. By describing the extent of these problems and their underlying causes accurately, managers are able to better formulate effective strategies for dealing with them. Policy analysis often begins by describing the extent and characteristics of problems and the factors associated with them.

Second, data are used to *describe policies and programs.* What are programs and policies expected to achieve? How many services are programs expected to provide? What are some milestones of achievement? How much will a program cost? These questions involve quantifiable answers, such as the number of national guardsmen brought in to assist with search and rescue efforts after a major hurricane, or the number of evacuees for whom officials expect to provide refuge. Policies and programs can be described in quite detailed ways, involving distinct program activities, the duration and geographic scope of activities, and staffing levels and area program budget data.

Third, programs produce much routine, administrative data that are used to *monitor progress and prevent fraud*. For example, hospitals produce a large amount of data about patient visits, who attended them, their diagnosis, billing codes, and so on. Schools produce vast amounts of data about student achievement, student conduct, extracurricular activities, support and administrative services, and so on. Regulatory programs produce data about inspections and compliance. In many states, gaming devices (such as slot machines) are monitored electronically to ensure that taxes are collected and that they are not tampered with. Administrative data assist in monitoring programs, and managers are expected to be familiar with these data.

Fourth, analysis is used to guide and *improve program operations.* Data can be brought to bear on problems that help managers choose among competing strategies. For example, what-if analysis might be used to determine the cost-effectiveness of alternative courses of action. Such analysis often is tailored to unique situations and problems. In addition, client and citizen surveys might be used to inform program priorities by assessing population needs and service satisfaction. Systematic surveys provide valid and objective assessments of citizen and client needs, priorities, and perceptions of programs and services. Systematic surveys of citizens and clients are used increasingly and are considered a valuable tool of modern management.

Fifth, data are used to *evaluate outcomes*. Legislatures and citizens want to know what return they are getting from their tax dollars. Did programs and policies achieve their aims? Did they produce any unexpected results? Most grant applications require public managers to be accountable for program outcomes. Public managers must demonstrate that their programs are producing effective outcomes and that they are doing so in cost-effective ways. This demand for outcome evaluation and monitoring far exceeds any requirement of proper funds management. Analysis can also be used to determine the impact of different conditions on program effectiveness, leading to suggestions for improving programs.

> **Getting Started**
> How are these uses of data and analysis present in your field?

Data and analysis are omnipresent in programs and policies. They are there at every stage, from the inception of programs and policies, to their very end. Of course, decisions are also based on personal observation, political consensus, anecdotal and impressionistic descriptions, and the ideologies of leaders. Yet data and analysis often are present, too, one way or another. This is because analysis is useful. Specifically, quantitative analysis aids in providing an objective, factual underpinning of situations and responses. Analysis, along with data, helps quantify the extent of problems and solutions in ways that other information seldom can. Analysis can help quantify the actual or likely impact of proposed strategies, for example, helping to determine their adequacy. At the very least, a focus on facts and objective analysis might reduce judgment errors stemming from overly impressionistic or subjective perceptions that are factually incorrect. As a result, managers are expected to bring data and analysis to the decision-making table.

COMPETENCY AND PROFICIENCY

Analysis requires competency and proficiency. The standards of accredited graduate programs in public administration and affairs recognize the importance of quantitative analysis. The accrediting organization for these programs, the *National Association of Schools of Public Affairs and Administration (NASPAA)*, requires that the "common curriculum components shall enhance the student's values, knowledge, and skills to act ethically and effectively in the application of quantitative and qualitative techniques of analysis."

NASPAA further stipulates that such skills should be applied to policy and program formulation, implementation, and evaluation, as well as to other decision-making and problem-solving activities.

Beyond this, at the time of this writing, the ***International Association of Schools and Institutes of Administration (IASIA)*** is planning for future accreditation of international programs, as well, and there is also discussion within NASPAA of providing accreditation for some foreign programs. The IASIA proposed standards of excellence were drafted in cooperation with a United Nations task force[1] and state that curriculum components should include the "application of quantitative and qualitative techniques of analysis" in such areas as "institutional and developmental economics," "policy and program formulation, analysis, implementation and evaluation," "decision-making and problem-solving," and "strategic planning." Other regional associations are also discussing accreditation standards. It seems that competency in quantitative data analysis in public administration and policy analysis has gained international acceptance.

The uses of data and analysis imply the need for six *competencies for analysis*. First, managers and analysts will have to be *familiar with data sources* in their lines of business. They will need to know what data are available and to what uses they are commonly put. For example, are they used for monitoring? For estimating service needs? For determining program efficiency? For describing community conditions? Beyond this, managers will also need to be able to determine the validity of these data and understand their limits. They will need to know whether data have been collected in ways that do not induce additional bias. Finally, managers will need to be able to develop new uses of data, for dealing with situations and problems as they arise.

Second, managers and analysts need competencies to *gather their own data*. Simply, existing data do not always address important issues at hand. For example, they may not be adequate to determine client needs or evaluate programs. The ability to collect new data implies familiarity with and competencies in conducting different types of research, such as archival research, or in conducting scientific population or program client surveys. Many managers value the ability of their staff to conduct these types of research. Client and citizen surveys are increasingly a staple of public management.

Third, public managers and analysts need to be able to *analyze the data*. Without analysis, it is not possible to generate meaningful information about program efficiency and effectiveness, for assessing whether a program is on track and for determining and identifying new client needs. Analysis requires competency in statistics. Analysis must be done in ways that shine light on important problems. It must also be done in ways that are sound, defensible, objective, and consistent with current practice.

Fourth, public managers and analysts need to be able to *communicate their results*. Communication requires the ability to explain complex or abstract concepts in ways that are accessible to different audiences. Results should be explained in simple ways without oversimplifying. Communication also involves effective writing and presentation skills; yes, analysts must also be able to produce clear, professionally looking graphs and charts that communicate their results to a diverse public. Communication is also often used to meet additional objectives of accountability and transparency.

Fifth, analysts must be able to bring to their analysis *the theory and practice of management and policy analysis*. Understanding the specific and unique problems of public and nonprofit programs and their context informs analytical tasks to be carried out. The needs of homeless people in New York City are different from those in Louisiana, as are the priorities of stakeholders and affected publics. Analytical tasks must be infused, from the start, with a clear sense of the specific program and contextual issues; without context or purpose, analysis is a blind exercise in technique only, not connected to purpose.

Sixth, analysts must have a sound and strong sense of *ethics*. Technical skills alone are not enough to ensure soundness of analytical purpose and practice; analysis also requires a commitment to being truthful, complete, mindful, and useful. Ethics affects how analysts and managers approach matters of analysis and communication and how they view the role of research and analysis in their field. Ethics affects which questions analysts and managers ask, and how they deal with them. Ethics is a hallmark of modern professionalism and a key to public service; it is discussed in greater detail in the next section.

These six competencies are to varying degrees grounded in the canons of scientific research and statistics. **Scientific research** is the careful, systematic process of inquiry that leads to the discovery or interpretation of facts, behaviors, and theories. The methods used for scientific research include standards and procedures for gathering, analyzing, and reporting data such as through surveys, focus groups, or archival research. Scientific research is distinguished from personal and other forms of research or inquiry by rather strict standards for accepting new facts and theories as knowledge, and by a process that includes other scientists in making such determinations. Science sets a high standard for what is considered to be valid knowledge. As a branch of science, **statistics** is the body of systematic knowledge and practice that provides standards and procedures for correctly analyzing one's data, and for drawing conclusions from them. Statistics is essential to program evaluation, performance management and forecasting, and underlies many policy recommendations.

Research and statistics provide essential frameworks and language that inform the six competencies described here. Research and statistics provide guidelines for determining what to measure, how to collect data, and how to draw conclusions from data. These guidelines help managers, for example, to evaluate the scientific validity of data, whether they use existing data or gather their own. Indeed, public management data often are incomplete, biased, or inaccurate in some way, and managers need to know how to address these matters. Some problems are correctable, whereas others warrant caveats. Knowledge of these standards can also help managers and analysts avoid problems, such as when they plan to collect their own data. This is not to say that all knowledge or information used by managers meets or should meet scientific standards, but the above competencies, as well as previously mentioned uses of data and analysis, do require careful attention to these matters. Knowledge of scientific standards and research processes, discussed in this book, cannot be ignored without sacrificing credibility.

Students and managers seeking to improve these competencies often experience different *stages of proficiency*. Respectively, these stages might be called the "know nothing," journeyman, technocrat, and sophisticated expert stages. Understanding these stages can help guide one's progress and development activity.

Know Nothing. Many people who are new to public and nonprofit management do not bring with them much background about data in their lines of business, or ways in which data might be used for improving program efficiency. This is not a problem but a fact. A good share of these students are reserved, skeptical, fearful, or even hostile about the uses of data and statistics. Then, they will need to acknowledge these feelings and work to become aware of ways in which data are usefully and correctly applied in management and policy analysis. To get beyond this stage, they will need to obtain a good foundation in research and statistics, and succeed in finding useful examples in each of the five areas of use described earlier.

Journeyman. People in this stage have worked for a few years in their lines of business. As such, they have usually seen some applications and are clear about the utility of data and analysis. They sometimes use data for monitoring program progress. However, lacking research and statistics skills, they often do not see themselves as being qualified to develop broader applications or even to analyze data in relatively simple ways. The purpose of this course is to provide readers with the necessary foundations and skills and to encourage the development of new uses of data and analysis in their lines of business. People at this level are often concerned about communicating their results and methods correctly, and this skill should also be focused on at this stage.

Technocrat. People in this stage have acquired varying levels of technical mastery of research and statistics. Some technocrats are highly skilled, whereas others have only a modest level of ability. A common problem is that technocrats are unable to integrate and guide their analysis with the substantive concerns of program and policies in their lines of business. They might even view themselves as statistics resource persons, rather than as managers and employees tied to specific programs and policies—the fifth competency (relating research and statistics to the theory and practice of management and policy analysis) is missing. The main challenge for technocrats is to learn how to put research and statistics in service of programs and policies. They need to put these substantive concerns on par with the technical analysis.

Sophisticated Expert. People in this stage have found the right balance between the development of policies and programs and the use of objective data and analysis to further decision making. They understand both. Because they have spent several years in their lines of business, they are familiar with the relevant existing data, they know the strengths and weaknesses of these data, they are familiar with a range of applications, and they are able to develop new applications and collect original data. They are well-rounded in the use of data. Sophisticated experts often have a positive orientation toward continuing, professional education. They may challenge themselves by writing articles for scholarly journals and making presentations at conferences.

> **Getting Started**
> At which stage of proficiency do you see yourself today? Which competencies and uses of data and analysis would further your career?

At whatever your stage of proficiency, think of how you can benefit from increased use of data and analysis. Competencies with data and analysis are increasingly used skills in public and nonprofit organizations. Whether positions are analytical, such as in policy analysis, budgeting, or information technology, or people oriented, such as in counseling, human resources, or social services, analytical skills are in demand for analyzing data, conducting surveys, and communicating quantitative findings to a broader audience. Program managers, city managers, and elected officials, too, require a solid grasp of analytical skills, for monitoring performance, detecting fraud, and improving productivity. Almost every department needs people with analytical skills, and jobs associated with analytical skills often command a salary premium.[2]

ETHICS IN DATA ANALYSIS AND RESEARCH

The effectiveness of data and analysis in decision making depends on more than just technical competency; it also depends on the ethical integrity with which analysis is performed and presented. When questions surface about the ethics of analysis, its credibility suffers, and people may be unwilling to give it much, if any, consideration. Specifically, there are three *areas of ethical concern:* (1) the integrity of purpose, (2) the integrity of the process of analysis and communication, and (3) the integrity of dealing with human subjects. When research and analysis are clear about these matters, and technically proficient, too, then the role of analysis in decision making and policy may be enhanced.

Scientific misconduct is generally understood as the violation of the standard norms of scholarly conduct and ethical behavior in scientific research. Though some research norms are codified by associations and employers, and others are sometimes stated explicitly in research grants and contracts, the scientific community has also reached a general understanding of what these standards are. Violations of the norms include and go beyond plagiarism and data falsification, which have been well popularized. As in any community, the failure to live up to stated and unstated norms can have harsh consequences. This section enumerates key principles and norms of research and analysis. Scientific misconduct, when considered by others as significant or severe, can cause not only one's diminished reputation, but also exclusion from participation and even expulsion and the possibility of career termination and legal action; however, showing that one's analysis meets high research ethics can increase both its credibility and quality. There is good reason, indeed, for taking the following discussion seriously.

First, managers need to be clear about the purpose of their analysis. Analysis often has *dual purposes*: (1) to further programs and policies, such as by making them more efficient or effective, and (2) to establish factual, objective truths that meet standards of scientific evidence and that hold up under scrutiny. The first purpose causes analysis to focus on matters that are relevant to the agency and its mission; analysts need to be forthright in disclosing what questions they considered, and those which they did not— no analysis can cover everything. The second purpose implies that analysts should be open to all facts, whatever they are, and ensure that all facts comply fully with standards of scientific evidence. Analysts must disclose and issue caveats for instances in which this is not the case. Ethics in analysis requires full disclosure of the purpose of the analysis, and all the biases, trade-offs, and shortfalls encountered along the way.

These dual purposes can come into conflict, forcing ethical choices and decisions. For example, what is a manager to do when careful analysis shows his or her programs to be less effective than hoped for? Should pursuit of mission cause a blind eye to facts that are contrary? Such results may indicate the need for further research or to consider future program changes. Consider another example: Should the agency intentionally ignore questions or analysis that could strengthen the arguments of those who advocate against the program or agency? Agencies cannot totally ignore their fiduciary responsibilities to society at large and thus their broader impacts. Such counterarguments should be taken into consideration in some way, and they need to be shown in analysis. These tensions are quite common in practice, and they cannot be ignored or swept under the rug.

Second, managers need to consider the integrity of the analysis and communication process. Many of these considerations are based on the *guiding principles of scientific research*—to be honest, objective, accurate, and complete. Analysts should not hide facts, change data, falsify results, or consider only data that support a favored conclusion. For example, data may be sketchy and incomplete, and management judgment is that such information is better used than ignored. In this case, the poor quality of the information needs to be stated clearly and a caveat given. Analysts should also fully report the sources of their data, data collection methodologies, and any possible gaps and shortfalls, and they should assess the impact of such shortcomings on their findings.

It is obvious that facts and findings should not be altered or manufactured in any way. That is outright lying, and people will be justly outraged to know that they have been deceived. Data fabrication and any study falsification are very serious forms of scientific misconduct, and many scientists feel that the omission of relevant counter-conclusions is equally serious. Regrettably, each year cases of scientific misconduct and fraud make headlines. It is equally important that analysis be as meticulous and objective as possible in testing its own findings. Findings should be checked for errors and inaccuracy. Conclusions should be examined for the possibility of alternative or rival explanations. The impact of assumptions, gaps, and bias should be examined. Doing so is not only proper, but it also strengthens study findings by providing detailed knowledge about their validity and robustness. The more that is known about the data and results, the more confidence that others may have in them.

Communication in research matters, and results should be presented in straightforward and nonmisleading ways. For example, analysis should not adjust scales to give the appearance of a significant increase when the increase is in fact minor and insignificant. Such misrepresentations are considered the same as lying with statistics. Findings should be communicated in ways that are straightforward and easy to understand, for both experts and nonexperts, without oversimplification or deception. These ethical norms are not merely standards for evaluating analysis that has already been undertaken and presented. Rather, these norms provide essential guidance to analysts throughout the entire analytical process, as they decide what to analyze, how to write up their findings, and how to present them.

Third, in recent years considerable attention has been given to the impact of research on the *well-being of human subjects* in research. Some key ethical principles in research involving people are that their participation should be voluntary and based on informed consent (that is, they should know what they are getting involved in), that information about them should be held confidentially, and that risks of harm to subjects should be minimized and reasonable in relationship to anticipated benefits. Concerns about the well-being of human subjects arose from various medical research experiments that intentionally misled patients and exposed them to great harm.

Some landmark examples of scientific misconduct involving humans in medicine include the Nazi war crimes during World War II, in which concentration camp prisoners were subjected to torture and poisonous injections to see how they would be affected. In the United States, the Tuskegee syphilis study (1930–1972) used as its subjects several hundred black males with untreated syphilis, without informed consent. Even after penicillin was found to be an effective antibiotic treatment in the 1940s, these black males were neither informed about nor offered treatment choices. In the Willowbrook study, 1963–1966, newly admitted children with mental handicaps were injected with hepatitis in order to track the natural history of the disease. Parents had to approve of the treatment, but approval was also necessary as a condition for admission into this overcrowded facility.

Regrettably, these cases do not stand alone. Instances of deceit and coercion, whether subtle or blatant, led to the development of the ethical principles described earlier. There are many other examples of research misconduct, too. For example, in one case, public health workers lost a confidential file of known AIDS patients that was later sold in a local nightclub. Most human subjects research is now overseen by institutional review boards (IRBs) to ensure that risks to subjects are reasonable and that possible harm is identified and minimized. These boards are committees at universities and other research institutions composed of scientists who evaluate the protocols of proposed research. The point is that we confront ethical issues in research pretty much every time we do research, and we need to learn from past errors. For example, what ethical issues are involved in the push to have the U.S. Food and Drug Administration approve some drugs early, before they have been fully tested? The notions of research not causing unnecessary harm and being upfront with participants are now fully established ethical principles. If analysis involves access to confidential data, then steps must be taken to ensure that these data are protected. The impact of research on human subjects must be considered and steps undertaken to minimize and address harmful impacts. Managers also need to be mindful of the negative impacts that their analysis can have. The interest of affected parties should be considered, for example, by ensuring that conclusions are accurate and fair. Table 1.1 provides an overview of important ethical principles.[3]

Table 1.1 ⎯⎯⎯⎯ ⌇⌇ Ethics in Research and Analysis

Be honest:
1. Do not hide facts, change data, falsify results, or use only data that support your conclusion.
2. Present results in straightforward and nonmisleading ways. For example, do not adjust scales to give the appearance of a significant increase when the increase is minor or insignificant. Also, do not suggest a level of precision that is not present.

Be complete:
3. Report all data and results that relate to a conclusion, not just those that support it.
4. Identify caveats and alternative explanations that may qualify your findings, even if no data exist to evaluate these caveats or alternative explanations.
5. Report the sources of your data, data collection methodologies, possible gaps and shortfalls, and impact on findings.
6. Be thorough, meticulous, and objective in your analysis, conclusions, and communications.

Be useful:
7. Try to produce information that can help your employer, other stakeholders, and the public interest.
8. Communicate information and results in ways that nonexperts can readily understand.

Be mindful:
9. Information is power; be aware of possible negative consequences. Address possible negative consequences of your analysis by considering further analysis, by considering the interests of affected parties, and by identifying relevant caveats in findings.
10. Respect the interests of human subjects whose data are being analyzed. They may have rights to privacy and "hold harmless" clauses. Obey research protocols.

SUMMARY

Analysis and data are commonly used by public and nonprofit managers to support decisions. Analysis is useful because it helps provide an objective, factual underpinning to situations and programs and helps quantify the extent of problems and solutions. At the very least, a focus on facts and objective analysis can help reduce judgment errors that stem from impressionistic or subjective perceptions. Analysis and data often are used to describe problems, programs, and policies; to assist in monitoring programs and in making decisions that might make them more effective or efficient; and to evaluate outcomes.

The effective use of analysis and data requires competency in the following areas: knowing existing data sources, their applications, and their limitations; having an ability to gather one's own data; having an ability to analyze data; being able to communicate findings; being able to guide analysis by the specific, substantive program and policy interests; and being aware of ethics practices. Managers who seek to increase their competency often experience different stages of proficiency: "know nothing," journeyman, technocrat, and the sophisticated expert.

The effectiveness of data and analysis in decision making depends on more than just technical competency; however, it also depends on the ethical integrity with which research is performed. Areas of ethical concern involve the integrity of the research purpose, the integrity of its analysis and communication, and the integrity of dealing with human subjects. Analysis in public and nonprofit organizations often serves dual purposes, namely, to promote programs and policies and to establish factual, objective truths that meet standards of scientific evidence. Analysis should be forthcoming about the purposes that it serves and about the ways in which these purposes have affected it.

KEY TERMS

Areas of ethical concern (p. 11)
Competencies for analysis (p. 7)
Dual purposes (of analysis) (p. 11)
Guiding principles of scientific research (p. 12)
International Association of Schools and Institutes of Administration (IASIA) (p. 7)
National Association of Schools of Public Affairs and Administration (NASPAA) (p. 6)

Scientific misconduct (p. 11)
Scientific research (p. 8)
Stages of proficiency (p. 9)
Statistics (p. 8)
Uses of analysis and data (p. 5)
Well-being of human subjects (p. 12)

Notes

1. United Nations Department of Economic and Social Affairs/International Association of Schools and Institutes of Administration, Task Force on Standards of Excellence for Public Administration Education and Training. (May 2008). *Standards of Excellence for Public Administration Education and Training.* Retrieved from www.iias-iisa.org/iasia/e/standards_excellence/Documents/Standards%20of%20Excellence%20English.pdf.

2. To learn more about salaries in public and nonprofit administration, take a thorough look at salaries at the Bureau of Labor Statistics "Occupational Employment Statistics" website, www.bls.gov/oes/current/oessrci .htm. For government, scroll down and select sector 99. For nonprofits, select NAICS 712100, museums, or select NAICS 813300, social advocacy organizations, and then the subgroup "community and social service occupations." For an interesting look at careers, visit www.naspaa.org/ students/careers/careers.asp. This site also offers salary information.

3. Table 1.1 deals with ethics in research and data analysis, but it is also useful to consider codes of professional conduct generally. Most professional organizations have such codes, such as the American Society for Public Administration (www.aspanet.org) and the International City/County Management Association (www.icma.org).

SECTION II

Research Methods

This section examines research methods and their application to public and nonprofit management as well as to policy analysis. *Research methodology* is the science of methods for investigating phenomena. Research methods are used in almost every social science discipline. The chapters in this section provide an in-depth examination of the research methods that managers and analysts need to be familiar with, so that they can gain the competencies described in Chapter 1, such as to gather, analyze, and communicate facts and findings in their lines of work.

In this brief introduction, we offer a few distinctions that shape a useful perspective. First, research methods are used in all fields of science. Research methods are not unique to public administration or policy analysis, but the problems and purposes to which research methods are put do shape their importance and application. For example, being able to conduct a citizen survey or program evaluation is more important in public administration than, say, in international relations. Here, we examine research methods that address some important problems that public and nonprofit managers and analysts commonly face: (1) evaluating the past performance of programs and policies, (2) managing and monitoring the present performance of programs and policies, and (3) forecasting the future of programs, policies, and community conditions. Different fields have different problems and, hence, different emphases and applications in their research methods.

Second, many fields distinguish between two research purposes. Generally, the purpose of **basic research** is to develop new knowledge about phenomena such as problems, events, programs, or policies, and their relationships. Here are some basic research questions in public and nonprofit management: What is the nature of citizen apathy? What is the nature of citizen voluntarism? Which factors affect voluntarism? What consequences does voluntarism have? Or, what are the activities and outcomes of programs or policies? And, why do some people have an aversion to statistics? These questions clarify the nature and relationships among phenomena by asking, generally, "What is this, and what consequences does it have?" This question can be asked with regard to events in the past, present, or future.

But research and analysis in public and nonprofit management also serve applied and highly practical purposes. **Applied research** is used to solve practical problems. Examples of applied research questions include the following: What can governments do to reduce citizen apathy? How can governments increase the use of certain programs? What can be done to minimize the impact of turnover among political appointees on program quality? What can be done to increase students' interest in statistics? These questions clearly have practical matters in mind. They often ask, "How can this be done or improved?"

Research begins by asking questions, and managers and analysts will encounter both basic and applied questions in their work. For example, program evaluation might involve basic research questions such as, "What is the program achieving?" Thereafter, it might involve applied research questions such as, "How can the program be made more effective?" Both kinds of questions are important, and research methods help managers and analysts formulate and address them. Indeed, questions about improving programs presume knowledge of what these programs do and what they have achieved. Learning to ask questions that are both useful and answerable is surely an objective of this course.

Third, after raising questions, managers and analysts must choose among a broad range of research methods to answer their questions. Research methods often are classified as quantitative or qualitative in nature. **Quantitative research methods** involve the collection of data that can be analyzed using statistical methods. Such data typically are collected through surveys or compilations of administrative records, and they produce numbers used to describe (that is, to measure) the extent of societal problems (such as teenage violence or homelessness, for example), to monitor program operations, to determine program efficiency and effectiveness and to analyze by how much they can be improved, and to evaluate the impact of programs.

Qualitative research methods refer to the collection and analysis of words, symbols, or artifacts that are largely nonstatistical in nature. Such data often are collected through interviews, focus groups, and direct observation. Typically the purpose of qualitative research is to identify and describe new phenomena. Qualitative research provides a detailed, rich understanding of what is going on and why it matters to stakeholders, in their own words. Qualitative research is used to identify problems and the factors associated with these problems. It is also used to describe programs and policies, such as their priorities and methods of operation, as well as processes through which programs and policies affect outcomes. Qualitative research can also suggest ways in which programs might be improved.

Both quantitative and qualitative methods are indispensable in addressing questions of basic and applied research. Quantitative research requires solid knowledge of existing phenomena and how they are related to each other. Simply, before we measure something, we need to be certain that we know what we are measuring and that we are measuring the right thing. However, qualitative research does not provide much specific information about the magnitude of problems and phenomena, nor can it offer conclusive, statistical proof about the impacts of programs and policies. Hence, research in public management and policy analysis typically uses both quantitative and qualitative research methods.

Managers and analysts need a working familiarity with a range of basic and applied, quantitative and qualitative research methods. The chapters in this section reflect a diversity of purposes and methods, providing many examples of the distinctions described here. Chapter 2 introduces basic concepts of research and applies these concepts to program evaluation. Managers and analysts are often called upon to demonstrate the outcomes of public and nonprofit programs and policies. Program evaluation is an important method for holding people accountable, focusing on questions about how programs and policies performed in the past. The chapter explores experimental and quasi-experimental designs for evaluating programs and gives examples. Program evaluation demonstrates the use of both basic and applied research, and the need for both qualitative and quantitative research methods.

Chapter 3 addresses the problems of conceptualization and measurement that affect program evaluation and other research approaches in public management and policy analysis. For example, how are abstract concepts like democracy, apathy, safety, self-sufficiency, or congestion to be measured? The chapter discusses the problem of conceptualization, measurement validity, and the importance of measurement scales and levels.

Chapter 4 describes additional research methods for public managers and analysts. It deals with research on problems that involve the present (monitoring) and the future (forecasting). Specifically, it discusses performance measurement, which is increasingly used for program monitoring and to provide accountability. The chapter also applies criteria of validity, developed in Chapter 3, to the measures of performance measurement. Chapter 4 also examines common research methods for forecasting. The discussion of these methods is concise but encompassing and includes examples.

Chapter 5 looks at data collection methods. An important competency for analysts and managers is familiarity with the data sources in their lines of work. This chapter discusses uses and challenges of secondary data, administrative data, and survey data. It provides guidelines for conducting surveys, including sampling strategies and methods, and also notes the roles of qualitative data, such as interviews and focus groups. The workbook that accompanies this textbook includes many additional examples of the research methods and data collection strategies discussed in this chapter.

This book includes footnotes that serve a variety of purposes. Some provide additional clarification or examples, and others expand the material. Readers are encouraged to examine the footnotes. Finally, because public and nonprofit management draws on a multitude of fields, and public managers must work with professionals in different fields, readers will need to be familiar with some different but analogous terms and concepts. Throughout the book, analogous terms and concepts are clearly identified.

CHAPTER

2

Research Design

CHAPTER OBJECTIVES

After reading this chapter, you should be able to

- Distinguish between independent and dependent variables
- Describe the six steps of program evaluation
- Explain experimental and quasi-experimental designs
- Understand the importance of rival hypotheses
- Identify threats to validity in research design

This chapter introduces major concepts in social science research and applies them to program evaluation. Program evaluation, which helps managers and analysts to determine the outcomes of programs and policies, is an important and necessary skill for managers and analysts to have. This chapter also examines a variety of research designs commonly used in program evaluation.

INTRODUCING VARIABLES AND THEIR RELATIONSHIPS

Research is about establishing the nature of things. For example, assume that we are responsible for managing a program to reduce high school violence or that we are otherwise interested in this topic. One of the first steps that we need to take is to gain a solid understanding of this phenomenon, high school violence, by examining the ways in which it is manifested. We would want to know about its various forms such as verbal and emotional abuse; its physical manifestations such as shoving, hitting, and the use of weapons; and its racial and sexual manifestations, too. Thereafter, we would want to know the magnitude of each manifestation, such as how many fist fights, gun fights, or rapes occur. And we might want statistics on specific types of injuries, such as broken bones or concussions. Indeed, the frequency of these phenomena often is a key target for management and public policy.

The same is true for many other phenomena such as community conditions (for example, poverty or economic growth), events (such as wildfires or toxic spills), as well as the impacts of programs and policies (say, to increase the competitiveness of students or reduce the prevalence of certain diseases). We will want to first establish the manifestations of a phenomenon and then learn something about their magnitude. If we are interested in environmental quality, for example, we will want to know facts about the state of the environment and how it varies in different ways and in different locations. If we are in health care management, we will want to know the incidence of different diseases. If we are interested in inflation, we will want to know its current level, which factors such as energy prices or housing costs are responsible for recent changes, and how inflation varies in different parts of the country. Once we decide what we are interested in, we will want to know more about its manifestations and variations, and the ways in which policies or programs affect it.

Public and nonprofit management and policy typically involve phenomena that vary in some way. *Variables* are defined as empirically observable phenomena that vary. This is best illustrated by a few examples. "High school violence" is a variable because it is observable and varies across schools; violence is more common in some schools than in others, and we can observe the differences. "Environmental quality" is also a variable because it is observable and varies across locales, as do "diseases" and "inflation," for example. Variables are key to research, and they are everywhere. The number of students in classes is also a variable because different classes have different numbers of students, and the number of students in each class can be observed. By contrast, in a study of only female students, the variable "gender" does not vary and is therefore called a *constant*. Constants are phenomena that do not vary.

Getting Started

Can you identify important variables in your present or future line of work, such as services or program outcomes that vary in some way?

Attributes are defined as the specific characteristics of a variable, that is, the specific ways in which a variable can vary. All variables have attributes. For example, high school violence can be measured as being absent, sporadic, occurring from time to time, or ongoing—these are the attributes of the variable "high school violence." Another example is the variable "gender." Gender varies in the population, and the attributes of gender are "male" and "female." The variable "race" often has more than two attributes (Caucasian, African American, Native American, and so forth). The variable "income" can have few or a nearly infinite number of attributes if income is measured as specific dollar amounts. In surveys, often each survey item is treated as a separate variable, and the response categories for each question are the variable's attributes. For example, the question "What is your gender?" is considered a variable, and the response categories "male" and "female" are its attributes.

Research usually involves both *descriptive analysis* and the study of *relationships* involving variables. **Descriptive analysis** provides information about the nature of variables—such as whether a high school violence problem exists and the extent or level of it. The preceding discussion gave examples of descriptive analysis. In our high school violence example, descriptive analysis can be used to show the nature of the perpetrators, the geographic areas in which such violence most often occurs, and the extent to which it is perceived as a problem. Descriptive analysis is useful in public management and policy because managers need to know the state of the world that they are trying to shape. They need to know, for example, the number of teenagers who have been hurt by others at school. This is simply a number—such as 5 percent.

Managers also want to know the causes of problems and the effectiveness of interventions. This involves examining **relationships**, that is, specifying which variables are related to each other, and the ways in which they are related. Indeed, research is not only about establishing the nature of phenomena, but also about their relationships. For example, we might want to examine whether students who participate in anger management classes describe themselves as being less angry or less prone to acting out against others. Specifically, we want to know whether participation in anger management class decreases the extent of acting out by students. We might also examine the effect of other conditions—such as drug use or gang participation—on high school violence. By knowing how programs and conditions affect outcomes, managers can better recommend and pursue alternative courses of action. Most studies involve both descriptive analysis and an examination of relationships.

Relationships in social science are distinguished by whether they are *probabilistic* (occurring sometimes) or *deterministic* (occurring each time). For example, when we say that anger management reduces high school violence, we are not implying that this always occurs, for each student. Some students might even become more violent, perhaps learning new ways of expressing their anger. Rather, we mean that, *on average*, the number of violent incidents will decrease. The number of incidents will decrease for some students more than for others, and for still others it will not decrease at all; the relationship is probabilistic in nature. Many relationships in the social world are probabilistic.

When social scientists say, "anger management reduces high school violence," they typically mean that in most instances anger management reduces high school violence. They usually also have a standard in mind, such as anger management reducing high school violence at least 95 out of 100 times. Sometimes, social scientists adopt an even stricter standard, such as at least 99 out of 100 times. By adopting such standards, social scientists provide information about probabilistic relationships with a relatively high degree of confidence.[1]

Relationships also are distinguished as being either *causal* or *associational*. **Causal relationships** show cause and effect, such as the impact of anger management programs on high school violence, the impact of employee compensation on workplace productivity, or the impact of environmental policies on water quality. In these instances, one variable is assumed to affect another. By contrast, **associations** are relationships that imply no cause and effect. For example, it is said that in Sweden a relationship exists between the number of storks and the number of childbirths; both increase in the spring. Does this imply that storks really do bring babies, at least in Sweden? No, of course it doesn't. The appearances of storks and new babies are unrelated; they have no cause-and-effect relationship.[2]

Getting Started

Can you identify examples of causal relationships and associations in your area of interest?

Among causal relationships, we further distinguish between *independent variables* and *dependent variables*. **Dependent variables** are variables that are affected by other variables (hence, they are dependent on them). **Independent variables** are variables that cause an effect on other variables but are not themselves shaped by other variables (hence, they are independent). For example, in a study of the impact of anger management on high school violence, anger management is the independent variable that affects high school violence, which is the dependent variable. Causal relationships are commonly thought of in the following manner:

Independent Variable(s) $\rightarrow$ Dependent Variable

An important step in any research is specifying the dependent and independent variables. Doing so brings clarity and direction to the research. Although many studies examine several relationships, most evaluations focus on explaining only a few dependent variables. In our example, we wish to examine the impact of anger management on high school violence:

Independent Variable   *Dependent Variable*

Anger Management   →   High School Violence

Of course, our evaluation needn't be limited to studying just this relationship, but specifying relationships in this manner helps concentrate our attention on (1) accurately determining the level of high school violence and (2) examining whether anger management is associated with it. We might also study the effect of gun control laws (independent variable) on this dependent variable, or other relationships such as the effect of homework assistance (independent variable) on academic performance (dependent variable). Distinguishing between independent and dependent variables is a cornerstone of research, program evaluation, and policy analysis; it is essential to clarifying and sharpening one's thinking about which variables are being studied and how they are related to each other. It is fundamental to communicating to others about what is being studied. *Distinguishing between independent and dependent variables is an essential skill that managers and analysts will want to practice.*

> **Key Point**
> Distinguishing between independent and dependent variables is basic to research.

A literature review of scholarly (research) and professional articles can often help to further develop and clarify our thinking about independent and dependent variables. Oftentimes, managers and analysts are interested in a phenomenon, such as school violence, and perhaps one or two factors associated with it. Previous studies may suggest ways of measuring high school violence and perhaps provide a critical review of alternative measures. Researchers might have also taken different perspectives on the causes of high school violence, leading them to consider different independent variables. Research might have evaluated the effect of independent variables in different settings, though not necessarily yours. Past research can help further define variables and the relations of interest among them.

Program evaluation is often intended to stake a claim of *causation.* In our example, managers might want to argue that anger management has caused the decline in high school violence. You may have heard the expression "correlation does not prove causation." This is true. Causation requires both (1) *empirical (that is, statistical) correlation* and (2) *a plausible cause-and-effect argument.* These two **criteria for causality** must be present. Statistical analysis tests whether two variables are correlated, but causality also requires a persuasive argument (also called theory) about how one variable could directly affect another.[3] Regarding the impact of anger management on high school violence, a plausible theory might readily be written up. Anger management training teaches people how to identify anger and release it in ways that are nonviolent toward others. Thus, both statistical correlation and a persuasive theoretical argument are required to stake a claim of causation.

How difficult can it be to make a theoretical argument of cause and effect? Examining, say, the relationship between gender and high school violence, we have yet to make a plausible cause-and-effect argument. If we lack specific evidence (especially evidence that might persuade a skeptical audience) that gender, defined by reproductive organs and hormones, causes violence, then we best regard this relationship as a mere correlation, that is, an association. Empirical correlations remain mere associations until analysts have argued, in persuasive and exacting detail, how one variable can plausibly cause another.

Finally, relationships that have not yet been empirically tested (that is, established) are called *hypotheses*. For example, a study hypothesis might be that, on average, female teenagers are less prone to violence than males. Then, empirical data will need to be collected and analyzed in order to prove the hypothesis either true or false for the population from which these data are drawn. Subsequent chapters in this book discuss how to analyze data and draw conclusions about hypotheses. Academic research studies are usually quite explicit about which hypotheses are being tested and why they are relevant.

Getting Started

Look around you—select a relationship and identify the independent and dependent variables in it.

This brief introduction lays out important concepts that are used over and over again in research. Quite simply, when we do research, we see the world existing of variables and their relationships. We also identify the attributes of variables, and ask whether relationships are deterministic or probabilistic, causal or only associational, tested (established) or hypothesized.

PROGRAM EVALUATION

Program evaluation can be defined as the use of social science research methods to determine whether, and in what ways, a program works. Program evaluation involves the description of programs, conditions, and events, as well as the analysis of relationships, such as the impact of programs on outcomes. Program evaluation uses both quantitative and qualitative methods to describe programs and analyze their relationships.

How difficult can it be to document program outcomes? There usually is more to program evaluation than meets the eye. Among the first challenges is to find out what the program is expected to accomplish. Consider the following example. In response to growing concerns about teen violence, many communities and states have created after-school programs. The idea, according to elected officials and supported by the public, is to get teenagers off the streets and into supervised environments. As a public manager, your job is to implement such a program. Funding guidelines require that you document the success of the program.

Now, you must figure out what the program is expected to accomplish. You might be surprised to learn that sometimes little thought has gone into identifying specific outcomes for such programs, or that some elected officials and experts have different views. Some advocates only want teenagers off the streets, but others expect them to learn something as well. Still others feel that anger management should be taught. Even if you are responsible only for program evaluation, oftentimes you will find yourself formulating program outcomes.

Next, assume that you and others agree that anger management is one of several appropriate activities for the after-school program. Specifically, the after-school program will teach students to recognize and deal with anger in appropriate ways. You might even try to target so-called high-risk students. How will you measure the success of your anger management efforts? Should you ask students whether they feel less angry? Should you ask their parents and teachers as well? Should you ask teachers to record the number of classroom incidents, such as student outbursts? Should you do all of this? If so, in what way?

Suppose you decide to ask teachers to track classroom incidents. Which incidents should be tracked? Is it appropriate to compare different classroom incidents across schools or classes? Should you develop baseline data, and if so, which? Also, how accurate do you think the teachers will be in their reporting and tracking? Are their responses likely to be biased in any way? Or suppose you decide to send a survey to parents. Do you need to send your survey to all parents? How many questions should you ask? What response rate is appropriate? How do you avoid biased questions?

Finally, consider the possibility that the number of classroom incidents drops during the course of your anger management program. How do you know that the drop is due to the anger management course? Could teachers and parents have become more involved in anger management themselves? What if some students who are known to be angry and violent were transferred out of the school? In short, how sure can you be that any changes are due to the after-school program?

Getting Started

Select a program in your area of interest (or workplace) that is a candidate for program evaluation. Which relationship(s) would you focus on?

These questions are hardly academic. Elected officials and senior managers expect others to have answers to such questions, regardless of whether they concern after-school programs, prison overcrowding, environmental protection, or national security. Determining which outcomes ought to be measured and measuring their attainment in credible ways are activities germane to all public programs and policies. Public departments need people with skills to assess program outcomes; program evaluation applies social science methods to these issues.[4]

Six Steps

Program evaluation usually involves six steps. The purpose of these steps is to help researchers and managers identify and address relevant concerns in an orderly manner. These steps help ensure that evaluation is done in objective and scientifically valid ways—evaluation findings must be credible and stand up under the light of public scrutiny—and that conclusions and recommendations are embraced by those who have the power to bring about change. Program evaluation must include opportunities for stakeholders to have input; study conclusions must be credible, relevant, and consistent with opportunities for change. The following *six steps of program evaluation* provide a strategic roadmap that combines these dual needs—to be both responsive and objective:

1. *Define the activity and goals that are to be evaluated.* What are the key objectives and constraints according to key decision makers? What are the main objectives and concerns according to program staff? How do clients and others outside the program view it? What is the key target population of these activities and goals?
2. *Identify which key relationships will be studied.* Which program outcomes does the evaluation measure? Which factors are hypothesized to affect these program outcomes? Which counter-explanations are considered?
3. *Determine the research design that will be used.* Will a control or comparison group be used? Is there a need for developing a baseline of current performance? Are periodic or follow-up measurements foreseen and, if so, over what time period?
4. *Define and measure study concepts.* Which study concepts require detail in measurement? Which concepts require little detail? Will existing data be used, and how accurate are they? Will new data be gathered through, for example, a survey or focus group? If so, who will undertake such a project, and how long will it take? What statistical requirements must

the data meet for subsequent analysis? What resources and expertise are needed for data collection and program evaluation? What suggestions do key decision makers and others have for improving measurement?

5. *Collect and analyze the data.* Which statistical techniques will be used for data analysis? What type of conclusions are researchers seeking from the data? Do the data meet the requirements of different statistical techniques?

6. *Present study findings.* How, and to whom, will conclusions be presented? Can presentations be part of other consensus and decision-making processes? Can preliminary feedback about tentative findings be obtained from key decision makers and others? Who requires a detailed analysis and presentation? Who requires only a brief overview of main findings? What should the final report look like, and to whom should it be sent?

Previously we dealt with some matters pertaining to the first two steps. In our example, the activity is anger management as an after-school program. This program will teach students to recognize and deal with their anger. At this point, we might further specify that the program targets high-risk students, though it may include other students as well. The preceding questions prompt us to make finer specification. Also, assume that after further interviewing school administrators, teachers, and students and their parents, additional program objectives are formulated, in addition to reducing high school violence. These additional objectives might be to keep students safe after school, to improve academic performance, to reduce disruptive classroom behavior, to reduce violent behavior outside school, and to provide opportunities for getting involved in other, "fun" activities such as sports and music. The latter might seem far removed from anger management objectives, but program clients sometimes view such activities as useful motivators for continued participation.

Regarding the second step, while participation in anger management is examined for its impact on the specified outcomes, it is recognized that other factors might play a role, too. For example, gang participation and drug use is likely to reduce the effect of anger management training as a result of strong countervailing peer pressures and addictive impulses. Also, a lack of parental interest in their children's education is a likely negative factor. On the other hand, being transferred to a low-violence school might reduce violence. Thus, program evaluation will need to consider additional circumstances along with the impact of anger management training. Such circumstances are part of steps 2 and 3 and are discussed later in this chapter. Step 4, the definition and measurement of study concepts, is discussed in Chapter 3.

Rival Hypotheses and Limitations of Experimental Study Designs

The purpose of research design is to help ascertain that outcomes, such as reduced high school violence, are occurring and plausibly related to the program and not to other factors. But what if, parallel to anger management, another program aimed to reduce student access to weapons? Disallowing weapons in school (for example, by using a metal detector at the school entrance to check for them), is a concomitant activity that might also reduce high school violence. Real life surely has many things going on at the same time. The possibility of effects from other factors requires researchers to consider (and determine) the extent to which a change in the dependent variable is indeed caused by the independent variable under study (here, anger management). Studies usually consider multiple factors affecting their dependent variables which strengthens study conclusions about relationships among key variables.

Alternative explanations for observed outcomes are called ***rival hypotheses***, and variables used to measure rival hypotheses are called ***control variables***. Control variables are empirical, just as dependent and independent variables are, but they get their name from their research role: to test whether relationships between independent and dependent variables hold up under the presence of alternative, rival explanations for the observed pattern of outcomes. They are sometimes also called confounding variables, referring to concomitant activities that also explain outcomes and, hence, complicate efforts to establish a causal effect of programs or policies on outcomes. In our example, the presence of a weapons access policy, a concomitant event, is certainly a control variable that the manager will want to take into account. Indeed, the credibility of study conclusions often rests on the extent that pertinent control variables have been included in the research.[5]

Rival hypotheses (and their associated control variables) can be dealt with through (1) experimental design and (2) statistical control. ***Experimental designs*** address rival hypotheses through the use of control groups, which are similar to the study group in all aspects *except* that members of the control group do not participate in the intervention. You may be familiar with control groups through literature that describes the effectiveness of medical treatments. In ***classic, randomized experiments***, participants are randomly assigned to either a control or an experimental (or study) group. The assignments are random to ensure that any observed differences between these two groups are due only to the treatment and not to any other factor. Random assignment ensures that the two groups are similar, and baseline data are used to further rule out any chance differences in the groups' respective starting conditions. Further, neither the participants of the control and study groups nor their doctors are told whether they are receiving the experimental treatment or the ineffective placebo (they both look alike), because doing so might cause patients or their doctors to alter their behavior. In short, everything is done to ensure that the *only* difference between the groups is that one gets the treatment and the other does not. The logical inference, then, is that any difference *must* be due to the experimental treatment. The research design rules out every other factor.

Programs and policies are the public management equivalent of clinical interventions. Unfortunately, classic, randomized experiments are notoriously difficult to implement in public administration and policy because it is generally legally and ethically impossible to deny citizens or jurisdictions programs and policies. In our example, we do not envision randomly assigning teenagers to after-school programs. Some parents would be outraged if their children were denied access to the anger management program. They might even sue. It is also unclear what the "placebo" intervention might be in our example; it is absurd to suggest that subjects might participate in an anger management program that is intentionally designed to be ineffective. The problems of rival hypotheses are real, but the classic, experimental design is seldom a feasible strategy for addressing this matter in public administration and policy analysis.

The fact that we are unable to conduct classic, randomized experiments in public programs does not mean that we cannot use comparison groups or baseline measurements. Indeed, doing so can add valuable information to our program evaluation. For example, it would be interesting to compare high school violence among schools, of which only some have anger management programs. The term *comparison group* rather than control group would then be used, because the comparison group is not similar in all ways to the experimental group but for the intervention; other differences may exist, but they can help rule out some alternative explanations. Indeed, comparison groups, and before-and-after tests, are important to making defensible conclusions about a program's effectiveness.

But the presence of comparison groups that are not assigned according to experimental design procedures means that we can no longer rely on the research design itself to rule out the presence of rival hypotheses; rather, we must use **statistical control strategies** to account for rival hypotheses. This involves (1) identifying plausible rival hypotheses, (2) collecting data about them, and (3) using *statistical techniques* to examine their impact on high school violence, relative to anger management. Specifically, we ask, What is the impact of anger management on high school violence, controlled for these other factors? The statistical techniques for analyzing data in this way are discussed later in this book; however, this

> **Getting Started**
> Identify control variables that are relevant in your selected program evaluation.

approach obviously requires that analysts identify relevant control variables and collect data about them prior to analysis. Hence, the need to identify relevant rival hypotheses is determined early in program evaluation, during step 3.

QUASI-EXPERIMENTAL DESIGNS IN PROGRAM EVALUATION

Comparisons between experimental and comparison groups that do not meet the standard of classic research designs are called *quasi-experimental designs*. These designs may lack (i) randomization, (ii) baseline (or pretest) measurement, or (iii) a comparison group. However, comparison groups and baselines often provide important information that help evaluate the effectiveness of programs and policies. Without a baseline, it is harder to persuade others that a program has had an impact. Comparison groups provide a useful reference, for example, when comparing outcomes across different populations. Before-and-after measurements, comparison groups, and baselines all help make study results more persuasive.

First, suppose we know that before a crime mitigation program the level of crime in city A is a level 5 (measured on whatever scale) and after the program (of say, education) the level of crime has dropped to a 3. The drop in crime of [5 − 3 =] 2 points shows a change. Without a before (also called "pre-") measurement, we might not know whether a change had occurred.

What if we failed to take a before measurement or no relevant crime data are available? Maybe a policy analyst is asked to evaluate the program only after it has already been in place. Well, the art of research is to find solutions. An alternative approach, then, might be to ask people, after the program had been implemented for some time, whether they perceived that crime had lessened. However, this method might be a bit less accurate, as perhaps people might have been influenced by concomitant stories about crime, and peoples' memories may also be selective in what they recall. Clearly, it is better to have taken a before measurement. Moreover, the after-the-fact subjective assessment could provide for some triangulation of one's findings!

Second, suppose also that we have a comparison group—a city (let's call it city B) with similar composition and crime rates as in our city that saw the improvement (city A). Say, now, that we find that the level of crime in city B stayed about a constant 5.4 over the study period, but the crime level in city A dropped from 5 to 3. If no other factors might explain such divergent experiences, then having information about the comparison group seems to further strengthen our finding. Indeed, assume that someone might argue that crime fell because economic conditions improved; such an argument would be ruled out if the same economic conditions were also experienced in both cities. Of course, lacking randomization, analysts will have to argue that city B is indeed a valid comparison group for city A. In our example, analysts might find a comparison school in which students have similar test scores, similar socioeconomic backgrounds, similar academic and extracurricular programs, and similar arrest and felony rates. These data must then be gathered and the variables used as control variables to statistically control for any differences that might exist.

Third, consider the role of baselines in which before-and-after measures span a longer time. Baselines can help deal with several problems, such as declining effects over time or increases that have been going on since well before the study intervention. Some policy interventions have effects that taper off over time. In our example, high school violence might be recorded on a monthly basis, 6 months prior to and perhaps up to 12 months after the intervention, producing time series data. The efficacy of the intervention might be suggested by a change in trend after the sixth month, controlled for any intervening confounding variables, of course. One such possibility is suggested below:

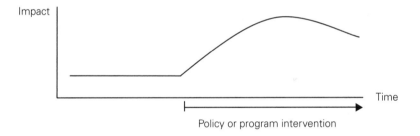

Policy or program intervention

The additional observations, before and after the start of the intervention, allow analysts to research important questions on the persistence of intervention impacts. In our example, the impact of anger management programs might reach a saturation point, beyond which further decreases in high school violence are not observed. This would indicate that some causes of high school violence are not related to anger. Or students might adopt new behaviors designed to mitigate or overcome the impact of anger management principles and practices. In this case, violence might begin to increase again after an initial decrease. Finally, how does the level of outcomes develop after the program ceases? Do students incorporate the new behaviors permanently, or do they go back to their old ways? A variety of such policy impact models can be examined toward the end of the intervention, when time series data are available.

It should now be clear that having randomization comparison groups, and baselines help strengthen conclusions about impacts or changes that might be observed. The above information is surely not as perfect as a study done under experimental conditions, but such a design may not be possible. Rather, analysts try to keep the possibility of being wrong about their statements as small as possible; they identify the most likely rival hypotheses and control variables in advance, and include data about them in their study methods. They caveat other factors. Of course, it not always possible to find comparison groups, or analysts may lack the resources (money) to gather data about them. The job of the analyst is to provide as much valid information as they can. Some examples of program evaluations are discussed in Box 2.1.

In Greater Depth . . .

Box 2.1   Program Evaluation in Practice

Program evaluations are undertaken by many organizations, some of which emphasize and excel in this activity. The Government Accountability Office (GAO, formerly the General Accounting Office) of the U.S. Congress provides numerous assessments each year and is highly respected. Some GAO reports evaluate program outcomes. For example, a GAO study of 23 adult drug court programs found that recidivism rates were 10–30 percent lower among participants than among those in comparison groups (GAO-05-219). In this study, a comparison group was developed for each of the adult drug court programs. Some comparison groups were contemporaneous, that is, consisting of defendants who were eligible for the adult drug court program but who received conventional case processing. Other, historical comparison groups were developed from individuals who completed conventional case processing before the adult drug court was implemented. In each case, comparison group participants were selected to closely match characteristics of those in the adult court groups regarding substance abuse, socioeconomic status, demographic profile, and criminal justice history. However, recognizing the possibility of selection bias (matching is not perfect), the study used statistical methods to control for individual differences between adult court and comparison group members.

In another study, the GAO examined how long it took the Departments of State and Commerce to issue export licenses, which are required for exporting

---

Box 2.1   *(continued)*

equipment and services that have military applications. The State Department issues licenses for items that have only military applications, and the Commerce Department issues licenses for items that have both military and commercial uses. Each year these agencies receive, respectively, 46,000 and 11,000 license applications (GAO-01-528). The study found little difference between these agencies; the State Department took 46 days to review an application, and the Commerce Department took 50 days. In making the comparison, the GAO was mindful to consider the nature and complexity of the application as a source of possible variation. Examples of GAO studies can be found at www.gpoaccess.gov/gaoreports/index.html.

However, many GAO reports are only descriptive, for example, providing information on what programs are doing, and focusing on issues of critical importance to the programs. For instance, a study of homelessness programs described what these programs do and examined the extent of coordination, which the GAO concluded that agencies should increase (GAO RCED-99-49). In other instances, the GAO examines the nature of oversight and accountability maintained by agencies and suggests ways in which that might be improved. Sometimes GAO reports examine an agency's potential for evaluation and recommend that the agency do a better job of maintaining and gathering data to enable meaningful evaluation.

The GAO is a good example of a government's ability to evaluate programs; reading a dozen or so of its reports can help increase your familiarity with program evaluation. However, as a government agency, the GAO is under considerable time pressure, too. Think-tanks such as the Urban Institute, the RAND Corporation, the Brookings Institution, and the American Enterprise Institute exemplify how program evaluation can be deeper and even more thorough when conducted by independent, nonprofit organizations dedicated to public policy research. Many of their evaluations, funded by government programs, are book length and sometimes use extensive methodologies. The websites of these organizations reveal the breadth of topics and programs that they have researched.

As an aside, we can view quasi-experimental research designs as variations on the classic, randomized design. Box 2.2 provides a stylistic representation of such designs. Design A is the classic, randomized design, showing randomization, a control group, pretests, and posttests. The designs under B are all lacking in one or more ways. Program evaluation almost

Box 2.2   Research Designs

Research designs can be characterized using the following notation, where R = randomization, X = intervention, and O = measurement. The following is based on the enduring, classic work of Donald Campbell and Julian Stanley.

A. The classic, randomized design is depicted graphically as follows. Any significant program impact would be indicated when (O2–O1) > (O4–O3). The placebo intervention is not shown, but if it existed it would be implemented between O3 and O4; it would be similar to X, except that it is intentionally ineffective.

	Pretest	Program	Posttest
Group 1:	R O1	X	O2
Group 2:	R O3		O4

B. Quasi-experimental designs vary from this design in several ways:

1. Research design with a nonrandomized comparison group:

	Pretest	Program	Posttest
Group 1:	O1	X	O2
Group 2:	O3		O4

2. One-group research design with posttest measure, only:

	Pretest	Program	Posttest
Group 1, only:		X	O2

3. Research design with comparison group and posttests, only:

	Pretest	Program	Posttest
Group 1:		X	O2
Group 2:			O4

4. One-group research design with pretest and posttest:

	Pretest	Program	Posttest
Group 1, only:	O1	X	O2

Source: Donald Campbell and Julian Stanley, *Experimental and Quasi-experimental Designs for Research* (Chicago: Rand McNally), 1963.

always uses a quasi-experimental design of some kind. As an example of a before-and-after design with comparison group (B1), in a study of innovative housing vouchers or mental health interventions, subjects with similar conditions might be assigned to different programs in similar cities that have similar neighborhoods. Some subjects might be followed who do not participate in any program; these subjects would make up the comparison group. Others might be assigned to a traditional program and others to one or more innovative programs. Outcomes would then be compared across these groups, controlling for rival hypotheses and differences that might exist among the different populations and local conditions.

A key task of research planning is to identify relevant rival hypotheses and control variables for one's program or policy, so that data of them are collected during the research process. This helps make subsequent analysis possible. Some careful thought has been given to types of rival hypotheses that researchers might consider, though not all of the following are relevant in every situation.

Threats to external validity are defined as those that jeopardize the generalizability of study conclusions about program outcomes to other situations. For example, suppose we evaluate one anger management program in one school setting and, on the basis of that evaluation, wish to generalize our study conclusions to anger management programs in all schools? Such a generalization might be invalid if conditions in these other schools differ from conditions in the school that was studied. Or perhaps there is something unique about the study population or about the students in the other schools that makes generalization problematic. If generalization is a study objective, then such concerns should be considered during the study design phase; we would need to choose program settings that can be generalized to other settings.

Threats to internal validity are those that stem from the study design and that jeopardize the study conclusions about whether an intervention in fact caused a difference in the study population. These threats often call into question the logic of study conclusions. *History* refers to events that are not part of the intervention yet occur during the intervention and affect study outcomes. For example, a shooting rampage among high school students elsewhere might temporarily reduce violence in other schools as that event is discussed and digested. Hence, history might explain the study outcomes. *Maturation* refers to the natural development of subjects in ways that affect study outcomes but that are not affected by the intervention. For example, students may themselves learn to control their anger, apart from any anger management program. People do grow up. Did the program control for this possibility? *Testing* refers to subjects changing their behavior because they are being tested rather than because of the intervention. For example, if high school violence is measured partly by asking students how many episodes of anger they experienced recently (however defined), asking them this question may cause some students to view anger as a problem, and they might take steps to reduce it. Any reduction in violence is then caused by the act of being tested rather than by the intervention itself.

Instrumentation refers to changes in outcomes resulting from the way in which an instrument (such as a survey) measures the outcomes. Perhaps violence is measured partly by observation, and observers become more attuned to different forms of violence over time. This will inflate later (for example, postintervention) measures of violence; the instrument (observation) measures more violence over time, regardless of whether more violence is occurring. *Statistical regression* refers to the fact that extreme scores tend to become less extreme over time; they regress toward the average. If we start out with students who all exhibit extreme violence of the worst kind, then it may not be possible for them to become any worse. Regardless of the intervention, the group is likely to improve. *Selection bias* refers to the problem that subjects may not be truly comparable between the experimental (intervention) and comparison groups. For example, the experimental group might have more at-risk students, as discussed earlier. *Mortality* refers to biases due to attrition of study subjects, for example, the transfer of angry students to other schools during the intervention. This event will reduce the incidence of violence, of course. *Imitation* occurs when some subjects in the comparison group learn of the intervention in the experimental group and begin imitating such behavior. In our example, students in classes that do not receive the anger management intervention might also see reductions in violence as a result of students talking with each other. *Rivalry* occurs when subjects in the experimental and comparison groups begin competing with each other. In our example, these students might compete with each other to be the least (or most!) violent.[6, 7]

The point of this lengthy list is to draw attention to concerns that analysts *may* want to consider in their research and evaluation. Most researchers consider at least a few or the most important rival hypotheses and threats to validity, as defined by the study context and the interests or concerns of their audience. Researchers sometimes talk with their audience in advance to help learn of others' study interests and concerns. Then, they think deeply about ways to increase the validity of their research, addressing others' concerns about inevitable study caveats. Research planning is key to success and involves (1) being clear about independent and dependent variables, (2) selecting important or relevant control variables, and

(3) when possible, extending the study design to cover before-and-after measures, comparison groups, and baselines. By planning carefully at an early stage, analysts increase the validity and acceptance of their work.[8]

SUMMARY

Social science research methods are often applied to many problems of management and analysis. Analysis typically involves a range of qualitative and quantitative research methods, and both basic and applied research focuses. Program evaluation is an example of such an application.

Variables, defined as observable phenomena that vary, represent a cornerstone concept in scientific research. Programs and policies usually attempt to affect variables in some ways (for example, by increasing or decreasing some social or economic conditions), and analysis often involves studying these changes.

Relationships in social science are distinguished by whether they are probabilistic (occurring sometimes) or deterministic (occurring each time). Relationships in social science are often probabilistic. Relationships are further distinguished as being either causal or associational. Causal relationships show cause and effect. When relationships are causal, independent and dependent variables can be distinguished. Independent variables are variables that cause an effect on other variables, and dependent variables are variables that are affected by other variables. Programs and policies are commonly conceptualized as independent variables causing changes in dependent variables, or outcomes.

The purpose of program evaluation often is to establish the effect of programs or policies on outcomes. A common concern is that other factors in addition to the program or policy (for example, events or processes) also affect outcomes. These alternative explanations for outcomes are referred to as rival hypotheses, and the variables associated with them are called control variables. The analytical task is to identify these rival hypotheses, collect data for the control variables, and use statistical methods to take their impact into account.

Program evaluation often uses quasi-experimental research designs. Such designs typically use before- an after-measurement, comparison groups and/or baseline measurement in a variety of ways. The theory of quasi-experimental research design includes consideration of different types of rival hypotheses, which are distinguished as threats to internal or external validity. Familiarity with these categories can help analysts to identify rival hypotheses. Studies often include a few important rival hypotheses and control variables.

KEY TERMS

(includes bold italic terms in the Section II introduction)

Applied research (see section introduction) (p. 18)

Associations (p. 24)

Attributes (p. 22)

Basic research (see section introduction) (p. 18)

Causal relationships (p. 24)

Classic, randomized experiments (p. 30)

Constant (p. 22)

Control variables (p. 30)

Criteria for causality (p. 25)

Dependent variables (p. 24)

Descriptive analysis (p. 23)

Experimental design (p. 30)

Hypothesis (p. 26)

Independent variables (p. 24)

Program evaluation (p. 26)

Qualitative research methods (see section introduction) (p. 19)

Quantitative research methods (see section introduction) (p. 18)

Quasi-experimental designs (p. 32)

Relationships (p. 23)

Research methodology (see section introduction) (p. 17)

Rival hypotheses (p. 30)

Six steps of program evaluation (p. 28)

Statistical control strategy (p. 31)

Threats to external validity (p. 37)

Threats to internal validity (p. 37)

Variables (p. 22)

Notes

1. In Chapter 10, we provide a more specific, technical definition of level of confidence, in our discussion of statistical significance.

2. Consider another example. In Louisiana a relationship exists between the increase in population and the state's shrinking in size each year. Does this mean that the weight of more people is causing the state to sink? No. The shrinking size is caused by erosion of coastal wetlands, not the weight of more people. These are unrelated events; the relationship is an association, only.

3. Two concerns are sometimes raised: (1) that the independent variable must precede the dependent variable in time and (2) that neither is caused by other variables; see the discussion of *spurious relationships* in note 5.

4. A variety of books address program evaluation. The leading text is Peter Rossi et al., *Evaluation: A Systematic Approach,* 7th ed. or later (Thousand Oaks, Calif.: Sage, 2003). See also *Exercising Essential Statistics,* the workbook that accompanies this textbook, for other references and exercises.

5. Control variables can affect the relationship between the independent and dependent variables in several ways. Different authors use different names to indicate these effects, but shown here is one approach. All three

examples involve control variables. In the following graphic, moderating variables affect the way in which the independent variable affects the dependent variable, for example, sabotaging a class in which the instructor helps students learn to control their anger.

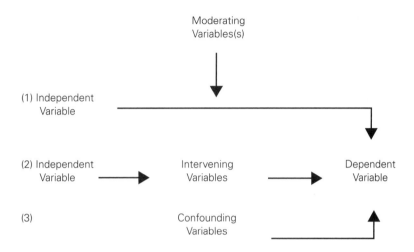

Moderating
Variables(s)

(1) Independent
Variable

(2) Independent   Intervening   Dependent
Variable   Variables   Variable

(3)   Confounding
Variables

Sometimes a variable gives rise to two variables, when in fact no relationship exists between the two variables. This is called a spurious relationship, as is shown below. For example, the time of year (spring) is a spurious variable that gives rise to both storks and childbirths.

Variable 1   Variable 2

Confounding
Variable

Bottom line: Regardless of how control variables affect variables, the point is to identify rival hypotheses (control variables) that may affect study conclusions.

6. A useful acronym for remembering these threats to internal validity is "Mis Smith": maturation, instrumentation, selection, statistical regression, mortality, imitation, testing, and history. The classic source for these distinctions is Donald Campbell and Julian Stanley, *Experimental and Quasi-experimental Designs for Research* (Chicago: Rand McNally, 1963). The text includes, additionally, the term *rivalry.*

7. Even the classic, randomized research design is subject to some of these validity threats. Threats to external validity (generalizability) are a problem

in any setting, and problems of history and mortality also may be present. It is not a given that the experimental and control groups experience the same intervening events (history), and they may have different rates of attrition (mortality). Testing might affect both groups, too. To address the problem of testing, a modification of the classic, randomized research design is the Solomon four-group design:

	Pretest	Program	Posttest
Group 1:	R O1	X	O2
Group 2:	R O3		O4
Group 3:	R	X	O5
Group 4:	R		O6

In this design, groups 3 and 4 allow the researcher to control for the impact of pretesting on groups 1 and 2.

8. For example, in a simple posttest design with no comparison group, the evaluation of anger management should consider whether any intervening effects (history) occurred that could have affected students' levels of anger and violence. Analysts will want to examine and account for possible maturation, statistical regression, and sample bias effects on the results. They also will want to assess subjects' knowledge of other efforts used elsewhere (which could give rise to imitation or rivalry) and ensure that the assessment method is accurate (minimizing effects of instrumentation).

CHAPTER

3

Conceptualization and Measurement

CHAPTER OBJECTIVES

After reading this chapter, you should be able to

- Appreciate the challenge of measuring abstract concepts
- Implement methods for measuring abstract concepts
- Distinguish between different levels of measurement
- Apply a variety of Likert scales
- Create index variables
- Understand criteria for assessing measurement validity

Measurement is a foundation of science and knowledge. How well phenomena are measured affects what we know about them, and rigor in measurement increases the validity of analytical work. This chapter discusses key concepts of measurement and shows how to apply these measurements in analytical work such as program evaluation. This chapter also shows how to make index variables.

MEASUREMENT LEVELS AND SCALES

A *scale* is defined as the collection of attributes used to measure a specific variable. For example, the variable "gender" is commonly measured on a scale defined by the specific attributes "male" and "female." Scales are important because they define the nature of information about variables. For example, we can measure incomes by asking respondents for their exact income or by asking them to identify their income using prespecified income brackets. Scales vary greatly—some are unique to the variables they measure, such as the Richter scale, which measures the strength of earthquakes; others are used for many different purposes, such as response scales found in survey questionnaires. Managers should be familiar with different types of scales so that they can adapt them to their needs.

Measurement scales are distinguished by their level of measurement. There are four **levels of measurement**: *nominal, ordinal, interval,* and *ratio*. A variable that has, for example, an ordinal-level measurement scale is commonly referred to as an ordinal-level variable or, simply, as an ordinal variable. The importance of the measurement level is threefold: (1) it determines the selection of test statistics (highly relevant to subsequent chapters), (2) it affects the amount of information collected about variables, and (3) it affects how survey and other types of questions are phrased.

A **nominal-level scale** exhibits no ordering among the categories. It provides the least amount of information. For example, the variable "gender" has a nominal scale because there is no ordering among the attributes "men" and "women." We cannot say that "men" are more than "women," regardless of any coding scheme that assigns numbers to these categories; they are nominal categories, only. "Region" is another common nominal scale: no ordering exists among the values of North, South, East, and West.

By contrast, an **ordinal-level scale** exhibits order among categories (hence, the name *ordinal*), though without exact distances between successive categories. "Order" means that categories can be compared as being "more" or "less" than one another. For example, assume that we measure teenage anger by asking adolescents whether they feel irritated, aggravated, or raging mad. Clearly someone feeling "raging mad" is more angry than someone who feels only "aggravated," who in turn is more angry than someone who feels "irritated." "Distance" means that we can measure how much more one category is than another. Ordinal scales lack distance. Although we can say that "raging mad" is more angry than "aggravated," we cannot say *how much* more angry "raging mad" is than "aggravated. Collectively, ordinal- and nominal-level variables are called **categorical** (or **discrete**) **variables**.

> **Key Point**
> A scale is a collection of attributes used to measure a specific variable.

Likert scales are a common type of ordinal scale. Developed in 1932 by Professor Rensis Likert, these scales are now a staple in surveys that measure attitudes. The responses used on Likert scales come in many variations, such as "strongly agree," "agree," "somewhat agree," "don't know," "somewhat disagree," "disagree," and "strongly disagree." Survey respondents are read statements (for example, "I feel safe at school") and are then asked, after each statement, to respond by selecting one of the responses. Likert scales demonstrate order and the absence of distance between categories: "strongly agree" is a higher level of agreeing than just "agree," but we cannot say how much more. Likert scales are so popular because they have been widely tested and are easy to use and adapt. Box 3.1 provides further examples of these important scales.[1]

In Greater Depth . . .

Box 3.1   Likert Scales

Likert scales are ordinal-level scales; several major variations are shown below. Five-point scales are identical to seven-point scales in the first three examples, except that they omit the categories of "somewhat." Some surveys (for example, some political polls) also lack the category "don't know" or "can't say," thereby forcing respondent answers. This approach is objectionable academically, because it fails to measure accurately the responses of those who genuinely "don't know" or "can't say" while overestimating adjacent categories.

1. Please indicate your agreement with the following statements, using the following scale:

    7 = Strongly Agree   3 = Somewhat Disagree
    6 = Agree   2 = Disagree
    5 = Somewhat Agree   1 = Strongly Disagree
    4 = Don't Know / Can't Say

    Students who are violent should be removed from class.   ①②③④⑤⑥⑦
    I would like us to have anger management classes.   ①②③④⑤⑥⑦
    There should be an after-school homework assistance program. ①②③④⑤⑥⑦

2. How important are the following items to you? Please use the following scale:

    7 = Very Important   3 = Somewhat Unimportant
    6 = Important   2 = Unimportant
    5 = Somewhat Important   1 = Very Unimportant
    4 = Don't Know / Can't Say

(continued)

Box 3.1 *(continued)*

Feeling safe in my neighborhood   ①②③④⑤⑥⑦
Putting those who commit crimes in jail   ①②③④⑤⑥⑦
Seeing more guards in school   ①②③④⑤⑥⑦

3. How satisfied are you with the following school facilities? Please use the following scale:

7 = Very Satisfied	3 = Somewhat Dissatisfied
6 = Satisfied	2 = Dissatisfied
5 = Somewhat Satisfied	1 = Very Dissatisfied
4 = Don't Know / Can't Say	

Basketball courts   ①②③④⑤⑥⑦
Computer lab   ①②③④⑤⑥⑦
School library   ①②③④⑤⑥⑦

4. How frequently do you use the following school services?

7 = Very Frequently	3 = Very Rarely
6 = Frequently	2 = Never
5 = Occasionally	1 = Don't Know
4 = Rarely	

School counselor   ①②③④⑤⑥⑦
School nurse   ①②③④⑤⑥⑦
School librarian   ①②③④⑤⑥⑦

Note: Additional examples of Likert scales can be found online. For example, see www.gifted.uconn.edu/siegle/research/instrument%20Reliability%20and%20 Validity/Likert.html. (October 15, 2005).

Interval- and *ratio-level scales* exhibit both order and distance among categories. We can say that someone who exercises daily does so seven times more often than someone who exercises only weekly. Someone who earns $75,000 per year makes exactly three times that of someone making $25,000. The *only* difference between interval and ratio scales is that the latter have a true "zero" (for example, income can be zero, but IQ cannot). The distinction between ratio- and interval-level variables is typically of little relevance to public and nonprofit administration and policy analysis. Variables with interval- and ratio-level scales are also called ***continuous variables***.[2]

Box 3.2   Writing the Report

New researchers and analysts sometimes struggle to write up their methods and results in professionally appropriate ways. What must be written? How must it be written? How can the report be made to appear professional? The adage that practice makes perfect is true but of insufficient guidance. Here are some *writing tips* and pointers that may help:

1. Collect 6–10 reports that are suitable examples of the kind of report you are looking to write. Subject matter is less important than the depth and nature of analysis, the report length, and its methodological sophistication. Study these reports very, very carefully. How is the report organized (table of contents)? What types of graphs and tables are presented? What do the appendices (if any) cover? Which of the issues mentioned in the chapters so far do they deal with? How do the reports deal with these issues? What aspects of these issues do they raise, and what language do they use in addressing them? Learn from these examples. Emulate them.

2. Develop an outline. The outline is your template, your strategy that tells you what you need to write. Therefore, draft an outline that is suited for you, modeled on the example reports. Decide what parts your report should have, and then write each part. The broad outline of many reports is as follows: executive summary, introduction, literature review, methods, results, conclusion, and appendices. Analytical reports are built piecemeal. Often, parts of different sections are generated in the research and analysis processes.

   The literature review is particularly helpful in that it brings to us what others have done before; even someone doing a comparables study for a local government labor negotiation wouldn't start from scratch. The traditional literature review is sometimes supplemented by reports and documentation reflecting the experiences of other jurisdictions and agencies.

3. Language matters. The words that come to you first may not be or sound very professional. Most analysts write several drafts; some write as many as 10 or 20. Ultimately you should write reports in the third person, using the active voice and present tense. Present your ideas clearly and concisely. Use short sentences rather than long and convoluted ones. Write down the thoughts and language that come to you, but then rework what you have written as often as necessary. Technical writing is very different from writing an English essay or fiction. Identify your audience, and write for it.

4. Details, details. Check the grammar. Format the report. Make it look professional. Double-check that you have made all of the arguments that need to be made. As you write, consult the example reports for additional ideas and arguments that you might make. Let others look over your work and make comments from which you can learn.

In general, we strongly prefer having more information about variables than less. Therefore, continuous-level scales are preferred over ordinal-level scales, which in turn are preferred over nominal-level scales. We also prefer ordinal and nominal scales that have more rather than fewer categories. Of course, a variable such as "gender" cannot be made ordinal or continuous, and it can have only two categories. Likewise, some variables can only be ordinal and cannot be continuous.[3]

The development of measures and scales is a precise task. We must avoid scales that are incomplete, ambiguous, or overlapping. An *incomplete scale* might omit "zero" as a response category when asking respondents how many fist fights they witnessed. An *ambiguous scale* is one that asks respondents to answer a question about the presence of violence "on a scale of 1 to 10" without defining each value. Respondents may have different definitions of any specific value, such as the value of "6." In an *overlapping scale,* at least one response is covered by more than one category. An example of such a scale is one that measures income with brackets $20,000–$40,000 and $40,000–$60,000. It is better to use $20,000–$39,999 and $40,000–$59,999. Another example is measuring "fist fights" and "scuffles" as separate categories.

Problems with measurement scales can affect the validity of one's findings. Measurement scales should be complete and unambiguous, with unique categories for each response. Of course, other measurement challenges also exist, such as well-known problems of using leading (or biased) survey questions as well as samples that are biased or restricted in some way; these matters are discussed further in Chapter 5.[4] We now turn to another measurement topic, that of measuring abstract concepts.

CONCEPTUALIZATION

Many important matters of public and nonprofit management and analysis involve abstract concepts, such as notions of democracy, effectiveness, volunteerism, citizen satisfaction, and, yes, high school violence and anger. The rigor with which study concepts are defined (such as the level of anger or high school violence) enhances the validity of our efforts. ***Measurement validity*** simply means that something measures or reflects what it is intended to. This is identified as step 4 in the six-step model of program evaluation (see Chapter 2). A research task needs to be clear about what is being studied. For example, how should we measure the concept "high school violence?"

In this regard, variables must be distinguished from concepts. Whereas variables belong to the realm of directly observable phenomena, concepts belong to the realm of ideas. ***Concepts*** are abstract ideas that are observed indirectly, through variables. Processes of concept measurement typically have two steps. First we need to be clear about the meaning of the concept and, in particular, identify all the relevant dimensions of the concept. This is called **conceptualization.** Then we need to identify and define the variable(s) that will be used to measure the concept and its dimensions. This is called **operationalization.**

This process is best explained through an example. Suppose we want to measure the concept "student anger." First we need to be clear about what "student anger" means. What is the essence of this concept?[5] How might we best define it in the context of our study? Because our program aims to reduce and control manifestations of anger and violence that can be disruptive, we might define "student anger" as "a strong emotion of displeasure by students that may be triggered by, or directed toward, specific or general grievances." Of course, this is not the only way to define the concept, and certainly some other definitions might be better. Perhaps you know of a better definition? We can justify this definition, however, through criteria that are commonly used for this purpose: consistency with generally understood meanings of the concept (here, anger), consistency with expert understandings and studies, and being relevant and central to the program and its evaluation.

Next, and still part of conceptualization, we need to ask whether any discernible, distinct dimensions of this concept should be considered and measured separately? Assume that we identify the following three dimensions to the concept "student anger": (1) emotions of anger, (2) thoughts (cognition) of anger, and (3) physical rage. Each dimension stands alone and can be measured separately. For example, some students might have thoughts of anger but little emotion associated with these thoughts, and vice versa. Some may have rage and emotion but little cognition. These are different dimensions of anger. Only after the dimensions of "student anger" have been identified can the analytical task shift toward developing a process for measuring these dimensions (that is, operationalization).

It is not a given that this concept will or should always have these dimensions. Complex concepts and those that are key to the research design are usually conceptualized with greater rigor than those that are simple or less key to the program or evaluation. In the case of evaluating the anger management program, "student anger" is an important concept and one that managers and analysts will want to examine carefully. Yet this concept might not be of much importance in a study about, say, student achievement. Such a study might choose to measure "student anger" in only a cursory way, perhaps as just a single item (for example, "How angry do you usually feel?"). Decisions about study rigor and the importance of specific study concepts drive thoroughness.

> **Key Point**
> There are different ways to conceptualize any concept, and some are more rigorous than others.

When study concepts are conceptualized with rigor and thoroughness, analysts need to determine how many concept dimensions they will identify and measure. An imprecise guiding principle is that analysts should be true and comprehensive with regard to their concepts. Typically two to five dimensions are used in rigorous conceptualizations, usually based on (1) the consensus of past studies, (2) whether concept definitions include disparate facets or dimensions, (3) program needs that might suggest dimensions, and (4) practical constraints in the ability to collect data.[6] Our example of conceptualizing "student anger" reflects judgments that it is a key study concept requiring rigor, that the three identified dimensions reflect a comprehensive and appropriate understanding of the concept, and that the concept is relevant to program management.

Analysts must justify their choices about the conceptualization and operationalization of study concepts. An important perspective is that no correct number of dimensions or variables exists, only bad or lacking ones.[7]

Another example involves the conceptualization of "high school violence." Assume that after defining this concept, conducting a brief litera-ture review, and talking with program officials, we reach a consensus that "high school violence" has three dimensions: (1) use of weapons, (2) inap-propriate physical contact (occurring without weapons and not involving sanctioned physical contact during sports activities), and (3) verbal assaults. These are seen not as degrees of violence, but as three different dimensions (or types) of violence. Students can have physical contact without necessar-ily using weapons or involving verbal assault. These dimensions of violence can be measured separately.

OPERATIONALIZATION

As we discussed earlier, the development of specific measures is called opera-tionalization. This process develops the specific variables that will be used to measure a concept. Three approaches to operationalization are (1) to develop separate measures for each dimension, (2) to develop a single set of measures that encompass the dimensions, or (3) to develop a single measure. These three strategies reflect a *declining* order of rigor.

The *first* strategy is the most comprehensive approach—measuring each dimension separately. By way of example, Table 3.1 lays out the basic measurement strategy for conceptualizing and operationalizing the three dimensions of "high school violence."

Whereas the table shows a mix of objective data and subjective assess-ments, this is not always the case nor is it always necessary. Student perceptions might be assessed through a survey in which students are asked to evaluate such statements. Typically 5–10 questions are used to measure each dimension.

Table 3.1 ———〜〜〜— Measuring High School Violence

Dimension	Measurement
1: Use of weapons	Number of students caught using weapons Student perception of presence of weapons (guns, knives, other)
2: Physical contact	Number of fights and scuffles reported to administrators Number of inappropriate physical contacts reported to administrators (sexual and nonsexual) Student perception of fights, scuffles, and inappropriate physical contact (sexual and nonsexual)
3: Verbal assaults and threats	Number of harassment allegations brought to administrators Student perception of verbal assaults and threats

For example, the following questions might be used to assess student perceptions of inappropriate physical contact at school (dimension 2):

> Please tell me which of the following you experienced in or around school, during the last month, which were not part of any normal sports activity:

I was involved in a fight or scuffle.
I was physically injured in a fight or scuffle.
I was pushed or tripped by someone who, I believe, tried to injure me.
I was touched sexually in ways that were unwanted by me.
I was struck by someone with an object (such as a stick or stone).
I was assaulted in some way but not injured.
I was physically hurt in some other way (please specify). . . .

This is certainly not the only way to assess student perceptions of "inappropriate physical contact." Some assessments might ask different questions. Unwanted sexual contact is included as a form of violence. As indicated in the table, objective data might also be included for each dimension. In the same way, survey items would be developed to measure the other two dimensions, "use of weapons" and "verbal assaults and threats." The correct and complete development of study measures finishes the process of operationalization. Chapter 5 provides additional guidance on developing survey questions and collecting data.

The *second,* less rigorous (but still comprehensive) approach is to develop questions that each measure a different aspect of high school violence, without specifying and developing these questions into measures of the three dimensions. Such an approach might be necessary because of data limitations (for example, limited space on surveys) or because other study concepts are more important. Although less thorough than the first approach, the following question might be considered a measure of high school violence:

> Please indicate whether you strongly agree, agree, don't know, disagree, or strongly disagree with each of the following statements:
>
> At least one of my classmates has carried a gun to school.
> Some students in my class regularly carry knives to school.
> Students in my class regularly get involved in fights and scuffles.
> There is inappropriate sexual contact or gesturing occurring in my class.
> People try to hurt others in my class through tripping, pushing, or shoving.
> People in my class threaten each other with physical violence.
> People in my class vandalize each other's property.
> People in my class regularly insult each other.

Note that the list encompasses the three dimensions identified earlier. Whether this measure suffices depends on the manager's needs for more specific information and on validation (discussed later in this chapter). Sometimes this second approach develops into the first approach as analysts give more careful consideration to the distinct dimensions of the concept.

The *third* approach is decidedly nonrigorous, using a single survey item to measure the concept. For our current example, such an item might read as follows:

> Please indicate whether you strongly agree, agree, don't know, disagree, or strongly disagree with the following statement:
>
> My high school is a violent place.

While not biased, this item does not provide any information about specific aspects of the phenomenon. As noted earlier, this approach is typically used when the concept is of quite minor importance to the program or evaluation. In our example, however, we want more information than would be obtained from this single item.

Getting Started

Identify an abstract concept, and practice conceptualizing it using the three strategies described here.

Finally, an important question is whether any best set of measures exists for measuring a concept. The *theorem of the interchangeability of indicators* states that if several measures are equally valid indicators of a concept, then any subset of these measures will be valid as well. In other words, there are many valid ways to measure a given concept.

The analyst's task is to choose one approach and then justify that that approach is valid. The challenge of justification is discussed later in this chapter.

INDEX VARIABLES

An *index variable* is a variable that combines the values of other variables into a single indicator or score. For example, the consumer price index is a variable that combines the prices of common consumer goods and services into a single score. Index variables are common, for example, measuring the economic outlook, infant and child health, environmental quality, political stability, volunteerism and giving, culture in cities, and so on. Managers and analysts frequently encounter index variables in their work.

Index variables are also commonly used to empirically measure abstract concepts and multifaceted, encompassing phenomena. In the preceding section, we developed a strategy for measuring different dimensions of high school violence. Some variables measure violence that involves weapons, other variables measure inappropriate physical contact, and still other variables measure verbal assaults and threats. How can these disparate measures be combined into one aggregate measure of high school violence?

The logic of index variable construction is simple: the values of the measurement variables are simply summed. The term *measurement variable* refers to the (observed) variables that make up the index; it has no bearing on any measurement scale or data collection strategy and is used to distinguish these variables from the index variable. When respondents score low on measurement variables, the resulting index score is also low, and vice versa. Table 3.2 shows how an index variable is created by simply adding up the values of the measurement variables that constitute the dimension or concept. Thus, when respondents score high on measurement variables, the resulting index score is high. When one or more of the measurement variables are missing from an observation, the value of the

Table 3.2 ⎯⎯⎯⎯⎯ᴧᴧᴧ⎯ Creating an Index Variable

Observation	Measure 1	Measure 2	Measure 3	Measure 4	Index
567	1	2	2	4	9
568	4	1	1	1	7
569	4	2	2	4	12
570	5	5	5	5	20
571	1	2	—	1	—
572	1	1	1	1	4

index variable for that observation is missing, too, as shown for observation 571. Note that whereas measurement variables might be ordinal (for example, measured on a five-point Likert scale), the resulting index variable often is continuous. In the example in Table 3.2, the index variable can range from a minimum of 4 to a maximum of 20. Of course, statistical software does the addition.

> **Key Point**
> An index variable combines the values of other variables into a new, single measure.

This logic is applied to other indexes, too. For example, the consumer price index is based on price changes for a bundle of goods. The sum of all prices is determined in each period, and the periods are then compared with each other. An index of municipal cultural activity might sum the number of performances, renowned organizations, and cultural facilities (museums, theaters, and the like).

To continue our example of high school violence, in our second approach we simply sum the values of each of the survey items and in this way construct an index measure of high school violence. The values of these items are summed for each observation, in exactly the same manner as in Table 3.2. But in our first, more rigorous approach, we follow a two-step process for creating the index measure. In the first step, we construct index variables for each of the three separate dimensions (use of weapons, inappropriate physical contact, and verbal assaults and threats). In the second step, we sum the values of these three index variables, for each observation, which then results in a new, "super" index of "high school violence." The latter index is clearly grounded in the three dimensions of high school violence.

A practical problem with index variables is that individual components sometimes have different scales or ranges. For example, if one variable can range from 0 (min) to 10 (max), and the other from 0 (min) to 1,000 (max), then the former will likely not have much impact on the aggregate measure, the index. Especially if most values of the latter variable are between, say, 300 and 800, then adding the values of the first variable, ranging between 0 and 10, will not much affect the aggregate score. To address this problem, analysts can rescale each of the variables being summed, so that each has the same range, such as 0 to 100. One way to do this, in the preceding case, would be to multiply each value of the first variable by 10 and divide each value of the second variable by 10. (However, other approaches exist.[8])

Although index measures are not very difficult to make, a key issue is their validation. The resulting index variable must be established as a valid measure of the underlying concept being measured. The next section discusses how we go about doing that.

MEASUREMENT VALIDITY

It is always important to think about the validity of what we do. Earlier, in Chapter 2, we discussed validity with regard to drawing study conclusions; here, we discuss it narrowly with regard to measurement. Measures must be shown to be valid measures of the phenomena and concepts that they measure. Measurement validity simply means that variables really measure what they are said to measure. Considerable thought has gone into the different strategies that can be used to establish measurement validity. Analysts are not expected to use all or even most of these strategies, but they are expected to justify their variables in some way.[9]

An important form of validation is theoretical—a persuasive argument that the measures make sense. One argument is that the measures are reasonable, common-sense ways of measuring the underlying concept. This is called *face validity*. Measuring "gender" by asking respondents whether they are male or female is a reasonable, common-sense method. Some respondents may erroneously indicate the wrong gender, but such numbers will likely be few and not affect study conclusions in any material way. In the case of high school violence, however, the justification is more elaborate. But again we can argue that the measures used are reasonable, common-sense ways of measuring the specific variables and underlying concept.

Regarding index variables, another argument is that they should encompass the (broad) range of aspects of the concept and its dimensions. For example, variables measuring "physical exercise" should not be skewed in some biasing way, perhaps underemphasizing individual sports in favor of team sports. Whether "student anger" is measured in a comprehensive or simple way, it should not be biased against certain forms of student anger. This form of validity is called *content validity*. The very simple operationalization given earlier ("How angry do you usually feel?") avoids this problem by not specifying any specific form of anger. In the case of "high school violence," we measure a broad range of aspects, especially those that ought to be included in such a study.

Empirical evidence can also be mustered in several ways. First, variables can be validated by comparing them with other measures or sources. For example, the measure "physical contact without weapons" might be triangulated by records of the school nurse (treatment of scrapes and bruises) and a student survey. Although such correlation does not prove that the measure is valid, certainly the lack of correlation would raise some eyebrows. Comparison with external sources is sometimes called *criterion (or external) validity* (not be confused with threats to external validity, discussed in Chapter 2). Some researchers also refer to this as *triangulation*. When the variable correlates as expected, additional validity is provided.

Second, we might ask respondents on the same survey about physical contact without weapons and compare that response with other responses, such as regarding physical injuries incurred at school. Such comparison against internal sources is called *construct (or internal) validity*. Although this comparison does not provide absolute proof (respondents may receive injuries at school for reasons unrelated to high school violence), it may provide some reassurance and, hence, a measure of validity. Certainly a lack of correlation would require further inquiry and explanation.

Getting Started

How can you validate your conceptualized measure?

Third, regarding index variables, the variables used to measure a concept should be strongly associated (or correlated) with each other. This is because each index variable measures different but related dimensions. When variables are not highly related, analysts should consider whether, perhaps, one or more of the variables measure some other concept. The correlation of measurement variables is called *internal reliability* (or internal consistency, not be confused with threats to internal validity, discussed in Chapter 2). *Cronbach alpha* (also called *alpha* or *measure alpha*) is a statistical measure of internal reliability that is often cited in research articles that use index variables.[10] Although you need not be concerned about the exact calculation of this measure,[11] alpha can range from 0 to 1, where a 1 indicates perfect correlation among the measurement variables, and a 0 indicates the lack of any correlation among the measurement variables. Values between 0.80 and 1.00 are desired, and they indicate high reliability among the measurement variables. Values between 0.70 and 0.80 indicate moderate (but acceptable) reliability. Alpha values below 0.70 are poor and should cause analysts to consider a different mix of variables. Although index variables with alpha scores below 0.70 should be avoided, values between 0.60 and 0.70 are sometimes used when analysts lack a better mix of variables. Analysts usually collect a few more variables than are minimally needed because they cannot know, prior to reliability analysis, which variable mix will have a sufficiently high alpha score to lend empirical support for the index measure. This is especially relevant for one-dimensional measures of complex concepts, such as the less rigorous measure of "high school violence" discussed earlier in this chapter.

Finally, descriptive analysis is used to examine the range of values of (index) variables. If most values of a variable are "high," then little will be known about those who score "low." Being mindful of this problem helps analysts avoid inappropriate generalizations to categories (for example, subpopulations) about which little empirical information has been collected. For example, if most of our respondents indicate that high school violence is a serious problem, then little will be learned about factors associated with high school violence among those who perceive it to be low, including, quite possibly, strategies causing some schools to have low levels of high school violence. Descriptive analysis is also used to examine whether observations with missing values in their index variables create a pattern of bias, perhaps systematically excluding some group or groups of observations, for example, such as minorities or pregnant teenagers for whom some items may have been irrelevant or in some way troublesome.

In sum, a plethora of strategies exists for assessing measurement validity. Analysts are not expected to use all of these approaches, but they should use some strategies to justify their measures. In scientific research, this usually requires some up-front consideration because, after data have been collected, it may be too late to collect more observations as needed for validation.

An obvious and final question is this: what is an analyst to do if one or more of the strategies described in this chapter show variables to be less valid than hoped for? Perhaps the measures of internal and external validity provide mixed results, and the alpha measure is marginal at best. If this happens, the analyst needs to add a caveat to his or her results. However, with foresight and planning, analysts usually gather a broad range of variables so that adequate supporting evidence from face and construct validity are available.

SUMMARY

The four measurement levels of variables are nominal, ordinal, interval, and ratio. A general guideline is that measurement scales are preferred that give as much information as possible about variables. Nominal-level scales exhibit no order among attributes, ordinal-level scales exhibit order but no distance between attributes, and interval- and ratio-level scales exhibit both order and distance. Variables with interval- and ratio-level scales are sometimes called continuous variables, and variables with nominal- and ordinal-level scales are called categorical or discrete variables. A variable's measurement level is also important in the selection of statistical tests, discussed in later chapters. Likert scales are commonly used ordinal-level variables in surveys. There are many different types of Likert scales, assessing degrees of importance, satisfaction, agreement, and frequency, for example. Index variables sum the values of disparate variables and are used to measure concepts.

Rigor in measurement increases the validity of analytical work. When working with abstract concepts, analysts need to carefully identify the different dimensions of their concepts and then develop appropriate ways to measure each. Measures used by other studies can help guide analysts in this task, but they often must develop and validate their own measures.

Measures should be valid, and this chapter offers strategies for determining measurement validity. Four types of validity are face validity, content validity, *criterion validity*, and construct validity. Additionally, Cronbach alpha is used for index variables as a measure of their internal reliability. Analysts should examine their measures for validity and provide caveats to their results, as necessary.

KEY TERMS

Categorical variables (p. 44)
Concepts (p. 48)
Conceptualization (p. 49)
Construct validity (p. 56)
Content validity (p. 55)
Continuous variables (p. 46)
Criterion validity (p. 58)
Cronbach alpha (p. 55)
Discrete variables (p. 44)
Face validity (p. 55)
Index variable (p. 53)

Internal reliability (p. 56)
Interval-level scale (p. 46)
Levels of measurement (p. 44)
Likert scale (p. 44)
Measurement validity (p. 48)
Nominal-level scale (p. 44)
Operationalization (p. 49)
Ordinal-level scale (p. 44)
Ratio-level scale (p. 46)
Scale (p. 43)
Writing tips (p. 47)

Notes

1. Other types of ordinal-level scales exist, too, but they are much less common. For example, *Guttman scales* are based on a series of statements with increasing or decreasing intensity, for example, "I feel safe around my classmates," "I avoid classmates who are violent," and "I bring a knife to school to defend myself against my classmates." The scale assumes a consistent pattern in answering these statements. That is, those who agree with the last statement are unlikely to agree with the first statement too. A statistical coefficient is calculated that measures the extent to which such a consistent pattern exists. Guttman scales have become less popular in recent years, due to their rigidity and complexity. *Thurstone scales* use judges to assess and order a large number of such statements, from which a scale is then composed. The cumbersomeness of using panels also makes Thurstone scales unpopular. Somewhat more common are *semantic differential scales,* especially in psychological studies. These scales assume that people think in opposing pairs as they assess situations, such as "How do you feel about anger management classes as a method for reducing high school

violence?" Respondents are asked to indicate a point on each line that indicates their feeling:

Good	------------------	Bad
Smart	------------------	Dumb
Respectful	------------------	Disrespectful

2. Some texts refer to both interval and ratio scales as interval scales, which may cause confusion. Other texts refer to both as metric scales and often refer to nominal and ordinal variables as nonmetric variables. In this context, the term *metric* has no bearing on the metric system of measurement. We avoid using the terms *metric* and *nonmetric* here, to prevent any such confusion.

3. The following question is sometimes raised: how many categories must an ordinal-level variable have in order to be considered an interval variable? This question misses the point that the key theoretical distinction between ordinal and continuous variables is whether the distances between categories can be determined. Even so, in practice ordinal-level variables with seven or more categories are sometimes analyzed with statistics that are appropriate only for interval-level variables. This practice has many critics, but it is done, because interval-level statistics more readily address control variables and also because ordinal-level statistics sometimes don't work well with large tables. Nonetheless, the practice is controversial, and it is best to analyze ordinal variables with statistics that are appropriate for ordinal-level variables, discussed later.

4. Measurement validity is also discussed at the end of this chapter.

5. This can be regarded as an example of asking questions of basic research—see Section II introduction.

6. Many scientific studies in public administration and public policy use one to five dimensions per concept (thus some concepts have only one dimension), and operationalization is often limited to five to eight variables per dimension. A practical consideration is that, when working with existing data (also called secondary data), analysts often must use whatever variables are available. Conceptualization and operationalization may then be wanting, to say the least. Analysts must acknowledge study limitations (caveats) and argue that the analysis adds value and is the best available.

7. In addition to the strategies discussed here, empirical approaches such as *factor analysis* can be used to justify the number of dimensions (see Chapter 18).

8. A better way of addressing this is through standardization, a process discussed in Chapter 7.

9. Recall the other threats to internal and external validity discussed in Chapter 2. Some problems of validity deal with sample bias, such as a biased selection of administrative records or survey respondents. Other problems deal with testing and instrumentation, such as biased or leading questions on survey questionnaires. Guidelines for dealing with these problems are discussed in Chapter 5.

10. You can find such articles in public administration, for example, by Googling "cronbach" "public administration."

11. See note 8 in Chapter 14.

CHAPTER

4

Measuring and Managing Performance: Present and Future

CHAPTER OBJECTIVES

After reading this chapter, you should be able to

- Develop performance measures for programs and policies
- Understand the logic model
- Distinguish between measures of efficiency and effectiveness
- Identify criteria for evaluating performance measures
- Understand the goals of performance management
- Distinguish data-based and expert-based approaches to forecasting
- Understand the role of statistical forecasting models

Performance measurement provides a real-time assessment of what a program or policy is doing, what resources it is using, and what it has accomplished recently. Whereas program evaluation focuses on the past (what has a program policy achieved?), performance measurement focuses on the present (what is a program or policy achieving?). Performance measurement assists management by providing information and analysis that shape current understanding and decisions, such as about the efficiency and effectiveness of program operations. In addition, performance measurement provides key indicators about activities and performance, and measuring performance is a prerequisite for improving performance.

Managers also face questions about the future. What is the future expected to be like? What impact is the program or policy likely to have? A variety of methods are available to managers who are using forecasting to answer these questions. This chapter completes our discussion of research strategies for providing information about the past, present, and future of programs and policies.

PERFORMANCE MEASUREMENT

Performance measurement is defined as a process for assessing progress toward achievement of program goals. As an analytical process, it is designed to produce information on an ongoing basis to determine what a program or policy is doing and what results are being achieved. This process helps managers to improve program monitoring and accountability and, by focusing on measurable results, to improve program performance and stakeholder satisfaction, too.

Performance measurement is increasingly common. More and more grants require performance measurement. The United Way requires performance assessment in its funding process. The Government Finance Officers Association encourages the use of performance measurement in program budgets. The movement toward demonstrating that outcomes are achieved is occurring across sectors. Twenty years ago, organizations and their managers could merely report how many services were provided ("we provided services to 6,000 individuals in the previous year"), but this is not the case any longer. Funders, and that includes councils and boards, want to know what services were provided, and what differences these services made. This is a considerable shift, and one that demands heightened analytical skills for organizations and their managers.

Performance measurement developed from program evaluation.[1] Although program evaluation can be a thorough process, it often is quite cumbersome and may produce information that is neither ongoing nor timely for management purposes. By contrast, performance measurement aims to overcome this limitation and provide an up-to-date management information system. Performance measurement provides a system of *key indicators* of program activities and performance. These measures are based on systematic and quantitative information, thereby supplementing other, sometimes impressionistic sources of management knowledge. Performance measurement is not the sole basis for understanding

> **Key Point**
>
> Performance measures are key indicators of program activity and performance.

programs and policies, but it provides a snapshot that integrates important, frequently quantitative information about programs and policies.

The Logic Model

Public and nonprofit organizations are increasingly using the **logic model** to conceptualize program performance. This model defines a way to describe relationships among resources, activities, and results, and it can be applied to any program:

Performance measurement provides key indicators of the following components: inputs, activities, outputs, outcomes, and goals, and each program will have its own unique measures. Indicators should be chosen to reflect managers' and stakeholders' interests, and thereby to assist in meaningful monitoring and decision making. Programs and their managers are apt to vary in how they choose to measure inputs, activities, outputs, and outcomes. Standards and common practices for conceptualizing and operationalizing (that is, measuring) these indicators are not yet well established. Organizations are often encouraged by professional associations, by their boards, or by legislatures to develop their own measures. Some funding agencies may prescribe specific indicator measures, and even ways in which some data are to be collected, but organizations and their managers are still responsible for developing their performance measurement systems.

Some general criteria for performance measures are that they should be *relevant, understandable,* and *consistent* over time. Also, measures should be considered that are likely to be relevant for some time and thus become part of trend data over time. However, some performance measures typically reflect important but likely temporary concerns, too; these will likely not become part of any trend data. Beyond these standards, performance measures should also be *valid;* they should avoid problems of inaccurate and incomplete measurement, as discussed in Chapter 3. Clearly, snapshots are only as accurate and valid as their measures. Some information is based on existing data sources such as might be obtained from accounting or operations departments, but some indicators require new data collection.

Regarding the specific components of the logic model, **inputs** are defined as resources used by the program to produce its goods and services. Programs use financial, human, organizational, and political resources, but not all of these resources are quantifiable nor are they necessarily all key to program decision making. Inputs typically are measured as (1) total program costs, or subsets of costs, and (2) personnel costs or time involved in providing a service. Of course, personnel costs are a subset of total costs (that is, a partial measure), but they reflect key concerns related to service efficiency.

Input measures illustrate well the possibility of considerable measurement bias. First, inputs cover not just costs. They also include qualitative components such as organizational leadership and political commitment, which are essential and strategic for program success, and which managers should not take for granted. Second, cost measures are obtained from agency budgets and administrative records. These sources are usually agency-centric, that is, they do not take into account the sometimes-substantial services and in-kind contributions from other agencies. Third, costs are sometimes defined as costs to the agency and sometimes only as those budgeted to the program. As such, they exclude indirect and overhead costs, such as facilities and administrative services. These amounts can be significant. Managers need to be clear about what their costs data include and what they do not.

In our ongoing example of the anger management program, inputs might be measured as (1) total program costs, defined as (a) the direct cost of teachers and support staff administering the program, as well as (b) the costs of using school facilities beyond regular school hours, and (c) a markup of these costs that reflects customary indirect and administrative overhead charged by schools for after-school programs. The teacher and support staff costs can also be used as a separate, partial measure. Another partial input measure might be (2) the actual time spent by teachers on the anger management program; this includes preparing for and teaching the class and following up with students. Presumably these cost data can be collected frequently, which aids in monitoring. In this example, resources provided by community organizations are not included, such as guest speakers making presentations to students, which might be done pro bono or paid for by other grants.

Activities are defined as the processes, events, technologies, and actions that a program undertakes with its resources, to produce results. Examples include the number of police patrols, the number of permit applications that have been logged in and processed in some way, or the number of clients participating in a counseling program. These are clearly measures of effort. Activities performed are typically those that are key to furthering the principal missions and goals of the program. Indeed, programs are increasingly encouraged to think strategically, that is, to define their goals and then develop their activities from those goals. The main activities that are essential to furthering the missions of programs or agencies should be included. By contrast, incidental activities and the activities by other units supporting these key activities, such as fleet maintenance or information technology services, are excluded. These services are subject to their own performance measurement.

Some key measures of the activities of the anger management program are the number of hours that the anger management classes are taught and the number of students involved in these classes. These measures address different but key aspects of the overall activity. Additional measures might include special events conducted in connection with the program.

Outputs are defined as the immediate, direct results of program activities. The logic model recognizes that many public and nonprofit programs have long-term goals, such as ensuring public safety or achieving behavioral changes in a population of clients. These long-term goals are supported by immediate program results, such as arrests of delinquents, timely and accurate completion of permit applications, and successful completion of a course of treatment. These outputs are precursors to later outcomes. As key indicators, outputs often measure what are considered to be successful or desired immediate results of activities. Sometimes outputs are also designed to highlight and track possible problem areas in service delivery.

What might be useful output measures for our anger management program? Examples could include (1) the number of students who completed the anger management program, including any tests that might be administered, (2) the number of students who did not complete the program (obviously a possible problem area), (3) the percentage of the school's students who successfully completed the program, and (4) the percentage of the school's at-risk students who completed the program. Each of these measures provides managers with useful information. The first is a measure of success, the second a measure of failure; the third takes stock of the program's "footprint" on the school; and the fourth relates the program to its principal target group, students known to be prone to violence. Multiple output measures reflect different dimensions of program performance as well as managerial interest in these dimensions. Consistency among these measures may also provide a measure of validity regarding overall program performance.

Outcomes are defined as specific changes in behaviors or conditions that are measures of various aspects of program goals. *Goals* are commonly defined as the ultimate purposes of a program; outcomes are the specific measures of that attainment. Thus, if the goal is public safety, then outcomes might be measured as crime rates and public perceptions of public safety, for example. If the purpose of a counseling program is to help people increase their self-sufficiency by finding a job, then an outcome is likely the percentage or number of people who found a job. These are

> **Key Point**
> Outputs are the direct results of program activities, and outcomes measure goal attainment. Both are needed.

Table 4.1 ————〜〜〜— Anger Management Performance
Measures

Performance component	Performance measure
Inputs	Total program costs Teacher and support staff costs Teachers' hours
Activities	Program hours Students enrolled in program Special events
Outputs	Students who completed the program Students who withdrew from the program Students who completed the program (%) At-risk students who completed the program (%)
Outcomes	Gun and knife incidents Fights and scuffles Sexual assaults and harassment Teachers' perception of school violence Students' perception of school violence
Goals	Reduce school violence Create a safe school environment

meaningful measures of such goals. Even though outcomes are presumed to
be caused by outputs (see the logic model), they are conceptualized as
measures that reflect goals: *outcomes are measures of goal attainment.*

In our example, a key goal of the anger management program is to
reduce the level of high school violence. Chapter 3 conceptualized "high
school violence" as involving the dimensions of violence through weapons,
inappropriate physical contact, and verbal threats and assaults. Based on that
conceptualization, measures of "high school violence" might include (1)
incidents involving guns or knives reported to the administration, (2) fights
and scuffles, not involving guns or knives, reported to the administration,
(3) incidents of sexual assault and harassment reported to the administration, (4) teachers' perception of school violence, and (5) students' perception
of violence. Obviously the first three measures need some guidelines to
correctly measure incidents that involve, for example, both knives and sexual
assault. School administrators will likely keep detailed records about such
incidents, and this further informs management decisions. The last two
measures are stakeholder assessments. Subjective assessments (such as

through surveys) are commonly used to support objective data, and obtaining such assessments may provide a measure of external validation. However, whereas the objective data might be available on a monthly basis, subjective data might be gathered only once or twice yearly. Table 4.1 summarizes the anger management performance measures described here.

Further Examples

Performance measurement can be applied to many different programs. Here are some further examples and reflections.

Getting Started

Develop performance measures for a program of your choice.

Fundraising. Fundraising typically involves different activities and purposes: mass mailings and telethons for the purposes of recruiting first-time donors who usually contribute small amounts, galas and special events for regular donors who contribute modest amounts, and major giving campaigns among wealthier donors who may contribute large sums. Typical input measures are staff time and costs of fundraising activities, as well as volunteer time and expenses. Activity measures are the number and size of mass mailings, telethons, galas, and visits with potential major donors. Outputs are the immediate consequences of these events, including not just the pledges and moneys received during the events but also the number of first-time donors. Outcomes are measures of the goal, the total amount of money or in-kind contributions raised. This includes funds received that are not attributed to specific fundraising activities, such as annual donations that are routinely made.

Law Enforcement. Law enforcement involves many different activities, each of which requires attention to performance measurement. For example, many local government police departments engage in preventive patrols, traffic enforcement, crime investigations, vehicle accident investigations, neighborhood and community activities (for example, neighborhood watches, school activities), 9-1-1 and emergency response activities, records management, and administrative services. Police departments usually maintain extensive activity reports and are required to report crimes, such as the number of murders, rapes, and robberies; even though these data assist in performance measurement, specific performance measures must nonetheless be designed. What are the outputs and outcomes of detective activity? Outputs are completed crime investigations, but outcomes must speak to both criminal convictions as well as other goals such as crime deterrence and creation of safe communities. These latter aspects, crime deterrence and community safety, may well require the subjective assessments of citizens. Because these latter outcomes are also shared with other law enforcement activities such as patrols and neighborhood watches (different activities contributing to the same goal), this example illustrates well that managers need to conduct their own, informal investigation into factors affecting performance.

Public Works. Like law enforcement, public works involves many disparate activities. Public works may include road maintenance and repairs (including street sweeping and signage), drainage repairs and storm water management, fleet maintenance, plan review and permitting, lake management, code enforcement, grounds maintenance (for example, irrigation, mowing), and arbor care and beautification. It may also include parks management and water production, distribution, and billing activities. Typically, costs and activities are clearly defined, and outputs are measured by the successful and timely completion of these activities. For example, outputs of paved road repairs might include the number of repaired potholes, as well as the percentage of potholes filled within 48 hours. Similar measures could be readily developed for plan review or fleet maintenance.

Outcomes measure the goals of these activities, which often indicate community infrastructure conditions. For example, public works outcomes relating to roads might measure the percentage of roads that are paved; the condition of paved roads; or the percentage of roads that fall below standards for paving, cleanliness, signage, or beautification. This example illustrates that although performance measurement aims to provide up-to-date and timely information, in practice such assessments are probably undertaken only on an annual basis. Hence, outcome measurement may occur on a different cycle than other measurements. This is also the case when citizen surveys are involved. It may be argued that such outcomes do not change rapidly and require only annual measurement. Some time lag is a practical reality. Also, performance measurement may prompt jurisdictions to undertake a more extensive, accurate community assessment than they otherwise might do.

Global Assessment. Many jurisdictions and agencies prepare performance measurement reports focusing on their entire agency or jurisdiction, rather than on distinct services. These reports develop measures of progress toward attaining strategic goals, and often incorporate performance measures of specific programs that were developed using the logic model. For example, a city might have as its goal that citizens feel safe and might measure attainment of this goal by citizen perceptions of safety, various crime rates (for example, murder, rape, burglary, arson), alcohol-related and other traffic accidents, community preparedness for disasters and emergency management, and neighborhood watch activities. These measures provide a broad perspective, though they do not always relate to activities and resources, or distinguish outputs from outcomes. Likewise, federal agencies often prepare performance reports identifying major goals and the milestones or activities that suggest progress made toward these goals.

EFFICIENCY, EFFECTIVENESS, AND A BIT MORE

Based on the measures described in the preceding section, other performance measures are developed as well. *Effectiveness* is simply defined as the level of results; to say that a program is effective is to point to one or more key results. Thinking about effectiveness forces managers to think about evidence of program performance that is compelling and, often, succinct. Effectiveness is typically measured by one or more output or outcome measures. The number of students who completed the anger management program might be considered as a measure of program effectiveness. The number of assaults in high schools might be considered a measure of the effectiveness of school efforts to reduce violence and provide a safe environment.[2]

In some instances, managers describe the "effectiveness" of their programs according to some standard, such as exceeding 95-percent on-time delivery or helping 60 percent of program clients to find a new job within six months. However, such standards fall outside the definition of the term *effectiveness.* They are more appropriately referred to as program or policy benchmarks. *Benchmarks* are standards against which performance is measured. In the case of the anger management program, standards might be set for a very low number of scuffles and fist fights, and gun- and knife-related incidents. Benchmarks might also be set for stakeholders' perceptions of safety and violence. Setting performance standards goes to the essence of "managing by the numbers."

Different types of benchmarks can be distinguished. *Internal* benchmarks are standards that organizations base on what their own prior programs have achieved, or on what they feel is appropriate, irrespective of what similar organizations or programs are achieving. *External* benchmarks are standards that are based on the performance of other organizations and programs. Acknowledging that not all organizations can be among the very best (say, in the top 5 percent), in recent years external benchmarks are increasingly based on comparison with the performance of *peer organizations* (those that are similar to or in the same class as the organization), *aspirant organizations* (those that are one step above the class of the organization and in the class to which the organization aspires), and *exemplary organizations* (those that are among the top 5 percent in the country). These distinctions are helpful for management purposes. A practical problem is knowing what these standards are. Often, this is determined based on discussions with members of such organizations. Sometimes published or national standards exist, such as related to mowing grass or drinking water quality. Readers might note an analogy between using external benchmarks and using comparison groups as discussed in Chapter 2. In recent years, benchmarking has sometimes become identified with determining best industry practices, but this is a limited application of the concept.

Efficiency is defined as the unit cost to produce a good or service. It is calculated as the output or outcomes over inputs, or O/I. Efficiency indicators can be calculated in many different ways and should be chosen to reflect program management concerns. Examples include the number of arrests per officer (arrests/officer), the number of completed permit application reviews per inspector (completed reviews/inspector), or the number of clients who successfully found jobs per counseling program (new jobs/program). In our example, some measures of efficiency might be the number of students who have successfully completed the anger management program per hour of teaching time (students passing program/hour of teaching), or the average total cost of successfully completing the anger management program per student (program cost/student passing program). A useful measure of administrative efficiency might be faculty and staff time administering the program per student completion (administrative time or cost/student passing program). Obviously benchmarks can be set for efficiency measures, too.

A potential problem with measures of efficiency is that they may compete with those of effectiveness. In the preceding examples, efficiency can be increased by lowering standards for course completion or by reducing the quality of the course, both of which are undesirable for effectiveness. Efficiency measures need to be chosen and managed carefully. The earlier examples also avoid another problem—inaccurately ascribing outcomes to activities. Recall that performance measurement does not analyze the causes of performance. Calculating the cost of reducing assaults per hour of teaching the anger management program has little validity when, in fact, reducing high school violence involves other activities, too. Thus, efficiency measures often are based on calculating outputs per cost, rather than outcomes per cost. Efficiency measures are sometimes mistaken for cost-benefit measures, which are discussed in Box 4.1.

Efficiency also must be distinguished from workload ratio measures. *Workload ratios* are defined as the ratios of activities over inputs, or A/I. For example, a workload ratio is the number of students in anger management courses per teacher providing such courses. As many case managers know, distinguishing between workload ratios and efficiency measures is important: a high caseload of clients does not mean that they are being served well. Likewise, large class sizes do not mean that students are getting the attention they need. Therefore, efficiency measures—which are based on outcomes—may be more relevant. Many managers, however, mistake workload ratios for efficiency measures, for example, when they state that they are now teaching more students, or have larger class sizes, or are undertaking more patrols. These are

Box 4.1 Cost–Benefit Analysis

Efficiency measures are sometimes mistaken for those arising from cost-benefit analysis (CBA); however, CBA is fundamentally different from performance measurement. CBA uses a *comprehensive* approach to measurement; this means that *all* costs and benefits should be identified. One issue in undertaking such an analysis is the perspective that is taken. From the agency's perspective, costs borne by other agencies are not its costs. From society's perspective, these other costs are part of the total costs of providing goods or services and thus should be included. CBA typically provides a calculation of costs and benefits from both private and social perspectives. The term *private* connotes the perspective of a specific actor, such as a public or private agency; it is not used in any legal sense but rather is used to distinguish the agency from society as a whole.

CBA also deals with the thorny issue that not all costs and benefits are readily quantifiable. What are the benefits of an anger management program that provides as a benefit a safer environment for learning? How can we quantify this benefit of feeling safer? CBA uses some skillful approaches, such as trying to figure out how much parents might be willing to pay for a safer learning environment for their children, or trying to assess the cost differential of schools with different levels of safety. This is obviously no easy task.

The problem of assigning dollar values is illustrated in the familiar problem of putting a dollar value on the price of a human life. What is the dollar benefit of an environmental program or policy that saves lives? Some approaches use actuarial data of future earnings from life insurance policies, but many people find these approaches unsatisfying. When benefits are identified but not expressed in dollar values, the resulting analysis is usually called *cost-effectiveness analysis.* Also, CBA typically includes some costs and benefits that are identified but not quantified; these are assumed to have little effect on study conclusions even if they could be quantified. CBA must also deal with the time-value of money. Often costs occur in the present and near future, but benefits accrue in the more distant future. CBA must discount future values, reflecting the depreciating effect of future inflation, but the rate used to discount future dollars can greatly affect conclusions about the cost-benefit of proposed programs and policies.

not measures of efficiency but rather activities or workload ratios; they do not include accomplishments. In our example, an obvious workload measure is the number of students being taught anger management, or the number of such students per teacher. The former is a measure of the workload for the entire school, whereas the latter is a measure of the workload placed on the teachers.

In some jurisdictions, performance measurement is limited to developing measures of workloads, effectiveness, and efficiency, whereby the latter are based on outputs rather than outcomes. These limited measures serve the needs of managers. Outcomes are measured separately, sometimes at more aggregate levels such as through global assessments.

Equity measures are used to compare performance across different groups. For example, it is often useful to measure how different outcomes or activities affect different populations or target groups. In the matter of police patrols or arrest rates, for instance, it is useful to know whether these measures differ in particular sections of the jurisdiction or among members of different races. Equity measures can be analyzed for different groups of population, types of organizations, programs or services, and so on. These measures also relate to a fundamental public service value, namely, that public agencies often are required to serve entire populations, and cannot "cherry pick" customers or citizens that they would like to serve; by contrast, private organizations do not have this requirement. Because of the broad, all-encompassing nature of some public services, equity measures that compare service performance across districts or population groups can be especially salient.

Balanced scorecards are not really an application of the logic model but rather are a different way of providing a global assessment. Many balanced scorecards provide a descriptive focus on the organization's financial state, customer and stakeholder satisfaction, efficiency and effectiveness of delivery processes, and activities to promote learning and improvement within the organization. Some of these measures are typically provided through performance measurement efforts, but others, such as efforts to advance learning by organizational members, typically require additional measurement. When new concerns arise, managers and organizations readily adapt the notion of managing by key indicators to include these new measures.[3]

Key Point

With so many measures to choose from, managers will want to choose those that matter most to them and their stakeholders.

Given that many performance measures are available, how does a manager choose which ones to use? Recall that performance measurement is a system of key indicators used to provide a snapshot description of activities and performance. There is no one or even best set of performance measures. The snapshot should be useful and valid, and it should involve measures that are used consistently over time. The manager's task is to construct such a system for measuring activity and performance.

MANAGING PERFORMANCE

Once a manager decides on performance measures, the next step is to use these measures to improve services and management. *Performance management* is generally defined as including activities to ensure that goals are consistently being met in an effective and efficient manner. One part is the use of performance measures for improving accountability, service delivery, and managerial decision making, which is our focus here. *Performance analysis* is the use of statistics to gain an understanding of a program's performance and the factors affecting it.

Performance measures can be used in many aspects of management and policy making. They can assist managers to make effective resource allocation decisions. They can help stakeholders understand the progress and achievement made by an organization or a program. They can also facilitate an organization's strategic planning process by providing an effective way to assess the achievement of goals and missions. But most important, performance measurement is an effective tool to help managers improve services and managerial decision making. In our ongoing example, knowing which schools have a high level of violence can help draw attention to those schools. Further knowing when such violence occurs (time of the day), the grade level of students involved in violence, and their academic performance also helps to further focus and aid in diagnosis. Once an intervention is settled on and implemented, monitoring violence is an important part of performance management.

As a second example, the logic model introduced in this chapter can help managers to gain an understanding of a program's performance and the factors affecting it. It emphasizes the importance of the logical links in the service delivery process. Let's say that there have been increasing citizen complaints about slow response time in the emergency management of a metropolitan city. The director of the Fire and Rescue Service suspects that something is not going well in the emergency response process, described in the following graphic:

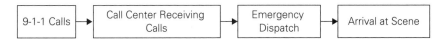

The response time is affected by how quickly a 9-1-1 call for emergency is answered at the Call Center; how quickly and accurately the Call Center dispatches the appropriate emergency response unit; and how quickly the emergency response unit arrives at the scene. The possible causes of slow responses (underperformance) include delayed answering of an emergency call, slow or inaccurate handling of the call at the Call Center, dispatching the wrong emergency response unit (for example, dispatching a fire protection unit in response to a call for a medical emergency), and slow response time within the unit. The preceding graphic is known as a *flowchart,* which is commonly used to identify problems in a process of operation. After developing the flowchart, the Fire and Rescue Service director decides to investigate all the possible causes to identify the true cause(s) of slow response, and data are collected and analyzed relating to the above "boxes."

This example shows how the logic model and performance measurement can provide accurate and meaningful performance information. Performance information can be brought into the daily or periodic activities of managing programs in which performance is assessed, monitored, and improved. Obviously, choosing one's performance measures well is key, and managers may give considerable attention to choosing measures that address their performance concerns and goals. More broadly, managers and agencies are increasingly thinking about developing performance databases that include a broad range of measures and allow for versatile analysis and support for ongoing program management. Though the idea is not new (it is used in many private companies, too), it emphasizes the growing need for professionals to design, develop, and maintain such databases, as well as for public managers who can analyze these data and use them in program management. As the saying goes, "what gets measured gets done," reflecting the emphasis that managers and stakeholders place on performance and the importance of instilling such emphases within the organization. Much benefit is to be gained from thinking about the use of better measurement for managing performance, and in bringing performance data into discussions with other managers and employees in program and policy operations.

One task of public managers is to help design useful performance measures and assist in the analysis and communication of performance information. Each program and policy is apt to have it is own unique performance measures. Even similar programs in different jurisdictions are likely to have different circumstances and priorities. Managers need to think clearly about the strategic purposes of programs and how information about their programs can be used in daily management of them. A performance information system also requires appropriate software, hardware, and statistical capabilities. The success of performance management also calls for the establishment of an organizational culture that fosters continual performance improvement, and some managers work closely with internal and external stakeholders in developing the relevant performance measures. The success of performance management depends on political, technical, and cultural capacities (support). Yet, performance expectations are increasingly being incorporated into managers' job descriptions, and performance measurement and management are important ways in which these expectations are put into practice. Chapters 6 and 7 provide statistical tools for performance monitoring, and Chapter 9 shows specific application of performance analysis. Statistical tools introduced in Chapter 8 and Sections IV and V focus on the ultimate goal of performance improvement.

PEERING INTO THE FUTURE: FORECASTING

How can we use information gathered from performance measurement and other sources to assist in answering questions about the future? Managers and analysts are often called upon to provide information about some future state: How many babies are likely to be born next year? How much will our revenue be three, four, and five years from now? How many business start-ups will there be three years from now? What is the likely quality of air and water 10 years from now? Managers and analysts are also expected to forecast the impact of alternative policies. For example, how is air quality likely to be affected in future years if the city adopts stricter rules for new permit applications? Or, how is the anger management program likely to affect high school violence in coming years?

A *forecast* is defined as a prediction about the future. Sometimes called a projection or prognosis, forecasting is different from planning. Whereas forecasting discusses what the future will look like, planning provides a normative model of what the future should look like, such as a specific vision for a city or school in the future. Planning often begins with forecasting in order to establish what the future is likely to look like, so that alternative futures or scenarios that might be preferred can be developed. Answers to the preceding questions require forecasting.

The problem of forecasting is, of course, that the future is somewhat unpredictable. Events are likely to happen that are beyond our scope or current vision. Thus, every forecast carries with it the caveat that it is based on current information and assumptions about the future. The current information is based on whatever is known about past, present, and future events. Forecasts are intended to guide decision makers today. Forecasting is an endeavor that informs decisions, but it is not a guarantee of what will happen. Tomorrow, based on new information, may warrant a different forecast. We need to be clear and forthcoming about our data, limitations, and assumptions. The challenge of forecasting is significant.

Separate research methods have been developed to deal with forecasting. These methods are generally distinguished by whether they are based on *statistical analysis* of trends and conditions or on *judgments* about situations and events. Statistical methods typically describe and aim to extrapolate quantitative trends based on past and present data. Statistical analysis and extrapolation use techniques ranging from the very simple to the highly complex. Analysis can involve no more than the simple extrapolation of the past few data points, but it can also analyze complex cyclical patterns and model other variables affecting past and present levels. Many of these techniques are discussed further, in Chapter 17, and they include validation strategies, too. Analysts will surely want to know how to make statistical forecasts, and we refer readers to Chapter 17.

Judgment-based methods often use experts to assess the likelihood of futures occurring. Experts can be brought together in groups, or as individuals. For example, the ***Delphi method*** is a forecasting method that asks experts to respond anonymously through written surveys using several rounds. After each round, summary opinions are provided, which are the basis for the next round, until, at last, one or more consensus-based opinions have materialized. A problem with this approach, however, is that it is quite time consuming, and experts may be disinclined to persist for more than a few rounds. Experts can also be asked to create different scenarios for what may happen, and the probability of these scenarios can be evaluated or "guesstimated." Decision trees can structure complex choices and follow consecutive events through to final outcomes. Experts can also use analogies and make comparisons with other contemporary or historical situations as a basis for forecasting what might occur in the present or future. In short, experts contribute a range of insights about what could occur, and they often are used in forecasting.[4]

Different approaches to forecasting are available. In general, the following six principles and practices should guide forecasting efforts. First, forecasting should use multiple methods, because single methods of forecasting are subject to large errors. Specifically, statistical trend forecasting may overlook factors that have yet to occur in the future, and experts are known to have been widely off in their opinions. The strategy is to learn something credible about the future from different forecasting methods, and to combine them. Analysts do well not to merely extrapolate an upward or downward trend in their data, but begin by identifying a full range of future scenarios and events. Consideration of these factors can lead to "what-if" scenarios and a range of probable forecasts that can inform decision making. This notion is captured in Figure 4.1.

Second, the longer the forecasting period, the more uncertain it is, as unforeseen events may occur and interactions among associated variables can have large effects. Thus, forecasts are thought to be more reliable for shorter periods—the spreadsheet example in Chapter 17 forecasts only a few periods. Third, all forecasts make assumptions and have limitations as to what factors are considered, and these assumptions and limitations should be stated clearly.

Figure 4.1  Outcomes under Alternative Scenarios

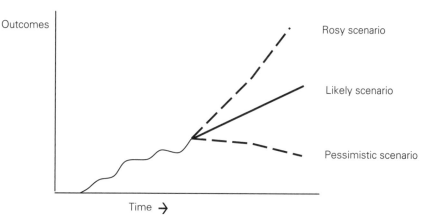

Forecasts are only as good as the data and expert judgments going into them; both should be as up-to-date and accurate as possible, and any unusual past events that affect data should be noted. Fourth, the accuracy of forecasts should be determined whenever possible. This can be done in several ways, such as by comparing predictions about the present against the observed reality of the present. For example, hurricane tracking forecasts often do this. It may also be possible to compare the accuracy of different previous forecasts.

Fifth, forecasts that incorporate more information about the past, present, and future are preferred over those that provide less. However, experts and judgmental methods may become overwhelmed by too much information, which is one reason quantitative, statistical methods are sometimes preferred. Sixth, forecasts using more complex methods are not always more accurate than ones made with simple methods. It is difficult to generalize about reasons for this; some events are difficult to forecast, and complex methods may make assumptions that turn out later to be invalid. Indeed, a bias exists in favor of simple forecasting methods that make full use of available information.

In sum, forecasting is not to be taken lightly. It is good to have trend data, but we need to think carefully about the future and not make rash assumptions that it will necessarily unfold as it has in the past. In 2004, New Orleans had not been flooded for almost 40 years; the last time was during Hurricane Betsy in 1965. One year later, in 2005, New Orleans was flooded in the wake of Hurricane Katrina, despite significant levee improvements. The past is only prologue—no more, no less. Statistical approaches to forecasting are described in Chapter 17.

Getting Started

Can you use your performance measures for forecasting?

SUMMARY

Managers deal with a range of questions about the present and future. Some questions deal with the current status of programs and policies, whereas others deal with the future, including the impact of programs and policies on community and other conditions.

Performance measurement describes present activities and results of programs. It provides a system of key indicators of program inputs, activities, outputs, outcomes, and goals. These components are described by the logic model. Performance measurement provides a snapshot that integrates important, quantitative information about programs and policies.

Performance measures should be relevant, understandable, consistent over time, and valid. Inputs are defined as resources that are used by the program to produce its goods and services. Activities are defined as the processes, events, technologies, and actions that a program undertakes with its resources to produce results. Outputs are defined as the immediate, direct results of programs. Outcomes are defined as specific measures that assess progress toward changes or program goals, which are defined as the ultimate purposes of programs. The challenge of performance measurement is to develop measures that are key indicators of these components, that are valid, and that are useful to management.

Performance management is the use of performance measurement in improving organizational or program effectiveness. The goal of performance management is performance improvement and accountability. Statistical analysis is a useful tool in achieving this goal. The success of performance management depends on capacities for making the political, technical, and cultural environments more favorable to performance management implementation.

Forecasting is about making predictions of the future. Forecasts are distinguished by whether they are based on statistical analysis of trends and conditions, or on judgments about situations and events. Forecasting should use multiple methods, and experts can provide input into statistical methods.

KEY TERMS

Activities (p. 64)
Balanced scorecards (p. 72)
Benchmarks (p. 69)
Delphi method (p. 76)
Effectiveness (p. 69)

Efficiency (p. 70)
Equity (p. 72)
Forecast (p. 75)
Goals (p. 65)
Inputs (p. 63)

Logic model (p. 63)

Outcomes (p. 65)

Outputs (p. 65)

Performance analysis (p. 73)

Performance management (p. 73)

Performance measurement (p. 62)

Workload ratios (p. 70)

Notes

1. Performance measurement was first developed in the late 1970s and was developed further in the 1980s. However, diffusion of performance measurement at all levels of government was greatly enhanced by the Government Performance and Results Act of 1993, which required its use in the federal government. Performance measurement became widely used by state and local governments, albeit with varying rigor, by the beginning of the twenty-first century.

2. This latter example illustrates well that "performance measurement does not analyze the causes of performance." It would be difficult to attribute the number of assaults in high schools to the anger management program alone; it is best described as a measure of the school's overall effort to reduce violence, which may include other activities, as well.

3. An example of a balanced scorecard, created by the U.S. Department of Energy, can be seen at http://management.energy.gov/726.htm (or Google "DOE Balanced Scorecard"). A variation of scorecards are dashboards. For an example, see dashboard.virginiadot.org or Google "VDOT dashboard."

4. Another approach involves putting people in an artificial situation involving role playing, gaming, or prediction markets. In role playing, managers or actors are asked to play out roles, given specific scenarios and constraints. Role playing shines light on actions that individuals might take, and their considerations and dilemmas that shape these choices. Gaming is similar but places players in a competitive situation with predetermined standards for "winning." A problem with using role playing and gaming for forecasting is that actual conditions may vary, of course. Prediction markets ask people to place bets with real money on future events, similar to future markets for stocks. For example, a bet might pay out $1 if a future event occurs and $0 if it does not. If the current price for this bet is, say, $.60, then the collective wisdom of people in this market is that the future event has a 60 percent chance of occurring. Bets could be placed on any future event, such as who might win the next presidency. The U.S. Defense Department created such a market for predicting the probability of future terrorist attacks but cancelled it after much public concern.

CHAPTER

5

Data Collection

CHAPTER OBJECTIVES

After reading this chapter, you should be able to

- Identify sources of data in your field
- Describe how data can be used for program evaluation, performance measurement, and forecasting
- Evaluate the availability and validity of data in your field
- Develop and implement a scientifically valid survey
- Understand how to draw a random sample
- Input data in a spreadsheet

The previous chapters discussed how managers and analysts can address questions about the past, present, and future of their programs and policies. These strategies require the availability of data, of course. What sources of data exist? What do these sources contain? How accurate are the data in these sources? If accurate data do not exist, can new data be collected and, if so, how? How should data be collected? In particular, what kinds of samples are available and how should the data be gathered?

This chapter deals with these questions of data collection. Managers and analysts are expected to be familiar with the data in their lines of business, and to be able to generate new data when existing data are unsatisfactory. As managers and analysts take inventory of the data in their fields and build skills in collecting new data, they are likely to find new and sometimes surprising uses of data. The first part of this chapter looks at data sources, and the second part looks at sampling from these sources.

SOURCES OF DATA

Administrative Data

Public and nonprofit managers have access to a considerable amount of data about their programs and policies. *Administrative data* are those that are generated in the course of managing programs and activities. There are many sources of administrative data:

- Absenteeism records
- Accident reports
- Activity logs and reports
- Ad-hoc and other special reports
- Bank accounts
- Client accounts and information
- Client requests and complaints
- Customer comments and complaints
- Error logs
- External program reviews
- Financial monitoring and reporting
- Grant requests and reports
- Inspection and repair reports
- Inventory reports
- Litigation
- Mandated studies
- Permit reviews and approvals
- Progress and completion reports
- Time cards and program staffing data
- Work orders

Programs vary greatly in their administrative data. Schools often have data about crimes and violent incidents that occur, which they may be required to report. They likely have data about their students' academic achievements from course work and standardized tests. They might have additional data on student participation in after-school activities (such as remedial language or math education), as well as information on students' special medical needs and psychosocial conditions such as problems at home, histories of violence, and so on. Schools also have other data concerning their teachers and staff, building and ground maintenance activities, and so on.

Among the first tasks of managers and analysts is to take inventory of available data and to determine the quality and uses of the data. Traditionally, administrative data have had three purposes: (1) to ensure that resources are not misused, (2) to determine the status of the organization's activities, and (3) to provide a record of what has been completed and accomplished. The first purpose often is associated with auditing and anti-corruption efforts, such as being accountable for how money is spent. The second purpose helps managers gain control over present activities and set priorities. Activity logs might be a first step toward developing project progress and completion charts. The third purpose has legal and accountability ramifications, documenting that agreed-upon objectives have been accomplished (for example, roads have been repaired, the class has been taught). Client complaints and inspection reports provide additional documentation about activities meeting standards.

Administrative data vary in their usefulness for program evaluation and performance measurement; the variables may or may not be those that are needed. Administrative data often are not collected with these purposes in mind, and sources of these data often cover many input and activity measures but lack data for many important output and outcome measures. For example, administrative data from road repairs are likely to include information about the amount of funding for repairs (input), the number of repairs undertaken in any reporting period (activity), and the number and miles of completed repairs (output). But data might be missing about the timeliness of key repairs and certainly about the condition of the roadways (outcome).

Performance measurement usually requires that additional administrative data be collected. Doing so adds a fourth purpose: monitoring key outputs and outcomes. This purpose goes well beyond providing a record of what has been completed and accomplished. In the case of road repairs, it requires that data be collected about the timeliness and efficiency of repairs, too. It also requires a comprehensive, perhaps annual or quarterly, assessment of the condition of roadways; this assessment could be part of an ongoing system that monitors street conditions. Similarly, many of the measures listed in Table 4.1, regarding the anger management program, might not even be gathered by schools if not required as part of a performance measurement and management system. Although teachers and administrators might monitor individual at-risk students, they might not identify and track that cohort in any systematic way. Hence, organizations that are committed to performance measurement are likely to require additional administrative data.[1]

Administrative data may also suffer from some quality challenges that must be acknowledged or overcome. Data are sometimes (1) missing or incomplete, (2) inaccurately reported, (3) subject to definitions that have changed over time and therefore cannot be compared, (4) not linked to particular events or clients, or cannot be disaggregated in necessary ways, (5) confidential and unavailable for analysis, or (6) insufficiently available in electronic format. These problems will need to be identified and addressed.

Analysts may also need to make reasonable adjustments that make it possible to relate data across time or cases. The rigor with which these problems are identified and addressed enhances the validity and credibility of administrative data. Recognizing that some problems are not easily or fully correctable (for example, past records may be irretrievable or incomplete), organizations may make the timeliness and quality of data collection a priority; many organizations are now investing in real-time, fully electronic ways of capturing their data. An objective of this activity is to ensure that data inaccuracies are inconsequential for purposes of validity and management. Some organizations take electronic collection a step further, using common enterprise software that makes administrative data from different departments available to senior managers throughout the organization. Overall, the availability and quality of administrative data have increased greatly during the past decade as a result of greater commitment to performance measurement and information technology applications.

Administrative data are also used in program evaluation and forecasting. Administrative data provide important descriptive information for program evaluation, but administrative data are generally not designed to provide adequate information about outcomes and factors affecting program outcomes (for example, rival hypotheses). Hence, program evaluation almost always requires data from additional sources, such as surveys, interviews, focus groups, and secondary sources discussed in the next section. Administrative data can also be used in forecasting, though usually in combination with expert judgment and secondary data about community conditions. Finally, the administrative data of other organizations, when available, is sometimes used to identify external benchmarks.

In short, administrative data assist in the management of programs and policies. Such data are essential for program evaluation and performance measurement, though typically they are insufficient or inadequate in some way. Managers and analysts should know what data are available to them and be able to assess the uses and validity of these data. Often, administrative data are complemented with data from other sources.

> **Getting Started**
>
> Identify administrative data in your field. How relevant are these data for the five uses described in Chapter 1?

Secondary Data

A broad range of studies and statistics available from public and private organizations provide important information for managers and analysts. These are sometimes called *secondary data*, referring to the fact that they were collected for some other purpose. An extraordinary amount of secondary data are available, and they are increasingly available through the Internet. For example, *FedStats* is a portal for statistics from many federal agencies, through which data can be accessed about health, education, incomes, housing, crime, agriculture, transportation, the environment, economic growth, and much more. These data are available at different levels of aggregation, such as at the state or city level. Nonprofit and other public organizations, including international organizations such as the United Nations and World Bank, also make secondary data available.[2]

An important task for managers and analysts is to know what specific data are available in their field, and how these data can help them. Secondary data are often used to describe communities in statistical terms (for example, how many crimes, how many cars), which in turn can contribute toward needs assessment, benchmarking, and outcome measurement. First, needs assessment involves determining the needs of members or organizations in a community. This activity also involves in-depth interviews and surveys of community members and leaders. Secondary data can buttress claims regarding widespread concerns about crime, low incomes, health, and so on. Second, comparisons or rankings of communities on issues such as education, crime, or economic growth commonly use secondary data, and benchmarking comparisons and rankings are sometimes reported in newspaper and magazine articles, too. Third, some community-level data may be relevant to public organization outcomes, such as secondary data pertaining to illiteracy, juvenile crime, student-teacher ratios, and so on.

Obviously the nature of data varies greatly across fields. Some areas have long histories of data collection, sometimes mandated by the federal government, whereas others have less data available. Some secondary data are available at very disaggregated levels, for example, at the level of individuals. Similarly, public statistics may be available at the level at which they were collected, such as for individual hospitals, schools, or cities. In other instances, only aggregated data are available, such as for entire states or school districts. These aggregated data can still be relevant, for example, in comparing one organization against a city or state average. Sometimes, agencies are willing to make available their raw data. Some cities use secondary data to prepare community indicators, which are global assessments of how well their community is doing.

Secondary data are also used in scholarly studies, such as to study relationships (for example, juvenile crime and drug use) and the control variables and circumstances that affect these relationships (for example, household income). Such in-depth uses have contributed to understanding limitations of secondary data. First, secondary data seldom provide managers and analysts with all of their data needs for their community; secondary data were not created with these needs in mind. Managers and analysts will typically use other data sources, too. However, secondary data may be more readily available and cheaper than those you collect on your own; there is thus an obvious bias toward using them when available. Second, biases may be found in secondary data as a result of uneven sampling; for example, school data may miss out on some schools or children, and these schools or children may be disproportionately in poorer districts or come from poorer or non-English-speaking households. The U.S. Census is well known for undercounting minorities and undocumented aliens. The significance of these biases varies greatly.

Third, data definitions may be unclear, unstable, or not suited for the study or management purpose. If unemployment is measured by those receiving unemployment compensation, this is likely an undercount because some people seeking employment do not file for unemployment compensation or even qualify for it. If we ask people whether they consider themselves unemployed, we might overestimate the amount of unemployment, because some people may not be sufficiently looking for employment. Likewise, whether or not a housing crisis exists depends on how it is measured: by the percentage of people living in a room (over-crowding), or by the percentage of income spent on rent or mortgage? Thus, we need to know the exact data definitions and ensure that they are reasonable for our purpose. No measure is perfect, but it might be embraced as an indicator.

Though secondary data may suffer from poor quality and problems of definition and sampling, managers and analysts are expected to know about and use the secondary data in their field. See Box 5.1, and plan to spend a few hours surfing the web to get to know new data sources in your area of interest.

> **Getting Started**
> Identify sources of secondary data in your field. Explore the data definitions for your program.

Surveys

Surveys collect information about the opinions and conditions of stake-holders. The most common forms are citizen, client, business, and employee surveys. Surveys provide important information about stakeholders that otherwise might be unavailable. For example, a survey of citizens or employees can identify concerns about the availability of child care services and after-school programs, and the quality of each. These may be important conditions that affect decisions, in this case about employment and child care. Knowledge of stakeholder preferences and conditions is often important in management decision making.

The argument for using surveys is that they provide systematic and objective information about stakeholder preferences and conditions. Managers usually know something about stakeholder problems and needs through their impromptu comments, calls, and complaints; through public hearings;

In Greater Depth . . .

Box 5.1 Getting to Know Data in Your Field

Data portals can provide good leads to data in your field. Below are some international and federal ones with which you should be familiar:

United Nations: *http://unstats.un.org/unsd/databases.htm* (data)
World Bank: *data.worldbank.org* (data)
Organisation for Economic Co-operation and Development: *stats.oecd .org*
CIA World Fact Book: *https://www.cia.gov/library/publications/the -world-factbook/*
International Social Survey Programme: *www.issp.org/page.php?pageId=4*
Federal government portal: *www.data.gov*
Federal data: *www.fedstats.gov* (includes data, reports)
U.S. Census: *www.census.gov* (see also "American FactFinder")
U.S. Government Accountability Office: *www.gao.gov* (reports)
U.S. Library of Congress: *thomas.loc.gov* (reports)

Additionally, you should research the websites of agencies and organizations in your specific field, such as federal agencies, national associations, state agencies, and counties and cities in your area. It is often surprising how much data exist. Banking associations, environmental associations, social services associations—they all have data that often are posted on their websites. Some research efforts also post data. The International Social Survey Programme, for example, includes data on in-depth topics from more than 30 countries. Some organizations also use existing surveys and aggregate these into useful measures (for example, see the Transparency International website, at www.transparency.org/policy_research/surveys_indices/cpi).

or through comments made by elected officials. Although this information is valuable, it seldom provides comprehensive and unbiased information. Those who call or complain have a specific agenda in mind; they are seldom representative of all citizens, clients, businesses, or employees. Surveys provide the necessary antidote of objectivity and comprehensiveness; they help prevent perceptions from becoming reality.

Surveys also supplement administrative and secondary data; when these sources are inadequate, managers need to collect their own information.

Surveys are varied, and the number and types of questions asked should depend on what you are trying to find out. Likert scales often are used (see Chapter 3), but other response formats may be used depending on the information sought. Some surveys are short,

Getting Started
How can a survey help managers in your field?

others longer depending on the audience and the issues being explored. Surveys are commonly used in program evaluation research and, increasingly, performance measurement. They are also used to aid community leaders in establishing community priorities and to determine how to address community needs. For example, in a growing community, a survey might be used to lay the groundwork for determining which roads to widen to cope with increased traffic, to determine the level of support for moving to a single waste hauler, or to measure community perceptions of the worst intersections in the city.

Four types of surveys are mail, Internet, phone, and in-person surveys. Here, we are referring to scientific, systematic surveys that use sampling methods discussed in the next section—not ad-hoc marketing surveys or pop-up surveys that are used for solicitation, for example. Each approach has somewhat different advantages, and the manager's experience with each type may vary according to the specific conditions assessed (see Table 5.1). Internet (or web-based) surveys have obvious advantages of low cost and high speed, but a continuing problem is often the lack of a list of email addresses from which one might sample. Internet surveys can be used when a list of email addresses is available; sometimes a mix of methods is used to include in the sample program clients whose email addresses are unknown or those who do not have email addresses.[3] A continuing problem with Internet surveys is the absence of a community list of email addresses; thus, phone surveys are commonly used for citizen surveys. Though not inexpensive, phone surveys can be completed quickly, and over 50 items can be asked when questions are easy and asked in a similar format.[4] For example, a typical lead-in might be, "I am going to read you a series of statements. Please tell me for each whether you strongly agree, agree . . . ," after which a series of short statements follows. A great deal of information can be gathered by using this format. A relatively recent development is the use of voice recognition software to assist interviewers in capturing responses to open-ended responses. For example, the analysis of open-ended questions such as "What three things do you like most [or least] about the program" provides useful information with high face validity. Despite the perception that people rarely answer phone surveys, the reality is that, because few citizens get calls on behalf of their governments asking them their opinions, many respondents are quite eager to contribute.

Table 5.1 ⎯⎯ ⌇⌇ ⎯ Comparing Mail, Internet, Phone, and In-Person Surveys

Criterion	Mail	Internet	Phone	In-person
a. Response rate	Variable	Variable	Variable	High
b. Amount of data	Highest	Low to Medium	Low to Medium	Low or High
c. Data collection	6–8 weeks	2–3 weeks	2–3 weeks	4–6 weeks
d. Cost per survey	Low to Medium	Low	Medium to High	Very high
e. Interviewer bias	Low	Low	Medium	Medium

Employee surveys are frequently conducted using confidential pen-and-paper survey. These are mailed to employees' homes or distributed at work. To ensure both high response rates and anonymity, employees sometimes are asked to complete the surveys simultaneously and then return them in blank envelopes. In theory, employee surveys can be conducted using a company's internal computer network, if employees have adequate trust that responses will indeed be kept confidential and anonymous.

Mail surveys continue to be used, though their cost and time advantages relative to phone and Internet surveys probably make them increasingly less attractive. When mail surveys are used, the appearance of the instrument should reflect high levels of professionalism in design and customer orientation; the instrument should look attractive and be easy for respondents to use. To reduce intimidation—mail surveys often are lengthy—they often are presented in a small booklet format, such as by folding legal-size paper twice. Mail surveys usually include a stamped return envelope, too. The idea is to make it easy for the respondent to complete the survey. In-person surveys are very expensive and seem to be increasingly rare. The U.S. Census uses them to conduct interviews that are extraordinarily lengthy, for example. (As an aside, our scientific surveys are very lengthy—sometimes over 200 items. Such length precludes using phone or Internet surveys. In the United States, these are mail surveys, but in smaller countries, researchers sometimes use more expensive in-person surveys to collect the data.)

Surveys are typically carried out using the following steps: (1) obtaining permission and resources for conducting surveys, (2) interviewing stakeholders to fully understand the study context and to specify study objectives, (3) obtaining a sample of the study population for surveying, (4) designing, testing, and improving a pilot survey, (5) implementing the final survey instrument, and (6) analyzing and reporting findings.

It is obvious that biased questions are a threat to validity. In addition, questions should be clear (that is, unambiguous and specific) and answerable by respondents.[5] Furthermore, double-barreled phrasing, leading (or biased)

phrases, and negative statements should be avoided. Consider the following examples. "Do you feel safe?" is ambiguous for the purpose of evaluating high school violence and should be clarified as, "How safe do you feel at school?" A leading question would be, "Could you ever think of hitting a classmate?" This question implies that it is undesirable or unacceptable to do so. A better question would be, "Have you thought about hitting a classmate during the last seven days?" An example of a double-barreled question is, "Do you feel that guns should be barred from school and that those who bring guns to school should be punished?" These two questions should be asked separately.

Regardless of the type of survey used, survey questions should be as easy as possible for respondents to answer while providing researchers with all the information they need. Formulating good questions is an art built on practice and continuous

> **Getting Started**
> How can a survey help managers in your field?

improvement. Beyond this, some other guidelines are that questions that deal with the same topic should be grouped together. Likert scales greatly assist in survey development because the same response scale can be used for many different items. The survey introduction should state the purpose of the survey and how results will be used, and all interviewers should follow the same script, with no variation; neither the interviewers nor the script should introduce bias. Many surveys go through numerous iterations and pilot testing before they are implemented. The CD that accompanies the workbook, *Exercising Essential Statistics,* includes examples of survey instruments, data, and reports. In short, surveys are increasingly used in management and analysis. Surveys allow managers and analysts to gather a considerable amount of information from their stakeholders.

Other Sources

Four other sources of data are *observers, actors, experts,* and *focus groups.* *Observers* are sometimes used to assess the condition of facilities and infrastructure, such as roads, public facilities, and park grounds. These assessments can be quite detailed, following extensive checklists and other structured reporting formats. For example, park grounds might be checked for litter, unsafe objects, grass length and condition, weeds, sign markings, pathway safety, condition of benches and playgrounds, paint and rust, and so on. Typically, considerable care is taken to ensure that all observers make their observations in the same manner, and reliability checks are conducted from time to time for this purpose. Observers should be carefully trained and evaluated to ensure that they are consistent in their assessments.

Actors are observers who are actively involved in what they observe. Role playing is sometimes used to assess frontline services, such as toll collection or welfare application processing. Actors usually participate as clients and assess services according to different conditions that they describe or represent. For example, actors are used to ensure that services are rendered irrespective of race or gender.

Experts are people with credible and typically advanced knowledge about a certain matter, They are used when objective data and stakeholder opinions and accounts alone are insufficient for making judgments about program outcomes. For example, landfill maintenance, analysis of medical records, and evaluation of the quality of higher education programs require a balance of objective facts and subjective opinion. In these cases, experts provide important information. Chapter 4 explored the idea of using experts in the context of forecasting. Experts can work either alone or collectively in coming to a consensus.

Focus groups are purposive samples used to generate insights about program services and goals. For example, a citizen focus group on law enforcement might be asked about perceptions of police officers in a juris-diction, as well as program needs and outcomes. Focus groups often are homogeneous, because different populations have different experiences and may drown each other out. For example, minorities and whites often have very different perceptions about law enforcement personnel. Although focus groups are valuable, the small number of focus group members (typically about 10–20) suggests that we cannot assume that the opinions of group members accurately reflect those of the larger group to which they belong. Generalization to the larger population is not possible. Also, focus groups do not provide much quantifiable data. Rather, focus groups are used to gener-ate insights into the reasoning, priorities, and experiences of participants.[6]

SAMPLING

After the research design has been selected, variables defined, and data sources selected, questions arise about how information will be collected. Among these questions is the matter of the target population. Specifically, about which population is information to be gathered, and how many members of the population need to be reached? The latter question refers to getting informa-tion from a sample, that is, a subset of a population. In public management, samples of citizens, clients, or employees are quite common. Three frequently asked sampling questions are (1) When is a sample needed? (2) How should samples be selected? and (3) How large should the sample be?

When Is a Sample Needed?
Although a **census** could be used to survey or count (tally) an entire group or population, such as all citizens in a jurisdiction or all program clients, doing so is often impractical. In these cases, a sample is used. Sometimes

data collection aims to conduct a census, such as when all employees or all clients are surveyed in a small program. However, some employees or clients may not respond, in which case the resulting response group is considered to be a sample.[7]

A *sample* is a selection, such as of citizens, from an entire population. In most surveys, the purpose of a sample is to make a *generalization,* or a statement about one group that is applied to another group or to a broader group. A statement made about a sample is held to be valid for the population from which the sample was drawn. Indeed, we are interested in knowing how a population, not just the sample, assesses something; we must be able to draw conclusions about the population.

Only representative samples allow generalizations to be made about an entire population. A *representative sample* is one that has characteristics similar to those of the population as a whole. Surveys are valid reflections of the general population only when they are based on a representative sample; the strategy of conducting a valid survey requires that a representative sample be obtained. Unrepresentative samples have a biased (or skewed) mix of characteristics (for example, a greater proportion of females) and do not lend themselves to generalization.

How Should Samples Be Selected?

Random sampling is the most accurate way to obtain a representative sample. In this process, each population member has an equal chance of being selected for the study sample. The list from which a sample is drawn is called a *sampling frame,* and one of the first tasks in conducting a survey is to acquire the sampling frame from which a sample is to be drawn. A common approach is to select participants blindly, thereby minimizing any researcher-induced bias. Two popular methods of random sampling are to assign a number to each population member and use computer-generated random numbers to select the sample, or to use randomly dialed telephone numbers to select participants for phone surveys. Another sampling method, *systematic sampling,* involves selecting a random number from the sampling frame and then selecting every nth member from the sampling frame. Note that chance (random selection) implies that representative samples are similar but not identical to the population; slight differences will exist between the sample and the population with regard to age, gender, income, and so on. In historical or archival research, sometimes a random sample of records is chosen when the entire population of records is too large for study.

> **Key Point**
> A representative sample is a sample that has similar characteristics as the population from which it is drawn. Random sampling is the most accurate way to obtain a representative sample.

Some threats to validity for surveys are inadequate sampling frames and unrepresentative samples. Ideally the sampling frame should closely match the survey population, but discrepancies will exist in practice. For example, a phone survey of citizens will miss out on households that have no phone. Some households may have only cell phones. This inaccuracy might be of minor significance, but in some cases such an inaccuracy might be very significant and should be acknowledged. Analysts must be aware of discrepancies between the population and the sampling frame.

Unrepresentative samples are another threat to validity. Two examples of unrepresentative samples are those based on customer comment cards and responses to enclosures in mass mailings such as utility bills. Although these efforts provide important information, they cannot be relied on for generalization. Those who complete customer comment cards are usually heavily skewed toward clients with gripes, though they typically include a few clients who offer praise. We cannot assume that their opinions reflect all clients. Enclosures in utility bills (and other mass mailings) may suffer from this problem, as well. Very few recipients return such enclosures, and we cannot assume that they are representative of all recipients. Community leaders typically want all citizens to receive a survey, but the resulting response sample often is a nonrepresentative sample based on self-selection. Rather, if generalization is the objective, then a random sample should be drawn.[8]

Finally, in recent years, studies of "exemplary practices" have been conducted. Organizations selected for such studies are selected not randomly but purposively, because of their exemplary practices. *Purposive sampling* is used to produce further insight, rather than generalization. These are not random samples. Often, these are case studies that are not even generalizable to other exemplary organizations, but the insights of how things are done are of great importance and most useful in improving public management. Likewise, case studies of policy impacts often are very useful in identifying unintended outcomes and program innovations that otherwise might not come to light. Research based on purposive samples can yield important insights, but the results are not generalizable.

> **Getting Started**
>
> Develop a strategy for obtaining a representative sample of your program clients.

How Large Should the Sample Be?

Large random samples will more accurately reflect characteristics of the population from which they are drawn. The term *sampling error* is defined as discrepancies (errors) that occur because random sampling procedures may cause sample statistics to differ from (unknown) population statistics. In a population, 30 percent of students might have an A, but a random sample might show 35 percent, leading to the conclusion that, in the population of students, 35 percent of students rather than 30 percent have an A. Of course, in practice one seldom knows these population statistics; that is why a sample is taken.

The sampling error is unknown, because the true values of population parameters are unknown. However, the sampling error can be calculated for random samples as the range within which one can be 95 percent certain that the population estimate falls. Larger samples better mirror the population from which they are drawn and thus have smaller sampling errors. Sampling errors reflect *reliability,* the extent to which repeated sampling and measurement produces the same result. The relationship between sample size and sampling error for samples drawn from populations over 20,000 is shown in Table 5.2. For example, the sampling error of a survey with a sample size (n) of 300 is ±5.7 percent; if a survey finds that 73.4 percent of respondents favor a new road, then you can be 95 percent certain that, in the population from which the sample was randomly drawn, between 67.7 percent [73.4% − 5.7%] and 79.1 percent [73.4% + 5.7%] favor the road. This assumes, of course, that the finding is not subject to other survey errors, such as asking biased questions or having unrepresentative samples.

For populations greater than 20,000, *sampling errors are independent of population size.* The same sampling error applies for a survey of a medium-sized jurisdiction of 40,000 as for the entire United States or the world![9] Another consideration is that gains in accuracy must be balanced against cost and effort. Accuracy gains on samples over 1,200 are seldom justified. Most samples range between 200 and 800. Larger samples are required only when analyses include many subsets (for example, many districts for which data must be reported separately).

> **Key Point**
> Sampling errors are the discrepancies between values of population parameters and their sample estimates. Sampling errors are independent of population size, in large populations.

Decisions on sampling can be aided by some further practical considerations. First, small populations (say, less than 100 or 200) do not require sampling; rather, the entire population should be surveyed.

Table 5.2 ⎯⎯⎯⎯⎯⎯⎯⎯ Relationships between Sample Size and Sampling Error

Sample size	Sampling error (%)	Sample size	Sampling error (%)
100	± 9.8	500	± 4.4
200	± 6.9	800	± 3.5
300	± 5.7	1,200	± 2.8
400	± 4.9	2,000	± 2.2

Second, sometimes sampling frames are lacking, such as when clients are served on a walk-in basis and no record is kept of names. In that situation, managers randomly select days and times at which anonymous walk-ins are surveyed. Third, when the population includes subgroups of small numbers (for example, small minority groupings), *stratified sampling* is used. Stratified sampling first divides the sampling frame according to each subpopulation to be surveyed and then samples randomly within each subgroup. This approach gives members from small groups a greater chance of participation than members of large groups. Of course, study results must later be weighted appropriately to ensure unbiased conclusions. Such weighting is discussed in Chapter 6. Fourth, nonrespondents must be accounted for by using a greater initial sample. If a 50 percent response rate is expected and 400 completed surveys are desired, then a random sample of 800 participants should be drawn.

Finally, generalization assumes that nonrespondents answer in the same manner as respondents. *Nonresponse bias* (also known as nonresponse error) is the extent to which views of nonrespondents differ from those of respondents, thus affecting generalizability from the sample to the population. Low response rates merit concern about nonresponse bias; this, too, is a validity concern for surveys based on enclosures in mass mailings. The problem of nonresponse bias is usually dealt with by comparing sample and population demographics. When differences exist (for example, phone surveys sometimes oversample females), researchers can statistically weight survey responses to account for over- or undersampling and may conclude that the likely, known effect of such oversampling is minor. Of course, the best approach to this problem is to avoid over- and undersampling as much as possible. For example, in the case of phone surveys, the solution may be to monitor participation rates of females and at some point survey only males. Many surveys compare sample and population demographics and report these comparisons in their methods section (see Box 5.2).[10] In some cases, caveats may be needed in reporting results.

DATA INPUT

The result of data collection is data that are to be subsequently analyzed. Analysis uses one or more software programs, which typically expect data to be in a spreadsheet-like form. Most software programs can read Excel spreadsheets, and a starting point may be to put one's data in an Excel spreadsheet that is subsequently either analyzed in Excel, or uploaded into another software program (for example, PASW/SPSS or Stata). Sometimes,

In Greater Depth . . .

Box 5.2   Writing Up Your Methods

The following excerpt is from a report of a citizen survey for a large county:

This study was conducted by the Florida Institute of Government and the Department of Public Administration at the University of Central Florida, on behalf of Orange County Government. The survey of Orange County residents focuses on government priorities, satisfaction with government services, and contact with public officials. Its purpose is to assist in updating the Orange County Strategic Plan.

The survey was developed with input from Orange County staff and includes items from an the earlier survey for the purpose of comparison. Calls were typically made between the hours of 1 PM and 6 PM on Saturdays and Sundays, and between 5:30 PM and 9:30 PM on Mondays through Thursdays. Some callbacks were made at other hours.

The survey protocol is provided in Appendix 4 [not shown here]. Random digit dialing was used to ensure a representative sample. This procedure involves selecting numbers at random from the appropriate exchanges in the Greater Orlando directory, and then substituting two randomly generated digits for the last two numbers. This allows the inclusion of new and unlisted numbers.

A total of 9,503 different telephone numbers were identified, and each phone number was dialed up to four times in order to contact potential interviewees. Of these 9,503 phone numbers, 3,669 (38.6 percent) were ineligible, because they were business or government offices, fax lines, disconnected or out of service numbers, or, in a few cases, exchanges with respondents living in nearby Seminole County. Some ineligible respondents occurred toward the end of the survey, when participation criteria were restricted to ensure demographic balance of the final sample. An additional 2,818 (29.7 percent) were never reached in four attempts. These were numbers at which no response, other than an answering message or a busy signal, was ever elicited. A total of 3,016 potential respondents were reached and asked to participate, which represents 31.7 percent of the total numbers selected and called. Of the 3,016 eligible respondents, 1,982 (65.7 percent) were unwilling or unable to complete the interview. The

(continued)

Box 5.2 *(continued)*

remaining 1,034 (34.3 percent) of eligible respondents participated and completed the interview.

The above procedures are designed to ensure a valid (that is, representative) sample of Orange County residents. A valid (or representative) sample is one that is adequate for generalizing study results to the entire population. In this regard, the following comparisons provide statistical evidence supporting the similarity between the sample and the Orange County population:

	Population	Sample
Age		
18–45	62.3%	62.8%
46–65	24.1	26.8
66+	13.6	10.4
Race		
White	81.5%	84.3%
Non-white	18.5	15.7
Gender		
Male	49.0%	43.9%
Female	51.0	56.1

The total sample size is 1,034 completed surveys. This implies a sampling error of no more than 3.2 percent. That is, we can be 95 percent certain that the population results are within ± 3.2 percent of the results reported in this study. The sample size was selected based on cost-effectiveness: to reduce the sampling error to, for example, 2 percent, requires a sample size of about 2,400, more than a doubling of effort.

analysts put data directly into a different software program. Three tasks follow data collection: data coding, data input, and data cleaning, all of which precede data analysis.

Data coding is the process of preparing data (from pen-and-paper surveys or from electronic or other sources) for input into statistical software programs. Analysts need to decide which variable names and labels will be used to reference specific survey questions, how they will code different responses, and how they will deal with missing values. These are routine but necessary matters in getting the data ready for analysis by statistical software programs.[11] Spreadsheets like Excel are computer application programs that arrange data into columns and rows; software programs expect each respondents' answers to be fully recorded in a separate row. Also, each spreadsheet column must be reserved for one unique variable that is to be analyzed. This is shown in Figure 5.1, for Excel. Note that the first row shows the variable names. The data start in row 2, for each separate observation (here, cities). The data for Akron (Ohio) are shown in row 2 (as much as can be shown in the figure). As column "AK" suggests, there are a lot of variables for each city. The point of data coding is to think of what the spreadsheet will look like for one's dataset.

Data input (also known as data entry) is the activity of recording these data in statistical software programs. This is sometimes a manual process, such as when data must be transcribed from pen-and-paper surveys or published statistical tables into electronic form. More often, this is a process of uploading a data spreadsheet into a statistical software program. This step usually requires some adjustments or recoding, and it requires careful attention to detail to ensure that the uploaded data are as intended. For example, data labels and strings (text, rather than numbers, as well as missing responses and data) must be appropriately recognized and read by the software program, and missing values must be addressed.[12]

Remember the expression "garbage in, garbage out"? *Data cleaning* is the process of identifying and removing reporting and recording errors. Most data have some errors. The quality of results is only as good as the quality of the data that are used. Errors include mistyped values, errors that arise in the process of uploading, and other implausible values that have been recorded. Data cleaning is aided by univariate analysis, and examples are shown in Chapter 7. It is common practice to assume that unexamined data usually contain various errors that must be identified and removed. Without data cleaning, such errors may introduce bias to your results.

> **Key Point**
> Most data have reporting and recording errors. The point of data cleaning is to find them.

Data cleaning usually consists of several activities. First, analysts identify implausible values in their data that they then remove or correct. For example, a variable "age" that has a value of "999" certainly requires further investigation. This might be a coding error or it might be that the value is used to indicate a missing value, in which case analysts should ascertain that "999" is defined in their software program as a missing value for this variable.

Figure 5.1 —— ᴧᴧᴧ— Data Input in a Spreadsheet

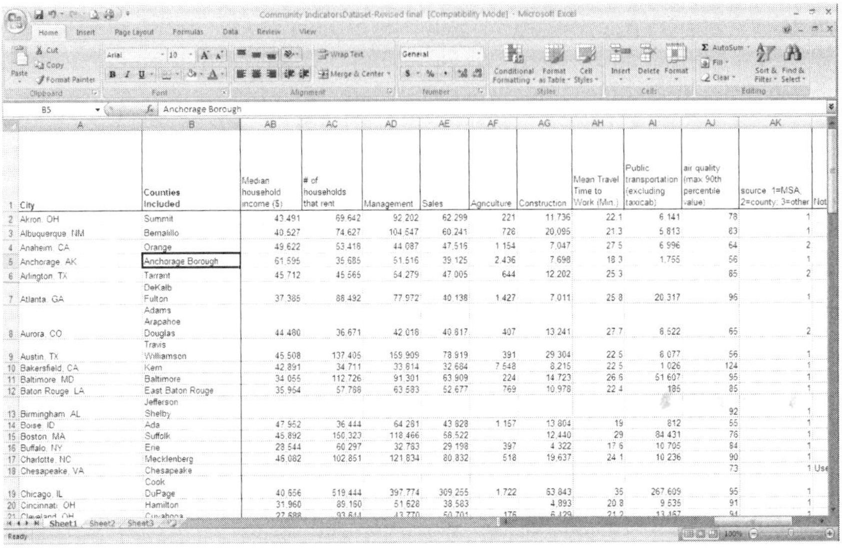

Analysts can examine the highest and lowest values of their variables and ascertain whether they are plausible. Second, analysts ascertain that their dataset is complete and accurate. To this end, the number of observations (records) in the dataset is verified against the number of records in the source (paper or electronic). In addition, a random sample of records in the statistical software is compared against corresponding records in the original data source; analysts will want to ensure that the data in these records match exactly. Analysts might also compare whether statistics (for example, the mean) are identical between variables in the statistical software program and the original data source. When this not the case, problems with variables or groups of observations may be indicated. Only *after* the analyst has determined that the data are complete and free from data-coding and data-entry errors can data analysis proceed further.

PUTTING IT TOGETHER

Conducting research and analyzing data clearly involve many different aspects. The six steps of program evaluation, discussed in Chapter 2, provide an organized way to look at the different activities and considerations involved. Below is a summary proposal—for evaluating an after-school program—that integrates elements of the previous chapters in this book. In some ways, we can think of proposals as final reports that lack data analysis or conclusions.

Proposal for Evaluating an After-School Program

In recent years, new after-school programs have been implemented in our region. The purpose of this proposal is to outline a strategy for evaluation. Input has been sought and obtained from many sources, including county management, school administrators, teachers, and a panel of school psychologists. We also conducted two focus groups with school students. A consensus exists that school violence is an important problem and that an after-school program presents an opportunity to reduce it. However, many observers believe that the benefits of after-school programs extend beyond the current issue of school violence, and we were encouraged to evaluate other outcomes, too.

The main after-school activities whose outcomes we will evaluate are the homework assistance and anger management components. Student participation in after-school programs often is voluntary, although many schools have made an effort to ensure that those teenagers participate who they believe are prone to violence, socially isolated, or academically at risk.

To better determine the impact of these after-school programs, we will include after-school programs that vary in their use of anger management and homework assistance. A few after-school programs provide only recreational activities, and we feel that those are an appropriate comparison group for these others programs. Although no baseline data have been gathered to date, we propose to gather such data as soon as the proposal is approved. Baseline data are important in evaluating the impact of these programs.

We will focus our efforts on a variety of well-targeted outcome measures. With regard to anger management, we will focus on students' knowledge of anger management principles, their ability to identify anger in themselves and others, the strategies they use to release anger in nonviolent ways, and their willingness to help others use such strategies. With regard to homework assistance, we will focus on the utilization of this service, the areas in which it is most often used, and perceptions of increased valuation of academics and study discipline. With regard to high school violence, we will assess violence with weapons, physical violence without weapons, and verbal assaults.

While after-school programs could affect violence and improve academic ability, other factors contribute to these outcomes as well. This evaluation acknowledges these other factors and will collect information about the following variables for purposes of statistical control: student access to weapons, student social isolation, peer pressure exerted by violence-prone groups, school enforcement of nonviolence policies, teacher awareness of teenage violence predictors, and teacher and staff commitment to reducing teenage violence. We will also consider student academic performance, composition of student household (number of parents and siblings living with student), gender, and race.

We will collect data from a variety of sources. School records track incidents of physical violence, though such records vary in accuracy regarding that which is recorded. Rather, the primary sources will be students and teachers. On a quarterly basis, teachers will be asked to participate in a survey about violence in their classes, and on the impact of the after-school programs on students who are in their classes. Also, students will be given a test of their knowledge of anger management principles, as well as an assessment of the usefulness and impact of homework assistance. The latter assessment is, of course, administered only to those who participate in such homework assistance. Both the teacher and student surveys include items regarding the other control variables mentioned above.

We intend to survey all teachers and a sample of students participating in these programs. We anticipate surveying about 100 teachers and a sample of 300 students (which has a sampling error of 5.6 percent). Detailed information about the measurements and survey instruments and protocols is provided in the appendix [not shown here].

SUMMARY

Managers and analysts can use several sources of data for program evaluation, performance measurement, and forecasting. These sources are administrative data; secondary data; survey research; and other sources such as observers, actors, experts, and focus groups. Managers and analysts are expected to be familiar with the data in their field and to be able to develop and integrate data from these different sources to meet their needs.

Sampling involves selecting a group for study from the population being examined. Studies that rely on generalizability (that is, most surveys) require representative samples. Such samples are obtained through random sampling, in which each population member has an equal chance of being selected. The size of the sample depends on the required sampling error; larger samples have smaller sampling errors and are thus more accurate. Some threats to validity are unrepresentative samples (for example, customer comment cards, enclosures in mass mailings) and low response rates, which may also result in unrepresentative samples.

KEY TERMS

Actors (p. 89)
Administrative data (p. 81)
Census (p. 90)
Data cleaning (p. 97)
Data coding (p. 96)
Data input (p. 97)
Experts (p. 90)
Focus groups (p. 90)
Generalization (p. 91)
Nonresponse bias (p. 94)

Purposive sampling (p. 92)
Random sampling (p. 91)
Representative sample (p. 91)
Sample (p. 91)
Sampling error (p. 92)
Sampling frame (p. 91)
Secondary data (p. 83)
Stratified sampling (p. 94)
Types of surveys (p. 87)

Notes

1. In recent years, many managers and analysts have contributed to their organizations by helping them collect more or better data. Some organizations have hired employees who are responsible for managing the organization's data needs for performance measurement.
2. Managers should be familiar with the following useful portals: www.fed stats.gov; www.worldbank.org/data; www.secondarydata.com (select "general sources"); and for state-level data, www.census.gov/sdc.
3. For example, Survey Monkey is a popular tool that makes producing a web-based survey relatively easy.
4. Examples of such lengthy and comprehensive phone surveys are shown on the CD that accompanies the workbook *Exercising Essential Statistics*. The workbook also provides further references (resources) for doing surveys.
5. Although respondents may have opinions about school safety, they are apt to be unfamiliar with specific options. Thus, "Do you want anger management programs?" may be unanswerable by those who are unfamiliar with such programs. It would be best to precede this question with, "How familiar are you with anger management programs?" Some of the best survey questions follow the K.I.S.S. rule: Keep It Simple, Stupid.
6. As noted by an anonymous reviewer, "One of my pet peeves is the tendency for community and nonprofit leaders to insist on a tool that is inadequate to the task. I have had people ask me to do randomly selected focus groups so they can generalize. This of course is not possible."
7. Although the term *census* is usually limited to a population, tallies are also taken of all program resources, activities, and results. Shortfalls in such counts are problematic, suggesting that the organization has achieved less than it really has. Organizations usually undertake considerable control to

ensure that such important tallies are highly accurate and complete. Although gaps and inaccuracies can be estimated, analysts are conservative in making such guesses; they often are difficult to justify and may induce errors of their own. Recall that the ethics of research includes being objective and avoiding any appearance of tampering with data (see Chapter 1).

8. Of course, there are good reasons why elected officials would like all citizens to receive the survey: it is good public relations, and it gives every citizen the chance to speak up. Some interesting responses might be obtained, but we need to acknowledge that the sample is unrepresentative.

9. Small populations have smaller sampling errors. For results that vary by ±5 percent, populations of 5,000 require samples of 357; populations of 1,000 require samples of 278; populations of 500 require samples of 217; populations of 300 require samples of 168; and populations of 200 require samples of 132. Populations of 100 require samples of 79, suggesting that a census would require only a modest amount of additional effort. Numerous Internet sites provide sample size–estimation tables. One such site is the DSS Research "Researcher's Toolkit," www.dssre search.com/toolkit/secalc/error.asp. The sampling errors shown are maximum estimates, which are commonly used. Specifically, they are based on the assumption that 50 percent of respondents answer in a specific way.

10. In some cases, researchers may be able to determine some differences between respondents and nonrespondents by surveying a sample of questions among those who did not respond—the fact that some were unwilling to participate in the full survey does not mean that they won't be willing to answer just a few questions. The results of this so-called nonrespondents' survey are then compared against those of the respondents' survey, allowing for further weighting and for determining the extent of any nonresponse bias. This approach is common in scientific research but less so in practitioner research.

11. The workbook that accompanies this text includes a manual with examples for data coding and data input into SPSS or any other statistical software program. The workbook also includes an SPSS user's guide.

12. Some software programs require a bit more information than Excel. For example, PASW/SPSS has a second screen that allows users to specify characteristics of their variables—we refer to the PASW/SPSS workbook tutorial for relevant screen shots. This text minimizes discussion of specific software, as a range of appropriate software exists.

Descriptive Statistics

Descriptive statistics provide important summary information about variables, such as their average, frequency distribution, and other measures that describe variables in helpful ways. Descriptive statistics are used widely in public and nonprofit management and analysis. For example, knowing how much pollution is occurring, the percentage of citizens favoring improved parks, or the average rate of absenteeism is often meaningful information that affects public decision making. This descriptive information can also be used for subsequent comparisons against past performance, against the performance of other jurisdictions, and across respondent or jurisdictional characteristics such as gender or area incomes. Descriptive statistics are a staple of analysis—arguably much of what practitioners use is based on descriptive statistics. Even though managers and analysts must also master advanced concepts and techniques, those discussed here are a backbone of analysis.

This section discusses many useful descriptive statistics and shows how to use them. It recaps essential concepts from Section II, such as variables, attributes, and levels of measurement. In Section III, Chapters 6 and 7 describe strategies for analyzing single variables, also called ***univariate analysis***. There are two basic types (or families) of univariate statistics. One tells us about *central tendency* (also known as averages), and the other discusses *dispersion,* such as is examined through frequency distributions. For example, we might want to know the average crime rate in past months, and also whether monthly rates vary a lot or a little. Univariate, descriptive statistics are sometimes also called *summary statistics.*

Chapter 8 discusses descriptive statistics for analyzing two or more variables. For example, we might want to compare the average crime rate among two or more high schools, or want to know whether violence varies by gender or age. The analysis of two variables is also called **bivariate analysis**. The approach described in Chapter 8 uses categorical variables to construct contingency tables) and a combination of categorical and continuous variables to construct pivot tables. Chapter 9, new to this edition, examines real-world examples to further hone readers' skills with descriptive statistics, including additional approaches to performance analysis (first mentioned in Chapter 4). Chapter 9 provides further guidance and examples for getting results from one's data. Although tables are used widely for analysis, descriptive statistics have limited use for analyzing such bivariate relationships; the analysis of contingency tables is revisited and extended in Chapter 10 (Section IV).

The strategies discussed here are rather straightforward, but a lot of mileage is to be had from them. Much of what public managers do in practice uses these strategies.

CHAPTER

6

Central Tendency

CHAPTER OBJECTIVES

After reading this chapter, you should be able to

- Identify three statistics of central tendency
- Calculate the mean, median, and mode
- Know appropriate uses of the mean, median, or mode
- Address problems of missing data
- Know when and how to weight data
- Estimate measures of central tendency from grouped data

The first family of univariate analysis is *measures of central tendency,* which provide information about the most typical or average value of a variable. Although measures of central tendency are popularly referred to as averages, they are in fact three separate measures: the *mean, median,* and *mode.* Analysts frequently use these types of measure when reporting on, for example, high school violence, housing starts, pollution, and the like. Analysts should always indicate which measure is being used.

Chapters 2 and 3 introduced important research concepts. It is worth reviewing these concepts here, because the discussion that follows illustrates their relevance. Succinctly, *variables* are key to research and are defined as empirically observable phenomena that vary. High school violence, housing starts, and pollution are examples of empirical phenomena that vary. Management and policy is very much about changing or shaping variables in some way to make society better off—with a bit less high school violence, more affordable housing, less pollution, and so on. *Attributes* are defined as the characteristics of a variable, that is, the specific ways in which a variable can vary. For example, high school violence can be measured as being "absent," "sporadic," "occurring from time to time," or "ongoing"; these are the attributes of the variable "high school violence." The variable "gender" has two attributes, namely, "male" and "female"; and so on.

A *scale* is defined as the collection of specific attributes (or values) used to measure a specific variable. There are *four* levels of measurement scales: *nominal, ordinal, interval,* and *ratio.* Because many statistics require that variables have certain levels of measurement, managers and analysts must be able to determine the level of measurement for their variables. A *nominal-level scale* is one that exhibits no ordering among the categories. "Gender" is a nominal variable: we cannot say that "male" is more than "female" or vice versa. By contrast, an *ordinal-level scale* is one that exhibits order among categories but without exact distances between successive categories. Likert scales, which are common on surveys, are examples of ordinal scales. A typical example of a Likert scale is one with the following response categories: "strongly agree," "agree," "don't know," "disagree," and "strongly disagree." Variables with nominal- and ordinal-level scales are referred to as *categorical variables.*

Interval- and *ratio-level scales* exhibits both order *and* distance among categories. For example, someone who earns $75,000 per year makes exactly three times that of someone making $25,000. The *only* difference between interval and ratio scales is that the latter have a true "zero" (for example, height can be zero, but IQ cannot). Variables with interval- and ratio-level scales are sometimes referred to as *continuous variables. Variables, attributes,* and *measurement scales* are of critical importance in statistics. Readers are encouraged to review the more extensive discussions of these concepts found in Chapters 2 and 3.

THE MEAN

> **Key Point**
>
> The mean is what most people call the "average," but the median and mode are also used as measures of central tendency.

The *mean* (or arithmetic mean) is what most people call "the average," but analysts should use the word *mean* to avoid confusion with other types of averages. Mathematically, the mean is defined as *the sum of a series of observations, divided by the number of observations in the series.* The term is commonly used to describe the central tendency of variables, such as the mean number of crimes, public safety inspections, welfare recipients, abortions, roads under repair, and so on. The mean is appropriate for continuous variables. Mean calculations are essential to most analyses and are used in almost every report.

The following example shows how to calculate the mean. Although computers and hand calculators are typically used to calculate the mean, you should also understand how to do so by hand. Assume that a sample of eight observations of variable x has the following values (or data elements): 20, 20, 67, 70, 71, 80, 90, and 225 ($n = 8$). Obviously, variable x is just a name that could refer to anything, such as the level of violence, educational attainment, arrests, test scores, and the like. A series of values (such as 20, 20, 67, . . .) is also called an *array*. For the above values, the mean is calculated as follows:[1]

$$\sum_i x_i / n = (20 + 20 + 67 + 70 + 71 + 80 + 90 + 225)/8 = 643/8 = 80.38.$$

This equation is probably not new to you, though the notation might be. As a second example, the mean of 15, 25, and 50 is [(15 + 25 + 50)/3 =] 30. The notation $\sum_i x_i$ means "the sum of all values of (variable) x," as shown above. In our example, this notation is shorthand for $\sum_{i=1}^{8} x_i$, which specifies adding the first eight values of x, in the order shown. In this example, $x_1 = 20$, $x_2 = 20$, $x_3 = 67$, and so on. Because our variable has only eight values, there is no need for the notation $\sum_{i=1}^{8} x_i$. Also, n is used to indicate that the observations are a sample. If the observations had constituted the entire population, we would have used a different notation: N (or $\sum_i x_i / N$). This is just a matter of notation, which affects neither the definition nor the calculation of the mean.

Calculating the mean is straightforward, indeed, but managers and analysts may encounter some practical issues that, for the most part, concern the data rather than the formula itself. These concerns are relevant to other statistics, too, and illustrate some important matters. First, variables often have missing data. For example, data may be missing for some clients, about some services, or for some years. We do not like to guess the values of these missing data because it is difficult to credibly justify such guesses. The most common approach is to exclude such observations from calculations; if we do not know x_5, then we generally do not guess it, either. The incidental exclusion of a few observations from among many (say, hundreds) will usually not bias results in any material way. Indeed, most analyses have a few missing observations. Bias may occur, however, when the proportion of missing data is large. Then analysts need to acknowledge that an extensive amount of data is missing and will need to add an appropriate caveat to their report. Obviously it is best to avoid using variables that have many missing values.[2]

> **Getting Started**
>
> Practice calculating the mean using your statistical software program.

Second, calculations of means usually result in fractions (for example, "the mean number of arrests is 8.52 per officer"). The presence of fractions implies that distances between categories are measured exactly, hence, that variables are continuous (that is, interval or ratio level). However, analysts frequently have ordinal variables, such as responses to survey questions that are based on a five- or seven-point Likert scale (see Box 3.1). Because fractions are not defined for ordinal scales, analysts should avoid writing, "On average, respondents provide stronger support for item A (3.84) than item B (3.23)." Rather, analysts might write, "On average, respondents provide stronger support for item A than item B. For example, "whereas 79.8 percent agree or strongly agree that . . . , only 65.4 percent agree or strongly agree that . . . ." The latter phrasing is also easier for many readers to understand or relate to. Nonetheless, this recommendation is not always followed; fractional reporting of ordinal-level variables is commonplace in analytical reports and data tables.[3]

Third, caution should be used with time series data (discussed in depth in Chapter 17). Briefly, dollar values should typically first be expressed as constant dollars (that is, adjusted for inflation), before applying the formula to calculate the mean. Today's dollars do not have the same purchasing power as yesterday's dollars; thus, they first need to be made comparable. The mean assumes that data elements are measured in the same units, including the same kind of dollars.

Fourth, in some cases the mean can be misleading. For example, suppose that most hospital patients stay either one or five days after some type of surgery. Other patients stay other lengths of time, but these lengths are much less frequent. Then we could say that the most common lengths of stay are one and five days. The mean leads us to a single value (say, maybe about three days), which is a poor measure of central tendency in this case because of the two values that occur most often. Though this is not a common situation, awareness of such possibilities may lead analysts to consider the distribution of variables as well (see Chapter 7) and not to rely only on measures of central tendency for summarizing and describing their variables.

Finally, in some cases it may be necessary to use a *weighted mean,* which is defined as a mean for which the observations have been given variable weights. The assignment of weights usually reflects the importance or contribution of each observation relative to other observations. This approach is often taken when measures are based on different population sizes. For example, consider the central tendency of a crime rate of 2.3 percent in city A, with a population of 500,000, and a crime rate of 4.5 percent in city B, with a population of 250,000. Then the mean can be expressed as either [(2.3% + 4.5%)/2 =] 3.4 percent across cities, or as [{(2.3%*500,000) + (4.5%*250,000)}/(500,000 + 250,000) =] 3.0 percent in the region encompassing the populations of cities A and B. The latter is the weighted mean, reflecting the importance of each rate relative to the overall population.[5] Rather than asking which mean is best, it is important to understand the conceptual differences and choose accordingly. Weighted means are also used for adjusting over- and undersampling in surveys. For example, when minorities are undersampled, we might want to weight each of their responses more heavily in order to reflect their actual proportions in the population. Box 6.1 illustrates these calculations. Weighted data can be used to calculate other statistics, too. Each of the eight observations discussed earlier was weighted equally (20 + 20 + 67 + . . .), so using the weighted mean was not necessary.

The issues described here may or may not be germane in every situation. The essential lesson is to be mindful before applying any statistical formula. You need to understand your data and the purposes, definitions, and assumptions of statistical formulas (such as for the mean), and then critically examine summary statistics that result. By taking this approach, you will have increased confidence in the calculated results.

THE MEDIAN

A limitation of the mean is that its usefulness is greatly affected when the data include a few very large or very small values, relative to other values. In the earlier example, if x_8 (the eighth observation in the above sequence, which is 225) had been 950, then the mean for the array would be 171—more than double its initial value! A realistic example of this problem arises when calculating the mean household income in the small hometown of Bill Gates, one of the world's richest people. In that case, the mean is a poor summary statistic of the average household income in that jurisdiction.

The *median is* defined as the middle value in a series (or array) of values. Its value is, by definition, unaffected by a few very large or small values. The median should always be used when a few very large or very small values affect estimates of the mean. Indeed, most summary income statistics of populations report both means and medians because they can be so different. The median is appropriate for both continuous- and ordinal-level variables. The interpretation of the median is that half of the observations lie above the median, and the other half lie below it. To find the median, the data must be ordered from low to high and then the value of the middle observation determined. If the number of observations is

Box 6.1 Weighting Your Data

Weighted means are calculated easily. The formula for weighted means is $\sum_i w_i x_i / \sum_i w_i$, which means "identify the weights, then multiply each weight with the value of each observation, then add these values, and, finally, divide this number by the sum of all weights. Confused? Statistical computer programs can easily weight your data,[4] and the following hand-calculation demonstrates the process:

Value	Weight	Weighted Value
2	0.5	1
2	1.0	2
3	2.0	6
3	2.0	6

The unweighted mean is $(10/4) = 2.50$, and the weighted mean is $(15/5.5) = 2.73$.

Weighted means have many applications, including in survey research. Nonresponse bias is the bias that occurs because survey samples seldom match the population exactly: nonrespondents might have answered differently from respondents. Perhaps the best approach is to conduct a separate survey of nonrespondents and compare their responses with those of the initial respondents. But this method often is expensive and complicated. A second best approach, then, is to compare weighted responses against the actual responses (called unweighted responses). The weighted responses are those that would have been obtained if the sample distribution had perfectly matched that of known population demographics. Typically, census and other sources provide information about age, race, and gender. Consider the following demographics, reported in the workbook *Exercising Essential Statistics*:

	Population	Sample
Age		
18–45	62.3%	62.8%
46–65	24.1	26.8
66+	13.6	10.4
Race		
White	81.5%	84.3%
Non-white	18.5	15.7
Gender		
Male	49.0%	43.9%
Female	51.0	56.1

(continued)

Box 6.1 *(continued)*

Clearly, residents over 66 years of age are undersampled: their responses should be weighted by (13.6/10.4) = 1.308. In a bit more complex example, the weight assigned to every white female respondent of age 45–65 years is [(81.5/84.3)*(51.0/56.1)*(24.1/26.8)] = 0.790. (A few extra decimal places are given here to avoid introducing bias.) Likewise, the weight assigned to every non-white male respondent over 66 years is [(18.5/15.7)*(49.0/43.9)*(13.6/10.4)] = 1.720. (While this is a large value, there are few such respondents in the sample.) Analysts then compare weighted and unweighted responses to determine the extent of nonresponse bias, if any (see workbook). Keep in mind that weighted means are best-guess estimates.

uneven, the median is the value of the middle observation. If the number of observations is even, the median is the mean of the two observations that are nearest to the middle location of the array. This location is found through visual inspection or the formula $(n + 1)/2$, where n is the number of observations.

In our earlier example, variable x has an even (eight) number of observations, which have already been arrayed from low to high. The two middle values are 70 and 71 (at locations 4 and 5); so the median is 70.50 (at location $[(8 + 1)/2 =] 4.50$). If a ninth observation is added to variable x, for example, $x_9 = 275$, the median becomes 71. Note that these estimates are unaffected by the values of the highest or lowest values. If $x_9 = 875$, the median is still 71, because the value of this variable does not affect the value of the middle observation in the series. Note that having few very large or very small values can also be caused by data entry errors, for example, coding x_8 as 1,225, when it should be 225. This property of the mean is yet another reason for taking data cleaning seriously (see Chapter 5).

Getting Started

Find examples of the mean and median in your field

Examples of the median are common in demographic studies of income, in which a few individuals or households typically have very large incomes. Other examples include studies of average jail time served by inmates (some people serve very long sentences), average wait times for tax returns or class registration, and average jury awards (some people have received huge sums). In nonprofit organizations, the median can be useful for tracking fundraising donations (a few people might make exceptionally large donations), service needs (a few people or neighborhoods might make many requests, whereas most make only a few), and volunteer length of service (some volunteers help for many years, but many work for only short periods). A rule of thumb is that when the mean and median are considerably different, analysts should report both. For example, the U.S. Census reports both the mean and median incomes of U.S. households; in 1999 these were, respectively, $56,644 and $41,994, which are considerably different. When the mean and median are similar, it suffices to report only the mean. The measure of what constitutes a "considerable difference" is a judgment call informed by the magnitude of the difference and the study's context. Of course, the earlier cautions about missing data, fractional reporting, time series data, and weighted samples apply when calculating medians, too.

Finally, sometimes analysts have access only to already published, tabulated data tables, rather than having the actual observations as the basis for their calculations. Then, the data have already been grouped, such as by age or income categories. Census data often come in this format, for example. The appendix to this chapter describes how to calculate measures of central tendency for data that have already been grouped.

THE MODE

The *mode* is defined as *the most frequent (typical) value(s) of a variable.* The mode is appropriate for all levels of variable measurement. In our example, the mode of variable x is the value 20; it occurs twice in the array. Another example is that the mode of people living in households is two. Perhaps the mode of assaults on school grounds is five annually. The mode is used infrequently, but an advantage of the mode is that it can also be used with *nominal*-level data, which is not possible for calculating the mean and median.[6] However, when the mode is used as a measure of central tendency for nominal-level data, managers frequently turn to *measures of dispersion,* discussed in Chapter 7, to express the frequency with which the mode occurs. For example, a manager who is analyzing choices of clients or respondents among a range of program options (a nominal variable) will state the number or percentage of clients or respondents who most often chose the most popular program option (that is, the mode).

SUMMARY

Descriptive statistics of the average are commonly used by public managers and analysts. After managers and analysts have verified the accuracy of their data, they may wish to calculate measures of central tendency. There are three such measures: the mean, median, and mode. The most commonly used of these measures is the mean, defined as the sum of a series of observations, divided by the number of observations in the series. Weighted means reflect the importance or contribution of each observation relative to other observations or can be used to account for over- or undersampling. Caution should be exercised in using means with ordinal-level variables.

The median is defined as the middle value in a series (or array) of values. The median should always be used when a few very large or very small values affect estimates of the mean. The mode is defined as the most frequent (or typical) value(s) of a variable. Analysts should always indicate which measure is being used, rather than referring to any of these measures simply as the "average."

The mean is appropriate for continuous-level variables, whereas the median is appropriate for both continuous- and ordinal-level variables. The mode is appropriate for all levels of measurement. Managers and analysts should be mindful when variables are missing a great deal of data or involve time series data.

KEY TERMS

(includes bold italic terms in the Section III introduction)

Attributes (p. 106)

Bivariate analysis (see section introduction) (p. 104)

Categorical variables (p. 106)

Continuous variables (p. 106)

Descriptive statistics (see section introduction) (p. 104)

Grouped data (see appendix to this chapter) (p. 114)

Interval-level scale (p. 106)

Mean (p. 106)

Measures of central tendency (p. 105)

Median (p. 111)

Mode (p. 112)

Nominal-level scale (see also Chapter 3) (p. 106)

Ordinal-level scale (see also Chapter 3) (p. 106)

Ratio-level scale (see also Chapter 3) (p. 106)

Scale (see also Chapter 3) (p. 106)

Univariate analysis (see section introduction) (p. 103)

Variables (see also Chapter 2) (p. 106)

Weighted mean (p. 108)

NOTE: see also Chapter 3 and Glossary

APPENDIX 6.1

Using Grouped Data

The calculations described in this chapter have assumed that the analyst has data for each observation. This is the assumption used in statistical software programs. However, analysts sometimes only publish data that is already in a table format such as Table 6.1. **Grouped data** refers to observations that have already been grouped in different categories. The column labeled "Interval of" could refer to almost anything, such as the groupings of city sizes, students' test scores, motorists' speeds through toll booths with electronic collection, or regional water quality ratings. The ranges show the values of each category. Ranges are sometimes shown as footnotes to tables, which then show only categories and frequencies. The "Frequency" column counts occurrences. For example, there are 12 cities in category 1, 5 cities in category 2, and so on. The column "Cumulative frequency" shows the running total of frequencies of each category and may be absent from some grouped data tables.

Calculations of means and medians of grouped data are *best-guess estimates* and should be used *only when individual observations are unavailable.* Unfortunately, few computer programs can read tabular formats of grouped data, in which case calculations must be done by hand. *Note that your ability to make these calculations will not affect your understanding of other material in this book.*

The *mean of grouped data* is calculated in two steps. In the first step, the mean of the categories is calculated using the formula $\sum_i w_i r_i / \sum_i w_i$, where r is the row number and w is the number of observations in each row. An example speaks a thousand words. In Table 6.1, the weighted mean of categories is $[\{(12*1) + (5*2) + (18*3) + (36*4) + (14*5)\}/(12 + 5 + 18 + 36 + 14) = 290/85 =] 3.412.$[7]

In the second step, the *variable value* associated with this group mean value is determined. This requires interpolation in the following manner: The mean of the grouped data, 3.412, lies somewhere between categories 3 and 4. The estimate of the average variable value associated with category 3 is defined as the midpoint of its range, or $[(11 + 15)/2 =] 13$, and the midpoint of the value associated with category 4 is $[(16 + 20)/2 =] 18$. Then the variable value associated with the category location of 3.412 (which is 3.000 + 0.412) is defined as the midpoint estimate of the range associated

Table 6.1 ⎯⎯⎯⎯ ⋀⋀⋀ ⎯⎯⎯ Illustration of Grouped Data

Category	Interval of	Frequency	Cumulative frequency
1	1–5	12	12
2	6–10	5	17
3	11–15	18	35
4	16–20	36	71
5	21–25	14	85

with category 3 (that is, 13) *plus* 0.412 of the difference of these category midpoints, or [18 − 13 =] 5. Hence, the estimated value of the variable mean is [13 + (0.412*5) =] 15.06 (with rounding). An equivalent expression is that 3.412 "lies 41.2 percent from category 3 toward category 4," which is shown graphically below:

Variable value:	13	← 2.06 →		18
Category value:	3	3.412		4

The *median of grouped data* is estimated in an analogous way. The sample has a total of 85 observations; the median is defined by the value of the forty-third [(85 + 1)/2] observation when values are ordered. Examining the cumulative frequencies, we find that the median falls somewhere between the third and fourth categories:

Variable frequency:	12	17	35	43	71	85
Category value:	1	2	3 ← 0.222 →		4	5

The value of the forty-third observation lies [(43 − 35)/(71 − 35) =] 0.222 from category 3 toward category 4, with a category value of 3.222. Using the same method of interpolation described for the group mean, we calculate the corresponding variable value of category location 3.222 as [13 + 0.222*(18 − 13) =] 14.11. Note the difference between the estimated group mean and median. The linear interpolation used for calculating grouped means and medians assumes defined distances between categories, hence, a continuous level of variable measurement.

The *mode of the grouped data* is the most frequent observation. This is category 4, which has a midpoint value of 18. The mode of these grouped data is thus 18.

Notes

1. Additional examples can be found in the workbook. Also, as a matter of nomenclature, we distinguish between attributes (introduced in Chapter 2) and values. The term *value* refers to the actual, observed responses or measures of a variable, whereas *attributes* refers to the range of values that a variable can have. For example, the variable "gender" has three attributes (male, female, and unknown), even if none of the respondents state that they are male. A variable has as many values as observations, and as many attributes as the different values that a variable *can* have. However, when these terms are used synonymously, confusion can result.

2. On surveys, missing data may indicate a problem with how the question was phrased, indicating a problem with survey validity.

3. Some analysts feel that the mean should not be used with ordinal-level variables, but it does provide useful information. However, the mean is especially inappropriate for nominal-level variables. For example, we cannot say that the average region is 2.45, on a scale of $1 = $ Northeast, $2 = $ South, $3 = $ Midwest, and $4 = $ West. When working with nominal variables, we should describe response frequencies, such as "23.7 percent of employees live in the Northeast, 19.8 percent live in the West," and so on.

4. In SPSS, select Data $\rightarrow$ Weight Cases (and then select a variable by which to weight cases, such as the variable "weight" in the Box 6.1 example).

5. We can also express the formula in the text as $(2.3^*0.67 + 4.5^*0.33) = 3.0$.

6. The mode might be useful in the following instance: Consider the number of violent incidents in which all high school students are involved. The mode may well be 0, and the mean 0.2, for example. If only those who have experienced an incident are included, then the mode might be 2 and the mean 4.2, for example. In this case, the mode is used as a precursor to a better understanding of the distribution of the data.

7. Often, we report values to two decimal places, by default. However, on occasion we may wish to report values to more or fewer decimal places. Here, we report the result to three decimal places to avoid rounding errors that would become evident in the next paragraph.

CHAPTER 7

Measures of Dispersion

CHAPTER OBJECTIVES

After reading this chapter, you should be able to

- Make frequency distributions and report results
- Distinguish between a histogram and a stem-and-leaf plot
- Create line charts, pie charts, and other visual aids
- Define the standard deviation
- Understand the normal curve
- Understand a confidence interval

This chapter examines *measures of dispersion*, which provide information about how the values of a variable are distributed. These measures are the second family of univariate statistics (the first family is *measures of central tendency,* as discussed in Chapter 6). A common measure of dispersion in public and nonprofit management is the frequency distribution. Knowing what percentage of clients or employees score above a specific value is often a prelude to decision making. Such frequency distributions can then be used to make comparisons or create rankings. Frequency distributions often are reported in tabular form, but they are also the basis of many graphs—such as bar charts, pie charts, and line graphs used in presentations.

Measures of dispersion are also used in preliminary data analysis, such as for data cleaning and for generating a first understanding of one's data. The boxplot is a useful tool for data cleaning and is used in this chapter to discuss outliers (that is, unusually large or small values). Analysts need to know how to identify and deal with outliers. An interesting paradox is that knowing the mean or median often invites further questions about the distribution of variables (calling for the use of measures of dispersion), but preliminary analysis of variables' distribution often precedes the analysis of central tendency to ensure that data are clean and appropriate. As a result, analysts commonly first use boxplots for data cleaning, then analyze means and medians, and then examine frequency distributions. This is an important sequence to remember.

This chapter also provides an introduction to the normal distribution, which is relevant for continuous variables. Many continuous variables, such as height and IQ, are normally distributed. Such variables have certain characteristics and terminology with which managers and analysts need to be familiar. In addition, many of the statistical tests discussed in later chapters assume that continuous variables are normally distributed. Those chapters also describe tests for examining this assumption and strategies for dealing with situations when this assumption is not met.

FREQUENCY DISTRIBUTIONS

Frequency distributions describe the range and frequency of a variable's values. They are easy to create and understand, and they often are a prelude to generating data tables and attractive graphics. First we discuss frequency distributions for categorical (nominal or ordinal) variables, and then we look at frequency distributions for continuous variables.

The categories of ordinal or nominal variables often are used in frequency distributions. For example, if a variable is measured on a five-point Likert scale, then we can count, or determine the frequency of, the data elements for each category. Table 7.1 shows a common type of typical frequency distribution; it gives the number of respondents and the frequency of responses (as a percentage) for each item in an employee survey.[1] For example, 81.3 percent [22.8% + 58.5%] of the 969 respondents who answered this question agree or strongly agree that they are satisfied with their job. Likewise, percentages can be determined for other items, and comparisons made across items, too. For example, more respondents agree or strongly agree that they are satisfied with their jobs than agree or strongly agree that each individual is treated with dignity (81.3% versus 42.3%). Frequency distributions are often found in the main bodies of reports and sometimes are used in the statistical appendices of reports, showing the distributions of all survey items.

Table 7.1 ————〰️〰️—— Frequency Distribution: Employee Survey

Statement	Mean[a]	Strongly agree (%)	Agree (%)	Don't know (%)	Disagree (%)	Strongly disagree (%)	n
I am satisfied with my job at Seminole County	3.88	22.8	58.5	5.5	10.7	2.5	969
Seminole County is a good place to work compared with other organizations	3.64	15.4	53.6	14.1	13.1	3.8	969
Each individual is treated with dignity	3.02	8.1	34.2	18.6	29.6	9.5	967

[a] 5 = Strongly agree; 4 = Agree; 3 = Don't know; 2 = Disagree; 1 = Strongly disagree.

Table 7.1 also shows the number of observations for each item (n). Because of incidental missing responses, this number may be different for each item. If all items have the same number of observations, then this number can be reported just once, such as at the top or bottom of a table. Table 7.1 also shows the mean of each response. Frequency distribution tables commonly include mean item responses, and this additional information is sometimes used for ordering (ranking) the items. Of course, items can also be ordered on the basis of the percentages of those who agree or strongly agree with an item. Either approach results in the same ordering of the three items in Table 7.1.[2]

Frequency distributions are readily calculated by statistical software programs. However, when variables are continuous, analysts will have to construct their own categories, because otherwise the frequency distribution will likely have a large number of frequency table categories with just one or a few observations. A practical question is how wide each category should be. Although no hard-and-fast rules exist, analysts should avoid recoding in ways that mislead. To avoid perceptions of lying with statistics, a rule of thumb is that categories should be based on *category ranges of equal length,* unless compelling reasons exist that are explained clearly in the text of the report.[3]

Frequencies can also be shown in a ***histogram,*** as shown in Figure 7.1. A histogram shows the number of observations in each category and they are commonly found in reports. A histogram is useful because it provides a quick visual representation of the extent and nature of dispersion. A histogram allows the analyst to see how many observations are present in each category, although it does not show the value of each observation. Software programs often automatically generate category widths (shown in Figure 7.1

Figure 7.1  Histogram

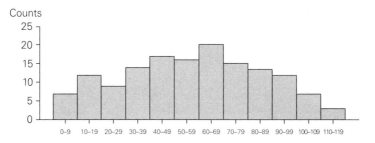

in increments of 10, the default used by SPSS for these data), but software users can also define these widths.[4] Analysts need to know how to make histograms, and it is a good idea to practice making them.[5]

Frequency distributions are a staple of analysis. Managers and analysts need to be able to describe them in plain terms that are readily understood by a broad audience. This matter is discussed in Box 7.1.

Graphical displays often aid in highlighting key results. Tables of frequency distributions, like the one shown in Table 7.1, can be used as the basis of displays that highlight important conclusions. Statistical software programs readily generate these graphs, which can be copied into other programs for further editing and word processing. Managers and analysts need to know how to create attractive graphical displays for their reports and presentations. *Bar charts* are graphs that show the frequency of occurrences through stacks (Figure 7.2); they are used with categorical data. Bar chart A shows options for three-dimensional effects and shading. Bar chart B is also called a Pareto chart, an ordering of categories according to their frequency or importance. This is a visually useful way of drawing attention to that which is important, as well as to the unimportance of other categories that, cumulatively, add very little to our understanding of the problem. Sources 5 through 7 seem barely worth debating. As a convention, bar charts are used with categorical variables, and the bars in such charts should not touch each other. Histograms are used with interval- and ratio-level variables, and their bars should touch each other, suggesting that these data are continuous (see Figure 7.1).

Pie charts typically are used to focus on equity: who gets the most (or the least) of what? Pie charts are used with categorical (often nominal) data, and they can be shown in various ways; Figure 7.2 also shows a pie chart with a slice that has been pulled out. *Line charts* are used with continuous data, partly to avoid displaying a very large number of bars. In the line chart shown in Figure 7.2, the lines show averaged occurrences each month. In this figure, two variables are shown in a way that highlights important trend differences.

Box 7.1 Writing It Up . . .

Effective communication of statistical findings is very important. People expect results to be written in a professional manner; otherwise, statistical analysis may well fall on deaf ears. New analysts often want and need to know how to write up their results.

In one sense, writing up statistical results is no different from any other writing. First, you need to know what you *want to say*. Second, you need to know what you *need to say about what you want to say*. Finally, you need to know *how to say it*. Regarding the first point, what you want to say often is either the result of an analysis or an argument that you wish to back up with statistical analysis. For example, you might want to inform an argument about education policy with an analysis of educational attainment. With a histogram or frequency distribution, you probably want to say something about the percentage of observations in one or more categories.

Second, people need to know that your conclusions are based on valid data and analysis. Thus, you will need to tell them what data you used, how they were collected, what they can be used for, and any known shortcomings. You also need to briefly state your analytical methods and show through your analysis that you are conversant with any issues or limitations that are pertinent to specific methods. Sometimes variables can be constructed or analyzed in different ways, and you might want to present a range of possible answers. In the case of a histogram or frequency distribution, in addition to matters of data validity, you might note if a large number of values were missing or if different ways of constructing categories might have led to different interpretations.

Third, you need to know how to say things. Generally you should state the facts as they are. It suffices to say, for example, that "53.4 percent of respondents disagree or strongly disagree with . . . ." Leave interpretations to the conclusion and discussion sections, where they should be clearly noted as such. As suggested in Box 3.2, it is useful to find several examples of write-ups that you like and then try to adapt the specific language to your needs. Then double-check the language to ensure that it is professional (using third person, present tense, and active voice) and that the report looks professional, too.

Figure 7.2 —⅄⅄— Graphical Displays

Bar chart A

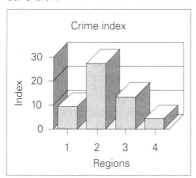

Bar chart B

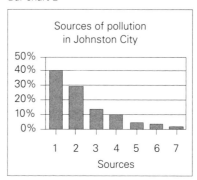

Pie chart

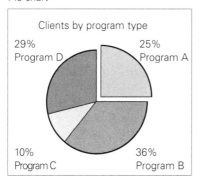

Line chart

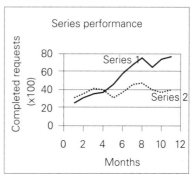

Visual representation is important for analysis and in the communication of study findings to a broader audience. Graphs and charts help draw out differences and inform analytical decisions about differences that matter. For audiences, graphs and charts succinctly summarize and communicate study conclusions, and demonstrate visually why they matter. Analysts are increasingly expected to use visual representations in their reports and oral presentations; they are typically an important and essential part of PowerPoint presentations.

Getting Started

Practice making a frequency distribution and a bar chart with data from your area of interest.

STANDARD DEVIATION

Definition

Let's say that you teach a statistics course at college and you give five exams to two students. On a test scale from 0 to 100 with 100 being all correct, student

A scores 80, 72, 93, 72, and 95. Student B scores 87, 80, 83, 80, and 82. Which one performs better? Both students have the same average score, 82.2. So they perform at the same level based on the mean. But a closer look at these scores shows that student B has a much more consistent and predictable performance. Student B's scores center closely around the mean whereas student A's scores scatter all over so that they depart greatly from the mean. The **stan-** ~~dard deviation,~~ a popular measure of variability, is calculated based on the distance (or, dispersion) of individual observations (such as test scores, in our example) from their mean. Although computer programs calculate the standard deviation, for explanatory purposes we note that the standard deviation is defined as:[6]

$$s = \sqrt{\frac{\sum (x_i - \bar{x})^2}{n-1}}$$

where x_i is the i individual observation and $\bar{x}$ is the mean.[7] For example, when an observation lies far from its mean, $(x_i - \bar{x})^2$ is large, and when an observation lies close to the mean, $(x_i - \bar{x})^2$ is small. Likewise, when *most* observations are scattered widely around the mean, $\sum (x_i - \bar{x})^2$ is large, and when *most* observations are scattered narrowly around the mean, $\sum (x_i - \bar{x})^2$ is small. Thus, data that are widely spread around the mean will have a larger standard deviation than data that are clustered closely around the mean. This is shown in Figure 7.3.[8] In our example of statistical tests, s for student B is 2.88, much smaller than that for student A, 11.10. (Chapter 8 uses a similar analysis for a job promotion example.) In short, the standard deviation represents the "average" (or standard) distance of a set of values from the mean. A larger standard deviation indicates a more dispersed data distribution. Computer programs also calculate s^2, called the *variance* of a variable. However, this measure has no particularly important properties and is provided as information only.[9]

Figure 7.3 —— Small and Large Standard Deviation

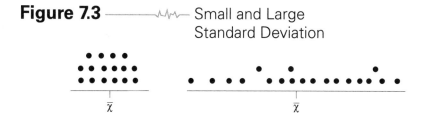

Small standard deviation   Large standard deviation

Some Applications of Standard Deviation

When variables are continuous, the question "How widely are the data dispersed around the mean?" is especially salient because continuous variables often have a large number of values that can be narrowly or (very) widely dispersed. By contrast, many ordinal-level variables have only a few different data values (for example, a five-point Likert scale) and thus may have a limited range. The ***normal distribution*** refers to the distribution of a variable that resembles a bell-shaped curve (Figure 7.4). The left and right sides of the curve mirror each other; they are symmetrical. Many variables are normally distributed, such as student scores, IQ scores, average crop yields, or counts of lightning flashes over time. However, in practice, almost no data are *exactly* normally distributed. Many analysts rely on *visual inspection* to determine distribution, supplemented with the statistics described in this section and in subsequent chapters. The sample data are not expected to match a theoretical bell-shaped curve perfectly because, given that they represent a sample, deviations due to chance selection should be expected.[10]

How Much More or Less? The *standard deviation* is a measure of dispersion that is calculated based on the values of the data. The standard deviation has the desirable property that, when the data are normally distributed, 68.3 percent of the observations lie within ±1 standard deviation from the mean, 95.4 percent lie ±2 standard deviations from the mean, and 99.7 percent lie ±3 standard deviations from the mean. For example, for the data shown below in the accompanying footnote,[11] the computer calculates the mean as 56.39 and the standard deviation as 27.43. Thus, when the data are normally distributed, about two-thirds of the observations will lie between 28.96 and 83.82. About 95 percent lie between the values of 1.53 and 111.25.

> **Key Point**
> The standard deviation is a measure of variability. When the data are normally distributed, 95.4 percent of observations lie within ±2 standard deviations from the mean.

Figure 7.4 —⟋⟍⟋⟍— Normal Distribution: Bell-Shaped Curve

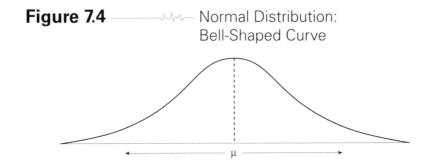

By extension, the distributional properties of the standard deviation can also be used to determine what percentage of values lie above or below a given value. For example, what is the percentage of caseloads in which female welfare clients have more than 2.6 children, if the mean number of children in such caseloads is 2.20, the standard deviation is 0.44, and the variable is normally distributed? To answer this question, we need to compare our values against a table showing the percentages for the standard normal curve, which is defined as a normal distribution that has a mean of 0 and a standard deviation of 1. Such a curve is shown in Appendix A. The area under this curve is 1.00,[12] which means that an observation has a probability of 1.00 of being somewhere under the curve, and the areas to the left and right of the midpoint ($z = 0$) are 0.50, as the curve is symmetrical. Before we can use Appendix A, we need to transform our data into standardized values, so that we can compare them to the table in Appendix A. All data can be standardized by using the formula $z = (x_i - x^-)/s$, and the resulting values are called **z-scores** (or standardized values). Variables whose values have been standardized are called **standardized variables**.

We plug the above information into the z-score formula and find a standardized value of $[(2.60 - 2.20)/0.44 =]$ 0.91. For any given z-score, the question is what percentage of observations have values greater or smaller than it. Appendix A shows areas to the left of the midpoint; for $z = 0.91$, that area is shown as 0.3186 (see Figure 7.5). Thus, 81.86 percent [50% + 31.86%] of cases have a value less than the value that gave rise to this z-score (2.60), and $[1 - 0.8186 =]$ 18.14 percent have a larger value. Note that negative z-scores indicate a probability less than 0.50. For example, the z-score of caseloads with 1.65 children among female welfare clients in the same sample is $[(1.65 - 2.20)/0.44 =]$ −1.25. The area associated with 1.25 in Appendix A is 0.3944 (only positive values are shown), but negative z-score values indicate areas to the left of the mean, and so $[0.5 - 0.3944 =]$ 10.56 percent of caseloads have fewer than 1.65

Figure 7.5 ⎯⎯⎯ Standard Normal Distribution

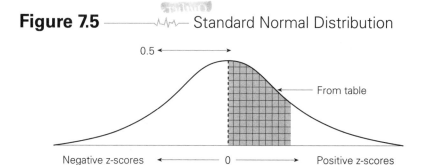

children, and [0.5 + 0.3944 =] 89.44 percent of caseloads have more than 1.65 children.

Calculating Confidence Intervals. The standard deviation is also used to calculate the **confidence interval,** defined as the range within which a statistic is expected to fall on repeated sampling. It is also used to estimate population means from samples. Random samples are often used to estimate population characteristics (see Section II), and statisticians have long worked on the problem that different random samples will yield somewhat different results. A confidence interval expresses how certain we can be that the real, but unknown population parameter falls within an interval. By convention, the term *parameter* refers to a population characteristic, whereas *statistic* refers to a sample characteristic.

The formula for calculating a 95 percent confidence interval of the mean (that is, the range within which the mean will fall in 95 of 100 samples) is $\bar{x} \pm (1.96^*s)/\sqrt{n}$. The measure $s/\sqrt{n}$ is also called the *standard error of the mean.* The value 1.96 is the z-value corresponding with 95 percent of the area under the standard normal distribution (0.475 on both sides) in Appendix A (see Section IV for a more in-depth discussion). For the data in note 5, using this formula, we expect the population mean to lie between [56.39 $\pm$ (1.96*27.43)/$\sqrt{124}$ =] 51.56 and 61.22. Likewise, the formula for calculating a 99 percent confidence interval is $\bar{x} \pm (2.58^*s)/\sqrt{n}$.

See Box 7.2 for further information about confidence intervals. Familiarity with the concept of confidence intervals helps guard against overly precise interpretations of surveys that are based on samples.

The preceding formula has considerable utility for managers and analysts. It provides a measure of how accurate the estimate of the mean is without having to consider or draw other samples; it is based only on the single sample at hand. It also prevents managers and analysts from having to stake their conclusions on a single number, such as 56.39. If the mean of data taken from some other sample or data in the next period is, say, 52.59, this value would still be within the realm of current findings.

Detecting Outliers. The standard deviation is also used to identify outliers in normally distributed variables. **Outliers** are values that are unusually (or extremely) small or large relative to other values in one's distribution. When variables are normally distributed, values that lie more than ±3 standard deviations from the mean are often considered outliers. Thus, for the data in the above mentioned footnote, values greater than [56.39 + (3*27.3) =] 138.68 or smaller than [56.39 − (3*27.3) =] −25.90 would be considered outliers. No such values are present. Outliers can be the result of data-coding errors (which should be either fixed or removed), or they may reflect actual but unusual values in the sample. Outliers matter because many public decisions are based on average behavior, rather than

In Greater Depth . . .

Box 7.2   Confidence Intervals

Pollsters typically use the term *sampling error* to indicate a 95 percent confidence interval. Thus, if survey results report that 79.5 percent of program clients are satisfied with a program, with a sampling error of, say, 3 percent, then the analyst is stating that he or she is 95 percent certain that between 76.5 percent and 82.5 percent of all clients are satisfied with the program. The probability of the estimate falling within the confidence interval, here 95 percent, is also called the confidence level.

The formula for calculating the 95 percent confidence interval for a proportion, p, such as from categorical variables, and based on a large sample ($n > 100$), is as follows:

$$p \pm 1.96^* \sqrt{[p(1-p)/n]}.$$

Sampling errors, such as those shown in Table 5.2, are usually calculated for $p = .500$, which produces the largest possible confidence interval. For example, the 95 percent confidence interval for $n = 124$ and $p = .500$ is $.5 \pm .088$, and for $p = .795$, it is $.795 \pm .071$.

The formula for calculating confidence intervals in small samples ($n < 100$) of continuous and normally distributed variables is analogous, but it uses the so-called t-distribution (discussed further in Chapter 12) to determine the constant. Appendix C shows that this value for a 95 percent confidence interval increases from 1.96 for a large sample to 2.086 for $n = 20$. For our sample, with mean = 56.39 and $s = 27.43$, we can be 95 percent certain that the population mean lies between $56.39 \pm [2.086^*(27.43/\sqrt{20})] = 43.60$ and 69.18. This larger interval than that shown in the text, for $n = 124$, reflects less certainty in our estimates because we have fewer observations. The theoretical underpinnings of confidence intervals involve inference and hypothesis testing (see Section IV).[13]

the unusual or uncharacteristic behavior of a few.[14] An important task of data cleaning and preliminary analysis is to distinguish *usual observations from unusual ones,* identify outliers, and decide whether they should be retained. Our position is that observations flagged as outliers generally should be retained when they are not coding errors, when they are plausible values of the variable in question, and when they do not greatly affect the

> **Key Point**
> The standard deviation can also be used to identify outliers.

value of the mean (of continuous variables). However, when outliers are present, their effect on final results should be studied, and analysts should report observations (outliers) that have been dropped from the analysis along with their reasons for doing so. When variables are not normally distributed, analysts can consider using boxplots for determining outliers (see Appendix 7.1).[15]

Normal Distribution? As discussed later, many statistics are based on the assumption that variables are normally distributed, and computers readily calculate measures that assist in determining whether data are normally distributed. *Skewness* is a measure of whether the peak is centered in the middle of the distribution. A positive value indicates that the peak is "off" to the left, and a negative value suggests that it is off to the right. *Kurtosis* is a measure of the extent to which data are concentrated in the peak versus the tail. A positive value indicates that data are concentrated in the peak; a negative value indicates that data are concentrated in the tail (giving the curve a "fat tail"). Values of skewness and kurtosis have little inherent meaning, other than that large values indicate greater asymmetry. A rule of thumb is that the ratio (absolute value) of skewness to its standard error, and of kurtosis to its standard error, should be less than two (these statistics are calculated by the computer). Large ratios indicate departure from symmetry. The respective ratios of skewness and kurtosis of our data, as calculated by the computer, are $|-0.06/0.22|$ and $|-0.73/0.43|$, which are both well below 2.0. Thus, our data are well centered; the tail is a little fat but not enough to cause us to worry about the normality of our data.[16]

> **Getting Started**
> Identify uses of the standard deviation in your area of interest, and verify calculations in the text on a computer.

These measures are used in conjunction with visual inspection efforts. Many computer programs can also superimpose a curve over a histogram to help tell analysts if their data are normally distributed. If this curve looks close to a perfect bell-shaped curve, the data are considered normally distributed. Many statistical tests discussed in Chapter 12 and beyond assume that variables are normally distributed; we return to this important matter in subsequent chapters.

SUMMARY

Measures of dispersion provide important information about the distribution of a variable's values, and they also help with data cleaning. Frequency distributions show the percentage of observations (for example, clients or employees) that score in or above a certain category. Frequency distributions often are reported in tabular form and are very common in reports. They are also used to generate graphs that are used in reports and presentations; such graphs are essential in helping analysts to communicate their findings to a broader audience.

The standard deviation is a very popular measure of variability that is calculated based on the distance (or dispersion) of individual observations (such as test scores, in our example) from their mean. When data are normally distributed, the standard deviation can also be used (1) to determine what percentage of values lie above or below a given value, (2) to calculate confidence intervals, which express the range within which a statistic is expected to fall, and (3) to determine whether specific values are outliers. This chapter also discusses measures that help determine whether distributions are normally distributed. The standard deviation has additional uses that are examined in Section IV of this book.

KEY TERMS

Bar charts (p. 120)
Boxplot (see appendix to this chapter) (p. 129)
Fences (see appendix to this chapter) (p. 130) Confidence interval (p. 126)
Frequency distributions (p. 118)
Interquartile range (p. 130)
Histogram (p. 119)
Kurtosis (p. 128)

Line charts (p. 120)
Measures of dispersion (p. 117)
Normal distribution (p. 124)
Outliers (p. 126)
Pie charts (p. 120)
Skewness (p. 128)
Standard deviation (p. 123)
Standardized variables (p. 125)
Z-scores (p. 125)

APPENDIX 7.1

Boxplots

A *boxplot* is a graphical device that shows various measures of dispersion. A boxplot is a useful tool for obtaining a quick, visual, and preliminary understanding of data. Computer programs readily provide boxplots for any number of variables. Though analysts also use other tools for their data cleaning, the boxplot offers much useful information, such as identifying outliers, which, for example, histograms or frequency distributions do not. Boxplots are appropriate for both continuous- and ordinal-level variables. The following calculations are shown only for purposes of conceptual understanding, given that software programs typically calculate the values obtained with boxplots. We use the same array as in Chapter 6, namely, 20, 20, 67, 70, 71, 80, 90, and 225.

Boxplots show statistics that are calculated on the basis of the location of data, such as the median. The figure below shows the boxplot for our example array. Because our example has eight observations, the median is defined as the value at location $[(n + 1)/2 =]$ 4.50 (see Chapter 6), that is, the mean of the values of the fourth and fifth observations, when all observations are ordered from the lowest to the highest values. This value is 70.50. The *first quartile* is simply the lowest quartile score (*it is not a range*). That location is defined as half the location of the median, hence, [4.50/2 =] 2.25. The variable value associated with this location (2.25) is defined as the value of the second observation plus one-quarter of the distance between the second and third observations. In our example, that value is calculated as [20 + 0.25*(67 − 20) =] 31.75. The *third quartile* is the third quartile score, or location [4.50 + 2.25 =] 6.75. The value is [80 + 0.75*(90 − 80) =] 87.50. Most computer programs also produce a statistic called the *midspread* (or *interquartile range*, IQR). The midspread is defined as the difference between the first quartile and the third quartile, hence, [87.50 − 31.75 =] 55.75. The *range* is simply the difference between the highest and lowest values, or [225 − 20 =] 205. Again, even though statistical software programs will calculate these values, you need to have a clear understanding of what these concepts mean.

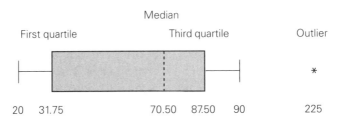

The boxplot also shows a singular observation with a value of 225 that is labeled "outlier." As mentioned in this chapter, *outliers* are extremes, or analyst-defined observations with unusual values relative to other values in the data. Boxplots also help analysts to calculate cut-off points beyond which any observations are statistically considered as outliers. These cut-off points are called, respectively, the inner and outer **fences**. The *inner fence* is an imaginary value that lies 1.5 times the midspread *below* the first quartile. For the data in our example, the inner fence is [31.75 − (1.5*55.75) =] −51.88. All our data are greater than the value of the inner fence; thus, our data show no outliers on this lower end. The *outer fence* is an imaginary value that lies 1.5 times the midspread *above* the third quartile. It is calculated as [87.5 + (1.5*55.75) =] 171.13. Our data has one observation that exceeds this value, $x_8 = 225$, which is therefore labeled an outlier.[17] Analysts might consider omitting x_8 from further analysis. Doing so greatly affects the mean, reducing it from 80.38 to 59.71. As expected, omitting x_8 does not much change the median, which goes from 70.5 to 70.0; the loss of the observation merely redefines the location of the middle observation. As discussed in the text, finding an outlier inevitably invites a decision about what to do with it, and the decision to retain or drop such an observation from analysis should be based on argument. Finally, the boxplot also shows two *whiskers* extending out from the first and third quartiles. The end points of these whiskers are the lowest and highest values of the variables that are *not* outliers. Together with the box (shown as the "area" between the first and third quartiles), these whiskers give analysts a quick visual image of the spread of the data. If the whiskers and box are relatively short, then the variable varies little in the sample. If the whiskers and box are long, there is more variation to talk about.

In short, boxplots are a great tool for data cleaning and preliminary data analysis, and they are easily produced by computer. They help identify outliers and provide valuable information about the distribution of data. Imagine the analyst who rushes head-long into producing detailed tables and reports, only to redo this work after outliers (and perhaps other problems, too) have been discovered in the data.

Notes

1. These data are from the Employees Attitudes dataset, which can be found on the CD that accompanies the workbook, *Exercising Essential Statistics.*
2. Both approaches are found in practice. As noted in Chapter 6, analysts should be mindful that fractional values (means) are not defined for ordinal variables. The write-up should report the percentages of data values in relevant categories.
3. Table 6.1 (see appendix to Chapter 6) shows how data for a continuous variable might be recoded into five categories. For example, categories for the data in Table 6.1 could have been created with unequal intervals (such as category 1 with range 1–14, category 2 with range 15–17, and category 3 with range 18–25), which would lead to a different conclusion.
4. In SPSS, category widths are often defined after the default histogram is generated; the editing options allow category widths (called "bin sizes") to be changed.
5. As an exploratory tool, many computer programs produce *stem-and-leaf plots* (in SPSS, Analyze → Descriptive Statistics → Explore). Stem-and-leaf plots show each value of a frequency distribution. For example, the stem-and-leaf plot below shows each value of the 124 observations of this variable. The left column is called the stem, and the right column is called the leaves. The observations are shown ordered from low to high, and the values are found by combining each stem with its leaves. The lowest number of the series is 002 followed by 003, 005, 008, 009, 010,

010, 011, 012, and 013, and so on. The five highest values are 103, 103, 110, 113, and 115. The median value is at location [(124 + 1)/2 =] 62.50, and is 058 (the sixty-second and sixty-third values, starting from lowest value 002 and counting forward, are both 58).

```
00   23589
01   0012344589
02   1123367
03   01134456889
04   00111223445567889
05   011233455568899
06   12223444445566778999
07   001235556899
08   01112234444
09   112334556
10   00233
11   035
```

6. To calculate the standard deviation for a population, divide by N.
7. Or, in "plain" English, the standard deviation is a measure of dispersion that is equal to the square root of the mean of squared deviations from the mean.
8. Standard deviations can also be calculated from grouped data (see the appendix to Chapter 6), using the following revised formula:

$$s = \sqrt{\frac{\sum w_i(x_i - \bar{x})^2}{n-1}}$$

where the is indicate the group categories. Consider an example. Referring to the data in Table 6.1, we first calculate the estimated group means of each category and then subtract these values from the previously calculated group mean. The estimated category means are 3, 8, 13, 18, and 23, respectively. Subtracting the value of the overall mean of 15.1, we get −12.1, −7.1, −2.1, 2.9, and 7.9. Then we take the squared difference of each—146.4, 50.4, 4.4, 8.4, and 62.4—weight each of these values by the number of observations in each category. Thus, the value for the first category is [12*146.4 =] 1,756.8, and subsequent values are 252.0, 79.2, 302.4, and 873.6. We add these numbers, get 3,264, and divide by 85, which is 38.4, and then take the square root, which is 6.2.

9. However, in Chapter 12 we will see that *variance* is used to explain the amount of variation in a variable.
10. But if the sample is consistent with a bell-shaped curve and if we had an infinite number of drawings, the sample would eventually look normal. This matter is taken up in Chapter 12.
11. The text uses the following values for the example: 2,3,5,8,9,10,10,11,12, 13,14,14,15,18,19,21,21,22,23,23,26,27,30,31,31,33,34,34,35,36,38,38,39,

40,40,41,41,41,42,42,43,44,44,45,45,46,47,48,48,49,50,51,51,52,53,53,54,
55,55,55,56,58,58,59,59,61,62,62,62,63,64,64,64,64,65,65,66,66,67,67,68,
69,69,69,70,70,71,72,73,75,75,75,76,78,79,79,80,81,81,82,83,83,84,85,85,
86,100,100,102,103,103,110,113,115.

12. A curve in which the area is 1.00 is also called a *density curve*.

13. Standard deviations also underlie the development of control charts, which are used in assessing production and service delivery processes. Control charts help managers determine the likelihood that unusually high or low performance is caused by chance. The upper and lower critical limits of control charts are defined as $UCL = \bar{x} + 3(s/\sqrt{n})$ and $LCL = \bar{x} - 3(s/\sqrt{n})$:

14. For example, decisions about educational programs are based on the mean attainment of students in those programs, expressed as "on average, enrolled students improved their XYZ ability by x percent more than students who did not enroll in the programs." Of course, irregular behavior draws attention in its own right, and public laws are often passed to address that. In addition, a lot can be learned from case studies of infrequent behavior.

15. Because boxplots do not assume variables to be normally distributed, they have broader use as a tool for data cleaning. However, boxplots cannot be used for constructing confidence intervals, and so both tools have their place.

16. Another rule of thumb is that both of the following measures should be less than ±1.96: *skewness*/$\sqrt{6/n}$ and *kurtosis*/$\sqrt{24/n}$. In our case, the respective values are −0.27 and 1.66.

17. Some computer programs, including SPSS, distinguish between outliers and extreme values. Then, outliers are defined as observations that lie 1.5 times the midspread from the first and third quartiles, whereas extreme values are observations that lie 3 times the midspread from the first and third quartiles.

CHAPTER

8

Contingency Tables

CHAPTER OBJECTIVES

After reading this chapter, you should be able to

- Create, interpret, and analyze contingency tables
- Understand the concept of a statistical relationship
- Discuss relationships in contingency tables
- Explain how pivot tables differ from contingency tables
- Generate pivot tables
- Transpose variables in pivot tables

After individual variables have been analyzed and results reported, analysts often turn to questions about relationships between variables. The study of relationships between two variables is called *bivariate statistics.* Some of these relationships aim at a better understanding of the effectiveness of programs and policies, whereas others help illuminate conditions under which programs and policies operate. For example, we might want to know whether participation in a teen anger management program is associated with lower rates of high school violence. If we have data on both variables, then we can examine the nature of the relationships between them. Similarly, we might examine whether participation in a teen pregnancy prevention program is associated with lower teen pregnancy rates. Gathering empirical information about relationships is a key step in determining program effectiveness.

We can also look at relationships across cities, rather than using program-level data. For example, we can ask whether average incomes are associated with different health problems, such as diabetes, hypertension, and HIV/AIDS. We can also use relationships to better understand characteristics of populations with which managers work. For example, if data are available on the economic status of program clients (such as annual household income or participation in food stamp programs), and also on their health conditions (such as hypertension or diabetes), then we can study quantitatively whether, for example, such diseases are more prevalent among clients with lower incomes. An understanding of this relationship may affect how programs are delivered, for example, ensuring that adequate transportation and funding is available for treatment.

Managers benefit from knowledge about relationships; it helps them improve program operations and understand program outcomes. It can help managers and policy makers by determining how, and which, variables affect key outcomes. This chapter introduces contingency tables, and subsequent chapters examine additional important statistics that managers and analysts need to consider.

CONTINGENCY TABLES

A *contingency table* expresses the relationship between two *categorical* variables. One variable is shown in rows and the other in columns. Each row and column shows the frequency of observations with specific values for both variables. Typically, row and column totals also are present. An example is given in Table 8.1 for data on the gender and year of promotion of employees. In this case, the manager or analyst wants to examine whether a relationship exists between gender and rate of promotion.

Table 8.1 ⎯⎯⎯⎯ Year of Promotion by Gender

Year	Gender		Total
	Male	Female	
1	14	8	22
2	16	14	30
3	7	22	29
4	6	8	14
Total	43	52	95

Regarding the anatomy of contingency tables, the term ***data cell*** is commonly used to refer to table cells that show the counts or percentages based on the values of the two variables.[1] For example, Table 8.1 shows that 14 male employees and 8 female employees received promotions within the first year. Each of these numbers is entered in a separate data cell. Table 8.1 also shows the row and column totals, which are called the ***marginal totals***; they are located in the margins of the table. The number of 95 total employees in the lower right-hand corner is called the ***grand total.*** The table also has clear column and row headings and a succinct but clear title, which avoids ambiguity. You should practice making contingency tables that are similar to this one in appearance (that is, neat and clear).

The placement of the variables in contingency tables depends on the nature of the relationship. In Chapter 2 we distinguished between causal relationships and associations. Causal relationships show cause and effect, whereby one variable affects another. The dependent variable is defined as the one that is affected (or caused) by the other, which is called the independent variable. When a relationship is causal (as determined by the analyst), the dependent variable is conventionally placed in the rows and the independent variable in the columns.[2] When two variables are only associated (with no causality implied), no preference exists regarding the location of variables.

> **Key Point**
> The placement of the two variables in a contingency table depends on the relationship of the variables, and the placement determines how results are interpreted.

We now examine how rates of promotion vary between men and women, that is, the relationship between these two variables. The absolute frequency counts in Table 8.1 do not tell us much. No conclusion can be drawn from the fact that 14 males and 8 females were promoted in the first year, because the sample has an unequal number of men and women. Rather, we need to compare the percentages of men and women promoted in each year. ***Column percentages*** are calculated by dividing each frequency by the column total. For example, [14/43 =] 32.6 percent of men and [8/52 =] 15.4 percent of women were promoted in the first year, and so on for subsequent years, too. The result is shown in Table 8.2. Note that each column adds up to 100 percent.

The examination of relationships in contingency tables is usually based on comparisons of column percentages or groups of rows. From Table 8.2 we see that men were indeed promoted at a faster rate than women. About 69.8 percent [32.6% + 37.2%] of men were promoted in the first two years, compared with only 42.3 percent [15.4% + 26.9%] of women. Conversely, a majority of women were promoted in the last two years, namely, 57.7 percent compared with only 30.2 percent of men. The conclusion is clear. Many software programs can produce both frequency counts and column percentages in the same table, hence, aiding analysis.

Table 8.2 ⎯⎯ Year of Promotion by Gender: Column Percentages

	Gender		
Year	Male	Female	Total
1	32.6%	15.4%	23.2%
2	37.2	26.9	31.6
3	16.2	42.3	30.5
4	14.0	15.4	14.7
Total	100.0	100.0	100.0
(n)	(43)	(52)	(95)

Table 8.3 ⎯⎯ Row and Total Percentages

A: Row Percentages				B: Total Percentages			
	Gender				Gender		
Year	Male	Female	Total	Year	Male	Female	Total
1	63.6%	36.4%	100.0%	1	14.7%	8.4%	23.1%
2	53.3	46.7	100.0	2	16.8	14.7	31.5
3	24.1	75.9	100.0	3	7.4	23.2	30.6
4	42.9	57.1	100.0	4	6.3	8.4	14.7
Total	45.3	54.7	100.0	Total	45.3	54.7	100.0
(n)	(43)	(52)	(95)				

A point of possible confusion is that computers can also calculate row percentages and total percentages. *Row percentages* show the percentages of men and women promoted within each year. For example, [14/22 =] 63.6 percent of employees promoted in the first year were men and [8/22 =] 36.4 percent were women. This is shown in Table 8.3. Likewise, [16/30 =] 53.3 percent of employees promoted in the second year were men, and [14/30 =] 46.7 percent were women. When row percentages are calculated, each row adds up to 100 percent. In our example, row percentages show the gender composition of each of the cohorts. Because we wish to know the cohort composition of each of the genders, we use column percentages. Analysts must be clear about what it is they are comparing; the row versus column placement convention described previously is designed partly to avoid this confusion. Tables in published reports usually show column percentages; row percentages are far less common.

Total percentages show frequencies as a share of all observations. For example, [14/95 =] 14.7 percent of all employees in the sample are males who were promoted within the first year, [22/95 =] 23.2 percent of all

Table 8.4 ————— Gender by Year of Promotion

Gender	Promotion (year)				Total
	1	2	3	4	
Male	63.6%	53.3%	24.1%	42.9%	45.3%
Female	36.4	46.7	75.9	57.1	54.7
Total	100.0	100.0	100.0	100.0	100.0
(n)	(22)	(30)	(29)	(14)	(95)

employees in the sample are females who were promoted within the third year, and so on. Such frequencies are sometimes useful when describing the sample, but they do not help address the question of whether differences in the rate of promotion exist across gender. Note that when total percentages are calculated, only the grand total adds up to 100 percent.

The preference for column percentages often affects the placement of variables. Typically, when analysts want to know the demographic distribution of a variable (for instance, gender composition of each cohort in our example), preferences for displaying column percentages will cause the demographic variable (such as gender, age, location, and the like) to be placed in rows and the other variable in the columns. Then column percentages show the demographic distribution of that variable. In our case, if we wish to show the demographic (gender) make-up of the promotion cohorts, and use column percentages, then we should show gender in the rows, as in Table 8.4. Confused? It is simply a matter of being clear about what the analyst wants to know, and then typically using column percentages to obtain that information.

Finally, in Chapter 2 we noted that "correlation does not prove causation." As with all statistical techniques, contingency table analysis sheds light on whether variables are empirically associated, but it does not address whether an explanation exists that establishes causality; this requires an additional cause-and-effect argument. Hence, if gender is causally related to promotion, then analysts will need to explain how that occurs. If gender is only associated with promotion rates, then no further explanation of cause and effect is required. Analysis often results in a thorough consideration of these matters.

> **Getting Started**
> Replicate Tables 8.1 and 8.2 on your computer.

RELATIONSHIP AND DIRECTION

When analysts state that a relationship exists between variables, what exactly do they mean? The *relationship* is sometimes broadly defined as two variables being associated with each other, possibly as one causing the other (see Chapter 2), but in statistics, relationships are defined in specific, technical terms. A *statistical relationship* means that as one variable changes, so too does another. Thus, if a relationship exists between gender and the rate of promotion, then the rate of promotion must change when the value of gender changes; males will have a different rate of promotion than females. If no relationship exists between gender and the rate of promotion, then the rate of promotion does not differ between males and females. Differences in the rate of promotion might be measured by mean rates of promotion, the percentage of employees promoted in first years, or in some other way.[3]

Relationships involving ordinal or continuous variables are characterized as having a positive or negative direction. A *positive relationship* means that large values of one variable are associated with large values of the other variable *and* that small values of one variable are associated with small values of the other variable. People are well familiar with graphs such as the one shown in Figure 13.2. A *negative relationship* implies the opposite: large values of one variable are associated with small values of the other variable *and* vice versa. The idea of relationship did not arise in the earlier example because gender is a nominal variable. It makes no sense to say that the relationship between gender and promotion is positive or negative.

However, if we were to look at promotion rates by age, then we could talk about a positive or negative relationship. For example, if it takes older workers more time to be promoted than younger workers, then we can say that a positive relationship exists between the age and the number of years that it takes to be promoted.

To determine the direction of a relationship in a contingency table (that is, whether it is positive or negative), we can focus on the distribution of column percentages, though this does not always work. As a brief example, Table 8.5, part A, shows a positive relationship, as small values of the column variable are associated with small values of the row variable, and large values of the column variable are often associated with large values of the row variable. When a relationship is positive, the relative frequencies (percentages) of the cells in the upper left and lower right corners will be large. Conversely, a negative relationship means that small values of the column variable are often associated with large values of the row variable, and vice versa. This is shown in Table 8.5, part B.

> **Key Point**
>
> A statistical relationship means that as one variable changes, so too does another. The direction of relationships is determined by the sign of the statistics.

Table 8.5 ——— ⁓⁓ Positive and Negative Relationships

A: Positive relationship			B: Negative relationship		
	LO	HI		LO	HI
LO	65%	29%	LO	31%	62%
HI	35	71	HI	69	38

However, the direction of a relationship can be difficult to determine in large tables through visual inspection alone. Studying the corner cells may be inconclusive; the pattern may be unclear. Several statistics are available that provide quantitative measures of relationships and of their direction, and these statistics are discussed in Chapters 11 and 14.[4] Positive values of these test statistics indicate a positive relationship, and negative values indicate a negative relationship.

In addition to the direction of relationships, it is also important to consider the ***practical relevance of relationships***, that is, whether the relationship of one variable to another results in large enough changes to be of practical importance. The term *practical relevance* is sometimes also called "practical significance," as opposed to "statistical significance"; not every statistically significant relationship is also practically relevant. In the previous example, are men promoted a lot or only a little faster? Such practical relevance often is of great importance to policy makers and managers. One way to express a sense of the difference is to ask how much longer it takes women to get promoted than men. Applying the descriptive techniques in Chapter 2, we find that the mean promotion rate is 2.12 years for men and 2.58 years for women. So, on average, men are promoted about 0.46 years faster than women. We can also state that it takes women $[(2.58 - 2.12)/2.12 =]$ 21.7 percent longer to be promoted than men.

We can flesh out this idea a little more. For example, comparing medians, we find that half of the men are promoted within two years, as compared with three years for women. We can also examine the percentile distributions. Whereas 25 percent of men were promoted within one year, the same percentage of women were promoted in two years. Or, using cumulative frequencies, we can say that whereas 69.8 percent of men were promoted within two years, only 42.3 percent of women were promoted within two years, as shown in Figure 8.1. Whether or not these differences are practically relevant ultimately rests with managers and elected officials; it is probably important whether men are promoted 4 percent faster, or 40 percent faster, and in what year these differences most often occur.

Searching for practical relevance and presenting results may involve some decisions regarding ethics. The data in Table 8.2 can be presented in

Figure 8.1 ———〰— Promotion Rates

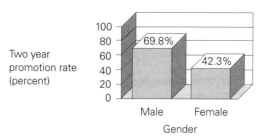

ways that indicate a large difference ("the rate of promotion is much faster for men than women; twice as many men get promoted than women in the first year") or a minute difference ("although men are promoted faster than women, the differences are quite small in the fourth year: 14 percent of men are promoted in the fourth year, as are 15 percent of women"). Both statements are based on parts of the data in Table 8.2. Consistent with Table 1.1 ("Ethics of Research and Analysis"), results should be presented in a complete and objective way. The task of the analyst is to be complete and to inform. Given the facts presented in Table 8.2, the analyst might better state something like this: "Men are promoted faster than women; 69.8 percent of men were promoted in the first two years, compared to 42.3 percent of women. More women were promoted in the third year (42.3% versus 16.2%), and both genders were promoted at nearly equal rates in the fourth year." We should present the facts as they are, complete and without bias or an attempt to spin.

PIVOT TABLES

Pivot tables take contingency tables a step further in an important way. They are used to analyze continuous variables, in addition to categorical variables. The contingency tables described earlier in this chapter are used to analyze only categorical variables.[5] Although *pivot tables* may appear to be similar to the earlier tables, they show statistics of one or more continuous variables for one or more categorical variables in the data cells. Consider the following example. Assume that in addition to data about employees' gender and year of promotion, we also have for each employee a performance evaluation score. The score is a continuous variable that ranges from 1 (low) to 10 (high). Table 8.6 shows the mean performance score for the combination of gender and year of promotion.[6]

Table 8.6 shows that mean performance scores are higher for both males and females who were promoted sooner than for those who were promoted

Table 8.6 ⎯⎯⎯⎯ᴧᴧ⎯ Mean Performance Scores by Gender and Year of Promotion

Year	Male	Female	Total
	Gender		
	Male	Female	Total
1	8.986	9.150	9.045
2	8.769	8.757	8.763
3	8.514	8.555	8.545
4	7.683	7.663	7.671
Total	8.647	8.563	8.601
(n)	(43)	(52)	(95)

later. For example, the mean score of males who were promoted in the first year is 8.986, compared with 8.769 among those promoted in the second year, 8.514 among those promoted in the third year, and 7.683 in the fourth year. The mean performance scores of females show a similar decreasing pattern for promotions in later years. Moreover, the performance scores of males and females are quite similar in each year of promotion.

Statistics reported in the data cells of pivot tables are not limited to means, of course. Statistical software programs can provide the full range of univariate statistics for continuous variables, such as median, standard deviation, range, minimum, maximum, skewness, and kurtosis. Pivot tables can calculate several of these statistics in the same table. Note that when categorical variables are reported in the data cells, continuous-level statistics are calculated, too. For example, if year of promotion is considered a variable to be reported in data cells, then pivot tables calculate continuous-level statistics, such as means, for this variable. The mean year of promotion is then shown as 2.12 for males, 2.58 for females, and 2.37 for the combined sample of male and female employees.

The term *pivot* is derived from the handy property that row and column variables can be readily transposed. **Transposing** means interchanging the locations of these variables; column variables become row variables, and vice versa. In addition, two or more variables can also be used in the same column or row, thereby creating a grouping structure as shown in Table 8.7. This can also be done in contingency tables. A *layer variable* is one that defines the subset of data used for subsequent data tables.[7] In this case, year of promotion is the layer variable. For illustrative purposes, assume that we have further data on the location of employees, in site A or B.

Note that gender is now grouped within each year of promotion. Table 8.7 shows, for example, that the mean performance score of females promoted within the first year in site A is 9.140. This score is nearly identical to that of

Table 8.7 ————〰️— Mean Performance Scores
by Gender and Year of Promotion

Year	Gender	Location A	Location B	Total
1	Male	9.150	8.767	8.986
	Female	9.140	9.167	9.150
2	Male	8.760	8.783	8.769
	Female	8.760	8.750	8.757
3	Male	8.750	8.200	8.514
	Female	8.617	8.531	8.555
4	Male	7.300	7.760	7.683
	Female	7.150	7.757	7.663
Total		8.830	8.435	8.647
(n)		(45)	(50)	(95)

males, 9.150. Note also that marginal totals show the mean performance scores for each gender by year; these are the same means shown in Table 8.6. Pivot tables can be used to quickly "drill down" your data, and many software programs allow users to graphically move around variables. With very little effort we can also group year of promotion within gender, or move both to the column. It also possible to create tables for only selected values of data; for example, we might produce a table like Table 8.6 for the A site only, or like Table 8.7 for female employees only. Pivot tables offer considerable flexibility, and an examination of the ease of constructing pivot tables in your software program is instructive.[8]

Be aware, however, that creating more data cells (compare Tables 8.6 and 8.7) implies that observations in the sample are distributed over more cells. This increases the possibility that some cells have very few observations. In our case, which involves a relatively small dataset, the number of men promoted in year 4 in site A is only 1 (not shown in Table 8.7). Surely, managers will not want to base policy decisions on just a single or a few observations. Larger tables do require larger datasets. Although no hard-and-fast rule exists regarding the minimum number of observations in each data cell, it is good practice to avoid creating tables in which any column or row has a large percentage of cells with fewer than five observations.[9] If this happens, the analyst should add a caveat to his or her findings or consider combining categories to eliminate cells with sparse counts. In Table 8.7, the categories of the third and fourth years of promotion might be combined to avoid a small number of frequencies in the fourth year by gender.

Getting Started

Develop a pivot table using one continuous and two categorical variables in your area of interest.

Pivot tables and contingency tables can be used for many analytical tasks. Box 8.1 examines how the univariate and bivariate techniques discussed in Chapters 6–8 are used to analyze community indicators.

The ease with which variables can be analyzed in so many different ways using pivot tables is highly appealing. But it also means that analysts need to know which calculations or comparisons they are looking for, rather than randomly trying out different analyses of variables. While blind analysis may reveal interesting and even important facts, eventually these facts must be understood and placed into context. The analytical process is usually a back-and-forth between empirical and theoretical inquiry. By way of example, Table 8.2 shows that males are promoted faster than women. We now ask: why is this so? Suppose that we entertain the rival hypothesis (see Chapter 2) that the promotion rate is different because men are more productive than women. That is, there is no gender discrimination per se. Regardless of your purposes, you will need to examine this possibility: either show that productivity differences (if any) do not explain gender discrimination (hence, gender discrimination really does exist), or show that the alleged gender discrimination is but an artifact of productivity differences.

Such reasoning underlies the construction of Table 8.6. As we already saw, Table 8.6 shows that the productivity scores of men and women are quite similar in years in which they are promoted. Hence, it might be that men are promoted faster based on their scores. However, reaching such a conclusion does not end the analytical inquiry. We might ask why men receive higher scores than women. Although discrimination might exist in how the productivity scores are assigned, a further hypothesis is that productivity scores might differ across work sites. Table 8.7 bears this out; the mean productivity score in site B is indeed lower than in site A (8.435 versus 8.830). Moreover, further analysis (not shown) indicates that women are more likely than men to work in site B (57.8 percent versus 46.5 percent). Perhaps then, there is something about site B that is problematic. . . . And so it goes. Empirical inquiry might not answer all questions, but it can answer some. This kind of reasoned inquiry, rather than mindless calculation or analysis, eventually brings analytical, quantitative insight to problems of management and policy. In short, analysis is the pursuit of understanding.[10]

SUMMARY

Contingency tables are used to analyze the relationships between two or more categorical variables. They help managers examine the impact of programs or policies; one variable is the policy or program, and the other is the outcome. Managers can also use contingency tables to examine how conditions differ among clients, employees, or jurisdictions. In this case, one variable is the

Box 8.1 Community Indicators

Many jurisdictions now report community indicators about conditions in their community. Indicators include general population characteristics—such as population size, age, and race—as well as indicators about literacy, housing, incomes, crime (for example, murder, rape, burglary), juvenile crime, health (various diseases such as AIDS) and exercise (walking, bicycling, swimming), educational attainment (test scores), environmental quality (air, water, and other pollution), transportation (road construction, accidents, commuting times, use of public transportation), and so on. These indicators track changes and improvements, and they help analysts to compare jurisdictions. Public and nonprofit organizations often use these data, for example, for program development.

Community indicators can be analyzed using the statistical techniques described in Chapters 6–8. For example, if indices are compared across jurisdictions, an index of overall community conditions might be developed that compares jurisdictions within a region. For example, measures such as average household income, educational attainment, crime rates, water quality, and commuting time might be compared by ranking one jurisdiction against others (see Chapter 3). The sums of these disparate ranks can be evaluated against other jurisdictions. Comparisons also can be made over time to show improvement (or lack thereof), or against other, comparable jurisdictions in other parts of the country.

Within a given measure such as crime we can also calculate the mean and median levels, expressed as either absolute (for example, number of crimes) or relative measures (for example, crimes per capita). We can also calculate standard deviations and percentiles. You may be able to determine in which percentile of crime, pollution, or income your jurisdictions falls. We can also examine relationships between indicators, for example, whether income is associated with health problems, home ownership, illiteracy, or transportation. We might find that some expected relationships hold up and others do not. Among those relationships that hold up, we might find many exceptions, for example, jurisdictions with low mean incomes that also have low levels of disease and crime. Such findings will prompt analysts to seek to better understand the specific conditions of these jurisdictions. Through all of these uses, community indicators are increasingly used to inform decision making and public policy debates.

condition and the other is a categorical variable describing clients, employees, or jurisdictions.

Contingency tables are used to calculate differences across categories, such as how employees vary in their rates of promotion, or how cities vary on community indices, or how clients vary in their program outcomes. Often, analysts calculate column percentages as a basis for making comparisons. Whether such differences are practically relevant depends on the judgment of analysts and managers. Contingency tables are also used to determine whether the relationship between ordinal variables is positive or negative.

Pivot tables are helpful extensions of contingency tables; they allow statistics to be calculated for continuous variables. These statistics are shown in the data cells of tables. The term *pivot* is based on the property that row and column variables can be readily transposed and grouped together. A limitation of tables that have many data cells is that they may require larger datasets. Contingency and pivot tables are essential and widely used to study relationships between variables.

KEY TERMS

Column percentages (p. 136)
Contingency table (p. 135)
Data cell (p. 136)
Grand total (p. 136)
Layer variable (p. 142)
Marginal totals (p. 136)
Negative relationship (p. 139)

Pivot tables (p. 141)
Positive relationship (p. 139)
Practical relevance of relationships
   (p. 140)
Statistical relationship (p. 139)
Transposing (p. 142)

Notes

1. In website programming, the term *data cell* describes all table cells, including row and column attributes and labels. In other instances, the term *data cell* is limited to cells at the intersections of row and column attributes, hence, excluding marginal and grand totals. We use the term here to refer to all cells that contain, well, data.

2. This convention often is violated, hence, making it a weak convention. Nonetheless, following it makes the analysis of tables easier when column percentages are used, as is commonly the case. Note that this convention is rather different from placing the dependent variable on the Y-axis in scatterplots and graphs, as discussed in Chapter 14.

3. The idea of variables varying together in some way is also expressed by terms such as *covary* and *correlate*. The prefix *co-* means together or jointly. Variables that are related to each other covary (when variable X varies, then variable Y varies in some way, too) and are thus correlated.

4. Kendall's tau-c (described in Chapter 11) is an example of such a statistic.
5. Whether one considers a pivot table as a type of contingency table or as something different is a matter of opinion. At this point in our discussion, we treat them as being different for illustrative purposes.
6. The terminology of *pivot tables* is not adopted uniformly or consistently. SPSS calls these tables "OLAP cubes," or On-line Analytical Processing (Analyze → Reports → OLAP Cubes). However, once these tables are created, analysts can edit and modify them by selecting graphical commands from the Pivot menu (Pivot → Pivoting Trays).
7. A layer variable is sometimes called a nesting variable. In this case, Table 8.6 would be called a nested table. However, this term is best reserved for statistical techniques (factorial designs) with which the term is traditionally associated.
8. See note 6. In Microsoft Excel, pivot tables are created by selecting from the menu bar Data → PivotTable and PivotChart Report.
9. It may be impossible to avoid all cells having sparse counts. Hence, the tenet concerns *most* cells in any one row or column.
10. Whether one calls this approach reasoned inquiry or post-hoc storytelling is a matter of perspective and opinion. In the end, truth must be told and supported by the facts.

CHAPTER

9

Getting Results

CHAPTER OBJECTIVES

After this chapter, you should be able to

- Apply the statistical concepts and tools introduced in Chapters 6–8
- Use graphic tools in analyses and presentations
- Understand and apply the analysis of outputs and outcomes
- Understand and apply the analysis of efficiency and effectiveness
- Understand and apply the analysis of equity
- Understand and apply quality-of-life analysis

In Chapters 6 and 7, we learned about measures of central tendency and dispersion. We also examined how to create contingency tables in Chapter 8. These are fundamental concepts in statistics, and they are very useful in daily management and policy making in public and nonprofit organizations. This chapter focuses on applying these statistical concepts to the real world. We use the performance management concepts introduced in Chapter 4 to present many of these applications.

Imagine that you are a management analyst for a human services agency in a city government. One important service the agency provides is a job training program for the city's unemployed or underemployed residents.

The goal of the program is to provide trainees with tools and skills that make them more marketable. Training activities offered include resume writing, network development, job interview skills, basic and advanced computer skills, personal financial management skills, and self-employment skills. Trainings are provided in 12-week cycles with multiple courses offered each cycle. Except for a mandatory program overview course, participation in all other courses is voluntary. But individuals must successfully complete at least three courses to receive a graduation certificate. To be eligible for the program individuals must be unemployed or underemployed (working less than 40 hours per week), and they must be of working age, as defined by federal law.

Program funding comes from a renewable federal grant matched by the same amount from the city's budget. The agency director wants you to conduct a performance analysis to justify the program's funding request for the new fiscal year. How do you do this? Where do you start?

ANALYSIS OF OUTPUTS AND OUTCOMES

Recall from Chapter 4 that program performance can be specified as program outputs or outcomes. *Output and outcome analysis* focuses on defining, calculating, and displaying output and outcome measures from a dataset.

Outputs are defined as immediate and direct results of program activities. The program activities in this case are the provision of training. What are immediate and direct results of the training? The many possibilities include the number of participants in a training course, the number of training courses completed by a participant, the number of training hours completed by a participant, and the like. Table 9.1 shows the number of training courses completed by 43 participants in the last training cycle, which offered six courses.

Table 9.1 ————〰〰— The Number of Courses Completed by Participants

Number of training courses	Number of participants
1	4
2	6
3	18
4	12
5	2
6	1

Figure 9.1 ⎯⎯⎯⎯⎯ᴧᴧᴧ⎯ Participation in Training Courses: A Bar Chart

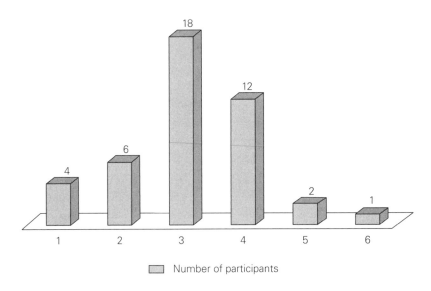

Number of participants

What are the mean, the median, and the mode of the number of courses completed? According to the formula for the mean (see Chapter 6), it is $[(1 + 1 + 1 + 1 + 2 + 2 + 2 + 2 + 2 + 2 + 3 + 3 + 3 + \ldots 4 + 5 + 5 + 6)/43 =]$ 3.12, indicating that, on average, participants completed a little more than three courses in the last training cycle. The median is 3, which is the middle number of courses completed. The mode is also 3—the most frequent number of courses completed: 18 participants completed three courses (see Figure 9.1).

Now, let's turn to the program outcomes. As defined in Chapter 4, outcomes are changes related to the program goal, which in our example is the improvement of employment. There are also many possible outcome measures: the number of participants who graduated from the program, the number or percentage of participants who found full-time jobs within 6 months of the training (that is, the employment rate), the increase in participants' annual incomes after graduation, and so on. Table 9.2 shows participants' full-time employment rates (within 6 months of the training) for the past four training cycles; Figure 9.2 shows these data in graphic form.

Sometimes, a little creativity in applying statistics can take you a long way. Let's say that you believe (hope) that graduates of the training program are more likely to find jobs. In other words, you want to know if

Table 9.2 ————〰️—— Full-Time Employment Rates for Job
Training Program Participants

Training cycle	Program participants (1)	Number employed within 6 months (2)	Employment rate (2)/(1)
1	38	5	13.16%
2	50	6	12.00%
3	47	3	6.38%
4	39	3	7.69%
Mean	43.5	4.25	9.81%

Figure 9.2 ————〰️—— Employment Rates for Four
Training Cycles: A Bar Chart

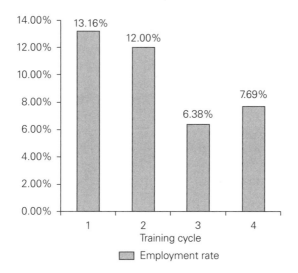

employment rates differ among participants who succeed or fail. To examine this, you need to compare employment rates for the two groups: the
participants who succeed (defined as receiving the graduation certificate)
and the participants who fail (those who don't receive the certificate).
Table 9.3 shows the data for these groups. Employment rates for the two
groups are presented in Figure 9.3. The employment rate is higher for the
successful group (10.29%) than for the group that failed (7.89%). These
results provide some evidence that the job training program may improve
employment rates for participants.

Note that in this analysis we presented the frequency distribution
(that is, the percentages) for the two groups. The analysis involves two

Key Point

Analysis of outcomes is becoming increasingly popular in public and nonprofit organizations because of citizens' and legislators' focus on service outcomes.

variables—training status (success or failure) and employment rate—which means it is in fact a tool of bivariate analysis. Nevertheless, this analysis can to some extent be seen simply as a calculation and presentation of one variable (employment rate) for two different groups. In that sense, it is the calculation of a univariate statistic (frequency distribution, in this case) for multiple times.

Table 9.3 ———〜〜〜— Does the Training Matter? A Comparison

	Program participants	Participants employed	Employment rate
Success in training	136	14	10.29%
Failure in training	38	3	7.89%

Figure 9.3 ———〜〜〜— Employment Rates for Two Groups

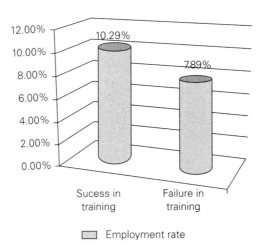

ANALYSIS OF EFFICIENCY AND EFFECTIVENESS

The employment training program produces a desirable outcome if it leads to more people being employed, but producing a desirable outcome does not necessarily justify the cost. Do you still want to fund the training program if it costs your agency, say, $10 million annually to operate? An output- or outcome-producing program does not mean that it is efficient or effective.

Efficiency and effectiveness analysis focuses on defining, calculating, and displaying efficiency and effectiveness measures from a dataset. As defined in Chapter 4, efficiency is the level of output by input, and effectiveness is the level of outcome by input. Let's look at an example of an efficiency and effectiveness analysis. One measure of effectiveness in education is the ratio of students who successfully graduate per instructor—the number of graduates/the number of instructors. A higher value indicates a more effective educational program because it indicates less consumption of resources (the instructors, in this case) to produce a desirable result (that is, the graduates). Table 9.4 shows this ratio for the past five years in two schools in a school district.

On average, both schools have graduated about 31 students per teacher. They are performing at the same level, according to the mean. However, to which school would you rather send your child? A closer look at the data shows a larger year-to-year performance difference at school A, from 19 to 47 graduates a year. The year-to-year difference at school B is much smaller, from 25 to 33 graduates a year. School B's performance is much more consistent and predictable. Figure 9.4 shows the performance differences graphically.

This performance variation, which is missed by looking at the mean, can be captured by the standard deviation introduced in Chapter 7. In fact, the standard deviation of school A is 13.35, much larger than that of school B (3.27). A larger standard deviation indicates a greater difference between individual observations (in this case, the graduation rates each year) and the average. Statisticians use the term *reliable* to describe a consistent and predictable performance. A performance is said to be reliable if the individual performances center closely around the average performance. A performance lacks reliability if individual performances scatter all over, departing greatly from the average performance.

Table 9.4 ———〰️— Graduation Rates (Number of Graduates per Teacher) at Two Schools

Year	School A	School B
1	19	33
2	43	25
3	26	32
4	47	32
5	19	32
Mean	30.8	30.8
Standard deviation	13.35	3.27

Figure 9.4 ⎯⎯⎯ Graduation Rates (Number of Graduates per Teacher) over Time: A Line Chart Analysis

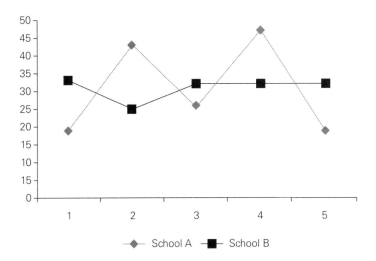

Let's look at another example of how to apply standard deviation in performance analysis. Some educational institutions in the United States link teachers' performance to students' academic performance, under the concept of "good teachers produce good students." Imagine there are two classes on the same topic, taught by two different teachers. Student performance is measured by a standardized test score on a 5-point scale, with 5 being the highest and 0 being the lowest. Students in class A have an average score of 3.00 and students in class B have an average score of 2.75 (this is an effectiveness measure). If you looked only at the average, you would conclude that students in class A perform better and you would reward the teacher of class A. But that logic may not work well if class A has a small group of students who get very high scores and the rest get average or very low scores. In that case, the individual scores of many students scatter away from the average—an indication of a large standard deviation. If students in class B, though having a lower average score, have a smaller standard deviation, their individual scores are close to the average. This means they have a more reliable performance than do students in class A. With additional information about the standard deviation of students' performance, you have a more complete picture of the two teachers and may want to rethink how to more fairly reward their teaching performance.

ANALYSIS OF EQUITY

Equity, defined as being equal in management practices and providing equal access to resources to all societal groups, is a democratic principle in public

Table 9.5 ———— ᴧᴧᴧ— Incentives and Affordable Housing Programs in 20 Cities: A Contingency Table Analysis

			Offer incentive to developers for the past five years		
			No	Yes	Total
Affordable housing projects for the past five years	No	Count	8	4	12
		% within offer incentive to developers for the past five years	80.0%	40.0%	60.0%
	Yes	Count	2	6	8
		% within offer incentive to developers for the past five years	20.0%	60.0%	40.0%
Total		Count	10	10	20
		% within offer incentive to developers for the past five years	100.0%	100.0%	100.0%

management and policy making. Measures of equity should be part of an organization's performance measurement system. *Equity analysis* focuses on showing how program resources, efforts, and outcomes vary across groups. An example of socioeconomic equity is the provision of affordable housing to the public. To increase access to affordable housing, a jurisdiction can provide incentives (such as tax benefits) for developers to build such housing. The contingency table analysis in Table 9.5 shows the possible impact of incentives on affordable housing projects in an urban area of 20 municipalities.

The table shows that, of the 10 cities that did not have incentives, 8 (or 80 percent) did not provide affordable housing projects for the past five years, and only 2 (or 20 percent) did provide affordable housing. Of the 10 cities that provided incentives, 6 (or 60 percent) had developed new affordable housing projects and 4 (40 percent) did not have new affordable housing projects. These results, also shown in Figure 9.5, indicate that government incentives may result in construction of more affordable housing.

QUALITY-OF-LIFE ANALYSIS

The performance of public organizations contributes to overall quality of life in a community. As stated in Chapter 8 (Box 8.1), many jurisdictions present quality-of-life measures (also known as community indicators) that

Figure 9.5 ———〜〜〜— Incentives and Affordable Housing Construction: A 3-D Pie Chart Analysis

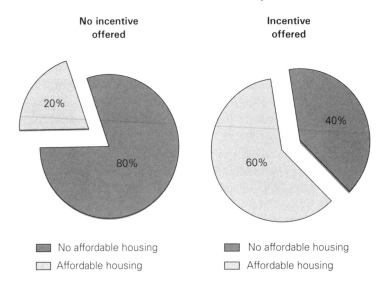

consist of measures of public safety, health care, transportation, economic development, environmental quality, education, and social and human services. *Quality-of-life analysis* focuses on defining, calculating, and displaying quality-of-life measures of a community, as based on some dataset. Let us look at an example to illustrate this type of analysis.

Myarea.org is a nonprofit organization devoted to creating a collaborative and comprehensive plan for an urban region of 2 million people. The organization, led by a group of leaders in public, private, and nonprofit organizations in the region, provides a forum for regional leaders to discuss and collaborate on planning and management issues of regional significance. It also provides training for regional leaders. The organization has developed a comprehensive community index to measure the quality of life in the region's 86 counties and cities. The index considers performance in 12 areas, including public safety, health care access, transportation, economic development, environmental quality, education, and social and human services. The index score and ranking of jurisdictions has been done once a year for the past 15 years.

The index has become popular among many jurisdictions in the region. These jurisdictions have used the index score and ranking to evaluate the performance of their jurisdictions relative to others in the region and to learn from those that perform better. For example, the city of Evergreen has ranked between 30th and 40th out of all 86 jurisdictions. The city manager

Table 9.6————— ⋀⋀— Budget and Quality-of-Life Index:
A Contingency Table Analysis

| | | | Budget increase or decline | | |
			Budget decline	Budget increase	Total
Ranking up or down	Ranking declined	Count	3	4	7
		% within budget increase or decline	50.0%	44.4%	46.7%
	Ranking improved	Count	3	5	8
		% within budget increase or decline	50.0%	55.6%	53.3%
Total		Count	6	9	15
		% within budget increase or decline	100.0%	100.0%	100.0%

believes the city's mediocre image is hurting its chances to attract business
and high-paid jobs and that one way to shake off the image is to move up in
the ranking. The city manager has long suspected that the ranking is associated with the city's level of expenditure (an input measure). Increases in
expenditures are associated with increases in the ranking, and budget
declines are related to declines in the ranking. He pulls out these statistics to
create Table 9.6.

The table shows that, in the 6 years (out of the past 15) when the budget
declined, half of the time (50 percent) the ranking increased and the other
half of the time it declined. During the nine years when the budget
increased, the ranking declined in four of those years (44.4 percent) and
increased in five of those years (55.6 percent). There is no evidence to indicate a relationship between expenditures and the ranking. This relationship
is also shown in Figure 9.6.

SOME CAUTIONS IN ANALYSIS AND PRESENTATION

Performance analysis is both art and science. Analysts encounter issues that
cause dilemmas in analysis, and other situations arise that require special
attention and treatment.

The Use of Multiple Measures
An organization's performance has multiple dimensions, and multiple
measures should be used to gain a complete picture. In the earlier example

Figure 9.6 ————〰〰— Budget and Quality of Life: A 3-D Bar Chart

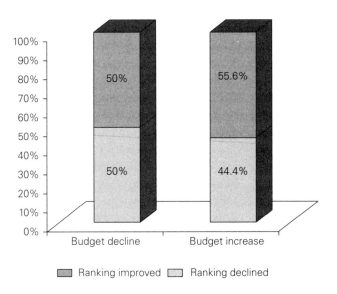

Ranking improved   Ranking declined

of an effectiveness analysis on the graduation rates at two schools, we drew two different conclusions if we looked at two different measures (the mean or the standard deviation) of graduation rates. Here is another example that demonstrates the importance of using multiple measures in analysis. A common measure of local police performance is the number of patrols. Let's assume that you are evaluating police performance in two police precincts in an urban city. The average number of patrols dispatched last month in precinct A was 38 daily, whereas the average in precinct B was 30. These results might lead you to believe that the police in precinct A perform better than those in precinct B, if you use the measure of numbers of patrols. However, let's say that the average patrol miles for each patrol in precinct A last month was 75, whereas in precinct B it was a higher 85. We might draw a completely different conclusion if we looked at this measure. Again, the lesson is that an analyst should always look at multiple measures to obtain a complete picture of an organization's performance.

On the flip side, however, it is important not to overwhelm one's audience with too many numbers. It is one thing to do a careful analysis, but what is presented is often but a subset of the full analysis. Your presentation should focus on a limited number of key performance indicators. You have to know what points you want to make, and then make them. Studies indicate that elected

> **Key Point**
> Using multiple measures gives a more complete picture of performance.

officials and the public are more interested in outcome measures than input or output measures. Use clear language, along with visually effective graphs that make your point. Studies also suggest that elected officials are interested in performance comparisons, so the demonstration of performance trends and results relative to those of other similar jurisdictions may also increase the audience's interest in your analysis.

Different performance scenarios may be given to demonstrate the possible impacts of performance indicators (a *what-if* analysis). For example, a worst-case scenario of a 15 percent budget cut might be linked to a 10 percent decline in police response times. By contrast, a best-case scenario of a 5 percent budget increase might lead to an improvement in police response times.

Treatment of Missing Values

What should you do when the data you need are missing? Missing values are a common occurrence in performance analysis. The reasons for missing values are many, such as clerical errors or omissions in data collection and processing, or changes in data collection protocols and procedures. For example, in revenue forecasting, a revenue category may be merged with other revenue categories for some time period, meaning that data from that revenue category will not exist for that time period.

Sometimes missing data can be simply ignored without significantly affecting your analysis. For example, in a revenue forecast, if the missing data happen to be the revenue from 10 years ago, you can simply use data from the last 9 years. In a survey of citizens' satisfaction about the services they received, missing responses of satisfaction from a few citizens should not cause a significant problem if enough citizens responded to the survey. As a general rule, analysts should not attempt to guess the values of missing values – we prefer to let them be missing, as justifications for our guesses may be uncertain. However, in some cases, missing values are needed in the analysis and estimates must be made to replace the missing data.

One estimate of a missing value is the average (the mean). For example, in the graduation rate data from Table 9.4, if the data for year 3 for school B were missing, you could use the average of the other four years to estimate the missing value [(33 + 25 + 32 + 32)/4 = 31]. If using the average to replace a missing value, you need to ensure that the missing data point is not a value that deviates largely from the mean (that is, outliers). Other possible replacements for missing values are the median or the mode.

Sometimes the use of the mean (or the median or the mode) is simply not accurate, and other factors have to be considered in estimating the missing value. Table 9.7 shows revenue data from the past six years with data missing for year 4. How do you estimate the missing value for year 4? A closer examination of the data shows an upward trend of revenue over time. The average, 15.6, may not be an accurate estimate if there is a trend in the

Table 9.7 ⟶ Missing Revenue Data

Year	1	2	3	4	5	6
Revenue	10	13	15	Missing	19	21

In Greater Depth . . .

Box 9.1 Unique Characteristics of Performance Analysis in the Public and Nonprofit Sectors

Performance analysis is used in public, nonprofit, and business settings as all organizations need to describe, monitor, understand, and evaluate performance. But differences exist in each sector. Public and nonprofit managers are judged much less often by their organizations' financial performance in revenue growth, profitability, and net cash flows. Furthermore, some unique aspects of public and nonprofit management in goal setting, decision-making structures, service delivery processes, and external environments result in unique conditions for analysis of public and nonprofit organizations.

First, the analysis serves stakeholders who have diversified, inconsistent, and sometimes contradictory interests. For example, whereas a high school administration wants high standardized test scores from students, parents want their children to learn skills in school that are not necessarily represented by test scores. This condition requires the analyst to have an acute understanding of stakeholders' diversified interests in the analysis and possible consequences of these interests on the analysis.

Second, most governments in the United States have an annual budgeting cycle, which means that performance measures should be sensitive enough to reflect policy changes and performance improvements within one year. This short funding cycle means that an analysis should be completed within 12 months or less. Data should be collected and analyzed and analysis reports written long before annual funding decisions are made. Moreover, the short funding cycle causes stakeholders to focus heavily on quick results. Performance measures used in the analysis should be sensitive enough to reflect policy changes and improvements resulting from performance interventions.

Box 9.1 *(continued)*

Third, because many public services are not tangible commodities that can be exchanged in the market, their output levels cannot be measured easily. For example, public safety (including police, the courts, and corrections) is an intangible service that cannot be sold in the market, which makes it difficult to measure its level of production.

Finally, most citizens or clients of public services—such as local police or fire protection—live in areas that have only one or a very few such providers. The absence of multiple service providers makes it difficult or impossible to compare the performance of service providers within the region. If a comparison is extended to include other regions, differences between regions may become apparent and it becomes necessary to control for demographic differences between regions. The comparison of an organization's own performance over time is perhaps more meaningful and more realistic to implement.

data because the average does not consider the incremental change caused by the trend. To consider the trend, you may want to use factors such as growth rate or incremental change in your estimate. For example, the incremental revenue changes prior to year 4 are $[13 - 10 =]$ 3 from year 1 to year 2 and $[15 - 13 =]$ 2 from year 2 to year 3, for an average of $[(3 + 2)/2 =]$ 2.5. Using this average incremental change, you can estimate the missing value for year 4 as the data in year 3 plus the incremental change, which is $[15 + 2.5 =]$ 17.5.

There are other more advanced methods to estimate missing values. For example, you can develop a model that specifies the parameters of key factors (variables) that influence the variable that has a missing value. In the preceding revenue data, you could specify a model that has the following parameter estimates: Revenue = 10 + 2*(Year). So the missing value in year 4 would be estimated as $[10 + 2(4) =]$ 18. The regression technique introduced in Chapter 14 is a tool that can be used to develop such a model. However, detailed coverage of other advanced methods in estimation is beyond the scope of this book.

SUMMARY

The descriptive statistical tools introduced in Chapter 6–8 can be applied easily to performance management in the real world. These tools can also be applied in other management and policy areas such as budgeting, financial management, human resources management, information and technology, and executive management. The essential analyses are (1) output and outcome analysis, (2) efficiency and effectiveness analysis, (3) equity analysis, and (4) quality-of-life analysis.

The ability to perform analyses is important—statistics is a skill that must be demonstrated in practice. Equally important is the capacity to present the results in a way that can be easily understood by people who lack much knowledge or training in statistics. The graphic presentations in this chapter were created using Microsoft Excel (see also Chapter 18 in *Exercising Essential Statistics*). The best way to learn statistics is through practice. The reader can profitably use the cases and examples of management and policy making found throughout this book to practice these skills.

KEY TERMS

Efficiency and effectiveness analysis (p. 153)

Equity analysis (p. 155)

Output and outcome analysis (p. 149)

Quality-of-life analysis (p. 156)

Inferential Statistics

This section examines the family of statistics commonly called *inferential statistics.* As the name implies, inferential statistics allow inferences to be made about characteristics of the population from which the data were drawn. A key application for these statistics is to address whether a relationship exists in the first place, and inferential statistics provide statistical evidence for answering this important question. Only if a relationship exists does it make sense to provide further description of its direction and practical importance. When no relationship exists, these later matters are irrelevant. Indeed, determining whether a relationship exists is the unresolved problem in Chapters 8 and 9. Many inferential statistics also provide information about the direction and strength of relations.

Different inferential statistics exist, and a key task of analysts is choosing the correct statistic to use. The rather broad range of tests reflects, in large measure, different measurement levels of variables and also somewhat different questions that might be raised. These matters drive the selection decision, and the Statistics Roadmap provided at the beginning of this book further assists. Specifically:

- When two variables are *categorical,* tests based on contingency tables should be used (Chapters 10 and 11).

- When one variable is *dichotomous* (for example, gender) and the other is *continuous,* the t-test should be used (Chapter 12); when one variable is categorical and the other is *continuous,* analysis of variance (ANOVA) can be used (Chapter 13).
- When both variables are *continuous,* simple regression analysis should be used (Chapter 14), and when three or more variables are analyzed, multivariate techniques should be used (Chapter 15).

Analysts are expected to know whether sufficient statistical evidence exists for claiming relationships they report. Though these statistics are not included in final reports and presentations, analysts are expected to be able to explain their statistical tests if called upon to do so. Being familiar with a broad range of inferential statistics is also essential statistical literacy for the professional to research literature in one's field. In keeping with the essentials character of this book, additional explanations and guidance are offered in detailed footnotes, which readers are encouraged to examine.

Chapter 10 defines essential statistical concepts involved in determining whether a relationship exists: hypothesis testing, statistical significance, critical values, degrees of freedom, test assumptions, confidence intervals, and other statistical terms. The chapter is the foundation for subsequent chapters. Chapter 10 shows how to test whether a relationship exists, and it does so using a practical example involving two categorical variables. The example uses the chi-square test statistic in a discussion of hypothesis testing.

Chapter 11 discusses measures of association that provide information about the direction and strength of relationships. Many of these measures also have tests of statistical significance associated with them; they are useful alternatives to chi-square. We also discuss a variety of nonparametric test statistics that can be used both to test hypotheses and to provide information about the direction and strength of relationships. Nonparametric statistics are characterized by having few or no test assumptions, which makes them relatively easy to use. *Note:* Depending on one's preferences, some readers may choose to skip over Chapter 11 or 13; the material in Section IV can be comprehended and mastered without these.

Chapter 12 discusses the t-test and its variants. The t-test is used to analyze relationships between one continuous and one dichotomous variable and is a staple of statistical analysis; many advanced tests borrow some aspects of t-tests. Although t-tests involve some cumbersome test assumptions, they are popular because they are relatively robust against violations of these assumptions. The chapter discusses the assumptions in detail and indicates how violations might be addressed. Because analysts sometimes want to use other tests, the chapter also provides nonparametric alternatives.

Chapter 13 examines ANOVA, which is useful when the independent variable is nominal and has three or more categories. This method extends the t-test. Managers and analysts are likely to encounter this method in fields that typically have such data (for example, experimental research in medicine and agriculture, and in education). ANOVA test assumptions are also discussed. ANOVA can be extended further, and bit of that discussion is also provided.

Chapter 14 examines the analysis of relationships between two continuous variables. Such relationships are tested primarily with Pearson's correlation coefficient, as well as with simple regression. Simple regression uses tests of the regression slope to determine whether a relationship exists. Many terms introduced in this chapter are essential to understanding subsequent chapters.

Chapter 15 transitions readers to the use of multivariate statistics, for relationships involving three or more variables. Multiple regression is used widely to test rival hypotheses and is a staple of such analysis. The chapter discusses the essential approach of a nomothetic explanation. It is foundational to be familiar with the test assumptions of multiple regression, and this chapter provides a good overview of them and discusses how to deal with assumption violations.

The chapters in this section provide a comprehensive selection of essential statistics. Together with the chapters on descriptive statistics from Section III, this material will offer analysts much of what they need to know. The presentation of these chapters also reinforces important tasks of analysts engaged in statistics. They must (1) understand the definition and purpose of a statistic, (2) ensure that a statistic is appropriate to the data and problem at hand, (3) understand and evaluate the test assumptions of a statistic, (4) apply the statistic to the problem at hand in ways that are mindful of those assumptions, (5) draw correct conclusions, and (6) communicate results in ways that are appropriate for both professional and general audiences. This sequence of events is practiced over and over again, and is consistent with the competencies identified in Chapter 1. The final section of this book additionally examines times series analysis and offers a survey of advanced statistics that managers and analysts may also find useful.

Hypothesis Testing with Chi-Square

CHAPTER OBJECTIVES

After reading this chapter, you should be able to

- Understand the process of hypothesis testing
- Define and apply the concept of "statistical significance"
- Test relationships among categorical variables
- Evaluate chi-square test assumptions
- Discuss how sample size affects statistical significance
- Consider tests involving control variables

Descriptive analysis goes only so far. An important task of statistics is to provide statistical evidence for determining whether relationships exist. This is essential to public policy, for example, establishing whether a program or policy had any impact, such as whether an anger management program affected classroom violence. It is also essential to science, establishing whether or not two variables are related. This chapter discusses general procedures for testing whether a relationship exists. This is also called *hypothesis testing*. Different statistical tests for hypothesis testing are used for different measurement levels of variables involved in relationships. This chapter, using chi-square, shows how to test for relationships between two categorical variables, but the process as described here is valid for other measurement levels, too. Only after the existence of any relationships has been established does it make sense to analyze them further.

WHAT IS CHI-SQUARE?

Chi-square (pronounced "ky-square") is a quantitative measure used to determine whether a relationship exists between two categorical variables. The Greek notation for chi-square is χ^2, which can be used interchangeably with its Latin alphabet spelling, chi-square. Many statistics quantify the relationship between variables in some way. We continue here with the example from Chapter 8 to illustrate the process of calculating chi-square and determining whether a relationship exists, but you are also encouraged to identify categorical variables in your field of interest.

In Chapter 8 we examined the relationship between two categorical variables, namely, gender and the year of promotion for a sample of employees. Managers are concerned that employees are promoted at unequal rates based on gender, raising the possibility of gender discrimination in the workplace. The data are shown again, in Table 10.1. We want to establish whether a

> **Key Point**
>
> Chi-square is a quantitative measure of a relationship between two categorical variables.

Table 10.1 ⟋⋀⟍ Year of Promotion by Gender: Frequencies and Percentages (frequency counts in parentheses)

Year	Gender Male	Female	Total
1	32.6%	15.4%	23.2%
	(14)	(8)	(22)
2	37.2	26.9	31.6
	(16)	(14)	(30)
3	16.2	42.3	30.5
	(7)	(22)	(29)
4	14.0	15.4	14.7
	(6)	(8)	(14)
Total	100.0	100.0	100.0
	(43)	(52)	(95)

relationship exists between gender and year of promotion. Table 10.1 shows both frequency counts and column percentages (in parentheses).

Chi-square provides a quantitative measure of the relationship between two categorical variables, first, by determining what the distribution of observations (frequencies) would look like if *no* relationship existed and, second, by quantifying the extent to which the observed distribution (such as in Table 10.1) differs from that determined in the first step. This section explains the calculation of chi-square, which is used in the next section for hypothesis testing (that is, determining whether a relationship exists).

What would the relationship in Table 10.1 look like if no relationship existed between gender and year of promotion? When no relationship exists between gender and the year of promotion, then men and women, by definition, do not differ in promotion rates. The column percentages in Table 10.1 will then be identical for men and women; they will not differ from the aggregate sample of all men and women. This distribution is shown in the right-hand, "Total" column. When no relationship exists between men and women, both men and women will be promoted at those rates. Hence, 23.2 percent of both men and women will be promoted in their first year, 31.6 percent will be promoted in their second year, 30.5 percent will be promoted in their third year, and 14.7 percent will be promoted in their fourth year.

The frequencies associated with these rates when no relationship exists are called **expected frequencies.** Table 10.2 shows these expected frequencies. For example, when no difference in promotion rates exists between men and women, 30.5 percent of 43 men, or 13.1 men, would have been promoted in their third year. Similarly, 30.5 percent of 52 women, or 15.9 women, would have been promoted in their third year. The other expected frequencies are calculated in similar fashion in Table 10.2.

Table 10.2 —————〰️—— Year of Promotion by Gender: Expected Frequencies

	A: Percentages			B: Counts	
	Gender			Gender	
Year	Male	Female	Total	Male	Female
1	23.2%	23.2%	23.2%	(23.2/100)*43=10.0	(23.2/100)*52=12.1
2	31.6	31.6	31.6	(31.6/100)*43=13.6	(31.6/100)*52=16.4
3	30.5	30.5	30.5	(30.5/100)*43=13.1	(30.5/100)*52=15.9
4	14.7	14.7	14.7	(14.7/100)*43=6.3	(14.7/100)*52=7.6
Total	100.0	100.0	100.0	43.0	52.0
(n =)	(43)	(52)	(95)		

Table 10.3 ⎯⎯⎯⎯⎯ ᖰᖰ⎯ Calculating Chi-Square

| Year | Male | | | Female | | | Total |
	Obs.	Exp.	χ^2	Obs.	Exp.	χ^2	χ^2
1	14	10.0	1.60	8	12.1	1.39	2.99
2	16	13.6	0.42	14	16.4	0.35	0.77
3	7	13.1	2.84	22	15.9	2.34	5.18
4	6	6.3	0.01	8	7.6	0.02	0.03
Total	43	43.0	4.87	52	52.0	4.10	8.97

Note: Obs. = observed frequency; exp. = expected frequency

Clearly, when the data indicate that no relationship exists between these variables, the values of observed and expected frequencies must be identical. Also, the greater the relationship, the greater the difference between the observed and expected frequencies. The *chi-square* statistic (χ^2) measures the difference between the expected and observed frequencies and is thus a quantitative measure of this relationship. Chi-square is defined in the following manner:

$$\sum_i \frac{(O_i - E_i)^2}{E_i}$$

where O_i is the observed frequency in a cell and E_i is the expected frequency in a cell. As is readily seen, when $E_i = O_i$, the chi-square value for that cell is zero. Using the frequencies shown in Tables 10.1 and 10.2 (part B), we find that the chi-square value of the first cell is $[(14 - 10)^2/10 = 4^2/10 = 16/10 =] 1.60$. Calculating chi-square for all of the cells yields 8.97, as shown in Table 10.3. *Of course, the value of chi-square is usually calculated by computer.*[1]

In short, when no relationship exists between the variables, chi-square equals zero. The greater the relationship, the greater the value of chi-square. Finally, note also that chi-square is always positive and that it provides no information about the direction of the relationship.[2]

HYPOTHESIS TESTING

We now use chi-square to determine whether a relationship exists between gender and promotion. This is called *hypothesis testing*. In our example, the hypothesis is that a relationship exists between gender and the rate of promotion; a hypothesis is a tentative statement about some relationship or condition that is subject to subsequent verification. The ***purpose of*** *hypothesis testing* is, simply, to determine whether a relationship exists. Specifically, we ask, "What is the probability that the above distribution of promotion rates among 95 men and women is consistent with a distribution in which men and women are promoted at *equal* rates?" That is, is a chi-square value of 8.97 sufficiently large to conclude that men are promoted at a faster rate than women?[3] A *key task* in statistics is to determine how large any measure of a relationship must be in order to say that it is "statistically significant." This part of hypothesis testing involves

- The null hypothesis
- The concept of statistical significance
- Critical values
- Steps to determine statistical significance

These issues are relevant to all statistical tests, such as chi-square tests, t-tests, and others discussed in this book.

The Null Hypothesis

Since statistics is a careful and cautious discipline, we presume that no relationship between variables exists and that any relationship that is found may have been obtained purely by chance. The *null hypothesis* states that *any observed pattern is due solely to chance* and that, hence, no relationship exists. Thus, the null hypothesis (that is, that no relationship exists) is assumed, and an objective of statistical testing is to examine whether the null hypothesis can be rejected. This idea is similar to the court of justice in which individuals are presumed innocent until proven guilty beyond a reasonable doubt. In our example, we presume that no relationship exists between gender and the rate of promotion.

In statistics the specific concern is that we may find a relationship in our sample when in fact none exists in the population. This may occur because of a fluke in our random sample. We endeavor to disprove this possibility. Another way of looking at this issue is that if we assume that a relationship does exist, we might be guilty of not trying hard enough to prove that it doesn't exist. By assuming that a relationship doesn't exist, we need only satisfy the standard of "reasonable evidence" in order to claim that it does exist. That standard is that it should be *very unlikely to find a relationship among variables* (that is, a test-statistic value such as chi-square) *of a certain (large) magnitude when in fact no relationship exists in the population.*

The null hypothesis is stated as follows:

H_0: No relationship exists between gender and the rate of promotion.

H_A: A relationship exists between gender and the rate of promotion.

H_0 is the null hypothesis, and H_A is called the *alternate hypothesis*. H_0 is also some-times called the straw man because we endeavor to "strike it down" or disprove it. The *alternate hypothesis* is the logical opposite of the null hypothesis; all possibili-ties must be accounted for between the null hypothesis and the alternate hypothesis.

In most instances, the null hypothesis is that *no relationship exists* between two variables, and the alternate hypothesis is that *a relationship does exist* between two variables. However, if the researcher has a priori informa-tion that a relationship can exist only in one direction (for example, that men can be promoted faster than women but that women cannot be promoted faster than men), then it is appropriate to state the null hypothesis as "men are not promoted faster than women" and the alternate hypothesis as "men are promoted faster than women." However, because, as is often the case, we cannot a priori rule out the direction of the relationship (it could be that women are promoted faster than men), we use the customary approach indicating that no relationship exists. If a relationship exists, we later can determine its direction.

Many scholars prefer to state these hypotheses as follows:

H_0: No relationship exists between gender and the rate of promotion in the population.

H_A: A relationship exists between gender and the rate of promotion in the population.

This usage clearly indicates that we are using sample data to draw inferences about relationships in the population. Indeed, we are not interested in our sam-ple, per se. Who cares about the preferences of, say, 500 citizens? We care about them only to the extent that their opinions *represent* those of the entire popula-tion. In the end, we want to know how the population, not merely a sample of it, thinks about something. We use a sample to infer conclusions about the popula-tion. To distinguish conclusions about the sample from those of the population, we use Greek letters to refer to the population. Then, the hypotheses are also written as follows:

$H_0: \mu_m = \mu_f$

$H_A: \mu_m \neq \mu_f$

where μ is the rate of promotion in the population, and the *m* and *f* subscripts stand for "male" and "female," respectively.

Statistical Significance

The phrase *statistically significant* often carries considerable weight in public discourse. To say that something is statistically significant is tantamount to throwing the weight of science behind a statement or fact. But what exactly does the phrase mean? ***Statistical significance*** simply refers to the probability of being wrong about stating that a relationship exists when in fact it doesn't. The phrase ***level of statistical significance*** refers to the level of that probability—in other words, *how often* we would be wrong to conclude that a relationship exists when in fact none exists, or how often we would incorrectly reject the null hypothesis when in fact it is true. One reason we might wrongly reject the null hypothesis is that our data are a random sample; had we drawn a different sample, we might have concluded otherwise (Box 10.1).

The statistical standard for significance is 5 percent in the social sciences; we are willing to tolerate a 1-in-20 chance of being wrong in stating that a relationship exists (that is, concluding that the null hypothesis should be rejected when in fact it shouldn't). Many researchers also consider a 1-in-100 (1 percent) probability of being wrong as an acceptable standard of significance. The latter is a stricter standard. We are less likely to be wrong stating that a relationship exists (when in fact it doesn't exist) when it is significant at the 1 percent level than when it is significant at only the 5 percent level.

We could set the bar even higher—for example, by choosing a level of significance of one-tenth of 1 percent—but doing so may cause us to conclude that no relationship exists when in fact one does. A standard of less than 1 percent is thus thought to be too risk averse. Why not settle for a 10 percent level of significance? If we did so, we would be accepting a 10 percent chance of wrongfully concluding that a relationship exists when in fact none does. Usually, that is thought to be too risky.[4]

By convention, 5 percent is usually thought to be the uppermost limit of risk that we accept. Thus, relationships that are significant at more than 5 percent (say, 6 percent) are said to be *not significant.* Only relationships that are significant at 5 percent or less are considered significant, and relationships that are significant at 1 percent or less are said to be *highly significant.* Another convention is that most relationships are reported as being significant only at the 1 percent or the 5 percent level. Thus, a relationship that is statistically significant at the 3 percent level is reported as being significant at the 5 percent level but not at the 1 percent level. A relationship that is significant at one-tenth of 1 percent is reported as being significant at the 1 percent level.

Finally, the phrase *level of significance* should not be confused with the term *confidence level.* The confidence level refers to the probability that an unknown population parameter falls within a range of values calculated from the sample (see Box 7.2). Sometimes the phrase *level of confidence* is taken as being synonymous with 100 percent minus the level of statistical significance; for example, a 5 percent level of significance is said to be the

In Greater Depth...

Box 10.1   An Introduction to Probability

Recall from Chapter 5 that obtaining information about an entire population is often impractical and that sample information is used instead. When we use sample information to estimate population parameters (for example, mean and standard deviation), there is a chance that our estimation is not accurate, which means a discrepancy exists between the estimate and the true parameter. Probability is an important concept when it comes to determining the accuracy of our estimation. Let's look at an example. Say that you work for a city of 10,000 residents (the population), and you are interested in citizens' satisfaction with city services. You asked a sample of 100 residents how happy they were with city services. You want to use the information from this sample to estimate the satisfaction of all 10,000 residents. Suppose that, out of the 100 in the sample, 60 (or 60 percent) said they were happy and the other 40 (or 40 percent) said they were unhappy. If you are about to ask one more person (your 101st subject), what is the chance, or probability, that person is happy about the services? It is 60 percent. By definition, the *probability* of a particular event (being happy, in this case) is the proportion of times that event would occur in a long run of repeated observations. The probability value goes from 0 to 1. A value of 0 indicates that the event does not occur, whereas 1 means that it occurs for sure.

Why is the concept of probability critical in statistics? Although 60 percent of respondents in your survey are happy with city services, you cannot really say that 60 percent of *all 10,000 residents* in your city are happy with the services. This is because the 60 percent is an estimate from a sample, and there is *always* a difference between a sample estimate and the true population parameter being estimated. Think about this: what is the chance that the true percentage of all residents who are happy about services is *exactly* 60 percent? It is very slim. So, there is a difference between the 60 percent and the true percentage. This difference, also known as the *sampling error* or *estimation error,* always exists when a sample is used to estimate a population parameter. This is why we have to use probability, not certainty, in statistical analyses. We often have to use the language of probability to describe the results of analyses based on samples.

same as a 95 percent confidence level. However, the phrase *level of significance* should be used in connection with matters of hypothesis testing.

The Five Steps of Hypothesis Testing

Recall the question asked earlier: How large should chi-square be so that we can conclude that a statistically significant relationship exists between gender and year of promotion or, in other words, so that we can reject the null hypothesis and accept the alternate hypothesis? All statistical tests follow the same *five steps of hypothesis testing*:

1. State the null hypothesis (in Greek letters).
2. Choose a statistical test.
3. Calculate the test statistic (t.s.) and evaluate test assumptions.
4. Look up the critical value (c.v.) of the test.
5. Draw a conclusion:

    If |t.s.| < c.v., do not reject the null hypothesis.
    If |t.s.| ≥ c.v., reject the null hypothesis.

We already discussed the first item and mentioned the second item in the introduction to Section III. Readers also may wish to consult the Statistics Roadmap at the beginning of this book for more detailed guidance on selecting test statistics. We have seen how to calculate the chi-square test statistic. Most statistical tests make assumptions about variables: we will soon address those of the chi-square test statistic. Now we discuss critical values. The *critical value* is the minimum value that a test statistic must be in order to rule out chance as the cause of a relationship. Technically, the critical value is the value above which the test statistic is sufficiently large to reject the null hypothesis at a user-specified level of significance.

> **Key Point**
>
> The null hypothesis states that no relationship exists. The critical value is the minimum value that a test statistic must be to reject the null hypothesis.

The following discussion is provided to enhance conceptual understanding because, again, computers do most of the work. The *critical value* of any test statistic is determined by two parameters: (1) the desired level of statistical significance and (2) the number of degrees of freedom (df). As stated earlier, by convention, analysts are interested in rejecting the null hypothesis at the 1 percent and 5 percent levels. The *degrees of freedom* address the practical, statistical problem that the magnitude of most test statistics is affected by the number of observations or categories. For example, the formula for calculating the chi-square test statistic requires us to calculate a value for each cell and then add them all up. All things being equal, the larger the number of cells, the larger the value of this test statistic. The degrees of freedom statistic controls for this problem.[5] (This also means that it is generally meaningless to compare the values of different chi-square test statistics based on tables of unequal sizes and, as we will soon see, unequal numbers of observations.)

Each type of statistical test has its own way of calculating degrees of freedom. The degrees of freedom for any chi-square test are defined by the formula $(c-1)*(r-1)$, where c is the number of columns in a contingency table and r is the number of rows. In Table 10.1, df $= (2-1)*(4-1) = 3$. If our table had six rows and four columns, the number of degrees of freedom would be $[(6-1)*(4-1) =]$ 15, and so on.

To determine the critical value of our test, we turn to a table of chi-square critical values (see Appendix B). The table shows the levels of significance in columns and the degrees of freedom in rows. Assume that we wish to test whether our previously calculated χ^2 test statistic (8.97) is statistically significant at the 5 percent level. The critical value at this level of significance and three degrees of freedom is shown to be 7.815. Thus, applying the very last step in the method for testing hypotheses, we evaluate the absolute value of 8.97 as indeed larger than the critical value. The absolute value is stated in step 5 because some test statistics, but not χ^2, can have negative values, and because the critical value is always positive. So, we conclude that *a relationship exists between gender and the rate of promotion at the 5 percent level of significance.* Alternatively, we can write that *a statistically significant relationship exists between gender and the rate of promotion* ($\chi^2 = 8.97$, p $< .05$). This important language is found in most analyses.

But is this relationship also significant at the 1 percent level? The critical value of this chi-square test at the 1 percent level and three degrees of freedom is 11.341. We evaluate that the absolute value of 8.97 is less than the critical value at this level of significance, and so we conclude that the relationship between gender and years of promotion is significant at the 5 percent level but not at the 1 percent level. We should always identify the highest level of significance, which in this instance is the 5 percent level. But if the test statistics had also been greater than the critical value at the 1 percent level, then the 1 percent level would be concluded.[6]

Getting Started

Replicate these results on your computer

Note some features of the table of chi-square critical values in Appendix B. First, at any given level of significance, the value of the chi-square critical values increases as the degrees of freedom increase. This is consistent with the problem mentioned earlier: contingency tables with more rows and columns will have larger test statistics simply as a result of having more cells. The degrees of freedom "compensate" for this fact. Second, at any given number of degrees of freedom, the value of the chi-square critical values increases as the level of significance decreases. This, too, makes sense because a 1 percent level of significance will have a higher threshold than a 5 percent level.

Statistical software programs calculate test statistics and report the level of statistical significance at which the test statistic is significant. For example, software output might have shown "p = .029," which indicates that the test statistic is statistically significant at the 5 percent level but not at the 1 percent level. The probability "p = .000" means that the relationship is highly significant, at better than the 1 percent level. The probability "p = .1233" or "p = .9899" indicates that the relationship is not significant. Software programs do not ordinarily report critical values at the 1 percent and 5 percent levels; rather, they show the level of significance at which test statistics are significant. Looking up critical values is a valuable exercise that increases conceptual understanding but one that you will need to do only sporadically.

Getting Started

Test whether a relationship exists between two variables of your choice.

Here is another example that you can follow to gain additional practice with hypothesis testing. Table 10.4 shows data

Table 10.4 ———〜〜— Training Participation and Employment

ID	Training participation	Employment status two years after the training session
1	Not participating	Not employed
2	Not participating	Employed
3	Participating	Employed
4	Not participating	Not employed
5	Participating	Employed
6	Not participating	Employed
7	Not participating	Not employed
8	Participating	Employed
9	Not participating	Not employed
10	Participating	Employed
11	Not participating	Not employed
12	Participating	Not employed
13	Participating	Employed
14	Not participating	Not employed
15	Participating	Employed
16	Participating	Employed
17	Participating	Not employed
18	Participating	Not employed
19	Not participating	Not employed
20	Participating	Employed

Table 10.5 ———⌇⌇⌇— Calculating χ^2 for Job Training Performance

	Training participation						
	Not participating			Participating			Total
	Obs.	Exp.	χ^2	Obs.	Exp.	χ^2	χ^2
Not employed	7.00	4.50	1.39	3.00	5.50	1.14	2.53
Employed	2.00	4.50	1.39	8.00	5.50	1.14	2.53
Total	9.00	9.00	2.78	11.00	11.00	2.27	5.05

Note: Obs. = observed count; exp. = expected count.

related to the effectiveness of training for 20 qualified unemployed individuals. The second column ("training participation") indicates the individuals' participation status, and the third column captures data regarding employment two years after the training session. You are asked to conduct a chi-square test to examine the relationship between training participation and employment status. What is your null hypothesis?

The null hypothesis is that there is no relationship between training participation and employment status. The alternate hypothesis is that training participation is related to employment. The calculation of chi-square is shown in Table 10.5.

The value of χ^2 is 5.05. This example has [$(2 - 1)*(2 - 1) =$] 1 degree of freedom. The critical value at the 0.05 level is 3.841 (see Appendix B). Because χ^2 ($= 5.05$) is larger than the critical value, we reject the null hypothesis and conclude that training participation is related to employee status at the 5 percent level.

Chi-Square Test Assumptions

Nearly all test statistics make *assumptions* about the variables that are used. *Assessing test assumptions is a critical task in statistical testing,* because violations of test assumptions invalidate test results. Analysts need to be familiar with the assumptions of different tests, and of ways for addressing violations of test assumptions. when they occur. There are three *chi-square test assumptions*. First, the variables must be categorical, which applies to our variables. Second, the observations are independent, as ours are. Independent samples are those in which each observation is independent of other observations in the sample. The concept of dependent samples is discussed more fully in Chapter 11, and typically involves experimental situations such as before-and-after measurement. Third, all cells must have a minimum of five expected observations. When this condition is not met, it is usually because the contingency table contains a large number of rows and columns relative to the number of observations. That is, the data are spread too thinly across too many cells. To correct this problem, simply redefine the data categories (that is, combine adjacent rows or columns) to create a smaller number of cells. Examination of Table 10.2 shows that our data meet this third assumption, too. The smallest expected frequency count is 6.3. If our data had violated this assumption, we would have combined rows or columns, recalculated results, and reported the revised conclusions. Some analysts, however, feel that this third assumption is too strong.[7]

Although chi-square is useful for testing whether a relationship exists, we have also noted some limitations: chi-square provides no information about the direction or strength of the relationship, and the third assumption may be problematic at times. For this reason, analysts often consider an alternative statistic, Kendall's tau-c, discussed below, which offers information about significance, direction, and strength, as well.

Statistical Significance and Sample Size

Most statistical tests are also affected by *sample size,* which has implications for the likelihood of finding statistically significant relationships. Specifically, it is easier to find statistically significant relationships in large datasets than in small ones. This is more than a statistical artifact; rather, it reflects that having more information makes us more confident of our conclusions, and vice versa. The sample size affects the statistical significance of many widely used test statistics, including chi-square.

For example, assume we had a sample of 950 employees, rather than 95 employees, with the same relative distribution as shown in Table 10.1 (see Table 10.6). It is easy to verify that the data in Table 10.6 are distributed in the same exact manner as shown in Table 10.1. But the added observations affect the calculation of the chi-square test statistic. The value of the chi-square test statistic in the first cell is $(O_i - E_i)^2/E_i$, or $[(140 - 100)^2/100 =]$ 16. This is exactly *10 times* that of the previously calculated value. Indeed, each cell value is 10 times larger, as is the chi-square test statistic, which now becomes 89.7. Yet, the chi-square critic value is still defined as $(c - 1)(r - 1)$. The critical value for rejecting the null hypothesis at the 1 percent level is still 11.341. Whereas previously we could not reject the null hypothesis at this level, we now succeed in doing so by virtue of *having more observations.* This phenomenon occurs with many other widely used test statistics, too.

Table 10.6 ⎯⎯⎯⎯⎯⎯⏦⎯ Year of Promotion by Gender: Observed and Expected Counts

| | A: Observed counts | | | B: Expected counts | |
| | Gender | | | Gender | |
Year	Male	Female	Total	Male	Female
1	140	80	220	100	121
2	160	140	300	136	164
3	70	220	290	131	159
4	60	80	140	63	76
Total	430	520	950	430	520

Of course, the opposite is also true: if we had tried to test for significance using only, say, 20 observations (instead of 95), we would have failed to reject the null hypotheses at even the 5 percent level. This reflects our having too little information to be sufficiently confident in our conclusions. By convention, many researchers prefer to test their null hypotheses on sample sizes of about 100 to a few hundred (say, 400). This is only a rough guideline. One implication is that analysts are neither surprised to find statistically significant relations in large samples, nor are they surprised to find the lack of statistical significance in small samples. Another implication is that, when working with large samples, analysts can find minute differences between groups to be statistically significant, even when the differences have very little practical relevance. Bigger samples are not necessarily better: they merely increase the importance of questions about the practical significance of findings. Box 10.2 discusses statistical power, which often is used to determine a minimum sample size.

In Greater Depth . . .

Box 10.2   Power and Sample Size

The level of statistical significance indicates how often we would be wrong to reject the null hypothesis when in fact it is true. However, another possible testing error occurs when we fail to reject the null hypothesis when in fact we should. The former is called a Type I (or α) error,

(continued)

Box 10.2 *(continued)*

		Decision	
		Reject	Accept
Null hypothesis	True	Type I (α) error	Correct
	False	Correct (Power, $1 - \beta$)	Type II (β) error

wrongfully concluding that a relationship exists. The later is called a Type II (or β) error, wrongfully concluding that a relationship does not exist.

If β is the probability of wrongfully concluding that a relationship does not exist when in fact it does (Type II error), then $1 - \beta$ is the probability of correctly rejecting the null hypothesis when we should. This probability, $1 - \beta$, is called ***statistical power***. The relationships between these concepts are summarized below:

A typical reason for Type II errors is that the sample size is too small relative to the relationships or differences for which we are testing; we just don't have enough statistical evidence to reject the null hypothesis. The purpose of analyzing power is usually to determine minimum sample size. It has been suggested that the power of tests should be at least .80. Formulas for calculating power vary from test to test; they depend on the sample size, the level of statistical significance, and the effect size (for example, difference between means). Effect size, too, is defined differently for different tests.[8] Typically, analysts use tables or power calculators, many of which are now available on the Internet.[9] Analysts err on the side of caution by postulating small effect sizes (that is, small differences between means or large standard deviations), thereby indicating a need for larger samples.

Finally, recall from Chapter 8 that once statistical significance has been established, analysts must turn to the task of establishing practical relevance. Are the differences between categories large or small? Are they large enough to warrant interest from policy makers? Are they large enough to conclude that programs and policy have a salient impact on society? This is the essential task that must follow up after statistical hypothesis testing. The descriptive techniques discussed in Chapter 8 regarding the analysis of contingency tables and the use of column percentages are essential to providing these answers, building on the results established here.

A NONPARAMETRIC ALTERNATIVE

Chi-square is a widely known and popular statistic, but it has some limitations. As we have seen, it provides no information about the direction or strength of relationships, and it is limited by some test assumptions (though they are not as cumbersome as some we will see later). Statisticians have developed alternative measures that overcome these limitations. For example, Kendall's tau-c belongs to the family of nonparametric statistics, discussed in Chapter 11, which derive their name from the fact that they have very few test assumptions. They are a bit less powerful, that is, able to determine the statistical significance of relations, but they are quite useful. Kendall's tau-c can be used as an alternative to chi-square. Here we only introduce Kendall's tau-c. The formula for Kendall's tau-c is given in Chapter 11, but as with chi-square, statistical software packages readily compute this statistic.

Kendall's tau-c provides information about the level of significance, as well as the strength and direction of relationships. Kendall's tau-c can vary from +1.00 to −1.00. A positive sign indicates a positive relationship and a negative sign indicates a negative relationship (see Chapter 8). A value of zero indicates that no relationship exists between the variables, and a value of |1.00| indicates a perfect relationship. Although there are no absolute standards, many analysts regard scores of less than |0.25| as indicating weak relationships; scores of between |0.25| and |0.50|, moderate relationships; and scores of greater than |0.50|, strong relationships. Beyond this, computers readily calculate the level at which Kendall's tau-c is statistically significant. Thus, this statistic provides three important pieces of information about any relationship: significance, direction, and strength. Another advantage of Kendall's tau-c is that it does not have the third test assumption of chi-square, that all cells must have a minimum of five expected observations. This assumption is unnecessary given the way that Kendall's tau-c is calculated (see Chapter 11).

Using the data from this chapter's example (see Table 10.1), the computer would calculate the value of Kendall's tau-c as .269, which is significant at the .029 level, indicating a positive and moderately strong relationship that is significant at the 5 percent level. However, in this example, the positive sign has no inherent meaning because the variable "gender" is a nominal variable. This example provides a good reminder to interpret outcomes in appropriate ways; it is senseless to describe the relationship in Table 10.1 as either a positive or a negative one. Also, the computer-generated value of chi-square is significant at the 0.16 level; Kendall's tau-c indeed determines the statistical significance of this relationship as a bit less than the chi-square test. But both statistics come to same conclusion, namely, that this relationship is significant at the 5 percent level.

The next few chapters provide more information on Kendall's tau-c and other nonparametric alternatives; we encourage analysts to become familiar with them. Though these statistics are a bit less powerful than chi-square, they are useful alternatives.

SUMMARY

When researchers assess the existence and nature of relationships between two variables, hypothesis testing and chi-square applications are invaluable tools. Hypothesis testing is an important step in data analysis because it establishes whether a relationship exists between two variables in the population, that is, whether a relationship is statistically significant. Processes of hypothesis testing involve

1. Stating the null hypothesis
2. Choosing the appropriate test statistics
3. Ensuring that data meet the assumptions of the test statistics
4. Calculating the test statistic values
5. Comparing the test statistic values against critical values and determining at what level a relationship is significant (or relying on the computer to calculate test statistics and to state the level at which they are statistically significant)

When analysts are confronted with two categorical variables, which can also be used to make a contingency table, chi-square is a widely used test for establishing whether a relationship exists (see the Statistics Roadmap at the beginning of the book). Chi-square has three test assumptions: (1) that variables are categorical, (2) that observations are independent, and (3) that no cells have fewer than five expected frequency counts. Remember, violation of test assumptions invalidates any test result. Chi-square is but one statistic for testing a relationship between two categorical variables; others are discussed in Chapter 11.

Once analysts have determined that a statistically significant relationship exists through hypothesis testing, they need to assess the practical relevance of their findings. Remember, large datasets easily allow for findings of statistical significance. Practical relevance deals with the relevance of statistical differences for managers; it addresses whether statistically significant relationships have meaningful policy implications.

KEY TERMS

Alternate hypothesis (p. 171)
Chi-square (p. 167)
Chi-square test assumptions
    (p. 177)
Critical value (p. 174)
Degrees of freedom (p. 174)
Expected frequencies (p. 168)
Five steps of hypothesis testing
    (p. 174)
Kendall's tau-c (p.181)
Level of statistical significance
    (p. 172)

Null hypothesis (p. 170)
Purpose of hypothesis testing (p. 169)
Replicaton (see appendix to this
    chapter) (p.185)
Rival hypotheses (see appendix to
    this chapter) (p.183)
Sample size (and hypothesis testing)
    (p. 178)
Statistical power (p. 169)
Statistical significance (p. 172)
Suppressor effect (see appendix to
    this chapter) (p.185)

APPENDIX 10.1

Rival Hypotheses: Adding a Control Variable

We now extend our discussion to rival hypotheses. The following is but one approach (sometimes called the "elaboration paradigm"), and we provide many other approaches in subsequent chapters. First mentioned in Chapter 2, *rival hypotheses* They are alternative, plausible explanations of findings. We established earlier that men are promoted faster than women, and in Chapter 8 (see "Pivot Tables") we raised the possibility that the promotion rate is different between men and women because men are more productive than women. We can now begin to examine this hypothesis formally using chi-square. Again, managers will want to examine this possibility as one of several.

Assume that we somehow measured productivity. Variables associated with rival hypotheses are called control variables. The control variable "productivity" is added to our dataset. To examine the rival hypothesis, we divide the sample into two (or more) groups, namely, employees with high productivity and those with low productivity. For each of these groups, we make a contingency table analysis by gender. If it is true that productivity, and not gender, determines the rate of promotion, then we expect to find no differences in the rate of promotion within the *same* level of productivity (high or low) because the differences exist across levels of productivity, and not by gender. Next, we construct a table (see Table 10.7). Note that the control variable "goes on top." We still have a total of 95 employees, 43 of whom are men and 52 of whom are women. For simplicity, and to avoid violating chi-square test assumptions (we must maintain a minimum of five expected frequencies in each cell), the variable "year of promotion" has been grouped, although this needn't be done in other instances. The relevant hypotheses are now as follows:

H1$_0$: No relationship exists between gender and rate of promotion among employees with high productivity.

H1$_A$: A relationship exists between gender and rate of promotion among employees with high productivity.

H2$_0$: No relationship exists between gender and rate of promotion among employees with low productivity.

H2$_A$: A relationship exists between gender and rate of promotion among employees with low productivity.

Chi-square test statistics are calculated for *each* of the two different productivity groups. We could find that one or both relationships are now statistically significant. When both relationships are not statistically significant, the result is called an **explanation** of the initial findings; that is, the statistically significant result has been explained away. Sometimes it is said that the previous relationship has proven to be

Table10.7 ⎯⎯⎯⎯⎯⎯ᴧᴧᴧᴧ⎯⎯ Year of Promotion by Gender: Controlling for Productivity

Year	Low productivity		High productivity	
	Gender		Gender	
	Male (%)	Female (%)	Male (%)	Female (%)
1–2 Years	47	22	85	52
3+ Years	53	78	15	47
Total	100	100	100	100
(n =)	(17)	(18)	(26)	(34)

spurious. When both relationships are statistically significant, the result is called a **replication** of the initial findings. When only one of the relationships is statistically significant, the result is called a *specification* of the initial findings. We would want to examine further the relationship that is not explained away. Finally, rarely does using a control variable result in uncovering statistically significant relationships that are otherwise insignificant. When this does occur, however, the result is called a **suppressor effect**. That is, the existing relationship is suppressed in the absence of the control variable.

Through our data, we obtain the following results. The chi-square test statistic for the relationship between gender and year of promotion among employees with low productivity is 2.39, which is not statistically significant ($p = .117$). Thus, we conclude that gender does *not* discriminate in the rate of promotion among employees with low levels of productivity. But the chi-square test statistic for the relationship between gender and year of promotion among employees with high productivity is 6.65, which is statistically significant at the 1 percent level ($p = .010$). Gender differences continue to explain differences in the rate of promotion among employees with high levels of productivity. This type of finding is called a *specification.*[10]

Although this approach allows us to test rival hypotheses, two limitations may be noted: results are sometimes inconclusive (for example, in the case of specification), and the added cells require a larger number of observations. Table 10.7 acknowledges this problem; rows were combined. In Chapter 15 we discuss multiple regression as an alternative for continuous dependent variables which is more much more commonly used than the approach mentioned here.

Notes

1. The CD accompanying the workbook *Exercising Essential Statistics* replicates these calculations on an Excel spreadsheet, called "Chi-Square." The computer-calculated value of chi-square is slightly higher, 9.043, due to rounding errors in calculating the expected frequency counts. This same result is achieved when using expected frequency counts with three decimal places. The expected frequency counts are then, for men: 9.976, 13.588, 13.115, and 6.321; for women: 12.064, 16.432, 15.860, and 7.644. Of course, maintaining three decimal places is more labor intensive for the illustrative, manually calculated example in the text, which retains only one decimal place in calculating the expected frequencies.

2. See Chapter 8 for a discussion of the direction of relationships.

3. It is commonly said that inferential statistics state the degree of certainty by which we can say that a relationship exists beyond chance alone. This is plainly said, and some academics will take issue with how this is phrased. People are free to make their own plain-sense interpretation of statistical formulas.

4. Such a level might be acceptable at times in administration, and scientists occasionally report a 10 percent level, too.

5. The concept of degrees of freedom is not easy to explain. Some texts explain it as the number of calculations that are not predetermined after others have already occurred. Succinctly, if an array (or column) has four data elements, and the sum total is also known, then after choosing the first three elements, the fourth element is predetermined: hence, we are free to choose only three elements, and the array is said to have three degrees of freedom, or $c - 1$.

6. For example, if the test statistic of our data had been, say, 15.0, then $p < .01$ rather than $p < .05$ would be concluded and reported. This is not the case here, though.

7. The rationale is to ensure that chi-square calculations are not unduly affected by small differences in cells with low counts. Note that the expected frequency is in the denominator of the chi-square formula. Some analysts feel that the standard of no cells with expected frequencies below 5.0 is too strict. They feel that (1) all cells should have greater expected frequency counts than 1.0 and (2) that no more than 20 percent of cells should have expected frequency counts lower than 5.0. The standard adopted in the text is more conservative. The point is, of course, that test statistics should not be affected by a few sparse cells.

8. This is defined as $(\mu_1 - \mu_2)/\sigma_{pooled}$, where $\sigma_{pooled} = \sqrt{[(\sigma_1^2 + \sigma_2^2)/2]}$. Small effect sizes are defined as those for which $\mu_1 - \mu_2$ is about .2 σ_{pooled}, medium effect sizes are about .5 σ_{pooled}, and large effect sizes are .8 σ_{pooled}. For a chi-square test, effect size is defined as the *Phi coefficient*, z, for two-by-two tables, $\sqrt{(\chi^2/N)}$, and as the contingency coefficient, C, for larger tables, $\sqrt{[\chi^2/(\chi^2 + N)]}$. Some of these measures are discussed in later chapters.

9. For example, see www.dssresearch.com/toolkit/spcalc/power.asp or http://power.education.uconn.edu/otherwebsites.htm.

10. This approach is rather inefficient: note that we had to combine categories in order to preserve an adequate number of observations in each cell. In subsequent chapters, we examine approaches that are

more efficient and more conclusive. Of course, when productivity is found to cause explanation or specification, you subsequently want to report on the bivariate relationship between the rate of promotion and productivity. That, of course, is a different relationship from the one discussed here.

CHAPTER 11

Measures of Association

CHAPTER OBJECTIVES

After reading this chapter, you should be able to:

- Understand the concept of "proportional reduction in error"
- Determine the strength and direction of relationships
- Know why Kendall's tau-c is increasingly used for tests involving two ordinal variables
- Test whether program or policy outcomes meet norms
- Test for relationships involving very small samples
- Test whether two or more evaluators agree in their rankings

Although chi-square is widely used for testing the statistical significance of relationships, it provides no information about the direction and strength of those relationships. Measures of association provide information about the direction and strength of relationships, and many of these measures also have tests associated with them for hypothesis testing; hence, they are very useful for analysis. This chapter discusses such statistics for two categorical variables. Many of these tests are referred to as *nonparametric statistics*, a name derived from the fact that these test statistics involve very few parameters or test assumptions. These statistical tests are easy to use, which makes them quite popular.

This chapter differs from Chapter 10 in that it covers a fairly broad range of statistics and situations. Some are alternatives to chi-square, and others are designed for specific situations such as testing significance in small samples. Working through the examples in this chapter will increase your familiarity with the process of hypothesis testing. Analysts and managers need to be familiar with the types of situations in which each of these statistics is used so that they can apply the appropriate statistics. Chapter 12 discusses additional nonparametric test statistics that can be used as alternatives to the test statistics discussed here.

THREE NEW CONCEPTS

We now introduce three concepts that extend the discussion of chi-square from Chapter 10: (1) Proportional reduction in error (PRE) is used to quantify the strength of relationships that involve categorical variables, (2) paired cases are used to measure the direction of such relationships, and (3) when dependent samples are involved, responses from one subject or observation are linked to the responses of another. It is assumed that readers will use computers to calculate statistics; the following formulas are provided only to enhance conceptual understanding.

PRE: The Strength of Relationships

Proportional reduction in error (PRE) is defined as the improvement, expressed as a fraction, in predicting a dependent variable due to knowledge of the independent variable. Frequently analysts want to know with how much certainty the knowledge of one variable can be used to predict another variable. For example, we may know that receiving welfare is statistically associated with having a low income, but to what extent is having a low income a good predictor of receiving welfare? If we know that a subject has low income, how certain can we be that that subject also receives welfare? PRE is used as a measure of the *strength of a relationship* between two variables, that is, the extent to which one variable is a good predictor of the other.

PRE can be calculated in several ways. The following example is purely illustrative because, in practice, computers are used. Assume that in a sample of 160 people, 90 people are not on welfare and 70 are on welfare (Table 11.1). If we guess that each person is not on welfare, we will be wrong 70 times. If we guess that each person is on welfare, we will be wrong 90 times. Hence, the mode (the most frequent category) is our best guess, because it results in fewer wrong guesses. However, when the level of income is also

Table 11.1 ⎯⎯⎯⎯⎯⎯⎯∿∿⎯ Welfare and Income

Receiving welfare	Income		Total
	Low	High	
No	40	50	90
Yes	60	10	70
Total	100	60	160

known, as well as the number of welfare recipients at each level of income, we make even fewer wrong guesses (or errors). If we know that welfare program participants have low income, we make 40 errors when we guess that everyone with low income in the sample receives welfare. Likewise, if we guess that the people with high income are not on welfare, we make 10 wrong guesses. Thus, the total number of mistakes when taking income into account is now 50, slightly less than the earlier 70 wrong guesses. The proportional reduction in errors (wrong guesses) can be defined as follows:

$$\frac{\text{Errors without knowledge of the independent variable} - \text{Errors with knowledge of the independent variable}}{\text{Errors without knowledge of the independent variable}}$$

> **Key Point**
>
> PRE is a measure of the strength of a relationship. Its value ranges from 0 to 1.

Applying this equation to our example, we find a PRE of $[(70 - 50)/70 =]$ 0.2857, or 28.6 percent, with rounding. In other words, as a result of knowing respondents' incomes, we are able to improve our guesses of their welfare situation by 28.6 percent.

PRE fractions range from 0.00 (no association or improvement in prediction) to 1.00 (perfect association or prediction). Although there are no absolute standards for PRE scores, many analysts regard scores of less than 0.25 as indicating a weak association, scores between 0.25 and 0.50 as indicating a moderate association, and scores above 0.50 as indicating a strong association. Thus, our calculated value of 28.6 percent is said to indicate a *moderate* association between these two variables.[1]

Paired Cases: The Direction of Relationships

Analysts often want to know the ***direction of a relationship***. For example, public managers may know that student participation in anger management classes is significantly associated with classroom violence, but is the association positive or negative? Teachers may hope that the relationship is statistically significant and negative, that is, that increased participation decreases violence (but then, who knows what students learn and apply?). Some methods for calculating PRE use an approach based on the concept of **paired cases**. This method distinguishes among similar, dissimilar, and tied pairs and is used to determine the direction of relationships. *Similar pairs* are pairs of observations that rank similarly low (or high) on both variables: both observations score high or low on both variables. *Dissimilar pairs* are pairs of observations that have reverse ranking on two variables—one observation scores high and the other low, and vice versa, on both variables. *Tied pairs* are those that rank similar on one variable and dissimilar on the other variable. The direction of relationships is determined by comparing the number of similar pairs against the number of dissimilar pairs. When there are more similar pairs than dissimilar pairs, the relationship is said to be positive. When there are more dissimilar pairs than similar pairs, the relationship is negative.[2]

Computers calculate the number of similar, dissimilar, and tied pairs, of course. For illustrative purposes, the number of similar pairs in Table 11.1 is calculated as 40*10 = 400. The number of dissimilar pairs is [50*60 =] 3,000. The number of tied pairs on "receiving welfare" is [40*50 + 60*10 =] 2,600, and the number of tied pairs on "income" is [40*60 + 50*10 =] 2,900. When the table is organized to show causal relationships, the number of tied pairs on "receiving welfare" is also called "the number of tied pairs on the dependent variable" (Ty), and the number of tied pairs on "income" is called "the number of tied pairs on the independent variable" (Tx). The calculations for larger tables follow the same logic but are more complex.[3]

Different statistics, discussed later in this chapter, make different uses of similar, dissimilar, and tied pairs in calculating PRE and the direction of relationships. However, all statistics have the following expression in their numerators: (number of similar pairs) − (number of dissimilar pairs). Hence, a positive value indicates a positive relationship between the variables, and a negative value indicates a negative relationship between the variables. In our example, the expression is negative (400 − 3,000), indicating a negative relationship between income and welfare. PRE statistics based on paired cases have a range of −1.00 to +1.00, which also provides information about the strength of the relationship. For example, a PRE test statistic based on paired cases with a value of −0.57 indicates a strong, negative relationship between two variables.

Dependent Samples

So far, the examples used in the text have involved independent samples. *Independent samples* are those in which the selection of one group (or sample) of subjects has no effect on the selection or responses of the other group (or sample) of subjects. For example, in a random sample of male and female employees, the selection of male employees has no effect on the selection of female employees, nor does it affect their responses. The sample thus consists of independent observations. *Dependent samples* (also called *related* samples) are those in which the selection of one subject in a sample does affect the selection of subjects in another group. For example, in before-and-after experiments, measures of subjects are taken at two points in time; those who belong to the first group necessarily also belong to the second group. The samples are thus necessarily linked though the same subjects. Moreover, the two measurements of each subject (before and after) are tied (or related) together; they are not independent observations. Such linkage violates the assumptions of many statistical tests that require independent samples.

Separate statistical tests exist for dependent samples. By convention, the following three situations constitute dependent samples: (1) the before-and-after test scores of subjects in (quasi-) experimental situations (including other repeated measures of subjects), (2) subjects who have been matched (or paired, that is, chosen as having similar characteristics), and (3) the ratings of evaluators. Matched subjects are necessarily linked across groups. When a group of evaluators rates the same set of items, the ratings of each item by different evaluators are regarded as repeated measures. Generally, *samples are assumed to be independent, except when the preceding scenarios are present, or when samples are necessarily correlated for other reasons.*[4] This chapter discusses, a bit later, some tests for dependent samples.

PRE ALTERNATIVES TO CHI-SQUARE

At the end of Chapter 10, we introduced Kendall's tau-c as an alternative to chi-square. We can now extend that conversation.

Data analysis often involves two ordinal variables, such as when citizen and client survey questions use five- or seven-point Likert scales. In analyses of relationships among two ordinal-level variables, four frequently calculated PRE-based statistics are *gamma* (γ), *Somers' d,* **Kendall's tau-b** (τ_b)**,** and **Kendall's tau-c** (τ_c). These statistics differ chiefly in the manner in which ties are taken into account, resulting in different estimates of PRE. Of these tests, tau-c is typically most conservative in estimating PRE and is therefore used widely.

Examination of the formulas for these statistics provides a sense of the differences. The following discussion is for illustrative purposes only, as computers calculate the statistics, of course. **Gamma** is defined as $(Ns - Nd)/(Ns + Nd)$, where Ns is the number of similar pairs and Nd is the number of dissimilar pairs. Gamma does not take tied pairs into account. By contrast, **Somers' d** is defined as $(Ns - Nd)/(Ns + Nd + Ty)$, where Ty represents ties on the dependent variable. Because Ty is in the denominator, the value of Somers' d is less than gamma γ; thus Somers' d is a more conservative estimate of the PRE. Somers' d is a **directional measure**, which means that the value of Somers' d depends on which variable is identified as the dependent variable; statistical software programs compute Somers' d for both possibilities. Tau-b is defined as $(Ns - Nd)/\sqrt{(Ns + Nd + Ty)(Ns + Nd + Tx)}$. It is symmetrical (that is, it does not depend on which variable is identified as dependent)[5] and is even more conservative than Somers' d. However, tau-b is appropriate only for square tables, which is an important limitation. Tau-c is developed from tau-b and is designed for nonsquare tables.[6] It is defined as $2m(Ns - Nd)/N^2(m - 1)$, where m is the smaller number of rows or columns, and N is the sample size. Tau-c makes an adjustment for the number of cases, as well as rows or columns, rather than for the number of pairs. These adjustments result in even more conservative estimates.

> **Key Point**
>
> Kendall's tau-c states the strength, direction, and significance of a relationship. It is widely used.

Computer programs provide a range of statistics in part because, depending on the unique features of one's data, the above generalizations may not always hold up. In some cases, the value of Somers' d may be less than that of tau-c, for example. Also, some analysts prefer the conceptual clarity of gamma, which does not make adjustments for ties. Nonetheless, Kendall's tau-c is widely used and reported as an alternative to chi-square for ordinal-level data; it is among the most conservative estimates, and many scientists have become familiar with it.[7] Also, unlike chi-square, these measures do not make assumptions about the number of expected frequencies, which further increases their ease of use.[8]

The use of these measures of association is shown in the following example. A human resources manager wants to know whether perceptions of the county as an employer are associated with feelings of fairness, especially in the area of work rewards. An employee survey is administered. The lead-in question is this: "Please evaluate the following statements by indicating whether you strongly agree, agree, disagree, or strongly disagree with the following statements. You may also state that you don't know." Two items are "I am satisfied with my job in Seminole County" and "The people who get promoted are the best qualified for the job." The results are shown in Table 11.2.

Table 11.2 ———〜〜— Comparing Ordinal-Ordinal PRE Measures of Association

Statistic		Value	Approx. sig.
Chi-square		253.17	0.000
Somer's d	Symmetric	0.323	0.000
	Dep = job satisf.	0.285	0.000
	Dep = promoted	0.372	0.000
Gamma		0.470	0.000
Kendall's tau-b		0.326	0.000
Kendall's tau-c		0.275	0.000

Note: Dep = dependent variables; sig. = significance.

The results show that job satisfaction is *significantly, moderately,* and *positively* associated with this measure of fairness for each of the test statistics. Table 11.2 also shows that tau-c has indeed the smallest PRE value and that all statistics are evaluated at the same level of statistical significance. A contingency table can be examined to determine practical significance (not shown here). Among employees who agree or strongly agree that the best people get promoted, 93.3 percent also agree or strongly agree that they are satisfied with their jobs; by comparison, only 69.1 percent of employees who disagree or strongly disagree that the best people get promoted also agree that they are satisfied with their jobs. Disagreeing that the best people get promoted also increases job *dis*satisfaction: 35.4 percent of employees who disagree or strongly disagree that the best people get promoted are dissatisfied with their jobs, as compared with only 3.2 percent of employees who agree or strongly agree that the best people get promoted.

When two variables are *nominal* level, **Goodman and Kruskal's tau** (τ_{yx}) is a test statistic with PRE interpretation. See Table 11.3 for an example of its use. Perhaps the analyst wants to know whether skill type affects job type, or vice versa. Because Goodman and Kruskal's tau is a directional measure, statistical software packages produce two measures of Goodman and Kruskal's tau that vary according to which variable is designated as the dependent variable. Goodman and Kruskal's tau is always positive (the question of direction is moot for nominal variables). For the data shown in Table 11.3, Goodman and Kruskal's tau is 0.016 (p = .579 > .05) when "job" is the dependent variable and 0.016 (p = .584 > .05) when "skills" is the dependent variable. Thus, the relationship between these two variables is not significant. The accompanying footnote discusses some other nominal-level measures that, though used less often, are provided by statistical software programs.[9]

Getting Started

Collect data for two ordinal-level variables, and calculate tau-c on a computer.

Table 11.3 ────〜〜── Job Applied For by Skills of Recipient

Job	Skills of welfare recipient			Total
	Word processing skills	Public speaking	Spread-sheets	
Clerk	14	5	10	29
Office assistant	15	10	20	45
Messenger	5	5	5	15
Total	34	20	35	89

BEATING THE STANDARD? THE GOODNESS-OF-FIT TEST

We now examine some tests for dealing with diverse situations that managers and analysts may encounter. For example, managers and analysts sometimes need to know whether a program or policy exceeds a standard or norm. The chi-square test discussed in Chapter 10 can also be adapted for this purpose. Assume we test 400 cars and find a 6 percent failure rate. Is that any different from a norm of 8 percent? You can readily think of other applications. For example, we might compare students who pass a test versus a stated norm, or clients who succeed in a treatment against a stated norm. We might look at water samples, housing, or anything else against a stated norm.

Regarding the chi-square test, program or policy outcomes are seen as observed frequencies, and the norm is used for calculating expected frequencies. Then we can examine whether a relationship exists between these variables. Such a test is a ***goodness-of-fit test***, a test of whether one distribution is similar to another. The two distributions for the cars example are shown in Table 11.4. The left data column shows the actual frequencies, and the right column shows the expected frequencies that would exist if the actual distribution was exactly consistent with the norm. Specifically, the actual frequencies are [0.06*400 =] 24 failed cars and [0.94*400 =] 376 passed cars. The expected frequencies are [0.08*400 =] 32 failed cars and [0.92*400 =] 368 passed cars. This definition and method of calculating expected frequencies is quite different from the test shown in Chapter 10.

The null hypothesis is that the two distributions are similar, and the alternate hypothesis is that they are dissimilar. Using the chi-square formula, $\Sigma(O_i - E_i)^2/E_i$, we calculate chi-square as $(24 - 32)^2/32 = 2.000$ for the failed category and as $(376 - 368)^2/368 = 0.174$ for the passed category. Thus, the chi-square test statistic is [2.000 + 0.174 =] 2.174. The degrees of freedom for this test is defined as the number of rows (r) minus 1, or [2 − 1 =] 1. From Appendix B, the chi-square critical value at the 5 percent level and df = 1 is 3.841. Because the test statistic is less than the critical value, |t.s.| < c.v., we fail to reject the null hypothesis. Hence, we conclude that the failure rate is *not different* from the prespecified norm of 8 percent. The failure rate is neither higher nor lower than the standard; it meets the standard.

Table 11.4 ⎯⎯⎯⎯⎯⎯⎯⎯ ᴧᴧ⎯ Test Failure Rates

	Actual (observed)	Norm (expected)
Passed	376	368
Failed	24	32

The above example can be expanded by considering more than just two response categories such as pass or fail. Assume that we just completed a citizen survey yielding 1,034 valid responses. We next want to know whether the age distribution of these respondents is consistent with that of the U.S. Census for the area. The lack of consistency may suggest problems of under- or over-sampling and, thus, possible bias that we might want to know about. Hence,

H_0: The age distribution of the sample is consistent with that of the population.

H_A: The age distribution of the sample is inconsistent with that of the population.

The results are shown in Table 11.5. Here, the census population frequencies are the expected frequencies, and the sample frequencies are the observed frequencies. With 1,034 completed survey responses, the expected frequency of the 18–45 age category is [1,034*0.623 =] 644. The expected frequencies of the other two categories are, respectively, [1,034*0.241 =] 249 and [1,034*0.136 =] 141; similarly, the observed (actual) frequencies are 649, 277, and 108. Using the usual chi-square formula, we find that the chi-square value for the first category (age 18–45) is [(649 – 644)^2/644 =] 0.039. The values for the second and third categories are calculated similarly and are, respectively, 3.149 and 7.723. Thus, the chi-square test statistic is 10.91 (with rounding). The number of degrees of freedom is $r - 1$, or [3 – 1 =] 2. The critical value at the 5 percent level of significance with df = 2 is 5.991 (see Appendix B); thus we conclude that the sample *is significantly different* from the population. Note that if the sample had consisted of only 300 completed responses, then the chi-square would have been 3.16, which is not significant.

Further inspection of Table 11.5 suggests that the researchers under-sampled older respondents and that they thus may want to reweight their findings to examine the effect, if any, of this undersampling on their conclusions. Note also that these calculations can be used to determine the number of surveys among those 66 years and older that should have been collected in order to avoid this problem. Perhaps researchers can continue surveying

Table 11.5 ⎯⎯⎯⎯ᴧᴧ⎯⎯ U.S. Census Response by Age Groups

Age	U.S. Census (%)	Survey sample (%)
18–45	62.3	62.8
46–65	24.1	26.8
66+	13.6	10.4

among that group. You can verify, by redoing the preceding calculations (using a spreadsheet), that completing another 12 surveys among the 66+ group (increasing the sample size to 1,046) reduces the chi-square test statistic to 5.955, which provides a sample that no longer is significantly different from that of the population.

DISCRIMINATION AND OTHER TESTS

Managers face a rather different kind of problem when they want to test for discrimination. In a typical scenario, assume that we want to test whether program staff is discriminating against minority clients by failing to provide them with services that are provided to other, white clients. To examine this possibility, we match up pairs of minority and white clients; each pair has similar equivalent conditions and are trained to provide similar responses to questions. Their main difference is race. This strategy is also used for testing discrimination in employment interviews or in bank lending practices. Pairs of majority and minority job (or loan) seekers are sent to interviews (or to apply for loans), intermingled with other candidates.

This scenario involves a *dependent sample* because the responses are linked to matched subjects. This scenario is also interesting in that we want to examine whether a pattern exists among dissimilar outcomes, only. The **McNemar test** determines the level at which dissimilar outcomes are statistically significant. For example, consider Table 11.6, in which each count compares the employment outcomes of the paired testers. The McNemar test compares whether the eight instances in which a white but not minority applicant received a job are significantly different from the one instance in which the minority candidate, not the white one, received the job. The test for these data is significant ($p = .039 < .05$), which means that this disparate outcome cannot be attributed to chance alone. The McNemar test ignores similar outcomes; thus, the same test result is obtained by examining the nine dissimilar outcomes, only. It ignores similar outcomes in which both testers are hired, such as when employers hire multiple candidates through the same interview process.[10]

The McNemar test is an example of a test designed for small samples (that is, those with small frequency counts). For *independent samples,* a variety of small-sample tests exists, often adaptations of chi-square. Although chi-square and Goodman and Kruskal's tau can be used for two-by-two tables with independent observations, some researchers argue that when analysts have small samples they should use **chi-square with the Yates' continuity correction**. Small samples bias the expected frequencies slightly upward; this bias is "corrected" by subtracting 0.50 from the difference of expected and observed frequencies, thus producing a more conservative test

Table 11.6 ⎯⎯⎯ᴧ√⎯ Employment Discrimination Test

| | White applicants | | |
Minority applicants	Hired	Not hired	Total
Hired	0	1	1
Not hired	8	2	10
Total	8	3	11

statistic. However, others argue that this correction overcorrects.[11] The *Fisher exact test* is used for two-by-two tables with small samples. It compares the observed table with all other possible tables that have the same marginal counts (that is, row and column totals). Based on this comparison, the test calculates the probability that the two variables are related.[12]

As an example, consider the following scenario. You are a senior staff member at a drug treatment center. Drop-out (discontinuation) rates among those undergoing treatment is an important problem. One of your contractors has proposed a new method that promises to reduce discontinuation. To test whether the system works, you implement it among a small sample of clients and want to compare the results with those who get the traditional method. The analytical task is clearly to align this problem with some method of statistical testing. Consider the outline of Table 11.7 as a way of structuring this problem. The right column shows clients using the new system; the left column shows outcomes among clients using the traditional treatment. Designed in this way, these are independent samples, and we can use tests that are appropriate for two-by-two tables and involve small samples. Note that although Table 11.7 appears similar to Table 11.6, this treatment scenario does not involve a dependent sample, nor are we interested in comparing only dissimilar outcomes.

Assume that the initial results are as shown in Table 11.7, which indicates that discontinuation decreased from [8/15 =] 53.3 percent to [5/15 =] 33.3 percent. Is this sufficient evidence to conclude that the decrease is statistically significant? The Goodman and Kruskal's tau test statistic for this test is 0.41 (p = .277), chi-square with continuity correction is 0.543 (df = 1, p = .461), and the Fisher exact test shows p = .462. Thus, the decrease is *not*

Table 11.7 ⎯⎯⎯ᴧ√⎯ New Treatment Test Results

| | Uses new treatment system | |
	No	Yes
No discontinuation	7	10
Discontinuation	8	5

statistically significant. Is this a problem for the manager or consultant? Probably not. Although we can ask how large the decrease has to be for it to be statistically significant,[13] a better managerial response is to acknowledge the decrease as "sizable" and ask how many more clients have to be involved for the difference as shown to be statistically significant. To this end, the raw data used to generate this table can readily be multiplied (copied and pasted) in statistical software programs, and we then conclude that about a fourfold increase, to 60 clients in each group, will show statistically significant results for these differences.[14] Then, Goodman and Kruskal's tau is 0.41 (p = .028), chi-square with continuity correction is 4.11 (df = 1, p = .043), and the Fisher exact test shows p = .042. Hence, the managerial response is thus to continue the alternative method, getting therapists' assessment and input into the new treatment; closely monitor continuation rates; and then reassess the alternative intervention for statistical evidence at a later date after more clients have been involved.

DO THE EVALUATORS AGREE?

Evaluators often are used to assess program or agency performance by providing qualitative judgments. ***Kruskal-Wallis' H test*** assesses whether programs differ in their ratings. Assume that 15 evaluators are each asked to evaluate one of three programs, and an index score is constructed of their evaluations. This is a test for *independent samples*; each evaluator evaluates only one program. The null hypothesis is that, on average, each program receives the same average ranking. The data are shown in Table 11.8 (for presentation, the variables are in separate columns; these data are entered in statistical software programs as one table with 15 observations and two variables). The group variable identifies the program. Note that the rating variable is shown as a continuous variable. Kruskal-Wallis' H assigns ranks to the rating variable, thus creating an ordinal variable from the continuous variable. Specifically, it does so by ranking the collective observations of all groups

Table 11.8 ——— ⋀⋀⋀— Ratings of Three Programs

Group	Rating	Rank	Group	Rating	Rank	Group	Rating	Rank
1	2.5	3	2	3.4	7.5	3	4.8	13
1	2.9	4	2	3.3	6	3	5.0	14.5
1	4.0	10.5	2	4.0	10.5	3	5.0	14.5
1	3.2	5	2	3.9	9	3	3.4	7.5
1	1.2	1	2	2.1	2	3	4.2	12
Mean		4.7			7.0			12.3

Table 11.9 ⎯⎯⎯⎯~~⎯⎯ Actual Ratings of Three Evaluators

Item	Rater 1	Rater 2	Rater 3
1	5	3	4
2	4	2	2
3	3	3	3
4	2	4	3
5	1	1	1

Table 11.10 ⎯⎯⎯⎯~~⎯⎯ Relative Ratings of Three Evaluators

Item	Rater 1	Rater 2	Rater 3
1	3	1	2
2	3	1.5	1.5
3	2	2	2
4	1	3	2
5	2	2	2
Mean rank	2.2	1.9	1.9

from high to low and then testing whether the means of the ranks of the groups are significantly different. Kruskal-Wallis' H has a chi-square distribution. The H test statistic for the data in Table 11.8 is 7.636 (df = 2, p = .022 < .05).[15] That is, the three programs vary in their mean ranking of evaluation scores. Information provided with this result shows that the mean rankings are, respectively, 4.70, 7.00, and 12.30.

Samples that involve evaluators often are dependent, however. Typically, a few evaluators assess different program items, and we want to know whether evaluators agree in their ratings. This occurs in program reviews, when outside experts assess programs or facilities such as hospitals or parks departments in connection with accreditation. It also occurs in regulatory inspections (do two or more inspectors or assessors agree?) and in the evaluations of trained observers. By convention, we assume that ratings are necessarily correlated because raters are typically consistent in their ratings. The data must be ordinal. The **_Friedman test_**, developed by the well-known economist Milton Friedman, uses data in the format shown in Tables 11.9 and 11.10 and has a chi-square distribution. The Friedman test ranks the evaluations of the three raters for each item (5 = highest). Table 11.9 shows that rater 1 has the highest ranking of item 1. The relative ranking of item 1 across the three raters is 3, 1, and 2 (Table 11.10) because rater 1 gives item 1 a higher rating than rater 3, who, in turn, gives item 1 a higher rating than rater 2. The ratings for item 2 are tied between the second and third raters.

The ranked ratings for item 2 are 3.00, [(1 + 2)/2 =] 1.50, and 1.50. The ranked ratings for item 3 are 2.00, 2.00, and 2.00 (they are all tied), and so on. Based on these rankings, the mean ranked ratings for each evaluator are determined, as shown in Table 11.10. The Friedman test statistic for these data is 0.545 (df = 2, p = .761 > .05). Thus, we conclude that the ratings of the evaluators are not different; *the evaluators agree with each other.* When columns and rows are reversed, the Friedman test assesses whether differences exist among the mean rankings of items. This test can also be used to examine test score changes in before-and-after situations. Then, the rows are subjects and the columns are the subjects' before-and-after scores.[16]

> **Getting Started**
>
> Discuss how these statistics can be used in your area of interest.

SUMMARY

Analysts are frequently confronted with categorical data. For example, many surveys (of employees, citizens, or program clients) involve categorical data, such as gender or income (when measured in brackets). Surveys also involve ordinal assessments, such as the extent to which respondents agree or disagree with certain statements. To analyze the extent and manner in which two variables are related to each other, analysts often use the PRE and nonparametric statistics discussed in this chapter. PRE-based statistics provide information about the statistical significance of relationships, as well as their strength and direction and are thus preferred to chi-square for testing relationships of categorical variables. Nonparametric statistics are used for rather special situations, such as comparing the ratings of two evaluators, significance testing that involves very small samples, and dependent samples (samples in which observations are correlated).

A plethora of PRE and nonparametric statistics exists. It would be a true challenge to memorize all the statistics discussed in this chapter. Rather, the task is to be familiar with the types of problems they address. Recognizing particular situations and problems will help analysts to know when to use each test. As bewildering as the array of tests might seem, clearly, the tests themselves are not particularly difficult to use. Indeed, they are rather straightforward:

- When both variables are ordinal, Kendall's tau-c is a commonly used PRE statistic for testing the significance, strength, and direction of the relationship between these two variables.
- When both variables are nominal, Goodman and Kruskal's tau is a PRE statistic used for testing the significance and strength of the relationship.

- When the sample is very small, statistics specifically designed for that purpose are used, such as the Fisher exact test.
- When a test of discrimination is needed, the McNemar test is used.
- When one variable is ordinal and the other is nominal, the scenario may involve a comparison of evaluators' rankings. Then, Kruskal-Wallis' H is used for independent samples, and the Friedman test is used for dependent samples.

This short list is an important resource for you as you learn to identify the particular situations that warrant the use of specific tests.

KEY TERMS

Chi-square with the Yates'
    continuity correction (p. 197)
Dependent samples (p. 191)
Direction of a relationship (p. 190)
Directional measure (p. 192)
Fisher exact test (p. 198)
Friedman test (p. 200)
Gamma (p. 192)
Goodman and Kruskal's tau (p. 194)
Goodness-of-fit test (p. 195)

Independent samples (p. 191)
Kendall's tau-b (p. 192)
Kendall's tau-c (p. 192)
Kruskal-Wallis' H test (p. 199)
McNemar test (p. 197)
Paired cases (p. 190)
Proportional reduction in error
    (PRE) (p. 189)
Somers' d (p. 192)
Strength of a relationship (p. 189)

Notes

1. Some authors suggest that values below 0.20 indicate weak relationships; between 0.20 and 0.40, moderate relationships; between 0.40 and 0.60, strong relationships; and above 0.60, very strong relationships. We suggest erring on the side of caution and thus using a higher standard.
2. This extends the earlier discussion about Table 8.5.
3. For example, see Chava Frankfort-Nachmias, *Social Statistics for a Diverse Society,* 2nd ed. (Thousand Oaks, Calif.: Pine Forge Press, 1999), chap. 7. Many books provide similar calculations. The example is provided for conceptual understanding only; the computer calculates test statistics.
4. Independent observations are also called independent samples, and dependent samples are also called paired or matched observations. The concept of paired observations should not be confused with that of paired cases, discussed as part of PRE.
5. Gamma, tau-b, and tau-c are symmetrical measures; only Somers' d is directional.

6. Although tau-c is designed for nonsquare tables, many scientists use tau-c for tables of any size. This reflects a bias toward more conservative estimates, and the fact that p-values of tau-b and tau-c are identical.

7. Tau-c can also be used when one variable is ordinal and the other is continuous, or when one variable is ordinal and the other dichotomous. When used with continuous variables, the estimates of tau-c may result in somewhat higher p-values, relative to statistics discussed in later chapters. For mixed ordinal-nominal data, analysts can consider the Mann-Whitney test described in Chapter 12, or the Friedman and Kruskal-Wallis' tests, discussed later in this chapter.

8. In addition to the statistics discussed here, many computer programs will produce additional measures of chi-square, but these often have little additional utility. The linear-by-linear association is the square of the Pearson's drop-out (discontinuation) rate correlation coefficient (see Chapter 14), multiplied by the sample size, minus one. The likelihood ratio is used for n-way tables, in which a third variable is added to the contingency table. See B.G. Tabachnick and L.S. Fidell, *Using Multivariate Statistics,* 3rd ed. (New York: HarperCollins), chap. 7.

9. SPSS produces a large range of statistics for nominal variables. Lambda is calculated using the PRE formula provided in the text. However, this results in a computational quirk that limits its usefulness; the value of lambda is zero when all of the category modes of the independent variable occur on the same category of the dependent variable, regardless of any association that may exist. Goodman and Kruskal's tau overcomes this computational problem by calculating association in a different way. Cramer's V is a chi-square-based measure that is corrected for the problem that χ^2 increases with sample size the number of cells. Cramer's V ranges from zero (no association) to one (perfect association) and is defined as

$$\sqrt{\frac{X^2}{n^* \, (rows - 1, \, columns - 1)}}.$$

Although not calculated as a PRE statistic, Cramer's V values below 0.25 are considered to indicate weak relationships, values between 0.25 and 0.50 to indicate moderate relationships, and values over 0.50 to indicate strong relationships. Many computer programs also produce the contingency coefficient, C (also called Pearson's coefficient of contingency), which is calculated as

$$\sqrt{X^2 / (X^2 + n)}.$$

C is calculated similar to V but has the disadvantage that its maximum value can be less than 1.0. Cramer's V overcomes this problem and is thus preferred. The uncertainty coefficient, U, is a measure that is quite similar to lambda and does not offer many advantages in this context. A formula for this statistic can be found in R.A. Cooper and A.J. Weeks, *Data, Models, and Statistics Analysis* (Oxford: Philip Allan, 1983), and other general statistics books.

10. The McNemar test statistic is defined as $\chi^2_{McNemar} = (|f_{0,1} - f_{1,0}|)^2/(f_{0,1} + f_{1,0})$.
11. The chi-square statistic with Yates' continuity correction is defined as

$$\sum_i \frac{(|O_i - E_i| - 0.5)^2}{E_i}.$$

12. The following measures may also be considered. Phi (ϕ) is defined as $\sqrt{\chi^2/n}$, and ranges from zero to one for two-by-k tables ($k \geq 2$). Phi-squared (ϕ^2) has a "variance-explained" interpretation; for example, a ϕ^2 value of 0.35 (or $\phi = 0.59$) means that 35 percent of the variance in one variable is explained by the other. Yule's Q is a measure of association with a PRE interpretation but without a test of statistical significance. Yule's Q is defined as follows. Assume the following two-by-two table:

A	B
C	D

Then, Yule's Q is $\frac{(AD) - (BC)}{(AD) + (BC)}$.

13. With the sample sizes of Table 11.7, the discontinuation rate of the alternative treatment would have to drop further to 13.3 percent (2 of 15 clients). Then, Goodman and Kruskal's tau is .180 (p = .022), chi-square with continuity correction is 3.750 (p = .53), and the Fisher exact test shows p = .50.
14. Another approach is to calculate power (see Box 10.2). Using the above continuation rates and $n = 60$ for each group, we find power to be 71.8 percent, which is indeed close to 80 percent.
15. The formula for H is

$$\frac{12}{n(n+1)}\left(\frac{T_2^2}{n_1} + \frac{T_1^2}{n_1} + \dots\right) - 3(n+1),$$

where T_i is the sum of ranks in group 1, and so on.
16. The Friedman test is quite sensitive to the number of items; it is best to have at least 10 rows.

CHAPTER

12

The T-Test

CHAPTER OBJECTIVES

After reading this chapter, you should be able to

- Test whether two or more groups have different means of a continuous variable
- Assess whether the mean is consistent with a specified value
- Evaluate whether variables meet test assumptions
- Understand the role of variable transformations
- Identify t-test alternatives

When analysts need to compare the means of a continuous variable across different groups, they have a valuable tool at their disposal: the t-test. T-tests are used for testing whether two groups have different means of a continuous variable, such as when we want to know whether mean incomes vary between men and women. They could also be used to compare program performance between two periods, when performance in each period is measured as a continuous variable.

The examples in this chapter differ from those in Chapters 10 and 11 in that in this chapter's examples one of the variables is continuous and the other is categorical. Many variables are continuous, such as income, age, height, case loads, service calls, and counts of fish in a pond. Moreover, when ordinal-level variables are used for constructing index variables (see Chapter 3), the resulting index variables typically are continuous as well. When variables are continuous, we should not recode them as categorical variables just to use the techniques of the previous chapters. Continuous variables provide valuable information about distances between categories and often have a broader range of values than ordinal variables. Recoding continuous variables as categorical variables is discouraged because it results in a loss of information; we should use tests such as the t-test.

Statistics involving continuous variables usually require more test assumptions. Many of these tests are referred to as *parametric statistics;* this term refers to the fact that they make assumptions about the distribution of data and also that they are used to make inferences about population parameters. Formally, the term *parametric* means that a test makes assumptions about the distribution of the underlying population. Parametric tests have more test assumptions than nonparametric tests, most typically that the variable is continuous and normally distributed (see Chapter 7). These and other test assumptions are also part of t-tests.

This chapter focuses on three common t-tests: for independent samples, for dependent (paired) samples, and the one-sample t-test. For each, we provide examples and discuss test assumptions.

This chapter also discusses nonparametric alternatives to t-tests, which analysts will want to consider when t-test assumptions cannot be met for their variables. As a general rule, a bias exists toward using parametric tests because they are more powerful than nonparametric tests. Nonparametric alternatives to parametric tests often transform continuous testing variables into other types of variables, such as rankings, which reduces information about them. Although nonparametric statistics are easier to use because they have fewer assumptions, parametric tests are more likely to find statistical evidence that two variables are associated; their tests often have lower p-values than nonparametric statistics.[1]

T-TESTS FOR INDEPENDENT SAMPLES

T-tests are used to test whether the means of a continuous variable differ across two different groups. For example, do men and women differ in their levels of income, when measured as a continuous variable? Does crime vary between two parts of town? Do rich people live longer than poor people? Do high-performing students commit fewer acts of violence than do low-performing students? The t-test approach is shown graphically in Figure 12.1, which illustrates the incomes of men and women as boxplots (the lines in the middle of the boxes indicate the means rather than the medians).[2]

When the two groups are independent samples, the t-test is called the ***independent-samples t-test***. Sometimes the continuous variable is called a "test variable" and the dichotomous variable is called a "grouping variable." The t-test tests whether the *difference of the means* ($\Delta \bar{x}$, or $\bar{x}_1 - \bar{x}_2$) *is significantly different from zero*, that is, whether men and women have different incomes. The following hypotheses are posited:

H_0: Men and women do not have different mean incomes (in the population).

H_A: Men and women do have different mean incomes (in the population).

Alternatively, using the Greek letter μ to refer to differences in the population, H_0: $\mu_m = \mu_f$ and H_A: $\mu_m \neq \mu_f$. The formula for calculating the t-test test statistic (a tongue twister?) is

$$ t = \frac{\bar{x}_1 - \bar{x}_2}{\sqrt{s_p^2 \left(\frac{1}{n_1} + \frac{1}{n_2} \right)}} . $$

As always, the computer calculates the test statistic and reports at what level it is significant. Such calculations are seldom done by hand. To further conceptual understanding of this formula, it is useful to relate it to the discussion of hypothesis testing in Chapter 10. First, note that the difference of means, $\bar{x}_1 - \bar{x}_2$, appears in the numerator: the larger the difference of means, the larger the t-test test statistic, and the more likely we might reject the null hypothesis. Second, s_p is the pooled variance of the two groups, that is, the weighted average

Figure 12.1 ⎯⎯⎯⎯⎯⎯ The T-Test:
Mean Incomes by Gender

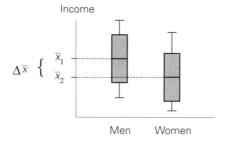

of the variances of each group.[3] Increases in the standard deviation decrease the test statistic. Thus, it is easier to reject the null hypotheses when two populations are clustered narrowly around their means than when they are spread widely around them. Finally, more observations (that is, increased information or larger n_1 and n_2) increase the size of the test statistic, making it easier to reject the null hypothesis.

The test statistics of a t-test can be positive or negative, although this depends merely on which group has the larger mean; the sign of the test statistic has no substantive interpretation. *Critical values* (see Chapter 10) of the t-test are shown in Appendix C as *(Student's) t-distribution*.[4] For this test, the *degrees of freedom* are defined as $n - 1$, where n is the total number of observations for both groups. The table is easy to use. As mentioned below, most tests are two-tailed tests, and analysts find critical values in the columns for the .05 (5 percent) and .01 (1 percent) levels of significance. For example, the critical value at the 1 percent level of significance for a test based on 25 observations ($df = 25 - 1 = 24$) is 2.797 (and 1.11 at the 5 percent level of significance). Though the table also shows critical values at other levels of significance, these are seldom if ever used. The table shows that the critical value decreases as the number of observations increases, making it easier to reject the null hypothesis.

The t-distribution shows one- and two-tailed tests. *Two-tailed t-tests* should be used when analysts do not have prior knowledge about which group has a larger mean; *one-tailed t-tests* are used when analysts do have such prior knowledge. This choice is dictated by the research situation, not by any statistical criterion. In practice, two-tailed tests are used most often, unless compelling a priori knowledge exists or it is known that one group cannot have a larger mean than the other. Two-tailed testing is more conservative than one-tailed testing because the critical values of two-tailed tests are larger, thus requiring larger t-test test statistics in order to reject the null hypothesis.[5] Many statistical software packages provide only two-tailed testing. The above null hypothesis (men and women do not have different mean incomes in the population) requires a two-tailed test because we do not know, a priori, which gender has the larger income.[6] Finally, note that the t-test distribution approximates the normal distribution for large samples: the critical values of 1.96 (5 percent significance) and 2.58 (1 percent significance), for large degrees of freedom (∞), are identical to those of the normal distribution.

> **Getting Started**
> Find examples of t-tests in the research literature.

T-Test Assumptions

Like other tests, the t-test has *test assumptions* that must be met to ensure test validity. Statistical testing always begins by determining whether test assumptions are met before examining the main research hypotheses. Although t-test assumptions are a bit involved, the popularity of the t-test rests partly on the robustness of t-test conclusions in the face of modest violations. This section provides an in-depth treatment of t-test assumptions, methods

Key Point
The t-test is fairly robust against assumption violations.

for testing the assumptions, and ways to address assumption violations. Of course, t-test statistics are calculated by the computer; thus, we focus on interpreting concepts (rather than their calculation).

Four **t-test test assumptions** must be met to ensure test validity:

- One variable is continuous, and the other variable is dichotomous.
- The two distributions have equal variances.
- The observations are independent.
- The two distributions are normally distributed.

The *first assumption,* that one variable is continuous and the other dichotomous, usually does not present much of a problem. Some analysts use t-tests with ordinal rather than continuous data for the testing variable. This approach is theoretically controversial because the distances among ordinal categories are undefined. This situation is avoided easily by using nonparametric alternatives (discussed later in this chapter). Also, when the grouping variable is not dichotomous, analysts need to make it so in order to perform a t-test. Many statistical software packages allow dichotomous variables to be created from other types of variables, such as by grouping or recoding ordinal or continuous variables.

The *second assumption* is that the variances of the two distributions are equal. This is called **homogeneity of variances**. The use of pooled variances in the earlier formula is justified only when the variances of the two groups are equal. When variances are unequal (called **heterogeneity of variances**), revised formulas are used to calculate t-test test statistics and degrees of freedom.[7] The difference between homogeneity and heterogeneity is shown graphically in Figure 12.2. Although we needn't be concerned with the precise differences in these calculation methods, all t-tests *first* test whether variances are equal in order to know which t-test test statistic is to be used for *subsequent* hypothesis testing. Thus, every t-test involves a (somewhat tricky) two-step procedure. A common test for the equality of variances is the **Levene's test**. The null hypothesis of this test is that variances are equal. Many statistical software programs provide the Levene's test along with the t-test, so that users know which t-test to use—the t-test for equal variances or that for unequal variances. The Levene's test is performed first, so that the correct t-test can be chosen.

Figure 12.2 ———— ⌇⌇ Equal and Unequal Variances

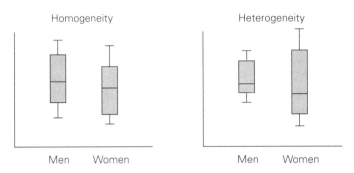

The term **robust** is used, generally, to describe the extent to which test conclusions are unaffected by departures from test assumptions. T-tests are relatively robust for (hence, unaffected by) departures from assumptions of homogeneity and normality (see below) when groups are of approximately equal size. When groups are of about equal size, test conclusions about any difference between their means will be unaffected by heterogeneity.

The *third assumption* is that observations are independent. (Quasi-) experimental research designs violate this assumption, as discussed in Chapter 11. The formula for the t-test test statistic, then, is modified to test whether the *difference* between before and after measurements is zero. This is called a *paired t-test,* which is discussed later in this chapter.

The *fourth assumption* is that the distributions are normally distributed. Although normality is an important test assumption, a key reason for the popularity of the t-test is that t-test conclusions often are robust against considerable violations of normality assumptions that are not caused by highly skewed distributions. We provide some detail about tests for normality and how to address departures thereof. Remember, when nonnormality cannot be resolved adequately, analysts consider nonparametric alternatives to the t-test, discussed at the end of this chapter. Box 12.1 provides a bit more discussion about the reason for this assumption.

A combination of visual inspection and statistical tests is always used to determine the normality of variables. Two tests of normality are the **Kolmogorov-Smirnov test** (also known as the K-S test) for samples with more than 50 observations and the **Shapiro-Wilk test** for samples with up to 50 observations. The **null hypothesis of normality** is that the variable *is* normally distributed: thus, we *do not* want to reject the null hypothesis. A problem with statistical tests of normality is that they are *very sensitive* to small samples and minor deviations from normality. The extreme sensitivity of these tests implies the following: whereas failure to reject the null

In Greater Depth . . .

Box 12.1 Why Normality?

The reasons for the normality assumption are twofold: First, the features of the normal distribution are well-established and are used in many parametric tests for making inferences and hypothesis testing. Second, probability theory suggests that random samples will often be normally distributed, and that the means of these samples can be used as estimates of population means.

The latter reason is informed by the *central limit theorem*, which states that an infinite number of relatively large samples will be normally distributed, regardless of the distribution of the population. An infinite number of samples is also called a sampling distribution. The central limit theorem is usually illustrated as follows. Assume that we know the population distribution, which has only six data elements with the following values: 1, 2, 3, 4, 5, or 6. Next, we write each of these six numbers on a separate sheet of paper, and draw repeated samples of three numbers each (that is, $n = 3$). We record the mean of each sample. Our first sample might consist of the numbers 2, 4, and 5; hence, we record the mean of $[(2 + 4 + 5)/3] = 3.67$. The next sample might be 1, 2, and 6, and so we then record the mean value 3.00. After we have taken about 30 or so samples (not quite an infinite number of samples, but getting there . . .), the histogram of recorded means will resemble a normal distribution with a mean of about 3.5. This number is also the population mean, namely, $[(1 + 2 + 3 + 4 + 5 + 6)/6] = 3.5$.

This theorem is important because it shows that we do not need to know the population distribution to estimate the mean of the population. Note that the population is not normally distributed; each value occurs just once, but the distribution of sample means is normally distributed. Further, although in practice we have only one sample, the central limit theorem states that we can use the normal distribution to create expectations about any sample mean. Our discussion of confidence intervals, in Chapter 7, demonstrates this point.

In short, parametric tests such as the t-test are based on these properties for their inferences and hypothesis testing and require variables to be normally distributed. Although nonparametric statistics do not require variables to be normally distributed, a bias exists toward using parametric tests because they are more powerful than nonparametric tests. Nonparametric alternatives to parametric tests often transform continuous testing variables into other types of variables, such as rankings, which reduces the information available about them.

hypo thesis indicates normal distribution of a variable, rejecting the null hypothesis does not indicate that the variable is not normally distributed. It is acceptable to consider variables as being normally distributed when they visually appear to be so, even when the null hypothesis of normality is rejected by normality tests. Of course, variables are preferred that are supported by both visual inspection and normality tests.

Remedies exist for correcting substantial departures from normality, but these remedies may make matters worse when departures from normality are minimal. The *first* course of action is to identify and remove any outliers that may affect the mean and standard deviation. The *second* course of action is **variable transformation**, which involves transforming the variable, often by taking $\log(x)$, $\sqrt{x}$, or x^2 of each observation, and then testing the transformed variable for normality. Variable transformation may address excessive skewness by adjusting the measurement scale, thereby helping variables to better approximate normality.[8] Substantively, we strongly prefer to make conclusions that satisfy test assumptions, regardless of which measurement scale is chosen.[9] Keep in mind that when variables are transformed, the units in which results are expressed are transformed, as well. An example of variable transformation is provided in the second working example.

Typically, analysts have different ways to address test violations. Examination of the causes of assumption violations often helps analysts to better understand their data. Different approaches may be successful for addressing test assumptions. Analysts should not merely go by the result of one approach that supports their case, ignoring others that perhaps do not. Rather, analysts should rely on the weight of robust, converging results to support their final test conclusions.

Working Example 1

Earlier we discussed efforts to reduce high school violence by enrolling violence-prone students into classes that address anger management. Now, after some time, administrators and managers want to know whether the program is effective. As part of this assessment, students are asked to report their perception of safety at school. An index variable is constructed from different items measuring safety (see Chapter 3). Each item is measured on a seven-point Likert scale (1 = strongly disagree to 7 = strongly agree), and the index is constructed such that a high value indicates that students feel safe.[10] The survey was initially administered at the beginning of the program. Now, almost a year later, the survey is implemented again.[11]

Administrators want to know whether students who did not participate in the anger management program feel that the climate is now safer. The analysis included here focuses on 10th graders. For practical purposes, the samples of 10th graders at the beginning of the program and one year later are regarded as independent samples; the subjects are not matched. Descriptive analysis shows that the mean perception of safety at the beginning of the program was 4.40 (standard deviation, *SD* = 1.00), and one year later, 4.80 (*SD* = 0.94). The mean safety score increased among 10th graders, but is the increase statistically significant? Among other concerns is that the standard deviations are considerable for both samples.

As part of the analysis, we conduct a t-test to answer the question of whether the means of these two distributions are significantly different. First, we examine whether test assumptions are met. The samples are independent, and the variables meet the requirement that one is continuous (the index variable) and the other dichotomous. The assumption of equality of variances is answered as part of conducting the t-test, and so the remaining question is whether the variables are normally distributed. The distributions are shown in the histograms in Figure 12.3.[12]

Are these normal distributions? Visually, they are not the textbook ideal—real-life data seldom are. The Kolmogorov-Smirnov tests for both distributions are insignificant (both p > .05). Hence, we conclude that the two distributions can be considered normal. Having satisfied these t-test assumptions, we next conduct the t-test for two independent samples. Table 12.1 shows the t-test results.

The top part of Table 12.1 shows the descriptive statistics, and the bottom part reports the test statistics. Recall that the t-test is a two-step test. We first test whether variances are equal. This is shown as the "Levene's test for equality of variances." The null hypothesis of the Levene's test is that

Figure 12.3 ⎯⎯⎯⎯⎯⎯⎯∿∿⎯ Perception of High School Safety among 10th Graders

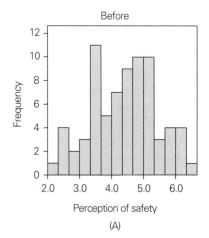
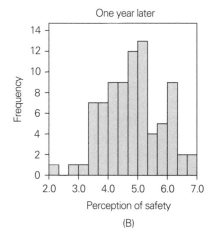

(A)   (B)

Table 12.1 ———〜〜— Independent-Samples T-Test: Output

Group statistics			
Group	**N**	**Mean**	**SD**
One year later	82	4.805	0.962
Before	74	4.399	1.008

	Step 1:				Step 2:		
	Levene's test for equality of variances				T-test for the equality of means		
Variable	**F**	**p**			**t**	**df**	**p (2-tailed)**
High school safety	0.177	0.675	Equal variances assumed		2.576	154	0.011
			Equal variances not assumed		2.570	150.57	0.011

Note: SD = standard deviation.

variances are equal; this is rejected when the p-value of this Levene's test statistic is less than .05. The Levene's test uses an F-test statistic (discussed in Chapters 13 and 15), which, other than its p-value, need not concern us here. In Table 12.1, the level of significance is .675, which exceeds .05. Hence, we accept the null hypothesis—the variances of the two distributions shown in Figure 12.3 are equal.

   Now we go to the second step, the main purpose. Are the two means (4.40 and 4.80) significantly different? Because the variances are equal, we read the t-test statistics from the top line, which states "equal variances assumed." (If variances had been unequal, then we would read the test statistics from the second line, "equal variances not assumed."). The t-test statistic for equal variances for this test is 2.576, which is significant at p = .011.[13] Thus, we conclude that the means are significantly different; the 10th graders report feeling safer one year after the anger management program was implemented.

Working Example 2

In the preceding example, the variables were both normally distributed, but this is not always the case. Many variables are highly skewed and not normally distributed. Consider another example. The U.S. Environmental Protection Agency (EPA) collects information about the water quality of watersheds, including information about the sources and nature of pollution. One such measure is the percentage of samples that exceed pollution limits for

Figure 12.4 ⎯⎯⎯⎯⎯⎯⎯⎯ Untransformed Variable: Watershed Pollution

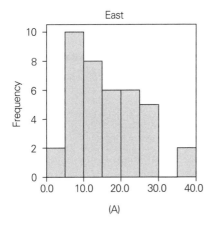
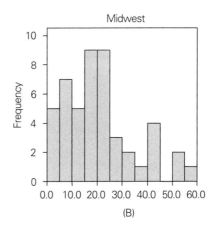

ammonia, dissolved oxygen, phosphorus, and pH.[14] A manager wants to know whether watersheds in the East have higher levels of pollution than those in the Midwest.

An index variable of such pollution is constructed. The index variable is called "pollution," and the first step is to examine it for test assumptions. Analysis indicates that the range of this variable has a low value of 0.00 percent and a high value of 59.17 percent. These are plausible values (any value above 100.00 percent is implausible). A boxplot (not shown) demonstrates that the variable has two values greater than 50.00 percent that are indicated as outliers for the Midwest region. However, the histograms shown in Figure 12.4 do not suggest that these values are unusually large; rather, the peak in both histograms is located off to the left. The distributions are heavily skewed.[15]

Because the samples each have fewer than 50 observations, the Shapiro-Wilk test for normality is used. The respective test statistics for East and Midwest are .969 (p = .355) and .931 (p = .007). Visual inspection confirms that the Midwest distribution is indeed nonnormal. The Shapiro-Wilk test statistics are given only for completeness; they have no substantive interpretation.

We must now either transform the variable so that it becomes normal for purposes of testing, or use a nonparametric alternative. The second option is discussed later in this chapter. We also show the consequences of ignoring the problem.

To transform the variable, we try the recommended transformations, $\log(x)$, $\sqrt{x}$, or x^2, and then examine the transformed variable for normality. If none of these transformations work, we might modify them, such as using

Figure 12.5 —— Transformed Variable: Watershed Pollution

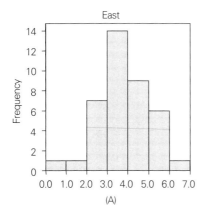
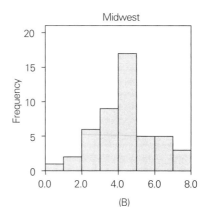

$x^{1/3}$ instead of $x^{1/2}$ (recall that the latter is $\sqrt{x}$).[16] Thus, some experimentation is required. In our case, we find that the $x^{1/2}$ works. The new Shapiro-Wilk test statistics for East and Midwest are, respectively, .969 (p = .361) and .987 (p = .883). Visual inspection of Figure 12.5 shows these two distributions to be quite normal, indeed.

The results of the t-test for the transformed variable are shown in Table 12.2. The transformed variable has equal variances across the two groups (Levene's test, p = .119), and the t-test statistic is −1.308 (df = 85, p = .194). Thus, the differences in pollution between watersheds in the East and

Table 12.2 —— Independent-Samples T-Test: Output

Variable: watershed pollution

	Step 1:			Step 2:		
	Levene's test for equality of variances			T-test for the equality of means		
	F	p		t	df	p (2-tailed)
Transformed	2.479	0.119	Equal variances assumed	−1.308	85	0.194
			Equal variances not assumed	−1.347	80.6	0.182
Untransformed	4.537	0.036	Equal variances assumed	−1.723	85	0.089
			Equal variances not assumed	−1.801	80.6	0.075

Midwest are not significant. (The negative sign of the t-test statistic, −1.308, merely reflects the order of the groups for calculating the difference: the testing variable has a larger value in the Midwest than in the East. Reversing the order of the groups results in a positive sign.)

For comparison, results for the untransformed variable are shown as well. The untransformed variable has unequal variances across the two groups (Levene's test, p = .036), and the t-test statistic is −1.801 (df = 80.6, p =.075). Although this result also shows that differences are insignificant, the level of significance is higher; there are instances in which using nonnormal variables could lead to rejecting the null hypothesis. While our finding of insignificant differences is indeed *robust*, analysts cannot know this in advance. Thus, analysts will need to deal with nonnormality.

Variable transformation is one approach to the problem of nonnormality, but transforming variables can be a time-intensive and somewhat artful activity. The search for alternatives has led many analysts to consider nonparametric methods.

TWO T-TEST VARIATIONS

Paired-Samples T-Test

Analysts often use the paired t-test when applying before and after tests to assess student or client progress. Paired t-tests are used when analysts have a *dependent* rather than an independent sample (see the third t-test assumption, described earlier in this chapter). The **paired-samples t-test** tests the null hypothesis that the mean difference between the before and after test scores is zero. Consider the following data from Table 12.3.

Table 12.3 ——————— ᜟᜟᜟ— Paired-Samples Data

Before	After	Difference
3.2	4.3	1.1
3.2	4.3	1.1
4.0	3.8	−0.2
2.4	3.5	1.1
3.0	3.3	0.3
4.0	4.4	0.4
4.3	4.2	−0.1
3.8	3.3	−0.5
2.9	3.9	1.0
3.8	4.2	0.4
2.5	3.8	1.3

The mean "before" score is 3.39, and the mean "after" score is 3.87; the mean difference is 0.54. The paired t-test tests the null hypothesis by testing whether the mean of the difference variable ("difference") is zero. The paired t-test test statistic is calculated as

$$t = \frac{\bar{D}}{s_D / \sqrt{n}},$$

where D is the difference between before and after measurements, and s_D is the standard deviation of these differences. Regarding t-test assumptions, the variables are continuous, and the issue of heterogeneity (unequal variances) is moot because this test involves only one variable, D; no Levene's test statistics are produced. We do test the normality of D and find that it is normally distributed (Shapiro-Wilk = .925, p = .402). Thus, the assumptions are satisfied.

We proceed with testing whether the difference between before and after scores is statistically significant. We find that the paired t-test yields a t-test statistic of 2.43, which is significant at the 5 percent level (df = 9, p = .038 < .05).[17] Hence, we conclude that the increase between the before and after scores is significant at the 5 percent level.[18]

One-Sample T-Test

Finally, the **one-sample t-test** tests whether the mean of a single variable is different from a prespecified value (norm). For example, suppose we want to know whether the mean of the before group in Table 12.3 is different from the value of, say, 3.5? Testing against a norm is akin to the purpose of the chi-square goodness-of-fit test described in Chapter 11, but here we are dealing with a continuous variable rather than a categorical one, and we are testing the mean rather than its distribution.

The one-sample t-test assumes that the single variable is continuous and normally distributed. As with the paired t-test, the issue of heterogeneity is moot because there is only one variable. The Shapiro-Wilk test shows that the variable "before" is normal (.917, p = .336). The one-sample t-test statistic for testing against the test value of 3.5 is –0.515 (df = 9, p = .619 > .05). Hence, the mean of 3.39 is *not* significantly different from 3.5. However, it is different from larger values, such as 4.0 (t = 2.89, df = 9, p = .019). Another example of this is provided in the Box 12.2.

Finally, note that the one-sample t-test is identical to the paired-samples t-test for testing whether the mean $D = 0$. Indeed, the one-sample t-test for $D = 0$ produces the same results (t = 2.43, df = 9, p = .038).

In Greater Depth . . .

Box 12.2   Use of the T-Test in Performance Management: An Example

Performance benchmarking is an increasingly popular tool in performance management. Public and nonprofit officials compare the performance of their agencies with performance benchmarks and draw lessons from the comparison. Let us say that a city government requires its fire and medical response unit to maintain an average response time of 360 seconds (6 minutes) to emergency requests. The city manager has suspected that the growth in population and demands for the services have slowed down the responses recently. He draws a sample of 10 response times in the most recent month: 230, 450, 378, 430, 270, 470, 390, 300, 470, and 530 seconds, for a sample mean of 392 seconds. He performs a one-sample t-test to compare the mean of this sample with the performance benchmark of 360 seconds. The null hypothesis of this test is that the sample mean is equal to 360 seconds, and the alternate hypothesis is that they are different. The result (t = 1.030, df = 9, p = .330) shows a failure to reject the null hypothesis at the 5 percent level, which means that we don't have sufficient evidence to say that the average response time is different from the benchmark 360 seconds. We cannot say that current performance of 392 seconds is significantly different from the 360-second benchmark. Perhaps more data (samples) are needed to reach such a conclusion, or perhaps too much variability exists for such a conclusion to be reached.

NONPARAMETRIC ALTERNATIVES TO T-TESTS

The tests described in the preceding sections have nonparametric alternatives. The chief advantage of these tests is that they do not require continuous variables to be normally distributed. The chief disadvantage is that they are less likely to reject the null hypothesis. A further, minor disadvantage is that these tests do not provide descriptive information about variable means; separate analysis is required for that.

Nonparametric alternatives to the independent-samples test are the **Mann-Whitney** and **Wilcoxon tests**. The Mann-Whitney and Wilcoxon tests are equivalent and are thus discussed jointly. Both are simplifications of the

Table 12.4 ⎯⎯⎯⎯⎯∿⎯ Rankings of Two Groups

Group	Rating	Rank	Group	Rating	Rank
1	2.5	3	2	3.4	7
1	2.9	4	2	3.3	6
1	4.0	9.5	2	4.0	9.5
1	3.2	5	2	3.9	8
1	1.2	1	2	2.1	2
Sum		22.5	Sum		32.5

more general Kruskal-Wallis' H test, discussed in Chapter 11.[19] The Mann-Whitney and Wilcoxon tests assign ranks to the testing variable in the exact manner shown in Table 12.4. The sum of the ranks of each group is computed, shown in the table. Then a test is performed to determine the statistical significance of the difference between the sums, 22.5 and 32.5. Although the Mann-Whitney U and Wilcoxon W test statistics are calculated differently, they both have the same level of statistical significance: $p = .295$. Technically, this is not a test of different means but of different distributions; the lack of significance implies that groups 1 and 2 can be regarded as coming from the same population.[20]

For comparison, we use the Mann-Whitney test to compare the two samples of 10th graders discussed earlier in this chapter. The sum of ranks for the "before" group is 69.55, and for the "one year later group," 86.57. The test statistic is significant at $p = .019$, yielding the same conclusion as the inde-pendent-samples t-test, $p = .011$. This comparison also shows that nonparametric tests do have higher levels of significance. As mentioned earlier, the Mann-Whitney test (as a nonparametric test) does not calculate the group means; separate, descriptive analysis needs to be undertaken for that information.

> **Getting Started**
>
> Calculate a t-test and a Mann-Whitney test on data of your choice.

A nonparametric alternative to the paired-samples t-test is the **Wilcoxon signed rank test**. This test assigns ranks based on the absolute values of these differences (Table 12.5). The signs of the differences are retained (thus, some values are positive and others are negative). For the data in Table 12.5, there are seven positive ranks (with mean rank = 6.57) and three negative ranks (with mean rank = 3.00). The Wilcoxon signed rank test statistic is normally distributed. The Wilcoxon signed rank test statistic, Z, for a difference between these values is 1.89 ($p = .059 > .05$). Hence, according to this test, the differences between the before and after scores are not significant.

Again, nonparametric tests result in larger p-values. The paired-samples t-test finds that $p = .038 < .05$, providing sufficient statistical evidence to

Table 12.5 ───~᭺~── Wilcoxon Signed Rank Test

Before	After	Difference	Signed rank
3.2	4.3	1.1	8.5
4.0	3.8	−0.2	−2.0
2.4	3.5	1.1	8.5
3.0	3.3	0.3	3.0
4.0	4.4	0.4	4.5
4.3	4.2	−0.1	−1.0
3.8	3.3	−0.5	−6.0
2.9	3.9	1.0	7.0
3.8	4.2	0.4	4.5
2.5	3.8	1.3	10.0

conclude that the differences are significant. It might also be noted that a doubling of the data in Table 12.5 results in finding a significant difference between the before and after scores with the Wilcoxon signed rank test, $Z = 2.694$, $p = .007$.

The Wilcoxon signed rank test can also be adapted as a nonparametric alternative to the one-sample t-test. In that case, analysts create a second variable that, for each observation, is the test value. For example, if in Table 12.5 we wish to test whether the mean of variable "before" is different from, say, 4.0, we create a second variable with 10 observations for which each value is, say, 4.0. Then using the Wilcoxon signed rank test for the "before" variable and this new, second variable, we find that $Z = 2.103$, $p = .035$. This value is larger than that obtained by the parametric test, $p = .019$.[21]

SUMMARY

When analysts need to determine whether two groups have different means of a continuous variable, the t-test is the tool of choice. This situation arises, for example, when analysts compare measurements at two points in time or the responses of two different groups. There are three common t-tests, involving independent samples, dependent (paired) samples, and the one-sample t-test.

T-tests are parametric tests, which means that variables in these tests must meet certain assumptions, notably that they are normally distributed. The requirement of normally distributed variables follows from how parametric tests make inferences. Specifically, t-tests have four assumptions:

- One variable is continuous, and the other variable is dichotomous.
- The two distributions have equal variances.
- The observations are independent.
- The two distributions are normally distributed.

The assumption of homogeneous variances does not apply to dependent-samples and one-sample t-tests because both are based on only a single variable for testing significance. When assumptions of normality are not met, variable transformation may be used. The search for alternative ways for dealing with normality problems may lead analysts to consider nonparametric alternatives.

The chief advantage of nonparametric tests is that they do not require continuous variables to be normally distributed. The chief disadvantage is that they yield higher levels of statistical significance, making it less likely that the null hypothesis may be rejected. A nonparametric alternative for the independent-samples t-test is the Mann-Whitney test, and the nonparametric alternative for the dependent-samples t-test is the Wilcoxon signed rank test.

T-tests and their nonparametric alternatives provide information about whether two group means are significantly different. Analysts will need to further assess the magnitude of these differences, and to determine whether they are practically significant. Chapter 13 discusses analysis of variance, or ANOVA, which can be used when means are compared across three or more groups, rather than the two groups of a dichotomous variable.

KEY TERMS

Central limit theorem (p. 211)
Heterogeneity of variances (p. 209)
Homogeneity of variances (p. 209)
Independent-samples t-test (p. 207)
Kolmogorov-Smirnov test (p. 210)
Levene's test (p. 209)
Mann-Whitney test (p. 219)
Null hypothesis of normality (p. 210)
One-sample t-test (p. 218)
One-tailed t-tests (p. 208)

Paired-samples t-test (p. 217)
Robust (p. 210)
Shapiro-Wilk test (p. 210)
Student's t-distribution (p. 208)
T-test test assumptions (p. 209)
T-tests (p. 206)
Two-tailed t-tests (p. 208)
Variable transformation (p. 212)
Wilcoxon signed rank test (p. 220)
Wilcoxon test (p. 219)

Notes

1. Some research suggests that nonparametric tests may not be as robust as thought when variances of groups of rankings are substantially unequal.
2. Boxplots are shown for ease of presentation. It is more appropriate, theoretically, to show two normal distributions, but that clutters the presentation. In any event, continuous data can be presented in boxplots.
3. The formula for the pooled variance is

$$s_p^2 = \frac{(n_1 - 1)s_1^2 + (n_2 - 1)s_2^2}{n_1 + n_2 - 2}.$$

When $s_1 = s_2$, the value of s_p is affected by the relative number of observations in each group, that is, n_1 and n_2. The computer calculates the pooled variance, of course. For more on this topic, see David Howell, *Statistical Methods for Psychology*, 3rd ed. (Belmont, Calif.: Duxbury Press, 1992), 181–187.

4. The name *Student's t* is derived from W.S. Gossett, who used "Student" as a pseudonym in the early twentieth century to protect his identity. Legend has it that Gossett was concerned that his employer, an agro-industrial company, might want to protect the formula as a trade secret because of competitive advantages: the t-test enables very efficient testing of samples.

5. See Box 10.2. The decision to require a higher critical value is not without cost; it could increase Type II errors. However, many analysts prefer to err on the side of caution.

6. Even though studies have shown that men typically have higher incomes than women, this need not always be the case. In any specific setting, in any specific industry, at any point in time, women could have higher incomes.

7. The revised formula for calculating the t-test when variances are unequal is

$$t = \frac{\overline{x}_1 - \overline{x}_2}{\sqrt{\dfrac{s_1^2}{n_1 - 1} + \dfrac{s_2^2}{n_2 - 1}}}.$$

See Howell, *Statistical Methods for Psychology*, for the revised formula for calculating degrees of freedom.

8. Students often want to know how they can transform variables. In most software packages it is simply a matter of specifying something like: newvar = sqrt(oldvar) or newvar = lg10(oldvar). Students also ask what transformation works best. This is largely unknown. It is a matter of trial and error.

9. Some students initially consider variable transformation to be "playing with the data." However, we need to consider that the ancient development of the common measurement scale (1, 2, 3, 4, 5 ...) is as arbitrary as any other scale that might have been chosen (such as 1, 4, 9, 16, 25 ...). The fact that the common measurement scale is frequently useful from the perspective of satisfying test assumptions should not lead us to assign supreme considerations to it or to be reluctant to try other measurement scales that work better in other situations. It is far more important to ensure that the variables are normally distributed for the purpose of test validity.

10. With a Cronbach alpha measure of 0.79, the analyst concludes that the index measure has adequate reliability (see Chapter 3).

11. The data in this example are real, but the reported scenario is fictitious.

12. SPSS readily produces these plots as part of the Analyze → Descriptive Statistics → Explore routine.

13. Software output may also include the 95 percent confidence interval for estimates of the difference. When t-tests are insignificant, the interval will include the value zero, indicating that no difference between the means can be ruled out. When t-tests are significant, the interval will not include the value zero.

14. For more information about this measure, visit www.epa.gov/iwi. See also the Watershed dataset on the CD accompanying the workbook *Exercising Essential Statistics* to replicate the results given here. The index variable is called "conpolut" in the dataset.

15. This conclusion is further indicated by the measures of skewness: East (.519) and Midwest (.912). Based on the test described in Chapter 7, skewness/se(skewness) for the two regions is, respectively, [.559/.378 =] 1.48 and [.912/.343 =] 2.65, which confirms the considerable departure from zero for Midwest. The measures of kurtosis are −.113 and .406.

16. This conclusion is consistent for a wide range of root variable transformations that result in a normal distribution (for example, using x^{35}, not shown, rather than the root variable $\sqrt{x}$.

17. In paired tests, degrees of freedom are defined as $n - 1$ (where n is the number of *pairs* or, equivalently, difference scores).

18. In many t-tests the output includes a 95 percent confidence interval of the difference. This is the range within which we can be 95 percent certain that the population difference lies. For this test, the range is between .032 and .927. Although this is a considerable range, it excludes the value zero, or no difference of the means.

19. The formula for calculating the Mann-Whitney test statistic is

$$n_1 n_2 + \frac{n_1(n_1+1)}{2} - T_1,$$

where T_1 is the sum of ranks for group 1, n_1 is the number of observations in sample 1, and n_2 is the number of observations in sample 2. The relationship between U and the Wilcoxon W test statistic is

$$U + W + \frac{m(m+2n+1)}{2},$$

where m is the number of observations in the group that has the smaller number of observations, and n is the number of observations in the group that has the larger number of observations.

20. By contrast, the p-value for comparing groups 1 and 3 in Table 11.8 is .016. We may note that using the Kruskal-Wallis' H test for these two groups yields the exact same level of significance.

21. Another, less powerful alternative is the sign test. It is conducted in the same manner as described in the text, but it compares only the number of positive and negative signs rather than the differences of the mean ranks. It is a very crude test that is generally not preferred. In the example in the text, the sign test finds p = .070, indicating that the mean "Before" score is not significantly different from 4.0.

Analysis of Variance (ANOVA)

CHAPTER OBJECTIVES

After reading this chapter, you should be able to

- Use one-way ANOVA when the dependent variable is continuous and the independent variable is nominal or ordinal with two or more categories
- Understand the assumptions of ANOVA and how to test for them
- Use post-hoc tests
- Understand some extensions of one-way ANOVA

This chapter provides an essential introduction to *analysis of variance (ANOVA)*. ANOVA is a family of statistical techniques, the most basic of which is the one-way ANOVA, which provides an essential expansion of the t-test discussed in Chapter 12. One-way ANOVA allows analysts to test the effect of a continuous variable on an ordinal or nominal variable with two or more categories, rather than only two categories as is the case with the t-test. Thus, one-way ANOVA enables analysts to deal with problems such as whether the variable "region" (north, south, east, west) or "race" (Caucasian,

African American, Hispanic, Asian, etc.) affects policy outcomes or any other matter that is measured on a continuous scale. One-way ANOVA also allows analysts to quickly determine subsets of categories with similar levels of the dependent variable. This chapter also addresses some extensions of one-way ANOVA and a nonparametric alternative.

ANALYSIS OF VARIANCE

Whereas the t-test is used for testing differences between two groups on a continuous variable (Chapter 12), *one-way ANOVA* is used for testing the means of a continuous variable across more than two groups. For example, we may wish to test whether income levels differ among three or more ethnic groups, or whether the counts of fish vary across three or more lakes. Applications of ANOVA often arise in medical and agricultural research, in

> **Key Point**
>
> ANOVA extends the t-test; it is used when the independent variable is categorical and the dependent variable is continuous.

which treatments are given to different groups of patients, animals, or crops. The F-test statistic compares the variances within each group against those that exist between each group and the overall mean:

$$F = \frac{s_b^2}{s_w^2}.$$

The logic of this approach is shown graphically in Figure 13.1. The overall group mean is $\bar{\bar{x}}$ (the mean of means). The boxplots represent the scores of observations within each group. (As before, the horizontal lines indicate means, $\bar{x}$, rather than medians.) Recall that variance is a measure of dispersion. In both parts of the figure, w is the within-group variance, and b is the between-group variance. Each graph has three within-group variances and three between-group variances, although only one of each is shown. Note in part A that the between-group variances are larger than the within-group variances, which results in a large F-test statistic using the above formula, making it easier to reject the null hypothesis. Conversely, in part B the within-group variances are larger than the between-group variances, causing a smaller F-test statistic and making it more difficult to reject the null hypothesis. The hypotheses are written as follows:

H_0: No differences between any of the group means exist in the population.

H_A: At least one difference between group means exists in the population.

Note how the alternate hypothesis is phrased, because the logical opposite of "no differences between any of the group means" is that at least one pair of means differs. H_0 is also called the **global F-test** because it tests for differences among any means.

The formulas for calculating the between-group variances and within-group variances are quite cumbersome for all but the simplest of designs.[1] In any event, *statistical software calculates the F-test statistic and reports the level at which it is significant.*[2]

When the preceding null hypothesis is rejected, analysts will also want to know which differences are significant. For example, analysts will want to know which pairs of differences in watershed pollution are significant across regions. Although one approach might be to use the t-test to sequentially test each pair of differences, this should not be done. It would not only be a most tedious undertaking but would also inadvertently and adversely affect the level of significance: the chance of finding a significant pair by chance alone increases as more pairs are examined. Specifically, the probability of rejecting the null hypothesis in one of two tests is $[1 - 0.95^2 =] .098$, the probability of rejecting it in one of three tests is $[1 - 0.95^3 =] .143$, and so forth. Thus, sequential testing of differences does not reflect the true level of significance for such tests and should not be used.

Post-hoc tests test all possible group differences and yet maintain the true level of significance. Post-hoc tests vary in their methods of calculating test statistics and holding experiment-wide error rates constant. Three popular post-hoc tests are the Tukey, Bonferroni, and Scheffe tests. The Scheffe test is the most conservative, the Tukey test is best when many comparisons are made (when there are many groups), and the Bonferroni test is preferred

Figure 13.1 ⎯⎯⎯⎯⎯⎯ ANOVA: Significant and Insignificant Differences

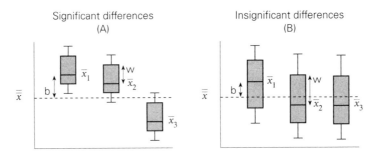

when few comparisons are made. However, these post-hoc tests often support the same conclusions.[3] To illustrate, let's say the independent variable has three categories. Then, a post-hoc test will examine hypotheses for whether $\overline{y}_{x1} = \overline{y}_{x2}, \overline{y}_{x2} = \overline{y}_{x3}$, and $\overline{y}_{x1} = \overline{y}_{x3}$. In addition, these tests will also examine which categories have means that are not significantly different from each other, hence, providing **homogeneous subsets**. An example of this approach is given later in this chapter. Knowing such subsets can be useful when the independent variable has many categories (for example, classes of employees).

Eta-squared (η^2) is a measure of association for mixed nominal-interval variables and is appropriate for ANOVA. Its values range from zero to one, and it is interpreted as the percentage of variation explained. It is a directional measure, and computer programs produce two statistics, alternating specification of the dependent variable.

Finally, ANOVA can be used for testing interval-ordinal relationships. We can ask whether the change in means follows a linear pattern that is either increasing or decreasing. For example, assume we want to know whether incomes increase according to the political orientation of respondents, when measured on a seven-point Likert scale that ranges from very liberal to very conservative. If a linear pattern of increase exists, then a linear relationship is said to exist between these variables. Most statistical software packages can test for a variety of progressive relationships.

ANOVA Assumptions

ANOVA assumptions are essentially the same as those of the t-test: (1) the dependent variable is continuous, and the independent variable is ordinal or nominal, (2) the groups have equal variances, (3) observations are independent, and (4) the variable is normally distributed in each of the groups. The assumptions are tested in a similar manner.

Relative to the t-test, ANOVA requires a little more concern regarding the assumptions of normality and homogeneity. First, like the t-test, ANOVA is *not robust* for the presence of outliers, and analysts examine the presence of outliers for each group. Also, ANOVA appears to be less robust than the t-test for deviations from normality. Second, regarding groups having equal variances, our main concern with homogeneity is that there are no *substantial* differences in the amount of variance across the groups; the test of homogeneity is a strict test, testing for *any* departure from equal variances, and in practice, groups may have neither equal variances nor substantial differences in the amount of variances. In these instances, a visual finding of no substantial differences suffices. Other strategies for dealing with heterogeneity are variable transformations and the removal of outliers, which increase variance, especially in small groups. Such outliers are detected by examining boxplots for each group separately. Also, some statistical software packages (such as SPSS), now offer post-hoc tests when equal variances are not assumed.[4]

A Working Example

The U.S. Environmental Protection Agency (EPA) measured the percentage of wetland loss in watersheds between 1982 and 1992, the most recent period for which data are available (government statistics are sometimes a little old).[5] An analyst wants to know whether watersheds with large surrounding populations have suffered greater wetland loss than watersheds with smaller surrounding populations.

Most watersheds have suffered no or only very modest losses (less than 3 percent during the decade in question), and few watersheds have suffered more than a 4 percent loss. The distribution is thus heavily skewed toward watersheds with little wetland losses (that is, to the left) and is clearly not normally distributed.[6] To increase normality, the variable is transformed by twice taking the square root, $x^{.25}$. The transformed variable is then normally distributed: the Kolmogorov-Smirnov statistic is 0.82 (p = .51 > .05). The variable also appears visually normal for each of the population subgroups. There are four population groups, designed to ensure an adequate number of observations in each.

Boxplot analysis of the transformed variable indicates four large and three small outliers (not shown). Examination suggests that these are plausible and representative values, which are therefore retained. Later, however, we will examine the effect of these seven observations on the robustness of statistical results. Descriptive analysis of the variables is shown in Table 13.1. Generally, large populations tend to have larger average wetland losses, but the standard deviations are large relative to (the difference between) these means, raising considerable question as to whether these differences are indeed statistically significant. Also, the untransformed variable shows that the mean wetland loss is less among watersheds with "Medium I" populations than in those with "Small" populations (1.77 versus 2.52). The transformed variable shows the opposite order (1.06 versus 0.97). Further investigation shows this to be the effect of the three small outliers and two large outliers on the calculation of the mean of the untransformed variable in the "Small" group. Variable transformation minimizes this effect. These outliers also increase the standard deviation of the "Small" group.

Using ANOVA, we find that the transformed variable has unequal variances across the four groups (Levene's statistic = 2.83, p = .41 < .05). Visual inspection, shown in Figure 13.2, indicates that differences are not substantial for observations within the group interquartile ranges, the areas indicated by the boxes. The differences seem mostly caused by observations

Table 13.1 ——— Variable Transformation

Population	N	Untransformed variable		Transformed variable	
		Mean (%)	Standard deviation	Mean (%)	Standard deviation
Small	31	2.52	4.30	0.97	0.50
Medium I	32	1.77	1.68	1.06	0.28
Medium II	30	2.79	6.80	1.07	0.38
Large	27	3.21	3.54	1.26	0.27

located in the whiskers of the "Small" group, which include the five outliers mentioned earlier. (The other two outliers remain outliers and are shown.) For now, we conclude that *no substantial differences* in variances exist, but we later test the robustness of this conclusion with consideration of these observations (see Figure 13.2).

We now proceed with the ANOVA analysis. First, Table 13.2 shows that the global F-test statistic is 2.91, $p = .038 < .05$. Thus, at least one pair of means is significantly different. (The term *sum of squares* is explained in note 1.)

> **Getting Started**
> Try ANOVA on some data of your choice.

Second, which pairs are significantly different? We use the Bonferroni post-hoc test because relatively few comparisons are made (there are only four groups). The computer-generated results (not shown in Table 13.2) indicate that the only significant difference concerns the means of the "Small" and "Large" groups. This difference (1.26 - 0.97 = 0.29 [of transformed values]) is significant at the 5 percent level ($p = .028$). The Tukey and Scheffe tests lead to the same conclusion (respectively, $p = .024$ and .044). (It should be noted that post-hoc tests also exist for when equal variances are not assumed. In our example, these tests lead to the same

Figure 13.2 ——— Group Boxplots

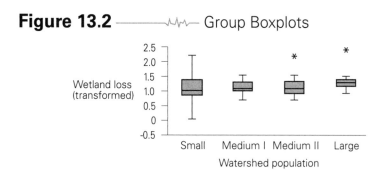

Table 13.2 ──────〰〰── ANOVA Table

	Sum of squares	df	Variance (s^2)	F-test	p
Between groups	1.203	3	0.401	2.907	.038
Within groups	16.002	116	0.138		
Total	17.205	119			

result.[7]) This result is consistent with a visual reexamination of Figure 13.2, which shows that differences between group means are indeed small. The Tukey and Scheffe tests also produce "homogeneous subsets," that is, groups that have statistically identical means. Both the three largest and the three smallest populations have identical means. The Tukey levels of statistical significance are, respectively, .725 and .165 (both > .05). This is shown in Table 13.3.

Third, is the increase in means linear? This test is an option on many statistical software packages that produces an additional line of output in the ANOVA table, called the "linear term for unweighted sum of squares," with the appropriate F-test. Here, that F-test statistic is 7.85, p = .006 < .01, and so we conclude that the apparent linear increase is indeed significant: wetland loss is linearly associated with the increased surrounding population of watersheds.[8] Figure 13.2 does not clearly show this, but the enlarged Y-axis in Figure 13.3 does.

Fourth, are our findings *robust?* One concern is that the statistical validity is affected by observations that statistically (although not substantively) are outliers. Removing the seven outliers identified earlier does not affect our conclusions. The resulting variable remains normally distributed, and there are no (new) outliers for any group. The resulting variable has equal variances across the groups (Levene's test = 1.03, p = .38 > .05). The global F-test is 3.44 (p = .019 < .05), and the Bonferroni post-hoc test

Table 13.3 ──────〰〰── Homogeneous Subsets

Population size (independent variable)	N	Subset for group 1 (mean watershed loss, transformed variable)	Subset for group 2 (mean watershed loss, transformed variable)
1	31	.9736	
2	32	1.0556	1.0556
3	30	1.0738	1.0738
4	27		1.2558
Sig.		.725	.165

Figure 13.3 ⎯⎯⎯⎯⎯⎯ Watershed Loss, by Population

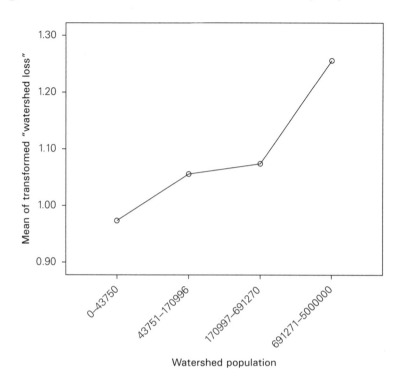

Watershed population

similarly finds that only the differences between the "Small" and "Large" group means are significant (p = .031). The increase remains linear (F = 6.74, p = .011 < .05). Thus, we conclude that the presence of observations with large values does not alter our conclusions.

We also test the robustness of conclusions for different variable transformations. The extreme skewness of the untransformed variable allows for only a limited range of root transformations that produce normality. Within this range (power 0.222 through 0.275), the preceding conclusions are replicated fully. Natural log and base-10 log transformations also result in normality and replicate these results, *except* that the post-hoc tests fail to identify that the means of the "Large" and "Small" groups are significantly different. However, the global F-test is (marginally) significant (F = 2.80, p = .043 < .05), which suggests that this difference is too small to detect with this transformation. A single, independent-samples t-test for this difference is significant (t = 2.47, p = .017 < .05), suggesting that this problem may have been exacerbated by the limited number of observations. In sum, we find converging evidence for our conclusions. As this example also shows, when using statistics, analysts frequently must exercise judgment and justify their decisions.[9]

Finally, what is the practical significance of this analysis? The wetland loss among watersheds with large surrounding populations is [(3.21 − 2.52)/2.52 =] 27.4 percent greater than among those surrounded by small populations. It is up to managers and elected officials to determine whether a difference of this magnitude warrants intervention in watersheds with large surrounding populations.[10]

Beyond One-Way ANOVA

The approach described in the preceding section is called *one-way ANOVA*. This scenario is easily generalized to accommodate more than one independent variable. These independent variables are either discrete (called **factors**) or continuous (called **covariates**). These approaches are called *n*-way ANOVA or ANCOVA (the "C" indicates the presence of covariates). **Two-way ANOVA**, for example, allows for testing of the effect of two different independent variables on the dependent variable, as well as the *interaction* of these two independent variables. An **interaction effect** between two variables describes the way that variables "work together" to have an effect on the dependent variable. This is perhaps best illustrated by an example. Suppose that an analyst wants to know whether the number of health care information workshops attended, as well as a person's education, are associated with healthy lifestyle behaviors. Although we can surely theorize how attending health care information workshops and a person's education can each affect an individual's healthy lifestyle behaviors, it is also easy to see that the level of education can affect a person's propensity for attending health care information workshops, as well. Hence, an interaction effect could also exist between these two independent variables (factors). The effects of each independent variable on the dependent variable are called **main effects** (as distinct from interaction effects).

To continue the earlier example, suppose that in addition to population, an analyst also wants to consider a measure of the watershed's preexisting condition, such as the number of plant and animal species at risk in the watershed. Two-way ANOVA produces the results shown in Table 13.4, using the transformed variable mentioned earlier.

The first row, labeled "model," refers to the combined effects of all main and interaction effects in the model on the dependent variable. This is the global F-test. The "model" row shows that the two main effects and the single interaction effect, when considered together, are significantly associated with changes in the dependent variable (p < .000). However, the results also show a reduced significance level of "population" (now, p = .064), which seems related to the interaction effect (p = .076). Although neither effect is

Table 13.4 ————〜⋏〜— Two-Way ANOVA Results

	Sum of squares	df	Mean square	F-test	p
Model	126.566	12	10.547	99.418	.000
Population	.798	3	.266	2.508	.064
Species	.191	2	35.663	.900	.410
Population*species	1.260	6	25.377	1.980	.076
Within groups	10.078	95	8.225		
Total	136.645	107			

significant at conventional levels, the results do suggest that an interaction effect is present between population and watershed condition (of which the number of at-risk species is an indicator) on watershed wetland loss. Post-hoc tests are only provided separately for each of the independent variables (factors), and the results show the same homogeneous grouping for both of the independent variables.

As we noted earlier, ANOVA is a family of statistical techniques that allow for a broad range of rather complex experimental designs. Complete coverage of these techniques is well beyond the scope of this book, but in general, many of these techniques aim to discern the effect of variables in the presence of other (control) variables. ANOVA is but one approach for addressing control variables. A far more common approach in public policy, economics, political science, and public administration (as well as in many others fields) is multiple regression (see Chapter 15). Many analysts feel that ANOVA and regression are largely equivalent. Historically, the preference for ANOVA stems from its uses in medical and agricultural research, with applications in education and psychology. Finally, the ANOVA approach can be generalized to allow for testing on two or more *dependent* variables. This approach is called multiple analysis of variance, or MANOVA. Regression-based analysis can also be used for dealing with multiple dependent variables, as mentioned in Chapter 17.

A NONPARAMETRIC ALTERNATIVE

A nonparametric alternative to one-way ANOVA is *Kruskal-Wallis' H test of one-way ANOVA*. Instead of using the actual values of the variables, Kruskal-Wallis' H test assigns ranks to the variables, as shown in Chapter 11. As a nonparametric method, Kruskal-Wallis' H test does not assume normal populations, but the test does assume similarly shaped distributions for each group. This test is applied readily to our one-way ANOVA example, and the results are shown in Table 13.5.

Table 13.5 ———~w~— Kruskal-Wallis' H-Test of One-Way ANOVA

a. Ranks	Population	N	Mean rank
Watershed loss	1	31	50.69
(transformed variable)	2	32	58.63
	3	30	55.98
	4	27	79.00
	Total	120	

b. Test results	Watershed loss (transformed variable)
Chi-square	10.703
df	3
Sig.	.013

Kruskal-Wallis' H one-way ANOVA test shows that population is significantly associated with watershed loss (p = .013). This is one instance in which the general rule that nonparametric tests have higher levels of significance is not seen. Although Kruskal-Wallis' H test does not report mean values of the dependent variable, the pattern of mean ranks is consistent with Figure 13.2. A limitation of this nonparametric test is that it does not provide post-hoc tests or analysis of homogeneous groups, nor are there nonparametric n-way ANOVA tests such as for the two-way ANOVA test described earlier.

SUMMARY

One-way ANOVA extends the t-test by allowing analysts to test whether two or more groups have different means of a continuous variable. The t-test is limited to only two groups. One-way ANOVA can be used, for example, when analysts want to know if the mean of a variable varies across regions, racial or ethnic groups, population or employee categories, or another grouping with multiple categories. ANOVA is family of statistical techniques, and one-way ANOVA is the most basic of these methods. ANOVA is a parametric test that makes the following assumptions:

- The dependent variable is continuous.
- The independent variable is ordinal or nominal.
- The groups have equal variances.
- The variable is normally distributed in each of the groups.

Relative to the t-test, ANOVA requires more attention to the assumptions of normality and homogeneity. ANOVA is not robust for the presence of outliers, and it appears to be less robust than the t-test for deviations from normality. Variable transformations and the removal of outliers are to be expected when using ANOVA. ANOVA also includes three other types of tests of interest: post-hoc tests of mean differences among categories, tests of homogeneous subsets, and tests for the linearity of mean differences across categories.

Two-way ANOVA addresses the effect of two independent variables on a continuous dependent variable. When using two-way ANOVA, the analyst is able to distinguish main effects from interaction effects. Kruskal-Wallis' H test is a nonparametric alternative to one-way ANOVA.

KEY TERMS

Analysis of variance (ANOVA) (p. 226)

ANOVA assumptions (p. 229)

Covariates (p. 234)

Factors (p. 234)

Global F-test (p. 228)

Homogeneous subsets (p. 229)

Interaction effect (p. 234)

Kruskal-Wallis' H test of one-way ANOVA (p. 235)

Main effect (p. 234)

One-way ANOVA (p. 227)

Post-hoc test (p. 228)

Two-way ANOVA (p. 234)

Notes

1. The between-group variance (s_b^2) is defined as $\sum (\bar{x}_k - \bar{\bar{x}})^2 / k - 1$, where the subscript k identifies groups, $\bar{x}_k$ is each of the group means, $\bar{\bar{x}}$ is the overall group mean (the mean of the means), and k is the number of groups. The within-group variance (s_w^2) is defined as $\sum_k \sum_i (\bar{x}_i - \bar{x}_k)^2 / (n-1)$, for each group, where $\bar{x}_i$ is the mean of group observations and n is the total number of observations (across all groups). The terms $\Sigma(\bar{x}_i - \bar{x}_k)^2$ are called "sums of squares." See also Table 13.2. Many textbooks demonstrate how to calculate these values.

2. F-test critical values are defined by two types of degrees of freedom: the degrees of freedom for the numerator is $k - 1$, where k is the number of groups. The degrees of freedom for the denominator is $n - k$, where n is the number of observations. For example, if there are 4 groups and 76 observations, then df (numerator) = 3, and df (denominator) = 72. Based on the F distribution (see Appendix E), the critical value of F(3,72) = 2.74 at the 5 percent level of significance (estimated based on table).

3. In SPSS, these tests are found through Analyze → Compare Means → One Way ANOVA → Post-Hoc.

4. In SPSS, these tests are found through Analyze → Compare Means → One Way ANOVA → Post-Hoc: Tamhane's T2, Dunnett's T3, Games-Howell and Dunnett's C tests.

5. This is the variable "wtldls92" on the CD that accompanies the workbook, *Exercising Essential Statistics.* The variable population, see further, is "watershed population" in the Watershed dataset.

6. The Kolmogorov-Smirnov test statistic is 3.11, p = .000 < .01. Skewness is 5.42, with a standard error of 0.20. This ratio greatly exceeds a value of 2.

7. See note 4.

8. In SPSS, this output is generated through Analyze → Compare Means → One Way ANOVA → Contrasts → Polynomial: Linear. The term *unweighted* simply means that all means are weighted equally, regardless of the number of observations in each group. This reflects our purpose. The weighted linear term, which weights the group means according to the number of observations in each group, should not be used.

9. These results are replicated for the untransformed variable, but only when numerous observations identified as outliers for each group are removed. The remaining untransformed variable is not normal for any group, but it does have homogeneous variances. The text findings for the transformed variables strengthen our conclusion that we should regard the stated differences as significant, not as a special case of the nonnormal, untransformed variable.

10. When only "typical" wetland losses are considered (that is, the removal of watersheds that are characterized as outliers in the example analysis), the mean wetland losses of watersheds with small and large surrounding populations are, respectively, 1.73 percent and 2.52 percent, suggesting a 49.2 percent greater wetland loss among watersheds with large populations. The question is whether this categorization of "typical" losses has any traction in public discourse.

CHAPTER

14

Simple Regression

CHAPTER OBJECTIVES

After reading this chapter, you should be able to

- Use simple regression to test the statistical significance of a bivariate relationship involving one dependent and one independent variable
- Use Pearson's correlation coefficient as a measure of association between two continuous variables
- Interpret statistics associated with regression analysis
- Write up the model of simple regression
- Assess assumptions of simple regression

This chapter completes our discussion of statistical techniques for studying relationships between two variables by focusing on those that are *continuous*. Several approaches are examined: simple regression; the Pearson's correlation coefficient; and a nonparametric alterative, Spearman's rank correlation coefficient.

Although all three techniques can be used, we focus particularly on simple regression. Regression allows us to predict outcomes based on knowledge of an independent variable. It is also the foundation for studying relationships among three or more variables, including control variables mentioned in Chapter 2 on research design (and also in Appendix 10.1). Regression can also be used in time series analysis, discussed in Chapter 17. We begin with simple regression.

SIMPLE REGRESSION

Let's first look at an example. Say that you are a manager or analyst involved with a regional consortium of 15 local public agencies (in cities and counties) that provide low-income adults with health education about cardiovascular diseases, in an effort to reduce such diseases. The funding for this health education comes from a federal grant that requires annual analysis and performance outcome reporting. In Chapter 4, we used a logic model to specify that a performance outcome is the result of inputs, activities, and outputs. Following the development of such a model, you decide to conduct a survey among participants who attend such training events to collect data about the number of events they attended, their knowledge of cardiovascular disease, and a variety of habits such as smoking that are linked to cardiovascular disease. Some things that you might want to know are whether attending workshops increases knowledge of cardiovascular disease and whether such knowledge reduces behaviors that put people at risk for cardiovascular disease.

Simple regression is used to analyze the relationship between two continuous variables. Continuous variables assume that the distances between ordered categories are determinable.[1] In simple regression, one variable is defined as the dependent variable and the other as the independent variable (see Chapter 2 for the definitions). In the current example, the level of knowledge obtained from workshops and other sources might be measured on a continuous scale and treated as an independent variable, and behaviors that put people at risk for cardiovascular disease might also be measured on a continuous scale and treated as a dependent variable.

Scatterplot

The relationship between two continuous variables can be portrayed in a *scatterplot*. A scatterplot is merely a plot of the data points for two continuous variables, as shown in Figure 14.1 (without the straight line). By convention, the dependent variable is shown on the vertical (or Y-) axis, and the independent variable on the horizontal (or X-) axis. The relationship between the two variables is estimated as a straight line relationship. The line is defined by the equation $y = a + bx$, where a is the intercept (or constant), and b is the slope. The slope, b, is defined as

$$b = \frac{\Delta y}{\Delta x},$$

Figure 14.1 ————〜〜〜Scatterplot

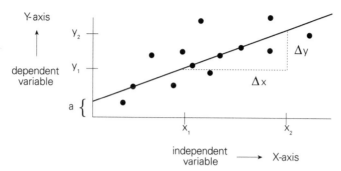

or $(y_2 - y_1)/(x_2 - x_1)$. The line is calculated mathematically such that the sum of distances from each observation to the line is minimized.[2] By definition, the slope indicates the change in y as a result of a unit change in x. The straight line, defined by $y = a + bx$, is also called the **regression line**, and the slope (b) is called the **regression coefficient**.

A positive regression coefficient indicates a positive relationship between the variables, shown by the upward slope in Figure 14.1. A negative regression coefficient indicates a negative relationship between the variables and is indicated by a downward-sloping line.

Test of Significance

The **test of significance of the regression coefficient** is a key test that tells us whether the slope (b) is statistically different from zero. The slope is calculated from a sample, and we wish to know whether it is significant. When the regression line is horizontal $(b = 0)$, no relationship exists between the two variables. Then, changes in the independent variable have no effect on the dependent variable. The following hypotheses are thus stated:

H_0: $b = 0$, or the two variables are unrelated.
H_A: $b \neq 0$, or the two variables are (positively or negatively) related.

To determine whether the slope equals zero, a t-test is performed. The test statistic is defined as the slope, b, divided by the standard error of the slope, $se(b)$. The standard error of the slope is a measure of the distribution of the observations around the regression slope, which is based on the standard deviation of those observations to the regression line:

$$\frac{b}{se(b)}.$$

Key Point

The significance of the slope tests the relationship.

Thus, a regression line with a small slope is more likely to be statistically significant when observations lie closely around it (that is, the standard error of the observations around the line is also small, resulting in a larger test statistic). By contrast, the same regression line might be statistically insignificant when observations are scattered widely around it. Observations that lie farther from the regression line will have larger standard deviations and, hence, larger standard errors. *The computer calculates the slope, intercept, standard error of the slope, and the level at which the slope is statistically significant.*

Consider the following example. A management analyst with the Department of Defense wishes to evaluate the impact of teamwork on the productivity of naval shipyard repair facilities. Although all shipyards are required to use teamwork management strategies, these strategies are assumed to vary in practice. Coincidentally, a recently implemented employee survey asked about the perceived use and effectiveness of teamwork. These items have been aggregated into a single index variable that measures teamwork. Employees were also asked questions about perceived performance, as measured by productivity, customer orientation, planning and scheduling, and employee motivation. These items were combined into an index measure of work productivity. Both index measures are continuous variables. The analyst wants to know whether a relationship exists between perceived productivity and teamwork. Table 14.1 shows the computer output obtained from a simple regression. The slope, *b,* is 0.223; the slope coefficient of teamwork is positive; and the slope is significant at the 1 percent level. Thus, perceptions of teamwork are positively associated with productivity. The t-test statistic, 5.053, is calculated as 0.223/0.044 (rounding errors explain the difference from the printed value of *t*). Other statistics shown in Table 14.1 are discussed below. The appropriate notation for this relationship is shown below. Either the t-test statistic or the standard error should be shown in parentheses, directly below the regression coefficient; analysts should state which statistic is shown. Here, we show the t-test statistic:[3]

$$\text{PRODUCTIVITY} = 4.026 + 0.223^{**}\text{TEAMWORK}$$
$$(5.05)$$
$$^{**}\ p < .01;\ ^{*}\ p < .05$$

The level of significance of the regression coefficient is indicated with asterisks, which conforms to the p-value legend that should also be shown. Typically, two asterisks are used to indicate a 1 percent level of significance, one asterisk for a 5 percent level of significance, and no asterisk for coefficients that are insignificant.[4]

Table 14.1 ——————ᴧᴧᴧ— Simple Regression Output

Model fit		
R	**R-square**	**SEE**
0.272	0.074	0.825

Dependent variable: Productivity

Coefficients

	Unstandardized coefficients			
Model	**b**	**SE**	**t**	**Sig.**
Constant	4.026	0.213	18.894	0.000
Teamwork	0.223	0.044	5.053	0.000

Note: SEE = standard error of the estimate; SE = standard error; Sig. = significance.

Table 14.1 also shows R-square (R^2), which is called the ***coefficient of determination***. R-square is of great interest: its value is interpreted as the percentage of variation in the dependent variable that is explained by the independent variable. R-square varies from zero to one, and is called a goodness-of-fit measure.[5] In our example, teamwork explains only 7.4 percent of the variation in productivity. Although teamwork is significantly associated with productivity, it is quite likely that other factors also affect it. It is conceivable that other factors might be more strongly associated with productivity and that, when controlled for other factors, teamwork is no longer significant. Typically, values of R^2 below 0.20 are considered to indicate weak relationships, those between 0.20 and 0.40 indicate moderate relationships, and those above 0.40 indicate strong relationships. Values of R^2 above 0.65 are considered to indicate very strong relationships. R is called the multiple correlation coefficient and is always $0 \leq R \leq 1$.

> **Key Point**
> R-square is a measure of the strength of the relationship. Its value goes from 0 to 1.

To summarize up to this point, simple regression provides three critically important pieces of information about bivariate relationships involving two continuous variables: (1) the level of significance at which two variables are associated, if at all (t-statistic), (2) whether the relationship between the two variables is positive or negative (*b*), and (3) the strength of the relationship (R^2).

The primary purpose of regression analysis is hypothesis testing, not prediction. In our example, the regression model is used to test the hypothesis that teamwork is related to productivity. However, if the analyst wants to predict the variable "productivity," the regression output also shows the SEE, or the ***standard error of the estimate*** (see Table 14.1). This is a measure of the spread of *y* values around the regression line as calculated for the mean value of the independent variable, only, and assuming a large sample. The standard error of the estimate has an interpretation in terms of the normal curve, that is, 68 percent of *y* values lie within one standard error from the calculated value of *y*, as calculated for the mean value of *x* using the preceding regression model. Thus, if the mean index value of the variable "teamwork" is 5.0, then the calculated (or predicted) value of "productivity" is [4.026 + 0.223*5 =] 5.141. Because SEE = 0.825, it follows that 68 percent of productivity values will lie 60.825 from 5.141 when "teamwork" = 5. Predictions of *y* for other values of *x* have larger standard errors.[6]

Assumptions and Notation

There are three **simple regression assumptions.** First, simple regression assumes that the relationship between two variables is *linear.* The linearity of bivariate relationships is easily determined through visual inspection, as shown in Figure 14.2. In fact, all analysis of relationships involving continuous variables should begin with a scatterplot. When variable relationships are nonlinear (parabolic or otherwise heavily curved), it is not appropriate to use linear regression. Then, one or both variables must be transformed, as discussed in Chapter 12.

Second, simple regression assumes that the *linear relationship is constant* over the range of observations. This assumption is violated when the relationship is "broken," for example, by having an upward slope for the first half of independent variable values and a downward slope over the remaining values. Then, analysts should consider using two regression models each for these different, linear relationships. The linearity assumption is also violated when no relationship is present in part of the independent variable values. This is particularly problematic because regression analysis will calculate a regression slope based on all observations. In this case, analysts may be misled into believing that the linear pattern holds for all observations. Hence, regression results always should be verified through visual inspection.

Third, simple regression assumes that the variables are continuous. In Chapter 15, we will see that regression can also be used for nominal and

Figure 14.2 ⎯⎯⎯⎯⎯⎯⎯⎯Three Examples of *r*

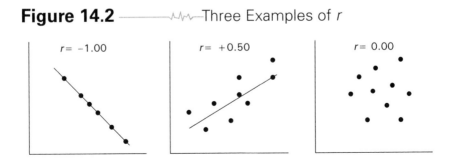

dichotomous independent variables. The dependent variable, however, must be continuous. When the dependent variable is dichotomous, logistic regression should be used (Chapter 16).

The following notations are commonly used in regression analysis. The predicted value of y (defined, based on the regression model, as $y = a + bx$) is typically different from the ***observed value of y***. The ***predicted value of the dependent variable*** y is sometimes indicated as $\hat{y}$ (pronounced "y-hat"). Only when $R^2 = 1$ are the observed and predicted values identical for each observation. The difference between y and $\hat{y}$ is called the regression *error* or ***error term*** (e). Hence the expressions

$$\hat{y} = a + b*x \qquad \text{and}$$
$$y = a + b*x + e$$

are equivalent, as is $y = \hat{y} + e$. Certain assumptions about e are important, such as that it is normally distributed. When error term assumptions are violated, incorrect conclusions may be made about the statistical significance of relationships. This important issue is discussed in greater detail in Chapter 15 and, for time series data, in Chapter 17. Hence, the above is a pertinent but incomplete list of assumptions.

> **Getting Started**
> Conduct a simple regression, and practice writing up your results.

PEARSON'S CORRELATION COEFFICIENT

Pearson's correlation coefficient, r, measures the association (significance, direction, and strength) between two continuous variables; it is a measure of association for two continuous variables. Also called the Pearson's product-moment correlation coefficient, it does not assume a causal relationship, as does simple regression. The correlation coefficient indicates the extent to which the observations lie closely or loosely clustered around the regression line. The coefficient r ranges from -1 to $+1$. The sign indicates the direction of the relationship, which, in simple regression, is always the same as the slope coefficient. A "-1" indicates a perfect negative relationship, that is, that all observations lie exactly on a downward-sloping regression line; a "$+1$" indicates a perfect positive relationship, whereby all observations lie exactly on an upward-sloping regression line. Of course, such values are rarely obtained in practice because observations seldom lie exactly on a line. An r value of zero indicates that observations are so widely scattered that it is impossible to draw any well-fitting line. Figure 14.2 illustrates some values of r.

> **Key Point**
> Pearson's correlation coefficient, r, ranges from -1 to $+1$.

It is important to avoid confusion between Pearson's correlation coefficient and the coefficient of determination. For the two-variable, simple regression model, $r^2 = R^2$, but whereas $0 \leq R \leq 1$, r ranges from -1 to $+1$. Hence, the sign of r tells us whether a relationship is positive or negative, but the sign of R, in regression output tables such as Table 14.1, is always positive and cannot inform us about the direction of the relationship. In simple regression, the regression coefficient, b, informs us about the direction of the relationship. Statistical software programs usually show r rather than r^2. Note also that the Pearson's correlation coefficient can be used only to assess the association between two continuous variables, whereas regression can be extended to deal with more than two variables, as discussed in Chapter 15. Pearson's correlation coefficient assumes that both variables are normally distributed.

When Pearson's correlation coefficients are calculated, a standard error of r can be determined, which then allows us to test the statistical significance of the bivariate correlation. For bivariate relationships, this is the same level of significance as shown for the slope of the regression coefficient. For the variables given earlier in this chapter, the value of r is .272 and the statistical significance of r is $p \leq .01$. Use of the Pearson's correlation coefficient assumes that the variables are normally distributed and that there are no significant departures from linearity.[7]

It is important not to confuse the correlation coefficient, r, with the regression coefficient, b. Comparing the measures r and b (the slope) sometimes causes confusion. The key point is that r does not indicate the regression slope but rather the extent to which observations lie close to it. A steep regression line (large b) can have observations scattered loosely or closely around it, as can a shallow (more horizontal) regression line. The purposes of these two statistics are very different.[8]

SPEARMAN'S RANK CORRELATION COEFFICIENT

The nonparametric alternative, *Spearman's rank correlation coefficient* (ρ, or "rho"), looks at correlation among the ranks of the data rather than among the values. The ranks of data are determined as shown in Table 14.2 (adapted from Table 11.8):

Table 14.2 ⎯⎯⎯ Ranks of Two Variables

Observation	Variable 1 value	Variable 1 rank	Variable 2 value	Variable 2 rank
1	2.5	2	3.4	3
2	2.9	3	3.3	2
3	4.0	5	4.0	5
4	3.2	4	3.9	4
5	1.2	1	2.1	1

In Greater Depth . . .

Box 14.1   Crime and Poverty

An analyst wants to examine empirically the relationship between crime and income in cities across the United States. The CD that accompanies the workbook *Exercising Essential Statistics* includes a Community Indicators dataset with assorted indicators of conditions in 98 cities such as Akron, Ohio; Phoenix, Arizona; New Orleans, Louisiana; and Seattle, Washington. The measures include median household income, total population (both from the 2000 U.S. Census), and total violent crimes (FBI, Uniform Crime Reporting, 2004). In the sample, household income ranges from $26,309 (Newark, New Jersey) to $71,765 (San Jose, California), and the median household income is $42,316. Per-capita violent crime ranges from 0.15 percent (Glendale, California) to 2.04 percent (Las Vegas, Nevada), and the median violent crime rate per capita is 0.78 percent.

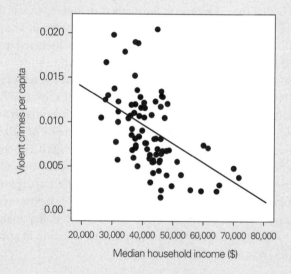

There are four types of violent crimes: murder and nonnegligent manslaughter, forcible rape, robbery, and aggravated assault. A measure of total violent crime per capita is calculated because larger cities are apt to have more crime. The analyst wants to examine whether income is associated with per-capita violent crime. The scatterplot of these two continuous variables shows that a negative relationship appears to be present:

(continued)

Box 14.1 *(continued)*

The Pearson's correlation coefficient is $-.532$ ($p < .01$), and the Spearman's correlation coefficient is $-.552$ ($p < .01$). The simple regression model shows $R^2 = .283$. The regression model is as follows (t-test statistic in parentheses):

$$\text{Violent Crime Per Capita} = .020 - 2.54*10^{-7**} \text{Household Income}$$
$$(-5.72)$$

$**\ p < .01.$

The regression line is shown on the scatterplot. Interpreting these results, we see that the R-square value of .283 indicates a moderate relationship between these two variables. Clearly, some cities with modest median household incomes have a high crime rate. However, removing these cities does not greatly alter the findings. Also, an assumption of regression is that the error term is normally distributed, and further examination of the error shows that it is somewhat skewed. The techniques for examining the distribution of the error term are discussed in Chapter 15, but again, addressing this problem does not significantly alter the finding that the two variables are significantly related to each other, and that the relationship is of moderate strength. With this result in hand, further analysis shows, for example, by how much violent crime decreases for each increase in household income. For each increase of $10,000 in average household income, the violent crime rate drops 0.25 percent. For a city experiencing the median 0.78 percent crime rate, this would be a considerable improvement, indeed. Note also that the scatterplot shows considerable variation in the crime rate for cities at or below the median household income, in contrast to those well above it. Policy analysts may well wish to examine conditions that give rise to variation in crime rates among cities with lower incomes.

Because Spearman's rank correlation coefficient examines correlation among the ranks of variables, it can also be used with ordinal-level data.[9] For the data in Table 14.2, Spearman's rank correlation coefficient is .900 ($p = .035$).[10] Spearman's p-squared coefficient has a "percent variation explained" interpretation, similar to the measures described earlier. Hence,

90 percent of the variation in one variable can be explained by the other. For the variables given earlier, the Spearman's rank correlation coefficient is .274 (p < .01), which is comparable to r reported in preceding sections.

Box 14.1 illustrates another use of the statistics described in this chapter, in a study of the relationship between crime and poverty.

SUMMARY

When analysts examine relationships between two continuous variables, they can use simple regression or the Pearson's correlation coefficient. Both measures show (1) the statistical significance of the relationship, (2) the direction of the relationship (that is, whether it is positive or negative), and (3) the strength of the relationship.

Simple regression assumes a causal and linear relationship between the continuous variables. The statistical significance and direction of the slope coefficient is used to assess the statistical significance and direction of the relationship. The coefficient of determination, R^2, is used to assess the strength of relationships; R^2 is interpreted as the percent variation explained. Regression is a foundation for studying relationships involving three or more variables, such as control variables. The Pearson's correlation coefficient does not assume causality between two continuous variables.

A nonparametric alternative to testing the relationship between two continuous variables is the Spearman's rank correlation coefficient, which examines correlation among the ranks of the data rather than among the values themselves. As such, this measure can also be used to study relationships in which one or both variables are ordinal.

KEY TERMS

Coefficient of determination, R^2 (p. 243)

Error term (p. 245)

Observed value of y (p. 245)

Pearson's correlation coefficient, r (p. 245)

Predicted value of the dependent variable y, $\hat{y}$ (p. 245)

Regression coefficient (p. 241)

Regression line (p. 241)

Scatterplot (p. 240)

Simple regression assumptions (p. 244)

Spearman's rank correlation coefficient (p. 246)

Standard error of the estimate (p. 244)

Test of significance of the regression coefficient (p. 241)

Notes

1. See Chapter 3 for a definition of continuous variables. Although the distinction between ordinal and continuous is theoretical (namely, whether or not the distance between categories can be measured), in practice ordinal-level variables with seven or more categories (including Likert variables) are sometimes analyzed using statistics appropriate for interval-level variables. This practice has many critics because it violates an assumption of regression (interval data), but it is often done because it doesn't (much) affect the robustness of results.

2. The method for calculating the regression coefficient (the slope) is called *ordinary least squares,* or OLS. This method estimates the slope by minimizing the sum of squared differences between each predicted value of $a + bx$ and the actual value of y. One reason for squaring these distances is to ensure that all distances are positive.

3. No consistent preference exists about what is shown in parentheses. The current practice in many political science journals is to report the standard error, but many public administrations report the t-test.

4. Some authors also identify other levels of significance, such as $p < .001$ or $p < .10$, but this does not affect study conclusions, of course.

5. The formula for R^2 is presented in Chapter 15, in our discussion of the F-test.

6. For predictions not based on the mean of x, the standard error of y is larger than the SEE, according to the following formula:

$$SEE' = SEE\sqrt{1 + \frac{1}{N} + \frac{\left(x_i - \bar{x}\right)^2}{(N-1)s_x^2}},$$

where s_x^2 is the variance of x, that is, $\Sigma(x - \bar{x})^2/(N - 1)$. As can be seen, $SEE' = SEE$ only when N is large and the predicted values of y are calculated for the mean value of x (that is, $x_i = \bar{x}$). Graphically, the relationship between SEE' and x is as follows:

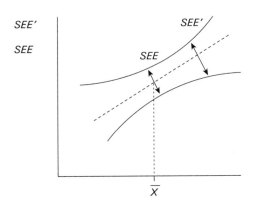

7. Based on visual inspection, these two variables are normally distributed. In addition, the Kolmogorov-Smirnov test (see Chapter 12) for the variable "teamwork" shows p = .084.

8. Pearson's correlation coefficient is also the basis for calculating Cronbach alpha, the measure of internal reliability discussed in Chapter 3. The formula for alpha is $\alpha = N^*\bar{r}/[1 + (N-1)^*\bar{r}]$, where N is the number of variables and $\bar{r}$ is the mean of the correlations among all the different pairs of variables that make up the measure. This formula clearly shows that alpha is bounded by zero and one: when $\bar{r} = 1$, then $\alpha = 1$, and when $\bar{r} = 0$, then $\alpha = 0$.

9. Spearman's rank correlation coefficient would also be used when assumptions of normality are violated, or when variables are related in nonlinear ways.

10. The formula for Spearman's rank correlation coefficient is as follows:

$$r_s = 1 - \frac{6\sum d^2}{n(n^2 - 1)},$$

where d is the difference between ranks in each observation (x,y). For the data shown in Table 14.2, consider the following calculation:

Observation	Variable 1 rank	Variable 2 rank	d	d^2
1	2	3	−1	1
2	3	2	1	1
3	5	5	0	0
4	4	4	0	0
5	1	1	0	0

Hence, the value of $r_s = 1 - [(6^*2)/5(25 - 1)] = 0.9$.

CHAPTER 15

Multiple Regression

CHAPTER OBJECTIVES

After reading this chapter, you should be able to

- Understand multiple regression as a full model specification technique
- Interpret standardized and unstandardized regression coefficients of multiple regression
- Know how to use nominal variables in regression as dummy variables
- Explain the importance of the error term plot
- Identify assumptions of regression, and know how to test and correct assumption violations

Multiple regression is one of the most widely used multivariate statistical techniques for analyzing three or more variables. This chapter uses multiple regression to examine such relationships, and thereby extends the discussion in Chapter 14. The popularity of multiple regression is due largely to the ease with which it takes *control variables* (or rival hypotheses) into account. In Chapter 10, we discussed briefly how contingency tables can be used for this purpose, but doing so is often a cumbersome and sometimes inconclusive effort. By contrast, multiple regression easily incorporates multiple independent variables. Another reason for its popularity is that it also takes into account nominal independent variables.

However, multiple regression is no substitute for bivariate analysis. Indeed, managers or analysts with an interest in a specific bivariate relationship will conduct a bivariate analysis first, before examining whether the relationship is robust in the presence of numerous control variables. And before conducting bivariate analysis, analysts need to conduct univariate analysis to better understand their variables. Thus, multiple regression is usually one of the last steps of analysis. Indeed, multiple regression is often used to test the robustness of bivariate relationships when control variables are taken into account.

The flexibility with which multiple regression takes control variables into account comes at a price, though. Regression, like the t-test, is based on numerous assumptions. Regression results cannot be assumed to be robust in the face of assumption violations. *Testing of assumptions is always part of multiple regression analysis.* Multiple regression is carried out in the following sequence: (1) model specification (that is, identification of dependent and independent variables), (2) testing of regression assumptions, (3) correction of assumption violations, if any, and (4) reporting of the results of the final regression model. This chapter examines these four steps and discusses essential concepts related to simple and multiple regression. Chapters 16 and 17 extend this discussion by examining the use of logistic regression and time series analysis.

MODEL SPECIFICATION

Multiple regression is an extension of simple regression, but an important difference exists between the two methods: multiple regression aims for *full model specification*. This means that analysts seek to account for *all of the variables that affect the dependent variable*; by contrast, simple regression examines the effect of only one independent variable. Philosophically, the phrase identifying the key difference—"all of the variables that affect the dependent variable"—is divided into two parts. The *first part* involves identifying the variables that are of *most* (theoretical and practical) *relevance* in explaining the dependent variable. In social science, this is called a **nomothetic mode of explanation**—the isolation of the most important factors. This approach is consistent with the philosophy of seeking complete but parsimonious explanations in science.[1] The *second part* involves addressing those variables that were not considered as being of most relevance.

Regarding the first part, the specification of the "most important" independent variables is a judicious undertaking. The use of a nomothetic strategy implies that a range of plausible models exists—different analysts may identify different sets of "most important" independent variables. Analysts should ask which different factors are most likely to affect or cause their dependent variable, and they are likely to justify, identify, and operationalize their choices differently. Thus, the term *full model specification* does not imply that only one model or even a best model exists, but rather it refers to a family of plausible models. Most researchers agree that specification should (1) be driven by theory, that is, by persuasive arguments and perspectives that identify and justify which factors are most important, and (2) inform why the set of such variables is regarded as complete and parsimonious. In practice, the search for complete, parsimonious, and theory-driven explanations usually results in multiple regression models with about 5–12 independent variables; theory seldom results in less than 5 variables, and parsimony and problems of statistical estimation, discussed further, seldom result in models with more than 12.

> **Key Point**
>
> We cannot examine the effect of all possible variables. Rather, we focus on the most relevant ones.

The search for parsimonious explanations often leads analysts to first identify different categories of factors that most affect their dependent variable. Then, after these categories of factors have been identified, analysts turn to the task of trying to measure each, through either single or index variables. As an example, consider the dependent variable "high school violence," discussed in Chapter 2. We ask: "What are the most important, distinct factors affecting or causing high school violence?" Some plausible factors are (1) student access to weapons, (2) student isolation from others, (3) peer groups that are prone to violence, (4) lack of enforcement of school nonviolence policies, (5) participation in anger management programs, and (6) familiarity with warning signals (among teachers and staff). Perhaps you can think of other factors. Then, following the strategies discussed in Chapter 3—conceptualization, operationalization, and index variable construction—we use either single variables or index measures as independent variables to measure each of these factors. This approach provides for the inclusion of programs or policies as independent variables, as well as variables that measure salient rival hypotheses.

The strategy of full model specification requires that analysts not overlook important factors. Thus, analysts do well to carefully justify their model and to consult past studies and interview those who have direct experience with, or other opinions about, the research subject. Doing so might lead analysts to include additional variables, such as the socioeconomic status of students' parents. Then, after a fully specified model has been identified, analysts often include additional variables of interest. These may be variables of lesser relevance, speculative consequences, or variables that analysts want to test for their *lack* of impact, such as rival hypotheses. Demographic variables, such as the age of students, might be added. When additional variables are included, analysts should identify which independent variables constitute the nomothetic explanation, and which serve some other purpose. Remember, all variables included in models must be theoretically justified. Analysts must argue how each variable could plausibly affect their dependent variable.

The *second part* of "all of the variables that affect the dependent variable" acknowledges all of the other variables that are not identified (or included) in the model. They are omitted; these variables are not among "the most important factors" that affect the dependent variable. The cumulative effect of these other variables is, by definition, contained in the error term, described later in this chapter. The *assumption of full model specification* is that these other variables are justifiably omitted only when their cumulative effect on the dependent variable is zero. This approach is plausible because each of these many unknown variables may have a different magnitude, thus making it possible that their effects cancel each other out. The argument, quite clearly, is not that each of these other factors has no impact on the dependent variable—but only that their *cumulative effect is zero.* The validity of multiple regression models centers on examining the behavior of the error term in this regard. If the cumulative effect of all the other variables is not zero, then additional independent variables may have to be considered. The specification of the multiple regression model is as follows:

$$y = a + b_1 x_1 + b_2 x_2 + b_3 x_3 + b_4 x_4 + \ldots + error$$

Dependent =	Independent variables in model	Variables not in model
variable	("most important factors")	("all excluded factors")
	+	
	("other included factors")	

Thus, multiple regression requires two important tasks: (1) specification of independent variables and (2) testing of the error term. An important difference between simple regression and multiple regression is the *interpretation of the **regression coefficients in multiple regression*** ($b_1, b_2, b_3, \ldots$) in the preceding multiple regression model. Although multiple regression produces the same basic statistics discussed in Chapter 14 (see Table 14.1), each of the regression coefficients is interpreted as its effect on the dependent variable, *controlled for the effects of all of the other independent variables included in the regression.* This phrase is used frequently when explaining multiple regression results. In our example, the regression coefficient b_1 shows the effect of x_1 on y, controlled for all other variables included in the model. Regression coefficient b_2 shows the effect of x_2 on y, also controlled for all other variables in

> **Key Point**
>
> The regression coefficient is the effect on the dependent variable, controlled for all other independent variables in the model.

the model, including x_1. Multiple regression is indeed an important and relatively simple way of taking control variables into account (and much easier than the approach shown in Appendix 10.1).

Note also that the model given here is very different from estimating separate simple regression models for each of the independent variables. The regression coefficients in simple regression *do not control* for other independent variables, because they are not in the model.

The word *independent* also means that each independent variable should be relatively unaffected by other independent variables in the model. To ensure that independent variables are indeed independent, it is useful to think of the distinctively *different types* (or categories) *of factors* that affect a dependent variable. This was the approach taken in the preceding example. There is also a statistical reason for ensuring that independent variables are as independent as possible. When two independent variables are highly correlated with each other ($r^2 > .60$), it sometimes becomes statistically impossible to distinguish the effect of each independent variable on the dependent variable, controlled for the other. The variables are statistically too similar to discern disparate effects. This problem is called *multicollinearity* and is discussed later in this chapter. This problem is avoided by choosing independent variables that are not highly correlated with each other.

A WORKING EXAMPLE

Previously (see Chapter 14), the management analyst with the Department of Defense found a statistically significant relationship between teamwork and perceived facility productivity (p <.01). The analyst now wishes to examine whether the impact of teamwork on productivity is robust when controlled for other factors that also affect productivity. This interest is heightened by the low *R*-square ($R^2 = 0.074$) in Table 14.1, suggesting a weak relationship between teamwork and perceived productivity.

A multiple regression model is specified to include the effects of other factors that affect perceived productivity. Thinking about other categories of variables that could affect productivity, the analyst hypothesizes the following: (1) the extent to which employees have adequate technical knowledge to do their jobs, (2) perceptions of having adequate authority to do one's job well (for example, decision-making flexibility), (3) perceptions that rewards and recognition are distributed fairly (always important for motivation), and (4) the number of sick days. Various items from the employee survey are used to measure these concepts (as discussed in the workbook documentation for the Productivity dataset). After including these factors as additional independent variables, the result shown in Table 15.1 is obtained. Comparison with Table 14.1 shows that *R*-square has increased greatly; it is now 0.274. Hence 27.4 percent of the variation in the dependent variable, "productivity," is now explained by the five independent variables in the model.

Table 15.1 ⎯⎯⎯⎯⎯⎯⎯⎯⎯ Multiple Regression Output

Model

R	R-square	Adjusted R^2	SEE
0.524	0.274	0.263	0.735

Dependent variable: Productivity

ANOVA table

Model	Sum of squares	df	Mean square	F	Sig.
Regression	64.239	5	12.848	23.809	0.000
Residual	169.980	315	0.540		
Total	234.219	320			

Coefficients

Model	Unstandardized coefficients		Standardized coefficients		
	b	SE	Beta	t	Sig.
Constant	2.064	0.301		6.850	0.000
Teamwork	0.166	0.040	0.202	4.166	0.000
Knowledge	0.267	0.050	0.263	5.391	0.000
Authority	0.200	0.035	0.288	5.804	0.000
Days sick	−0.011	0.020	−0.026	−0.543	0.587
Fairness	0.076	0.033	0.113	2.284	0.023

Note: SEE = standard error of the estimate; SE = standard error; Sig. = significance.

Regarding these independent variables, teamwork *remains statistically significant* ($p < .01$) *when controlled for all of the other variables in the model* (ability, authority, inducement, and fairness). The results also show that having adequate knowledge and authority are, statistically, positively associated with productivity (both $p < .01$). Perceptions of fairness in rewards and recognition are also associated with productivity at the 5 percent level of significance. The considerable increase in R-square reflects the addition of these significant variables. The number of sick days is not associated with productivity, when controlled for other variables. Note that the sign of the significantly associated variables is positive, as expected. We would have been piqued if it had been negative. We need not be concerned about the negative slope of sick days because this variable is insignificant (not significantly different from zero).

However, a key question is whether the model is fully specified. If the net effect on the dependent variable of all variables excluded from the model is not zero, then perhaps some other variable should be included that might affect our findings. The error term is examined to determine this possibility.

Recall that the net effect of all variables not included in the model is contained in the error term. When the net effect of such variables on the dependent variable is zero, *no relationship* exists between the error term and the predicted dependent variable. This relationship will be random, without pattern or shape. It is customary to plot the standardized error term (or residual) against the standardized predicted value of the dependent variable. This is called an **error term plot**. The concept of standardization (see Chapter 7) involves transformation such that variables have a mean of zero and a standard deviation of one. Then, if no relationship exists between these two variables, the scatterplot should be random and clustered around (0,0), as shown in Figure 15.1. This figure is *prima facie evidence* that the net effect of variables not included in the model is zero because the data points are randomly scattered. Later in this chapter, we discuss other violations of regression assumptions, and strategies for examining and remedying such assumptions. Then we extend the preceding discussion and will be able to conclude whether the above results are valid.

Again, this model is not the only model that can be constructed but rather is one among a family of plausible models. Indeed, from a theoretical perspective, other variables might have been included, too. From an empirical perspective, perhaps other variables might explain more variance. Model specification is a judicious effort, requiring a balance between theoretical and statistical integrity. Statistical software programs can also automatically select independent variables based on their statistical significance, hence, adding to R-square.[2] However, models with high R-square values are not necessarily better; theoretical reasons must

Getting Started

Find examples of multiple regression in the research literature.

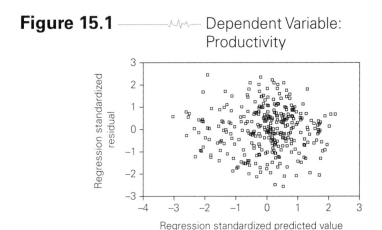

Figure 15.1 ⎯⎯⎯⎯ Dependent Variable: Productivity

exist for selecting independent variables, explaining why and how they might be related to the dependent variable. Knowing which variables are related empirically to the dependent variable can help narrow the selection, but such knowledge should not wholly determine it. We now turn to a discussion of the other statistics shown in Table 15.1.

FURTHER STATISTICS

Goodness of Fit for Multiple Regression

The model R-square in Table 15.1 is greatly increased over that shown in Table 14.1: R-square has gone from 0.074 in the simple regression model to 0.274. However, R-square has the undesirable mathematical property of increasing with the number of independent variables in the model. R-square increases regardless of whether an additional independent variable adds further explanation of the dependent variable. The *adjusted R-square* (or $\overline{R}^2$) controls for the number of independent variables. $\overline{R}^2$ is always equal to or less than R^2. The above increase in explanation of the dependent variable is due to variables identified as statistically significant in Table 15.1.

> **Key Point**
> R-square is the variation in the dependent variable that is explained by all the independent variables.

Adjusted R-square is often used to evaluate model explanation (or fit). Analogous with simple regression, values of $\overline{R}^2$ below 0.20 are considered to suggest weak model fit, those between 0.20 and 0.40 indicate moderate fit, those above 0.40 indicate strong fit, and those above 0.65 indicate very strong model fit. Analysts should remember that choices of model specification are driven foremost by theory, not statistical model fit; strong model fit is desirable only when the variables, and their relationships, are meaningful in some real-life sense. Adjusted R-square can assist in the variable selection process. Low values of adjusted R-square prompt analysts to ask whether they inadvertently excluded important variables from their models; if included, these variables might affect the statistical significance of those already in a model.[3] Adjusted R-square also helps analysts to choose among alternative variable specifications (for example, different measures of student isolation), when such choices are no longer meaningfully informed by theory. Empirical issues of model fit then usefully guide the selection process further. Researchers typically report adjusted R-square with their regression results.

Standardized Coefficients

The question arises as to which independent variable has the greatest impact on explaining the dependent variable. The slope of the coefficients (b) does not answer this question because each slope is measured in different units (recall from Chapter 14 that $b = \Delta y / \Delta x$). Comparing different slope coefficients is tantamount to comparing apples and oranges. However, based on the regression coefficient (or slope), it is possible to calculate the ***standardized coefficient,*** β (beta). Beta is defined as the change produced in the dependent variable by a unit of change in the independent variable when both variables are measured in terms of standard deviation units. Beta is unit-less and thus allows for comparison of the impact of different independent variables on explaining the dependent variable. Analysts compare the relative values of beta coefficients; beta has no inherent meaning. It is appropriate to compare betas across independent variables in the same regression, not across different regressions.

Based on Table 15.1, we conclude that the impact of having adequate authority on explaining productivity is $[(0.288 - 0.202)/0.202 =]$ 42.6 percent greater than teamwork, and about equal to that of knowledge. The impact of having adequate authority is two-and-a-half times greater than that of perceptions of fair rewards and recognition.[4]

F-Test

Table 15.1 also features an analysis of variance (ANOVA) table. The ***global F-test*** examines the overall effect of all independent variables jointly on the dependent variable. The null hypothesis is that the overall effect of all independent variables jointly on the dependent variables is statistically insignificant. The alternate hypothesis is that this overall effect is statistically significant. The null hypothesis implies that none of the regression coefficients is statistically significant; the alternate hypothesis implies that *at least one* of the regression coefficients is statistically significant. The F-test test statistic, 23.809, is statistically significant: hence, the overall effect of all independent variables jointly on the dependent variables is statistically significant. Analysts needn't rely on the global F-test for this information: the "Sig." (significance) column in the table of coefficients shows not only that at least one coefficient is statistically significant, it also shows which ones.[5]

As a point of information, the term *regression sum of squares* is a measure of the explained variation, $\Sigma(\hat{y}_i - \bar{y})^2$, and the *residual sum of squares* is a measure of the unexplained variation, $\Sigma(y_i - \hat{y}_i)^2$. These measures are shown graphically in Figure 15.2. *Total sum of squares* is defined as the sum of these measures. These measures are the basis for calculating R-square. Specifically, $R^2 = 1 - $ (residual sum of squares/total sum of squares). These values are shown in Table 15.1, from which we calculate R^2 as $[1 - (169.980/234.219) =]$ 0.274, which is shown as the value of R^2 in Table 15.1.[6]

Figure 15.2 —⌇⌇⌇— Regression and Residual Sum of Squares

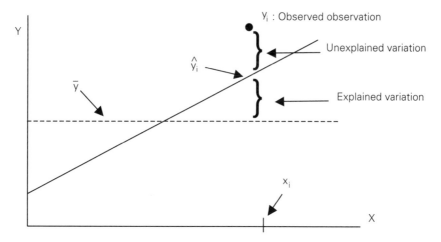

Y_i : Observed observation

Unexplained variation

$\hat{y}_i$

$\bar{y}$

Explained variation

x_i

USE OF NOMINAL VARIABLES

Multiple regression easily incorporates nominal variables as independent variables. However, a little transformation is required because the assumption of linearity suggests that it is not appropriate to regress a nominal variable against a dependent variable. Consider, for example, a nominal variable such as "Region" that is coded as West = 1, Northeast = 2, South = 3, and Midwest = 4. In this case, it would be incorrect to conclude that a predicted y value involving Midwest is four times that of West. Clearly, no such ordering exists among the values of this variable.

This difficulty is overcome by *recoding* the "Region" variable, creating *separate variables* for each of the response categories (except one, discussed below). Each new variable is dichotomous, having the value of one when it identifies the appropriate group, and zero otherwise. Such variables are called ***dummy variables*** because they take on only the values of zero and one. The recoding approach is shown in Table 15.2. Thus, for example, when Region = 1, the new variable West = 1, and West is zero in all other instances. Similarly, when Region = 2, the new variable Northeast = 1, and this new variable is zero in all other instances. The number of dummy variables is equal to the *number of categories minus 1*. This relationship results because the introduction of a variable representing the last category (Midwest) creates a perfect linear relationship among the independent variables: West + Northeast + South + Midwest = 1. For mathematical reasons,

Table 15.2 ⎯⎯⎯⎯ ⌇⌇ ⎯⎯ Recoding of Variables

Old Region	New Region		
	West	Northeast	South
1	1	0	0
2	0	1	0
3	0	0	1
4	0	0	0

when such perfect relationships exist among independent variables, it is not possible to calculate the regression coefficients.[7]

The implication of not including a variable identifying one of the categories is that results are interpreted as the effect on the dependent variable controlled for all independent variables in the model *plus the omitted category*. In our example, when the dummy variables are added to the model in Table 15.2, the regression coefficient of West shows its effect on productivity controlled for all other independent variables, including the effect of the Midwest, which is not entered into the regression.[8]

The corresponding regression model is then written as follows:

$$y = a + b_1 Northeast + b_2 South + b_3 West_3 + b_4 x_4 + b_5 x_5 + \ldots + error,$$

where *Northeast* = 1 when the observation is located in the Northeast; *Northeast* = 0 when the observation is located in the South, Midwest, or West; *South* = 1 when the observation is located in the South; *South* = 0 when the observation is located in the Northeast, Midwest, or West; *West* = 1 when the observation is located in the West; and *West* = 0 when the observation is located in the Northeast, South, or Midwest.

This interpretation is similar to considering the effect of gender on productivity, when the variable "gender" is coded as 0 = male and 1 = female. In that case, the regression coefficient of gender shows the effect of being female on productivity controlled for all other independent variables, including the effect of being male. There is no need to add a separate dummy variable for "male."

Dummy variables can also be used to identify control groups (for example, "exp" = 0) and experimental groups ("exp" = 1). Dummy variables are also useful for identifying observations at different time periods, for example, Time = 0 (before intervention) and Time = 1 (after intervention). This approach allows us to distinguish between two or more different groups and to determine whether belonging to a group (for example, getting treatment or not) has a statistically significant effect on the dependent variable. For example, a model might be specified as follows:

$$y = a + b_1x_1 + b_2x_2 + b_3x_3 + b_4x_4 + \ldots + error,$$

where $x_1 = 1$ if the observation belongs to the treatment group, and $x_1 = 0$ if the observation belongs to the control group. Dummy variables are also used in time series analysis to model the impact of policies over time (see Chapter 17).

> **Getting Started**
> Develop your own multiple regression model.

TESTING ASSUMPTIONS

Multiple regression is a powerful tool, but the technique includes assumptions that must be met. Many regression assumptions involve a test of the error term, which can help reveal problems with the model or data. Ideally, the relationship between the error term and the predicted dependent variable, shown in an *error term plot*, should be random (see Figure 15.1). However, several problems can occur that cause this pattern *not* to be random. The art of testing assumptions involves the analysis of these patterns. The following **multiple regression assumptions** exist: (1) no outliers, (2) no multicollinearity, (3) linearity, (4) no heteroscedasticity, (5) no autocorrelation, (6) no specification error, and (7) no measurement error. Although multiple regression is a powerful tool, analysts must also pay attention to these assumptions.

> **Key Point**
> Regression results cannot be assumed to be robust in the face of assumption violations.

Outliers

Outliers are observations with uncommon values, with regard to both single variables as well as combinations of variables. For example, although students with both high grade point averages (GPAs) and scholastic awards are not uncommon, any such student who commits frequent acts of school violence would likely be an outlier even among students who commit crimes. Outliers are common in multiple regression, and they are of concern because they may affect the statistical significance of regression coefficients.

This problem of outliers is shown graphically in Figure 15.3. Regression line A is estimated based only on the observations indicated with black dots. It is calculated without the uncharacteristic outlier, shown as the single starred observation; the regression slope is not significantly different from $b = 0$. Line B is the recalculated regression line that now includes the starred observation. The additional observation alters the direction of the regression line such that $b > 0$, leading to the conclusion that the independent variable is significantly associated with the dependent variable. Conclusions that are affected so strongly by just one or a few observations are not robust.

Figure 15.3 —⁓— Impact of Outliers

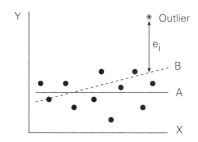

Detection. Outliers are commonly identified by the size of their residual. Note that the residual (or error, e_i, defined as $y_i - \hat{y}_i$) is larger for the additional starred observation than for any of the dotted observations in Figure 15.3. Outliers are usually first identified when the error term plot is examined (see Figure 15.4). Observations are defined as outliers when their residuals exceed ±3 standard deviations; clearly, such observations are unusual relative to others. Statistical software packages can flag residuals that exceed a user-specified value (such as three standard deviations) and produce error term plots.[9]

How to resolve. The effect of outliers on regression conclusions is examined by removing outliers, reestimating the model, and then examining conclusions for substantive robustness. Statistical software packages allow users to save residuals associated with each observation. These residuals are then used to remove from subsequent analysis any observations that are outliers. The primary concern is with significant coefficients that become insignificant, and vice versa. Change in the direction (sign) of regression coefficients is also of concern. The final reported results should be robust; hence, they should exclude outliers that substantively affect conclusions.

Figure 15.4 —⁓— Outlier Detection

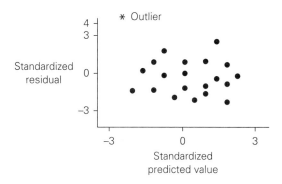

Multicollinearity

The problem of ***multicollinearity*** (pronounced "multi-KOH-li-nee-air-i-tee") is that two independent variables may be correlated to such a high degree that their effects on the dependent variable are indistinguishably similar. For example, in a study of high school violence, the variables "off-campus crimes" and "off-campus misdemeanors" might be highly correlated. In this case, the regression coefficients of these two independent variables might be statistically insignificant because, net of the other(s), they have little or no residual effect on the dependent variable, "high school violence." This problem is shown graphically in Figure 15.5. The black and white observations produce regression lines so similar that, given their respective standard errors, they are statistically indistinguishable.

Detection. Multicollinearity is more likely to occur as more independent variables are entered into the model. The more independent variables entered, the more likely that some will be highly correlated with each other. Multicollinearity is usually first suspected when the regression coefficients of independent variables in a multiple regression are statistically insignificant, even though in bivariate relationships they are known to be highly significant (for example, $r^2 > .60$). Computers readily calculate correlation matrices, which show these correlations for all pairs of variables. Computers also calculate the *variance inflation factor* (VIF) for each regression coefficient.[10] VIF is a measure of the effect of all other independent variables on a regression coefficient.[11] Values greater than 5 or 10 indicate multicollinearity; values of variables that do not exhibit multicollinearity are usually between 1.0 and 2.0. VIFs are routinely calculated by statistical software packages.

How to resolve. To correct for multicollinearity, researchers need to remove the collinear variables from the model. When the variables are substantively related, they might be combined to create a new index variable. For instance, in the example concerning high school violence, it might be possible to combine the variables "off-campus crimes" and "off-campus

Figure 15.5  Multicollinearity

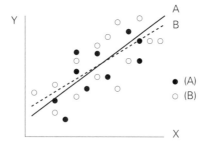

Figure 15.6 ——〰—— Curvilinear Relationship with Regression Line

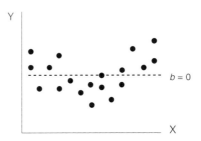

misdemeanors" into a single, new index variable. When variables are not substantively related to each other, analysts should consider substituting one of the collinear variables for a similar measurement that is less highly correlated with the other variables.

Linearity

Multiple regression estimates a *straight* regression line; it assumes that independent variables are *linearly* correlated with the dependent variable. *Curvilinear* relationships are relationships that are not linear, such as $y = \sqrt{x}$ or x^2. For example, certain forms of pollution have curvilinear relationships with population density. In these cases, a straight regression line is a poor fit, and regression coefficients underestimate the significance of the relationship. Hence, **linearity** is an important regression assumption, as well. In the worst cases, the regression coefficient will be estimated as being insignificant when it is not; this extreme problem is shown in Figure 15.6. Linear estimation is a poor fit for any curvilinear relationship.

   Detection. Diagnosis of curvilinear relationships centers on examining the curvilinear pattern of error terms, as shown in Figure 15.7. Subsequent

Figure 15.7 ——〰—— Detecting Curvilinearity

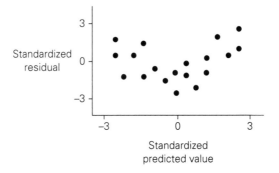

bivariate analysis is then used to identify *which* independent-dependent variable relationship is curvilinear. Many statistical packages also produce so-called *partial residual plots,* which show the relationship between the dependent variable and each independent variable, when controlled for other independent variables.[12] Using such plots, analysts decide whether the relationship is linear, curvilinear, or simply not present.

How to resolve. Curvilinearity is typically corrected by transforming the independent variable; square root, quadratic, and logarithmic transformations are used (see Chapter 12). For example, if a curvilinear relationship exists between the dependent variable and the independent variable x_1, then the initial relationship might be transformed in the following manner:

$$\text{Initial relationship: } y = a + b_1 x_1 + b_2 x_2 + \dots .$$
$$\text{Transformed relationship: } y = a + b_1 \sqrt{x} \; x_1 + b_2 x_2 + \dots .$$

Of course, any other transformation of x_1 that results in a linear relationship between y and this independent variable is acceptable. In rare instances, it may be necessary to transform the dependent variable when it is curvilinearly related to all or most independent variables.[13]

Heteroscedasticity

Heteroscedasticity (pronounced "heh-troh-SKUH-das-ti-ci-tee") is the problem of unequal variances of the error term. For example, when expenditures are examined by unit size, the residuals of larger units will vary more than those of a smaller size because larger jurisdictions and households with larger incomes usually have more discretion in their spending patterns than do those of smaller size. The extent to which heteroscedasticity occurs in public management and policy analysis varies with the nature of one's data or problems. Equal variance of the error terms is desired, which is called homoscedasticity. Unequal variances of the error term are a violation of random distribution of the error term, and they cause the statistical significance of regression coefficients to be underestimated. Heteroscedasticity usually occurs when data include heterogeneous subunits, such as households with greatly varying levels of income or jurisdictions of vastly different populations.

Heteroscedasticity is detected graphically by examination of the error term plot for unequal variance, as shown in Figure 15.8. The figure shows a trumpet-like distribution of the error terms, but the heteroscedasticity can also occur to the left or even in the middle if that is the range in which error terms have relatively larger variances. When heteroscedasticity is suspected, the error terms (e) may also be plotted against each independent variable ($x_1, x_2, \dots$) in order to determine *which* dependent-independent variable relationship is heteroscedastic.[14]

Figure 15.8 ⎯⎯⎯ᴧᴧ⎯ Heteroscedasticity

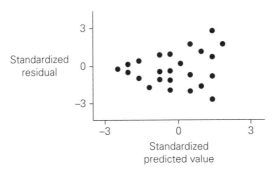

How to resolve. Heteroscedasticity is overcome by transforming one or more variables. The scale adjustment reduces the sizes of differences between variables, minimizing unequal variance. Often, a logarithmic transformation of *both* the dependent and the independent variables sufficiently corrects for the problem:

$$\text{Initial relationship: } y = a + b_1 x_1 + b_2 x_2 \dots.$$
$$\text{Transformed relationship: } \ln(y) = a + b_1 \ln(x_1) + b_2 \ln(x_2) + \dots.$$

The log transformation is useful when large error terms are associated with large values of the (in)dependent variables because the log transformation reduces large values much more than small values. However, this approach may fail when heteroscedasticity is caused by a more complex relationship between the error term and one or more variables. *Weighted least squares* (WLS) is a procedure that mathematically calculates the requisite transformation based on the observed variance and its relationship to a specific variable. WLS is available in most statistical software packages.[15] Box 15.1 illustrates the assumption testing carried out for the regression model examined earlier in this chapter.

> **Getting Started**
>
> Verify your understanding of regression assumptions.

Autocorrelation

Autocorrelation is the problem that successive observations are correlated with each other; they are not independent. This is a frequent problem with time series data, because values at $t = T$ are often good predictors of subsequent values at $t = T + 1$, which are then good predictors of other values at $T + 2$, and so on. This feature also causes error terms to be correlated with each other, when plotted in their time-ordered sequence, as shown in Figure 15.9. This is a violation of the assumption of the random distribution of error terms.

Box 15.1   Assumption Testing in Multiple Regression

Earlier in this chapter, we discussed the example of a workplace productivity analysis, the results of which are shown in Table 15.1. In that example, perceived productivity is the dependent variable, and teamwork, job knowledge, authority, sick days, and fairness are independent variables. Table 15.1 shows that $\overline{R}^2 = 0.263$, and teamwork, job knowledge, and authority are significant at the 1 percent level. Fairness is significant at the 5 percent level. How do we test for assumptions?

The first step is to plot the error terms against the predicted values. Figure 15.1, shown at the beginning of this chapter, is that error term plot. The error term plot does not show the presence of any outliers, which would have been indicated by values of the regression standardized residual (shown on the Y-axis) smaller than −3 or greater than +3. We do note that one observation has a value that is close to −3. To examine its impact on regression results (as we would have done for all observations with standardized residuals smaller than −3 or greater than +3), we remove this observation from the sample and rerun the regression model to test for robustness. We then observe that removing this observation does not affect the reported levels of statistical significance, which hence are robust for outliers.

We also test for multicollinearity. The reported values of the variance inflation factors (VIFs) are 1.025 for teamwork, 1.074 for job knowledge, 1.074 for authority, 1.011 for sick days, and 1.056 for fairness. These VIFs are well below the threshold of 5; thus, we conclude that multicollinearity does not affect the statistical significance of the independent variables. This result is reflected by the Pearson's correlation coefficients of the bivariate correlations among the independent variables. The largest bivariate correlation coefficient, r, is a mere 0.202, occurring between the variables "fairness" and "authority."

Although the scatterplot shown in Figure 15.1 does not suggest heteroscedasticity (there is no obvious trumpet-shaped pattern), the Park test (see note 14) does find evidence of slight heteroscedasticity between the error term and the variable authority (t-test statistic 2.69, $p < .01$). Using the weighted least squares procedure, we rerun the model with "authority" as the weight variable. Adjusted R-square is now slightly lower (0.237), but the levels of statistical significance reported earlier remain unchanged.

Finally, we see no evidence of curvilinearity in the plot. This is verified further by examining the partial regression plots of each of the independent variables. In all, then, we conclude that the previously reported results are robust. They are not affected by any of the potential problems noted.

Figure 15.9  Autocorrelation

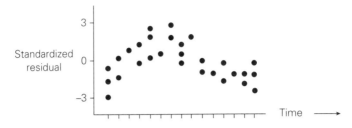

One problem of autocorrelation, which is also called *serial correlation,* is that it severely exaggerates the statistical significance of variables, leading to the erroneous conclusion that variables are statistically associated when they are not. Tests for detecting and addressing autocorrelation are discussed in Chapter 17. Typically, analysts do well to assume that problems of autocorrelation are likely to occur when working with time series data. For example, panel data collected and analyzed across different time periods are likely to have the problem of autocorrelation. By contrast, cross-sectional data rarely involve successive observations that are correlated with each other, which means that autocorrelation is not likely to be a problem.

Measurement and Specification

Multiple regression further assumes (1) that the model does not omit important variables, (2) that the model does not include irrelevant variables, and (3) that the variables are measured accurately (see Box 15.2). Unlike the assumptions discussed earlier in this chapter, detection and resolution are based largely on theoretical rather than empirical grounds. These problems are important and frequent threats to the validity of models.

As mentioned earlier in this chapter, full model specification allows for a family of plausible models. Random distribution of the error term does not imply that a given set of independent variables is the only plausible set; relevant, independent variables may have been excluded. **Specification error** involves both the omission of relevant variables and the inclusion of irrelevant ones. The effect of *omitting a relevant variable* is to inflate the value of t-test statistics of independent variables that are included. Analysts should ask whether any theoretically relevant (control) variable has been excluded from the model. Indeed, adding a relevant control variable may affect the observed levels of statistical significance. Excluding relevant variables also biases the estimate of the intercept, which may affect prediction. To avoid these problems, analysts need to give full, theoretical consideration to the broadest possible set of relevant variables when they are building statistical models.

In Greater Depth . . .

Box 15.2 An Application of Multiple Regression in Performance Management

Recall the example in Chapter 14, in which we mentioned a regional consortium of 15 local public agencies (in cities and counties) that provide low-income adults with health education. Assume you want to examine the relationship between health educational activities and the percentage of people who quit smoking as the result of the education (quit-smoking rate). Now, assume that you also suspect that the quit-smoking rate is affected by a person's smoking history. The longer a person smokes, the less likely he or she is to quit smoking. To examine the impact of the health education on the quit-smoking rate, you want to control for the impact of smoking history—you can do so by using multiple regression analysis. Let's say that these are the data you have collected:

Agency	Quit-smoking rate	Number of health educational events	Average number of years in smoking
1	0.04	22	20
2	0.13	45	10
3	0.09	32	15
4	0.08	38	15
5	0.04	45	21
6	0.05	43	15
7	0.1	31	12
8	0.05	19	15
9	0.09	24	15
10	0.03	20	16
11	0.11	40	10
12	0.04	38	15
13	0.045	30	19
14	0.08	21	15
15	0.04	23	18

Running these data produces the equation: Quit-smoking rate = 0.17155 + (0.00041∗Educational events) − (0.00758∗Smoking history), with $R^2 = 0.6730$ and adjusted $R^2 = 0.6186$. The F test shows that the

(continued)

Box 15.2   *(continued)*

model is significant at the .01 level (p for the F test is .001222). The test of the slope for "Educational events" shows that the slope is not statistically significant at the .05 level (t = 0.7259, p = .4818), indicating that health education may not reduce the smoking rate. However, the test of the slope for "Smoking history" indicates that it is statistically significant at the .01 level (t = −4.5287, p = .00069), indicating a significant, negative impact of the length of smoking history on the quit-smoking rate. So, what do you conclude?

The effect of *including irrelevant variables* is the opposite of that of omitting a relevant value; namely, it understates the importance of other independent variables. Analysts should ask whether all variables included in the model are theoretically sound. The problem of including irrelevant variables often arises as analysts verify how existing models hold up under the impact of a broader range of variables. Generally, irrelevant variables should not be included because they reduce the level of statistical significance of other variables, increase the possibility of multicollinearity, and work against model parsimony. Also, theoretically irrelevant variables cannot be justified, no matter how statistically significant they may be. Thus, a guarded stance regarding irrelevant variables is usually appropriate.[16]

Measurement error is defined as inaccurate measurement of the underlying study concept; variables that have measurement error are substantively invalid or have systematic biases. Measurement validity was discussed earlier as part of validating index variables (see Chapter 3). Accurate measurement is especially important for the *dependent* variable because inaccurate measurement may render it impossible for independent variables to achieve requisite levels of statistical significance. For example, inaccurate measurement of the dependent variable can occur when there are few categories, such as when using a dependent variable with a five-point Likert scale. This typically causes an upward or downward sloping pattern of the error terms. To improve measurement, an index variable, which increases the range of values and improves substantive relevance (by encompassing more dimensions of the concept), should be used. Researchers usually give heightened importance to measurement of the dependent variable.

SUMMARY

Multiple regression is a powerful and popular technique for taking control variables (rival hypotheses) into account. It uses two or more independent variables. Multiple regression can also use nominal, independent variables, which are transformed as so-called dummy variables. Analysts frequently encounter multiple regression in research articles. Multiple regression is a full model specification technique; that is, the technique seeks to account for all effects on the dependent variable. The popularity of multiple regression is due largely to its ability to control for all other independent variables in the model when estimating the relationships between each independent variable and the dependent variable.

Although multiple regression is quite powerful, it does not substitute for developing a thorough understanding of the bivariate relationships in which analysts are interested. Both before and after multiple regression is used, the nature, strength, and practical significance of bivariate relationships should be examined. Indeed, analysts often turn to multiple regression because they want to learn more about a previously discovered, significant bivariate relationship. They want to know whether a specific bivariate relationship remains significant when controlled for other variables. Thus, multiple regression usually follows bivariate analysis.

Finally, although multiple regression is used widely, it also has various test assumptions that must be met. Models should be specified correctly and variables measured without error. In addition, assumptions pertaining to the error term are that there should be no outliers, heteroscedasticity, multicollinearity, autocorrelation, or curvilinearity.

KEY TERMS

Adjusted R-square (p. 259)
Autocorrelation (p. 268)
Dummy variables (p. 261)
Error term plot (p. 257)
Full model specification (p. 254)
Global F-test (p. 260)
Heteroscedasticity (p. 267)
Linearity (p. 266)
Measurement error (p. 272)
Multicollinearity (p. 265)

Multiple regression assumptions
(p. 263)
Nomothetic mode of explanation
(p. 253)
Outliers (p. 263)
Regression coefficients in multiple
regression (interpretation of)
(p. 255)
Specification error (p. 270)
Standardized coefficient, β (p. 260)

Notes

1. Nomothetic explanations are contrasted by *idiographic* explanations, which identify all factors affecting a dependent variable. Idiographic models are quite difficult in multiple regression because the number of factors that affect dependent variables often is very large, including unique factors that affect only a small subset of observations. Because empirical data about all of these factors are typically missing, nomothetic strategies are used instead.

2. SPSS and other programs offer a range of selection approaches. Some methods select the variables that are the most significantly associated with the dependent variable ("forward selection"), other methods remove the variables that are least significantly associated with the dependent variable ("backward selection"), and still other methods use a combination of forward and backward selection strategies until no more variables can be either added or removed ("stepwise selection").

3. Some phenomena are quite complex to explain, and models that have these as dependent variables will have a low model fit. For example, it can be very difficult to explain last-minute voting decisions, especially in a parsimonious way. Also, many phenomena include random elements, and there are also measurement errors that affect model fit.

4. Statistical software packages can also produce part and partial regression coefficients. *Partial correlation* examines the correlation between the dependent variable and one independent variable, controlled for correlations that each has with the other independent variables in the model. *Part (or, semipartial) correlation* examines the correlation between the dependent and one independent variable, controlled for the correlation that only the dependent variable has with the other independent variables in the model. Part correlations show the incremental or unique impact of an independent variable. *Zero-order correlations* are simply the bivariate correlation coefficients of each independent variable with the dependent variable.

5. Although the global F-test is not particularly useful, one variation is the *partial F-test.* Here, the analyst wants to know whether including other independent variables adds to the explanation of the dependent variable. The initial model is called the restricted model (R), and the model with additional independent variables is called the unrestricted model (UR). The F statistic for testing the statistical significance of the additional variables is defined as follows:

$$F = \frac{\left[\left(R^2_{UR} - R^2_R\right)/m\right]}{\left[\left(1 - R^2_{UR}\right)/(N-k)\right]},$$

where N is the number of observations, k is the number of variables in the unrestricted model, and m is the number of variables in the unrestricted model minus the number of variables in the restricted model. To test this statistic, the denominator degrees of freedom (df) is defined as $(N - k)$ and the numerator degrees of freedom (df) is defined as m.

6. The formula for adjusted R-square shows the adjustment for the number of independent variables: $1 - [(\text{residual sum of squares})(n - 1)/(\text{total sum of squares})(n - p - 1)]$, where n is the number of observations (here, 321) and p is number of independent variables. From Table 15.1, we calculate adjusted R-square as $1 - [(169.980*320)/(234.219*315)] = 0.263$.

7. Statistical software packages vary in their response to this problem. SPSS automatically deletes one variable that causes the perfect correlation, whereas other programs report error messages.

8. For example, if we thought that performance were also affected by region, we could specify the model in Table 15.2 as follows: productivity $= f$ (teamwork, ability, authority, inducement, fairness, Northeast, South, West), where f indicates that productivity is a function of the variables between parentheses. Note that use of a dummy variable assumes that the regression models are statistically similar among all groups. If differences are suspected, analysts may also wish to run regression models for each separate group.

9. Other approaches exist for detecting influential observations. See any advanced text for a discussion of measures such as Cook's D. Measures of Cook's D greater than 1.0 may signal influential observations.

10. In SPSS, Analyze $\rightarrow$ Regression $\rightarrow$ Linear $\rightarrow$ Statistics: Collinearity Diagnostics.

11. VIF $= 1/\text{Tolerance}$, where Tolerance $= 1 - R^2$, and R^2 is calculated for the model in which an independent variable is predicted by all of the other independent variables.

12. Technically, partial residual plots show the relationship between the error term of the independent and dependent variables, when each is regressed against all of the other independent variables. Partial residual plots differ from partial regression plots, which are used to identify influential observations such as outliers.

13. A special instance occurs when the dependent variable is a fraction p, ranging from 0.0 to 1.0. Then, a so-called logit transformation, which is defined as $\ln[1/(1 - p)]$, is recommended.

14. Some analysts believe that this graphical approach can sometimes fail to detect heteroscedasticity. They suggest analyzing the relationship between e^2 and each independent variable. This is the *Park test*. Squaring of the error term causes a positive relationship to occur with the

independent variable if heteroscedasticity is present (see the figure, below). To determine whether a relationship exists between e^2 and x, the following simple regression is used. The log transformation is used to ensure that the relationship is linear, rather than curvilinear, which may occur because of the squaring:

$$\ln e^2 = a + b_1 \ln(x).$$

When the slope (b_1) is significant, a heteroscedastic relationship exists between the error term and the independent variable:

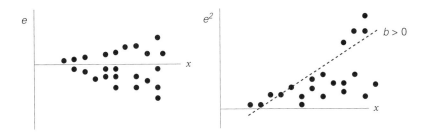

15. A thorough discussion of WLS is beyond this text. For a discussion and example of WLS, see SPSS, *Regression Models 10.0* (Chicago: SPSS, Inc., 1999 or latest edition), or Damodar Gujarati, *Basic Econometrics*, 3rd ed. (New York: McGraw-Hill, 1999).

16. Some analysts also consider as a criterion whether adjusted R-square increases as a result of adding a variable. Increases in adjusted R-square imply that more variance of the dependent variable is explained. However, the ultimate basis for including or excluding variables should be theoretical; it cannot be based solely on empirical considerations.

Further Statistics

This section examines additional statistical techniques of interest to public managers and policy analysts. Here we discuss advanced techniques with three important purposes in mind. First, familiarity with advanced techniques makes research articles and reports more accessible for managers and analysts. Managers and analysts are expected to keep abreast of state-of-art research in their fields, and they will want and need to know how to read these statistics. No one can be an expert in all techniques, but some comprehension is expected. To assist, we offer summaries that focus on a few key aspects of these techniques: What is the purpose of these techniques? What statistics are commonly reported in applications? What assumptions pertain to these techniques? What are some typical applications of these techniques? These are the key questions to ask when first encountering statistical techniques.

A second purpose of these chapters is to lay the groundwork for those who might want to pursue these techniques further. The initial discussion of important purposes and measures can assist and stimulate more advanced study. Finally, a third purpose is to help readers understand how to apply these techniques; hence, some discussions include considerable detail, such as the discussion on time series regression and non-regression-based fore-casting. Indeed, some courses might highlight techniques beyond those discussed in Section IV, and the material covered in this section will help toward that end.

Chapter 16 examines logistic regression, the technique used when the dependent variable is dichotomous. This method overcomes an important limitation of multiple regression, namely, the requirement that the dependent variable be continuous. Dichotomous dependent variables are quite common in political science, for example, when studying election outcomes or the occurrence of war. These events are seen as dichotomous; either something happens or it doesn't. Logistic regression can then be used to estimate the probability of these events occurring.

Chapter 17 discusses time series analysis, in regression and non-regression-based ways. First, we extend the discussion of multiple regression to time series data. In particular, this chapter addresses unique issues pertaining to regression assumptions associated with such data. It demonstrates how to use time series regression in the assessment of policy and program impacts, adding to the strategies discussed in Section IV. Second, we examine the regression-based approaches to forecasting. Forecasting helps managers make decisions about future events (see Chapter 4). Some regression-based approaches rely solely on extrapolation of single variables, whereas others incorporate the impact of independent variables. Regression-based forecasting typically requires at least 20 observations; when these observations are not available, managers and analysts will want to use spreadsheet-based methods of forecasting. Third, we examine non-regression-based methods of forecasting, which are quite common in budgeting, for example.

Chapter 18 discusses a few more statistical techniques that may be found in the literature. For example, it looks at path analysis, which is used when relationships between the dependent and independent variables are complex. The chapter notes techniques that are used when feedback loops are present. It also examines survival analysis, which is used when researchers want to study the decay of samples over time, such as factors that might cause students to drop out of educational programs over time. Finally, this chapter examines some techniques for exploratory data analysis. It emphasizes factor analysis, which is often used in social science research. However, it also briefly notes some other methods, such as discriminant analysis.

The chapters contained in this final section provide a survey of decidedly more advanced techniques, though others exist, as well. It is hoped that this discussion will provide a useful reference for managers and analysts to use when they encounter these statistical methods in research articles and reports.

CHAPTER
16

Logistic Regression

CHAPTER OBJECTIVES

After reading this chapter, you should be able to

- State why logistic regression is used when the dependent variable is dichotomous
- Estimate the probability of an event
- Identify and test assumptions of logistic regression
- Address assumption violations

This chapter discusses logistic regression, a technique used when the dependent variable is dichotomous. Logistic regression is often used in political science, for example, when analysts try to understand the probability of a dichotomous event such as winning or losing an election. Logistic regression is in many ways analogous to multiple regression, but the former uses different statistics and estimation methods, hence requiring separate discussion in this short chapter.

THE LOGISTIC MODEL

Logistic ("loh-GIS-tic") *regression* deals with situations in which the dependent variable is dichotomous. Examples of dichotomous variables include winning a political election, receiving a death penalty, and having an abortion. In these instances, the dependent variable is dichotomous by nature because it is impossible to win half an election or to be somewhat put to death.

The dichotomous nature of the dependent variable violates an assumption of multiple regression, discussed in Chapter 15, that the dependent variable should be continuous. The dichotomous dependent variable creates a statistical problem, namely, that the linear regression line is poorly suited to predict the dichotomous variable. This situation is shown graphically in Figure 16.1. When the straight regression line is used, predicted values of the dependent variable can be less than zero and greater than one. This is problematic if we want to interpret the predicted values as the probability that the dependent variable event occurs. Obviously, the chance of winning an election can neither be negative nor greater than one. To resolve this problem, an S-shaped curve (also called a logistic curve) is fitted to the observations. The values of this curve always lie between zero and one.

> **Key Point**
> A logistic model is used when the dependent variable is dichotomous.

The shape of the curve is defined by the following equation:

$$\text{Prob(event)} = 1/(1 + e^{-Z}),$$

where $Z = a + b_1 x_1 + b_2 x_2 + \dots$. In this model, Prob(event) is the probability of the event occurring. For example, if a dichotomous variable "war" is defined as going to war (war = 1) or not going to war (war = 0), then the formula calculates the probability of going to war. Z is also called the *logit*.

Figure 16.1 —— Logistic Curve

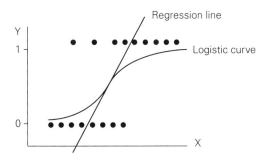

In addition to using a different estimation equation, logistic regression uses a different method for estimating the logistic curve. In multiple regression, coefficients are estimated by minimizing the sum of squared differences of observed and predicted values of each observation, or $\Sigma(y_i - \hat{y}_i)^2$ of each observation (see Chapter 15). This method is called ordinary least squares (OLS), and it produces the closest fit of the observations around the regression line. In logistic regression, the coefficients are estimated such that the likelihood of correctly predicting the observed events is maximized. An iterative process is used, called maximum likelihood estimation (MLE), in which successive models are evaluated until further improvements in correctly predicting observed events are no longer significant. This estimation method results in statistics that differ from those in multiple regression.

The different estimation method also causes logistic regression to have fewer assumptions than multiple regression. Logistic regression does not assume normally distributed error terms, and the dichotomous dependent variable makes homogeneity a moot point. However, it does assume that outliers are not present, and it also assumes full model specification, that the variables are measured and specified without error, and that no autocorrelation or multicollinearity is present. Logistic regression also assumes large samples. Recommendations vary but often suggest minimum sample sizes of at least 50 observations, and more when models include many independent variables.

A WORKING EXAMPLE

Assume, hypothetically, that data exist about teenagers who have been involved in incidents of classroom violence. We do not know how many incidents they have been involved in, only that they have been involved. Hence, the dependent variable is dichotomous. Assume further that we want to know whether gender, grade level, and scholastic attainment (grade point average, or GPA) are predictors of classroom violence. Data are available for 30 students who have been involved in such incidents, as well as for an additional random sample of 50 students who have not been involved. The population is drawn only from high school students. The results shown in Table 16.1 are obtained. This output yields many new statistics because the estimation methodology is different from that used in multiple regression.

The top row of Table 16.1 shows a variety of goodness-of-fit statistics. The first statistic, the **_log likelihood value_** (–2LL),[1] is analogous to the global F-test in regression (see Chapter 15). It assesses whether the model with independent variables is significantly better in predicting observed events than a model with no independent variables. The absolute value (66.001) has no interpretation, but the level of significance shows that this model

Table 16.1 ⎯⎯⎯ᴧᴧᴧ⎯ Logistic Regression Output

Model fit

Model	−2 log likelihood (−2LL) Sig. (base model)	Cox and Snell R^2	Nagelkerke R^2	Hosmer and Lemeshow test Chi-square	Sig.
66.001	0.000	0.392	0.535	8.397	.396

Dependent variable: Student classroom incident

Coefficients

Model	Unstandardized coefficients b	SE	Wald chi-square	Sig.
Constant	−7.405	5.202	2.027	0.155
Gender	−4.464	1.319	11.450	0.001
Education	1.558	0.544	8.212	0.004
GPA	−2.716	0.722	14.140	0.000

Classification table

Observed Variable	Group	Predicted Violence 0	1	Percent correct
Violence	0	44	6	88.0
	1	11	19	63.3
Overall percentage				78.8

Note: Sig. = significance; GPA = grade point average; SE = standard error.

with three variables is significantly better than the base (or null) model that lacks these variables. This is hardly a surprise, given that all three independent variables are statistically significant.

The Cox and Snell R^2 is analogous to R^2 in multiple regression, but it cannot reach a value of 1.0. The **Nagelkerke R^2** is a modification that overcomes this problem. The interpretation of the results shows that 53.5 percent of the variance in students involved in classroom incidents is explained by the model. The classification table at the bottom of Table 16.1 supports this finding. A **classification table** shows the percentage of corrected predicted observations. The minimum is 50 percent, indicating the lack of any useful prediction. Typically, standards of 80–85 percent indicate "good" model prediction. Our model falls somewhat short (78.8 percent correct); we acknowledge the desirability of a better model. Another goodness-of-fit statistic is the *Hosmer and Lemeshow test,* which compares the observed and predicted values. A good model fit has close correspondence between observed and predicted values and, hence, an insignificant chi-square value for this test. This is also shown in Table 16.1.

In addition to the above statistics, residuals can be calculated that measure the difference for each observation between the predicted probability of an event occurring and the observed probability (that is, group membership). This approach is analogous to calculation of the error term in multiple regression. Standardized residuals can be calculated,[2] and analysts can assess the effect of an observation whose standardized residuals exceed the absolute value of 2.58. Beyond this, logistic regression, like multiple regression, can flag other observations whose influence on coefficients and model fit can be examined.[3] In our case, further analysis shows that two observations might be classified as outliers, but removing them does not substantively alter or much improve the above results; hence, they are retained.

In short, a variety of statistics can be used to assess the overall goodness of fit. The classification table is a basic but very useful tool for understanding the predictive ability of the model. Regarding other assumptions, when working with time series data (which the above data are not), analysts need to follow the remediation processes described in Chapter 17. The possibility of multicollinearity is examined through the correlation matrix and the relationships of independent variables with the dependent variable as discussed in Chapter 15; no VIF test is available for logistic regression. Finally, a problem with logistic regression is that adding too many variables may result in solutions that are unstable, or regression coefficients that are inappropriate or no longer significant. Such problems may indicate *overfitting,* a term used in statistics to refer to models that have too many variables for the amount of data. When such estimation problems occur, analysts often need to use a model with fewer variables. (This problem is also relevant to multiple regression, but in practice it seems to occur far more often in logistic regression.)

Calculating Event Probabilities

The results in Table 16.1 show that all three variables are statistically significant. Gender, education (grade level), and GPA are all predictors of a student's becoming involved in a violent classroom incident. **Wald chi-square** is the test statistic used to determine the statistical significance of logistic regression coefficients. This statistic is analogous to the t-test, $b/\text{se}(b)$, in multiple regression. The Wald chi-square is defined as $[b/\text{se}(b)]^2$, and each variable has one degree of freedom.

The formula given earlier for the logistic curve can be used to calculate the probability of an event occurring. Using this formula, we can calculate the probability of a student's becoming involved in a violent incident for different levels of the independent variables. These calculations are readily performed on a spreadsheet (see Table 16.2), allowing for interesting what-if analyses. Positive logistic regression coefficients imply that probabilities increase, and negative logistic regression coefficients imply that probabilities decrease. For example, the negative coefficient of GPA means that increases in GPA are associated with lower probabilities of the event occurring, being involved in classroom incidents.

Key Point

A logistic model can estimate the likelihood of an event.

The results for 10th-grade students show that classroom violence is associated primarily with being male; for students with a GPA of 3.0, the probability of being involved in a violent classroom incident is much lower. The probability for the two groups are, respectively, 50.7 percent for males and 1.2 percent for females. Among 10th-grade males, the probability of being involved in a violent incident is affected greatly by school performance: for male students with a GPA of 2.0 the chance is 93.9 percent, but for those with a 4.0 GPA the chance is only 6.4 percent. Further analysis shows that the chance of violence increases with grade level; it is highest in the 12th grade. In particular, 12th-grade females with a 3.0 GPA have a 21.1 percent probability of being involved in a violent incident.

Getting Started

Verify these calculations.

Finally, the ratio of P(event)/P(no event) is called an *odds ratio*. The odds ratio is used to compare the probability of something occurring, as compared to it not occurring. This definition is not akin to the ordinary meaning of the word *odds* as it relates to probability. Rather, the odds ratio shows how much more likely it is that an event will occur than it will not occur. The odds ratio is calculated as follows:

$$P(\text{event})/P(\text{no event}) = e^Z,$$

where $Z = a + b_1 x_1 + b_2 x_2 + \ldots$.

Table 16.2 ⁓⁓⁓ Calculating Event Probability

Variables						Probability
Gender	Education	GPA	$a + bx + \ldots$	$e^{-(a + bx + \ldots)}$	$1/(1 + e^{-(a + bx + \ldots)})$
0	10	3.0	0.027	0.973	0.507
1	10	3.0	−4.437	84.521	0.012
0	10	2.0	2.743	0.064	0.939
0	10	4.0	−2.689	14.717	0.064
1	12	3.0	−1.321	3.747	0.211

Note: GPA = grade point averages; 0 = male; 1 = female.

In Greater Depth . . .

Box 16.1 Logistic Regression in Research

A variety of research situations prompt analysts to use logistic regression. For example, political scientists frequently use logistic regression to examine the adoption of voting practices, to analyze specific voting decisions, and to look at turnover among presidential advisors. Specifically, we could try to predict whether or not citizens vote, how they choose between two candidates, and whether or not presidential advisors are retained from one year to the next.

Another line of research examines factors involved in whether or not jurisdictions adopted specific policies, laws, or practices, such as clean air policies, domestic violence legislation, lottery policies, or even whether they were awarded empowerment zones for urban economic development by the federal government. Other studies look at the adoption of innovative policies and practices by states. Indeed, in this way, researchers can study many differences across cities, counties, states, or countries.

Still other uses include researching factors that explain recidivism among offenders, whether municipal bonds are issued with insurance, whether or not highly qualified employees want to work for government, and whether or not wars occur (and how long they last). Other studies explain whether or not respondents are likely to adopt conservative or liberal attitudes.

In short, logistic regression can be used on many and varied occasions.

This measure may be used to observe how the odds ratio changes when only one independent variable is changed, such as by one unit. For example, when GPA decreases by 1, Z increases by 2.716 (note the negative sign of this coefficient in Table 16.1), and the odds ratio is $e^{2.716} = 15.12$. This means that a decrease in GPA greatly increases the chances of being involved in a classroom incident. It bears repeating that these are hypothetical data. Box 16.1 discusses other uses of logistic regression.

A final thought. Logistic regression extends multiple regression by considering a dichotomous dependent variable. But what if the dependent variable has more than two categories, yet it is still not continuous? The dependent variable might be nominal with three or more categories. For example, we might want to predict parents' choice of a school voucher program out of

Getting Started

Find examples of logistic regression in the research literature.

three or more types. Or the dependent variable might be ordinal, such as a five-point Likert scale. Techniques for dealing with these situations are beyond the treatment of this text but are mentioned briefly in Chapter 18.

SUMMARY

Logistic regression is used when the dependent variable is dichotomous. It allows researchers to estimate the probability of an event occurring. The statistics used in logistic regression are somewhat analogous but nevertheless different from those used in multiple regression. A variety of statistics, such as the classification table, help researchers to assess logistic regression models. The most defining application of logistic regression is, however, the ability to predict the probability of an event occurring.

KEY TERMS

Classification table (p. 282)
Log likelihood value (p. 281)
Logistic regression (p. 280)
Logit (p. 280)

Nagelkerke R^2 (p. 282)
Odds ratio (p. 284)
Wald chi-square (p. 283)

Notes

1. The log likelihood is calculated as $-2*\log(\text{likelihood})$, hence, $-2LL$. The likelihood is a measure of how well observed values can be predicted. Better fitting models have smaller values of $-2LL$.
2. The standardized residual is defined as follows: $\text{residual}/\sqrt{[p(1-p)]}$.
3. These measures include, for example, Cook's D. Measures of Cook's D greater than 1.0 may signal influential observations.

CHAPTER
17

Time Series Analysis

CHAPTER OBJECTIVES

After reading this chapter, you should be able to

- Identify different techniques for analyzing time series data
- Test assumptions of time series regression, and address violations
- Use dummy variables to assess the impacts of policies in time series data
- Understand the uses of different regression-based forecasting techniques
- Undertake forecasts that are based on a few observations

This chapter presents an overview of techniques used in time series analysis, in three parts: (1) multiple regression of time series data, (2) regression-based forecasting, and (3) non-regression-based forecasting. Each part provides an overview of techniques, emphasizing major purposes, statistics, and applications. Some techniques are discussed in a bit more detail, providing readers with skills aiding in application.

TIME SERIES DATA IN MULTIPLE REGRESSION

Managers and policy analysts frequently use data that have been collected over time. Examples of these data include administrative data, such as activity logs, customer complaints, budget data, and inspection reports that have been completed or gathered in different periods, as well as survey data that are completed on a regular basis, such as client, citizen, and business surveys.

Time series data can be used with multiple regression, which is then called time series regression. The principles that apply to multiple regression—full model specification and the judicious selection of independent variables—also apply to time series regression. The same assumptions apply, as well: the dependent variable must be continuous; independent variables must be continuous or dichotomous (that is, dummy variables); and the error terms must meet the same assumptions as stated in Chapter 15 with regard to normality, homoscedasticity, and the absence of outliers. Independent variables must be linearly related to the dependent variable and not exhibit problems of multicollinearity.[1] The unique feature of multiple regression with time series data is the likely violation of error term assumptions in a new way, through autocorrelation (also called serial correlation). The discussion of multiple regression with time series data centers around detecting and correcting this problem.

Autocorrelation

With time series data, the assumption of random distribution of error terms is usually violated. This is because the adjacent, time-ordered values of observations are highly correlated with each other: knowledge of today's value is a good predictor of tomorrow's. **Autocorrelation**, also called **serial correlation**, reflects correlation in the order (or series) in which observations are measured. The error term plot, when plotted against the sequence of time-ordered observations, typically exhibits a "snake-like" pattern, as shown in Figure 17.1. Note that the figure examines the residuals against time (the order in which the observations are made) rather than the (standardized) predicted dependent variable $\hat{y}$. Plotting the error term against $\hat{y}$ will *not* show the pattern of Figure 17.1. The problem with autocorrelation is that it can severely exaggerate the statistical significance of variables, leading to the erroneous conclusion that variables are statistically associated when they are not.

Serial correlation is usually anticipated when working with time series data. It can be detected visually through the graph shown as Figure 17.1 or by calculating the **Durbin-Watson test statistic**. Statistical software packages do not always easily produce such a figure, and many analysts rely on the Durbin-Watson statistic. Values of the Durbin-Watson test statistic range

Figure 17.1  Autocorrelation

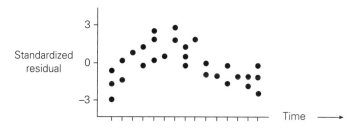

from 0 to 4. Values close to 2 indicate the lack of serial correlation; values closer to 0 and 4 indicate serial correlation. Values less than 2 indicate positive serial correlation, whereas values greater than 2 indicate negative serial correlation. Positive serial correlation occurs when successive error terms are positively correlated with each other, which is most common. Negative serial correlation implies the opposite.

Durbin-Watson critical values differ from other test statistics in two ways: each critical value has an upper and a lower limit, and the statistic tests for both positive and negative serial correlation. Software packages do not always produce the level at which the test statistic is statistically significant; analysts need to refer to the table of critical values in Appendix D. Critical values are determined by the number of observations (n) and number of independent variables (k). For example, when $n = 30$ and $k = 2$, the lower critical value (d_l) is 1.28 and the upper critical value (d_u) is 1.57 (p = .05). Values less than d_l and greater than $4 - d_l$ indicate the presence of correlation, but values between d_l and d_u, and $4 - d_l$ and $4 - d_u$, are considered inconclusive in determining serial correlation. These are critical values at the level of 5 percent significance. Figure 17.2 shows the critical regions for this test statistic. Thus, in the preceding example, values less than 1.28 and greater than 2.72 indicate autocorrelation; values between 1.57 and 1.28 and between 2.43 and 2.72 are inconclusive. Values between 1.57 and 2.43 indicate the absence of autocorrelation.

> **Key Point**
> Time series data typically violate regression assumptions. That needs to be addressed.

Figure 17.2  Durbin-Watson Critical Values

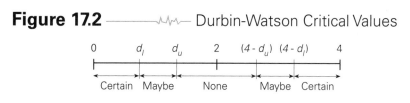

Correcting Autocorrelation

Two strategies are available for correcting serial correlation: the first strategy is to add a trend variable to the model, and the second strategy is to examine the relationship in so-called first-order differences.

The rationale for adding a trend variable is to control for the fact that over time many variables increase; the trend variable controls for growth over time and, hence, any spurious correlation between the dependent variable and independent variables. A **trend** (or counter) **variable** is simply a variable that records the order in which observations appear $(1, 2, 3, 4, 5, \ldots,$ shown as the variable "time" in Table 17.1). When adding a trend variable, we find that the relationship is changed in the following manner:

$$\text{Initial relationship: } y = a + b_1 x_1 + b_2 x_2 + \ldots$$
$$\text{Transformed relationship: } y = a + b_1 x_1 + b_2 x_2 + \ldots + b_n \text{Time}$$

A second strategy is to use **first-order differences**. These are the differences between successive observations, as shown below. The rationale for first-order differences (also called first-differences) is the logical proposition that if it is true that (the levels of) two variables are correlated with each other over time, then their increases also should be correlated over time. For example, the value of Δy for Time = 2 in Table 17.1 is the difference between the value of "vary" in Time = 2 and Time = 1, or $25 - 23 = 2$. The first observation is always lost because of the differencing. Statistical packages routinely calculate first-order differences. Thus, the relationship is transformed as follows:

$$\text{Initial relationship: } y = a + b_1 x_1 + b_2 x_2 + \ldots$$
$$\text{Transformed relationship: } \Delta y = a + b_1 \Delta x_1 + b_2 \Delta x_2 + \ldots$$

Relationships in first-difference form often eliminate problems of serial correlation because differenced data exhibit far more variability than do levels data. This is clearly shown in Table 17.1, in which the differenced data do not show the upward bias that the levels data do.

Table 17.1 ⌇⌇⌇ Calculating First-Order Differences

Time	Var y	Var x_1	Var x_2	Δy	Δx_1	Δx_2
1	23	1	5	.	.	.
2	25	2	8	2	1	3
3	27	4	10	2	2	2
4	29	5	13	2	1	3
5	31	6	18	2	1	5
6	30	8	16	−1	2	−2
7	33	9	14	3	1	−2
8	34	11	14	1	2	0

Comparing these two strategies, we see that the regression of first-order differences is considered a far more stringent test than adding a trend variable and is therefore preferred. Adding a trend variable is a prophylactic strategy that attempts to control for the problem. Regressing first-order differences is a preventive strategy that aims to avoid the problem.

Policy Evaluation

Time series data are excellent for evaluating the impact of a policy or program. Levels of performance or service utilization are tracked and compared with the moment or period in which a policy is implemented. Time series data are fundamental to the use of (quasi-) experimental designs in public management and policy, as discussed in Chapter 2.

Policy variables measure when and how policies affect the dependent variables. Policy variables are dummy variables that indicate when the policy has caused an effect. These variables can be modeled in different ways, as shown in Figure 17.3. The initial zeroes indicate the pre-policy time period, the first "1" indicates the first period in which the policy or program is implemented, and so on. These variables are easily added to any dataset, with values as shown in Figure 17.3.

The *pulse* and *period* variables reflect a policy or program that is used for only a limited time. For example, these policy variables might be used to measure, respectively, a one-time or limited-period intervention, such as a one-night or month-long effort by roadway police to apprehend drunken drivers. The period after the policy or program is terminated is called the post-policy period. By contrast, the *step* and *increasing impact* variables signify an ongoing policy or program. (By definition, no post-policy periods are associated with these ongoing programs or policies.) These variables differ only with regard to the level of impact over time. For example, some

Figure 17.3 ⎯⎯⎯⎯ Policy Variables

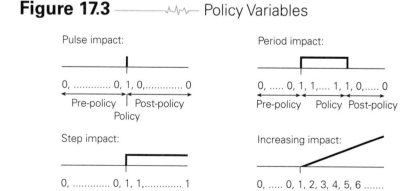

programs are plausibly hypothesized to have a near-constant effect over time, such as a permanent increase in the speed limit. However, benefit programs, such as after-school services, often have an increasing effect over time as more and more beneficiaries are affected by the policy or enrolled in the program. It is typically a matter of empirical trial-and-error as to which policy form best approximates the actual impact of the policy. To examine for policy impacts, the relationship without policy impacts is modified in the following way:

$$\text{Without policy impacts: } \Delta y = a + b_1 \Delta x_1 + b_2 \Delta x_2 + \dots$$
$$\text{With policy impacts: } \Delta y = a + b_1 \Delta x_1 + b_2 \Delta x_2 + \dots + b_r P_r + b_s P_s + \dots,$$

where $b_r P_r, \dots$ are alternative specifications of the policy impact, shown in Figure 17.3. The model can include different policy impact variables; P_r might model the pulse impact, P_s might model the step impact, and so on. A significant coefficient of any policy variable signifies that the policy has had an impact on the outcome, Δy. This model can also be written in levels form with an added trend variable.

Consider the following hypothetical example. In response to growing concern about classroom violence, discussed in Chapter 2, a high school has begun an anger awareness and management program. Teachers are asked to record the number of incidents that involve physical contact. The total number of weekly incidents is tallied. There are eight weeks of data from before the anger management program began and eight weeks of data since it began. The following data (average number of classroom incidents) are available on a per-classroom basis: 6.3, 6.4, 6.8, 7.0, 7.2, 7.3, 7.1, 7.5, 6.6, 6.5, 6.2, 6.0, 5.8, 5.5, 5.2, and 4.9. Is the decline sufficient to conclude that the program has a statistically significant impact? Table 17.2 shows the regression output. The dataset has 16 observations, one for each week. Values for the variable "trend" are 1, 2, 3, . . . , 14, 15, 16. Values for the variable "step impact" are 0, 0, 0, 0, 0, 0, 0, 0, 1, 1, 1, 1, 1, 1, 1, 1, and the values for the variable "increasing impact" are 0, 0, 0, 0, 0, 0, 0, 0, 1, 2, 3, 4, 5, 6, 7, 8. It also shows the results for the dependent variable in levels form with a trend variable. The first order of business is to determine whether the model violates regression assumptions. The Durbin-Watson test statistic is 1.597. With three explanatory variables and 16 observations, $d_l = 0.86$ and $d_u = 1.73$. Hence, the Durbin-Watson statistic is in the inconclusive range, and we decide that there is insufficient evidence of serial correlation. We also examine the error term plot and determine that no outliers are present. The results in Table 17.2 show that the program, modeled as both a step

> **Getting Started**
>
> Find examples of time series regression in the research literature.

Table 17.2 ———〜〜— Time Series Regression Output

Model fit				
R	R-square	Adjusted R-square	SEE	Durbin-Watson
0.989	0.979	0.973	0.125	1.597

Dependent variable: Violent classroom incidents (level)

Coefficients

Model	Unstandardized coefficients			
	b	SE	t	Sig.
Constant	6.221	.097	63.916	0.000
Trend	.162	.019	8.399	0.000
Step impact	−0.570	.126	−4.511	0.001
Increasing impact	−0.408	.027	−14.979	0.000

Note: SE = standard error; Sig. = significance.

and an increasing impact, is significantly associated with the reduction in classroom incidents. It shows that the anger management program reduces classroom incidents, and that this reduction increases over time. These results are plausible, as behavioral programs often have effects that increase over time.

The results find support in first-order difference form. Then, the Durbin-Watson statistic is 2.801, which is again in the inconclusive range. T-test test statistics are shown in parentheses:

$$\Delta \text{Incidents} = 0.171 - 0.668^{**}\text{Step} + 0.038 \text{ Increase}$$
$$(-3.43) \qquad (1.10)$$
$$^{**} p < .01; ^{*} p < .05.$$

This result is consistent with the earlier one because the dependent variable measures differences; the significance of the "step" variable suggests that the change in the number of incidents is constant; hence, the number of incidents decreases from one period to another.[2]

Lagged Variables

A *lagged variable* is one whose impact on the dependent variable is delayed. Even though a policy is implemented on a certain date, it sometimes takes time before measurable effects on the dependent variable occur. For example, the impact of the anger management program on classroom incidents might be delayed a little, perhaps because it requires a few time periods for the anger management program to be implemented fully, or because it takes students a few weeks before they begin to apply anger management. Thus, we wish to lag the effect of the program variable.

x_2	0	0	0	1	2	3	4	5	6	7
$x_{2, t-1}$	.	0	0	0	1	2	3	4	5	6
$x_{2, t-2}$	.	.	0	0	0	1	2	3	4	5

Statistical software packages can readily lag variables. For example, consider lagging the "increased impact" variable, identified as x_2. To indicate that the effect of this variable is lagged one time period, for example, the relationship "$y = a + b_1x_1 + b_2x_2 + \ldots$" becomes $y = a + b_1x_1 + b_2x_{2, t-1} + \ldots$. The notation "$t-1$" indicates the one-period lag. For illustration, x_2, $x_{2, t-1}$, and $x_{2, t-2}$ are shown above. An empirical question concerns the length of the lag: should x_2 be lagged one, two, three, or even more periods? Analysts can determine this on a trial-and-error basis. When effects are lagged, regression coefficients (and t-test statistics) often show a nice bell-shaped (or inverted-V) pattern for successive lags. For example, the regression coefficients of x_2 when lagged three through seven periods might be -2.25, 11.50, 73.89, 35.32, -1.83, suggesting that a lag of five is most appropriate, hence, $x_{2, t-5}$.[3]

On occasion, the dependent variable might be lagged, too: $y = a + b_1y_{t-1} + b_2x_2 + \ldots$. This signifies that the dependent variable is affected by its own immediate past: perhaps juvenile delinquency is seen as feeding on itself. The specification of a lagged dependent variable is called autoregression and further reduces problems of serial correlation. The Durbin-Watson statistic is not appropriate for autoregressive models. Instead, the Durbin h statistic is used.[4]

Regarding the preceding example, we find no evidence of lagged effect. For instance, the t-test statistics of the "increasing impact" variable are as follows: -14.979 (no lag), -12.869 ($t-1$), -11.680 ($t-2$), and -5.466 ($t-3$). These results are obtained by running the model separately for each lag. Thus, the impact of this variable is strongest when there is no lag. Similarly, the t-test statistics for the "step" variable are, respectively, -4.511, -0.873, -0.055, and -1.051. This, too, does not show a lagged impact.

STATISTICAL FORECASTING METHODS: A PRIMER

As discussed in Chapter 4, analysts and managers often face questions about the future: How many clients are we likely to have? What will their needs most likely be? How much revenue can the city expect? And so on. These questions are fundamental to the public and to nonprofit organizations. Chapter 4 also distinguished between statistical and nonstatistical approaches for addressing these questions. The principles and best practices of forecasting suggest that analysts should use a range of different approaches and that shorter forecasting periods are likely to be more accurate.

Here, we provide a brief primer on statistical forecasting methods. Quite simply, **statistical forecasting methods** use data about the present and past for forecasting. The simplest method is to forecast the immediate future as a replica of the past and present; what happened today and yesterday might happen tomorrow, too. This is a reasonable approach when events are well established. For example, if you normally drink coffee in the morning, you might do that tomorrow and in the immediate future, too. We might expect the level of high school violence tomorrow to be the same as today.

A problem with forecasting tomorrow based on today is that it does not take into account patterns of past trends. If there is a generally upward pattern, then the forecast for tomorrow might be revised upward, especially for a few time periods beyond tomorrow. The technique of **trend extrapolation** analyzes the pattern of past trends. Specifically, it analyzes (1) the presence of a general upward or downward pattern, (2) whether variations in the upward or downward pattern are cyclical (for example, seasonal fluctuations), probabilistic, or random in nature, and (3) uncharacteristic values that do not seem part of the trend. Thus, trend forecasting might note that I usually drink coffee (say, an 80 percent chance) and more often in the winter (a cyclical variation). In the case of high school violence, trend analysis might reveal such variations; perhaps school violence is more common on certain days (for example, Tuesdays), or in certain months of the year. Figure 17.4 shows an example of a forecast with upward and cyclical patterns of a program's workload. When policy makers and managers are aware of such trends, they can better anticipate and manage the future.

A limitation of trend extrapolation is that it is uninformed by factors that give rise to the trend and is ignorant of incidental factors that might

Figure 17.4  Workload

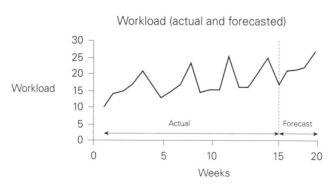

have affected or will affect it. Thus, trend forecasts are usually limited to but a few periods into the future, as shown in Figure 17.4. The accuracy of statistical forecasts may be enhanced further by considering other variables that affect trends. For example, local government revenues can be forecast not only as an extrapolation of past revenues but also by taking into account future changes in the taxable inventory of residential and commercial real estate; new office buildings or residential developments might soon be completed, for example, which add to the tax base. Similarly, future changes in the size of student cohorts associated with violence would shift the projected trend upward or downward. Analysts can adjust their trend forecasts based on these additional considerations, though some trend forecasting techniques can take such factors into account, as well. Obviously, some forecasts take into account several factors that are known to affect future trends.

Forecasting can also consider the impact of conditions that might occur, giving rise to a variety of what-if scenarios. The analysis of local government revenues might take into account the possibility of different assessment (tax) rates that might be considered as policy adoptions by council. The impact of economic conditions might be considered, too. These factors can then be used to identify a range of possible forecasts based on rosy, likely, and pessimistic scenarios. Revenue forecasts of the federal government typically involve such alternative scenarios (see Figure 4.1). Likewise, rosy, likely, and pessimistic scenarios can be identified for the impact of the anger management program. Again, experts can be used to help define such scenarios. All forecasting methods should acknowledge limitations of factors that are not considered. For example, even pessimistic scenarios for local tax revenues might need to acknowledge, through a caveat, that a catastrophic hurricane, or some other unforeseen event, might eliminate real estate and require temporary tax breaks.

Statistical modeling aims to forecast phenomena based on variables that significantly explain the phenomena in the present and past. When knowledge about likely future values of these explanatory variables exist, or can be guessed reliably, the future values of the phenomena can be predicted, too. This approach focuses on the dynamics giving rise to phenomena, rather than on trend extrapolation. These models are often statistically complex and some of them (for example, causal models) are discussed here and in Chapter 18. For example, a statistical model might identify 5 to 15 of the most important factors that explain changes in high school violence, and use statistical methods to determine the impact of each of these variables. By estimating future values of these variables, a manager can then estimate future levels of high school violence. A practical limitation of this approach is that the impact of policies and new conditions in the future must be estimated through the variables already included in the model; otherwise, they must be determined through the use of experts or past research studies, for example.

REGRESSION-BASED FORECASTING

Frequently, public managers and analysts are called upon to forecast. In this section, we provide some useful statistical forecast methods. To avoid confusion, the term *forecast* refers to the values of predicted observations in the *future*. By contrast, the predicted values of *known* observations are called predicted values, $\hat{y}$, not forecasts. Readers may also wish to familiarize themselves with Chapter 4, which discusses principles and general limitations of forecasting.[5]

Multiple regression often is of limited use for statistical forecasting because *future* values of independent variables are unknown. At best, when all of the independent variables are lagged, some near-term forecasts are possible, based on known values of independent variables. Rather, simple regression is then used to make forecasts in which "time" is the (sole) independent variable. Various advanced, statistical regression techniques estimate time series that take into account *trends* and *periodic* (for example, seasonal) fluctuations.[6] These advanced techniques are often used in financial forecasting, but they have found little application in public management and policy to date. There are four types of *regression-based forecasting* techniques: forecasting with leading indicators, curve estimation, exponential smoothing, and ARIMA (autoregressive integrated moving average).

Validation is critical in any forecasting. Generally, the first step in forecasting is ascertaining that the model accurately predicts current values. We cannot place much credence in forecasting a model that does a poor job of predicting today's known values. To this end, the models are recalculated based on a smaller sample that excludes recent observations. Recent observations are then used to compare the predicted and actual values. If the model is found to make accurate predictions of recent known values, which is usually determined by visual comparison of the actual and predicted values, then existing values are included and predictions are made of future conditions.

A limitation of regression-based approaches to forecasting is that they often require more observations than are available to managers; few managers have 20 or more time-based observations. Also, long series may include the effects of events that have since ceased. As a result, long trend series may not always be better for predicting the future. Hence, only a brief overview of each technique is provided here; later in this chapter, we examine spreadsheet-based approaches that do not require many observations.

Forecasting with Leading Indicators

Forecasting with leading indicators involves regression with independent variables that are all lagged (leading indicators). When independent variables are lagged, it is possible to forecast near-term observations by using the known, present values of the lagged independent variables to predict future values of the dependent variable. If the current predicted and observed values are close, then the forecasted values should be reasonably accurate. The usefulness of this approach is limited to forecasts that are no longer than the shortest of the lagged periods. Leading indicators are well-known in some fields, such as economics and business, where some indicators are seen as harbingers of future market changes. For example, manufacturing orders, building permits, and architecture billings are indicators of future construction activity. Leading indicators are used in other areas: environmental water quality is a leading indicator of certain fish stocks, for example, and student application requests are a leading indicator of student enrollment. It is useful to think of leading indicators in your line of work.

Curve Estimation

Curve estimation estimates the shape of a trend variable and makes forecasts based on it. Curve estimation is available in many statistical software packages. Typically, various linear, quadratic, and logarithmic models are estimated (fitted), where "time" is the sole independent variable. Thus, for example, a quadratic function is estimated as $y(t) = a + b_1 t + b_2 t^2$, and a logarithmic function is estimated as $y(t) = a + b_1 \log(t)$. Although R-square values are reported for each model, models should be selected that seem to best fit the observed curve. These models provide for level and trend but not for periodic effects (seasonality). If the analyst believes that a model fits accurately, then model parameters can be used as a basis for making forecasts. An example is shown in Figure 17.5. The figure shows linear, logarithmic, and

Figure 17.5 ⎯⎯⎯⎯⎯⎯⎯ Curve Estimation I

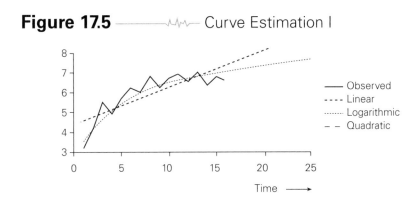

Figure 17.6 ⎯⎯⎯⎯ᴧᴧᴧ⎯ Curve Estimation II

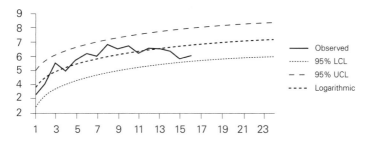

quadratic model results in vastly different forecasts. This is quite common with such estimations. Although the R^2 values of these models are quite respectable (respectively, 0.455, 0.747, and 0.895), both the linear and quadratic models seem way off the mark for even near-term predictions.

Curve estimation procedures can also be used to calculate confidence intervals. Confidence intervals are somewhat smaller for known values and become larger for forecasts that lie farther into the future. For the curves in Figure 17.6, the 95 percent level confidence intervals are considerable, varying from 60.87 to 62.31 for each of the estimated curves. Figure 17.5 shows the 95 percent confidence interval for the logarithmic curve.

Exponential Smoothing

Exponential smoothing is a technique that estimates the dependent variables based on their level, trend, and seasonality: $y(t) = f$ (level, trend, seasonality). The estimation methodology involves an iterative testing of alternative parameters that define level, trend, and seasonality components. There are four parameters: alpha (specifying the relative weight given to recent observations in calculating the current level), gamma (specifying the relative weight given to recent observations in determining the trend), and delta (specifying the relative weight given to recent observations in determining seasonality). In addition, some models also have a parameter phi, which specifies the extent to which the trend is dampened (that is, dies out) over time.

The computer conducts a so-called grid search, which is iterative testing of combinations of parameters to minimize the *sum of squared errors* (SSE, not to be confused with SEE; see Chapter 14), defined as the squared differences between actual and predicted values. The model with the lowest SSE best fits the observations. Predictions with exponential smoothing often rely heavily on recent observations. Then, forecasted values closely resemble the most recent observations, modified according to any trend that is present in the most immediate observations, and any seasonality that is present. This is shown in Figure 17.6. The forecasted values closely match the last observation. Note that the most recent observations are also devoid of any trend. Figure 17.7 does not include a seasonality component. If seasonality had been specified and present, the forecast would have been modulated to reflect the estimated seasonality. The model can also be made to give more weight to past observations. Then the forecasted values will show an upward trend. However, based on the criterion of choosing a model with the lowest SSEs, the above model is preferred. In this instance, the predicted observations do not always closely match the actual observations; the predicted values seem to follow actual observations by about one period. In fact, manually lagging the predicted values further reduces the SSE.[7]

ARIMA

Autoregressive integrated moving average (ARIMA) is a highly advanced technique often used for financial forecasting (for example, in stock markets), but it has found little application in public management and policy to date. ARIMA models require users to specify the nature of moving averages, autoregression, and seasonality. When the purpose is only prediction (not forecasting), independent variables can be used, too. The first step in ARIMA modeling is to make the data stationary, that is, to ensure that the variable has the same mean and variance across the entire range. This typically is achieved by taking first-order differences (described earlier in this chapter). The second step involves determining the nature of parameters through myriad diagnostics that are part of ARIMA procedures. The third step is estimation and evaluation of the model by comparing actual and predicted values (see the discussion of validation earlier in this chapter). Following these procedures, we came up with predicted values and forecasts, as shown in Figure 17.8. We used first-order differences and no seasonality.

Figure 17.7 —— Exponential Smoothing

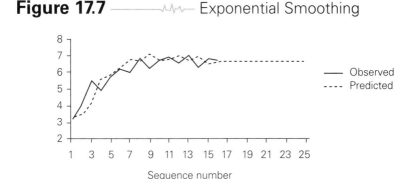

Figure 17.8 —— ⌇⌇⌇— ARIMA

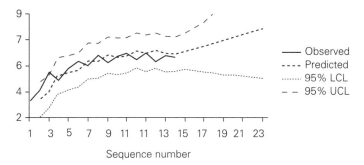

Sequence number

In comparison, ARIMA gives more weight to past observations than does exponential smoothing, resulting in the upward trend shown in Figure 17.8. ARIMA also produces confidence intervals. Forecasts that are farther into the future are more uncertain and thus have larger confidence intervals. The forecast methods described in the next section also give more weight to recent observations and increases; the smoothing of recent fluctuations quickly results in a constant forecast of about 6.7—the last observation, similar to the exponential smoothing forecast shown in Figure 17.7.

> **Key Point**
> Public managers often need to forecast revenues, expenditures, costs, manpower, service capacities, and the like. Regression is useful in forecasting.

NON-REGRESSION-BASED FORECASTING WITH FEW OBSERVATIONS

Managers are frequently asked to make forecasts on the basis of few previous observations. This problem sometimes is encountered when managers are asked to forecast budget expenditures on the basis of just a few years or months of prior data. The lack of an adequate number of observations makes the use of time series regression impractical. When one is working with expenditures and revenues, it is common to use constant dollars, that is, to remove inflationary growth from other sources of growth. Hence, expenditures are deflated before forecasts are made. Assume that annual inflation rates are as shown in Table 17.3 (in percentages). All data are first recalculated in constant year T dollars, which are then forecasted. This is shown in the table.[8] Inflation rates affect the current year's expenditures. Hence, $57.5 in $T - 1$ is equivalent to [$57.5*1.033 =] $59.4 in time period T. The amount $54.3 in Table 17.3 is equivalent to

Table 17.3 —— ᴧᴧ— Annual Inflation Rates: Percentages

Year	T–5	T–4	T–3	T–2	T–1	T	T+1	T+2	T+3
Inflation rate (%)	2.8	3.1	4.0	2.7	3.3	.			
Budget (current $s)	52.1	50.5	52.5	54.3	57.5	60.4			
Budget (constant $s)	60.9	57.4	57.9	57.6	59.4	60.4			

[$54.3*1.027*1.033 =] $57.6 in time period *T*. Any forecasted expenditures will now be net of any inflation. The result shows that despite the overall increase in current dollars, budget expenditures have been about level for most of the period; expenditures at time *T* are in fact less than at *T* – 5, when both are expressed in constant $t = T$ dollars.

Several approaches to forecasting data exist. Each approach has its own bias. A conservative approach is the use of **prior moving averages** (also called PMAs). In this approach, the average of the current preceding observations is used to predict the following period. The problem with this widely used approach is that it *under*estimates future values by basing forecasts on the average of the recent past. Typically, a time span of three periods is used; hence, the three most recent periods are used to predict the next period. At the end of existing observations, predicted observations become part of the series used to predict the next period, and so on. Whenever possible, actual rather than predicted values should be used. The results are shown in Table 17.4. For example, the predicted value of the budget in the *T* – 2 period is the mean of $60.9, $57.4, and $57.9 (see Table 17.3), which is $58.7. Similarly, the predicted value for the *T* – 1 period is the mean of $57.4, $57.9, and $57.6, which is $57.6. The forecasted value of the budget in period *T* + 1 is the mean of $57.6, $59.4, and $60.4, which is $59.1. Note that the values used to forecast the budget in *T* + 1 are the actual numbers, not the predicted numbers. The forecasted value in *T* + 2 is the mean of $59.4, $60.4, and $59.1, which is $59.6. Here, the value of *T* + 1 is the forecasted value because no actual value exists. Comparing predicted against actual values for purposes of validation, we see the downward tendency for *T* and *T* – 1.

Table 17.4 —— ᴧᴧ— Forecasted Budget Using PMA

Year	T–5	T–4	T–3	T–2	T–1	T	T+1	T+2	T+3
Predicted budget (constant $s)	.	.	.	58.7	57.6	58.3	59.1	59.6	59.7

A second approach, which we call *prior moving changes*, forecasts on the basis of *changes* in preceding periods. Often the average of the last three increases is used to predict the next period. Then future values are defined as the immediate past level plus the average of the last three increases. The idea is that future changes in expenditures should resemble past increases. Using the average increases of three prior years, we obtain the results shown in Table 17.5. For example, the change from $T-5$ to $T-4$ is [$57.4 – $60.9 =] $–3.50. The average of changes in the three periods prior to $T-1$ is the mean of $–3.5, $0.5, and $–0.3, which is $–1.1. Hence, the predicted value for $T-1$ is the actual budget of $T-2$, or $57.6 – $1.1, which is $56.5. The other values are calculated similarly. For example, the forecasted value of $T+1$ is calculated as the value of T, $60.4, plus the average of the last three increases ($–0.3, $1.8, and $1), or $0.83, which is $61.2. This is [$61.2 – $60.4 =] $0.8 higher than in time period T. (We prefer to use actual rather than predicted values whenever possible; hence, we use the actual value of $60.4 rather than the predicted value of $60.1.) This information is used to calculate the average increases for forecasts in the next time period, $T+2$, and so on. Comparing these two approaches, we find that forecasts based on average increases are far less conservative than those based on PMAs.[9] From the perspective of validation, we find that the predicted values of $T-1$ and T are slightly better than those using PMAs.

These results can sometimes be improved, or at least validated, through a third approach, which forecasts expenditures based on known *forecast ratios*. Tests involve other variables, such as work orders, client requests, or populations. Assume, for example, that expenditures are known to be related to the population size, the source of service requests. These forecasts can be triangulated by forecasts of population growth, shown below for $T+1$ and beyond. These forecasts are made as shown in Table 17.6. The average ratio is 0.227. Hence, the predicted budget for $T+1$ is [275*0.227 =] $62.4. These values seem consistent with

> **Getting Started**
> Verify these calculations.

Table 17.5 ⎯⎯⎯⎯⎯〰〰⎯ Forecasted Budget Using Average Changes

Year	T–5	T–4	T–3	T–2	T–1	T	T+1	T+2	T+3
Change from prior period		–3.5	0.5	–0.3	1.8	1.0	0.8	1.2	
Average change				–1.1	0.7	0.8	1.2	1.0	
Actual budget (constant $s)	60.9	57.4	57.9	57.6	59.4	60.4			
Predicted/forecasted budget (constant $s)					56.5	60.1	61.2	62.4	63.4

Table 17.6 ⎯⎯⎯⎯⎯⎯⎯ Predicted Budget: Forecast Ratio

Year	T–5	T–4	T–3	T–2	T–1	T	T+1	T+2	T+3
Budget (constant $s)	60.9	57.4	57.9	57.6	59.4	60.4			
Population	250	253	258	260	266	273	275	280	282
Ratio	0.244	0.227	0.224	0.221	0.223	0.221			
Forecasted budget (constant $s) Mean of all ratios							62.4	63.6	64.0
Forecasted budget (constant $) Mean of last three ratios							61.1	62.2	62.6

the forecasting approach based on prior moving changes. If the ratios of only the last three periods are used, whose mean is 0.222, then the forecasted values are somewhat lower. Of course, the credibility of these forecasts hinges on the constancy and theoretical justification of the ratio. If credible, the forecasted values heighten the importance of incorporating estimated demand in expenditure forecasts.

Forecasting with Periodic Effects

A rather different problem involves forecasting when data exhibit *periodicity* (or *seasonality*), that is, systematically fluctuating (or modulating) values. Some examples of these problems are daily activities that exhibit lower workloads on Mondays and weekly activities that exhibit more activity toward the end of the month. Table 17.7 lays out an example of such data. When only PMAs are used, the last three values of Month 4 will greatly overestimate the value of Week 1 in Month 5. This is because the three prior observations (the last three weeks in Month 4) fail to take into account that, on average, Week 1 activity levels are low for all months. The strategy of forecasting Month 5, Week 1, requires that we take this information into account. The methodology is a straightforward, albeit cumbersome, three-step process. First, average workloads are calculated for each period, on the basis of which a forecast is made for the entire Month 5. Specifically, we forecast an average for Month 5 as the average of Month 4 plus the mean increase of preceding months. Second, the mean deviations are determined for each week of the preceding months. Third, these deviations are used to adjust the weekly forecasts in Month 5. The calculations are done as follows.

The "Mean monthly activity" column clearly shows an upward trend. Because these are not expenditures, we do not deflate them. The first step is

Table 17.7 ————〰〰— Weekly and Monthly Activity: Forecasted Values

Month	Week	Activity	Mean monthly activity	Deviation from mean	Predicted activity for week 5
1	1	10		*−5.00*	
1	2	14		−1.00	
1	3	15		0.00	
1	4	21	15.00	+6.00	
2	1	12		*−4.75*	
2	2	15		−1.75	
2	3	17		+0.25	
2	4	23	16.75	+6.25	
3	1	14		*−4.00*	
3	2	16		−2.00	
3	3	16		−2.00	
3	4	26	18.00	+8.00	
4	1	16		*−3.25*	
4	2	16		−3.25	
4	3	20		+0.75	
4	4	25	19.25	+5.75	
Forecasted:					
5	1		20.67	−4.25	16.42
5	2		20.67	−2.00	18.67
5	3		20.67	−0.25	20.42
5	4		20.67	+6.50	27.17

to forecast all of Month 5. To this end, we calculate the *mean increase* from month to month. For example, the increase from Month 1 to Month 2 is [16.75 − 15.00 =] 1.75. In this manner, the mean increase is the mean of 1.75, 1.25, and 1.25, which is 1.42. Thus, it seems reasonable to forecast the average activity in Month 5 as 19.25 (the mean of Month 4) plus 1.42, which is 20.67.

Second, we calculate the deviations for each week and average them. For example, the mean deviation across all Week 1s (for each month) is the mean of −5.00, −4.75, −4.00, and −3.25, shown in italics, or −4.25. Similarly, mean deviations are calculated for other weeks. Third, the forecasted mean value for Month 5 is adjusted for these weekly deviations. For example, Week 1 in Month 5 is [20.67 − 4.25 =] 16.42. Values for other periods in Month 5 are calculated similarly. The results are shown in Table 17.7 and Figure 17.4.

SUMMARY

A vast array of statistical methods are available for analyzing time series data. Analysts use multiple regression when they need to understand the causes of past or present events. Although time series data and results must meet the same assumptions as discussed in Chapter 15, a principal concern is with autocorrelation, which is tested using the Durbin-Watson test statistic. Autocorrelation often is overcome by adding a trend variable or transforming the data into first-differences. This chapter also discusses how policies can be modeled using dummy variables.

Analysts have many techniques available to them for making forecasts; Chapter 4 discusses the importance of combining statistical and nonstatistical methods in forecasting. Regarding statistical methods, the basic choice is between using regression-based and non-regression-based methods. The former often are based on trend extrapolation, with or without other, independent variables. Techniques differ in how they deal with periodic fluctuations and with how much weight they give to recent rather than past observations.

Non-regression-based methods of forecasting typically use spreadsheets and are designed to deal with smaller numbers of observations. These forecasts, too, vary in how much weight they give to present or past observations, and whether they make forecasts that are related to other variables. In the business of making forecasts, analysts and managers do well to heed the principles of forecasting discussed in Chapter 4, and to rely on a range of plausible forecasts, rather than on any single approach.

KEY TERMS

Autocorrelation (p. 288)
Autoregressive integrated moving
    average (ARIMA) (p. 300)
Curve estimation (p. 298)
Durbin-Watson test statistic (p. 288)
Exponential smoothing (p. 299)
First-order differences (p. 290)
Forecast (p. 297)
Forecast ratios (p. 303)
Forecasting with leading indicators
    (p. 298)
Lagged variable (p. 293)

Periodicity (p. 304)
Policy variables (p. 291)
Prior moving averages (p. 302)
Prior moving changes (p. 303)
Regression-based forecasting (p. 297)
Seasonality (p. 304)
Serial correlation (p. 288)
Statistical forecasting methods
    (p. 295)
Statistical modeling (p. 296)
Trend extrapolation (p. 295)
Trend variable (p. 290)

Notes

1. Some time series data are also more likely to exhibit problems of multi-collinearity because, over time, many variables show similar upward or downward sloping patterns.
2. The Durbin-Watson test statistic may fail to detect autocorrelation when time series data are strongly seasonal or when a lagged dependent variable is used as an independent variable.
3. Statistical packages often have a cross-correlation function (CCF), which examines lags between two variables. This function is used to estimate the number of lags. The CCF should be used only when variables are stationary, that is, when they exhibit a stable mean and variances over time. This is typically accomplished by taking first-order differences. The discussion of CCF is beyond the scope of this text. See, for example, SPSS, *SPSS Trends 10.0* (Chicago: SPSS, Inc., 1999 or later editions).
4. Durbin h is defined as

$$(1-0.5DW)\sqrt{\frac{N}{1-N\left[se\left(b_{y_{t-1}}\right)\right]^2}},$$

where N is the sample size, DW is the Durbin-Watson statistic, and $[se(b_{y_{t-1}})]^2$ is the squared standard error of the regression coefficient of the lagged dependent variable (that is, b_1, in the model $\Delta y = a + b_1 \Delta y_{t-1} + b_2 \Delta x_2 + \ldots$). Durbin h is normally distributed; hence, values greater than $|h| > 1.96$ indicate serial correlation.

5. The methods discussed here concern statistical forecasting only and do not address the judgmental forecasting mentioned in Chapter 4.
6. Seasonal variation can also be modeled in multiple regression through dummy variables, for example, using dummy variables for spring, summer, and fall, or for different months.
7. In this regard, exponential smoothing with seasonal trend nearly identically matches the predicted observations shown in Figure 17.4. The mean discrepancy between these forecasts is 2.4 percent. Without seasonality, the fitted model merely shows the general trend.
8. For ease of calculation, only one decimal place is retained in the following data and tables. Actual results (such as when using a spreadsheet) will vary slightly due to rounding.
9. Some analysts might prefer using the average of prior expenditures, rather than the last expenditure, as the basis for future prediction. This

approach, of course, has a downward effect on prediction. For example, the prediction for $T-1$ is the average of T through $T-2$, or $57.6, $59.4, and $60.4, which is $59.1, plus the average increase of $T-1$ through $T-3$, $0.67, or $59.8. This value falls between the two approaches discussed in the text.

CHAPTER

18

Survey of Other Techniques

CHAPTER OBJECTIVES

After reading this chapter, you should understand

- How path analysis uses multiple dependent variables
- How survival analysis deals with events that have not yet occurred
- How factor analysis is used for exploratory purposes
- Other advanced, statistical techniques

This chapter provides an overview of several advanced statistical techniques. Each of these multivariate techniques expands on previous techniques in ways that help managers to work with some rather special situations. Three techniques are examined in some depth, and other advanced techniques are summarized more briefly. The techniques described in some detail are path analysis, survival analysis, and factor analysis. Managers and analysts are apt to come across these techniques in the research literature.

PATH ANALYSIS

Path analysis is a technique for estimating models with complex interrelationships among variables. Regression analysis does a poor job of modeling

Figure 18.1 —⌇⌇— Path Analysis

Relationship between job training, job interviews, and employment

complex reality. Linear regression assesses the impacts of all variables on one dependent variable; what if reality allows for indirect effects? Consider the following hypothetical scenario from a welfare employment agency. Unemployed persons are provided the opportunity to participate in job training, which includes training in job interview techniques as well as some remedial education. The question is whether the job training is successful. Managers suspect that job training affects employment (that is, whether a job seeker secures employment within a certain time) in the manner shown in Figure 18.1. Job training is hypothesized to increase the employment of job seekers, but it also causes them to participate in more job interviews because part of the job training includes interviewing skills. This, in turn, also increases employment. Thus, the hypothesized effect of job training is both direct and indirect. Figure 18.1 can be elaborated further by including the effects of having dependents and substance abuse problems (see Figure 18.2).

Path analysis is a causal modeling technique for estimating such complex models. However, an important limitation of path analysis is that it may not be used when feedback loops are present. Feedback loops are relationships in which two or more variables are directly or indirectly caused by each other; no such relationships are present in Figure 18.2. (Feedback loops would have existed *if* additional paths had been added that go from "job interviews" to "job training," or from "job interviews" to "having dependents." Of course, these additional paths make little theoretical sense in our model.)[1] Models without feedback loops are called ***recursive models***. When no feedback loops are present, each path can be estimated with ordinary least squares (OLS) regression.[2] Specifically, in this example, the following regression models are estimated:

Employment = a_1 + b_1 Job interviews + b_2 Job training + b_3 Dependents + e_1
Job interviews = a_2 + b_4 Job training + e_2
Job training = a_3 + b_5 Dependents + b_6 Substance abuse + e_3

Note that in causal models, the terminology of independent and dependent variables often is inconclusive: the variable "job interviews" is both an independent

Figure 18.2 ─────∿∿── Path Analysis

Relationship between job training, job interviews, and employment
with effects of dependents and substance abuse

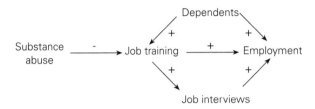

variable (causing employment) and a dependent variable (caused by job training, having dependents, and substance abuse). Then, causal modeling distinguishes between **exogenous variables,** which are variables that are unaffected
by other variables in the model (such as substance abuse), and **endogenous
variables,** which are affected by other variables (such as employment and job
interviews).

For each model, the impact of each variable is stated by the beta coefficient. Assume that the results in Figure 18.3 are available. The numbers
along the arrows are the beta coefficients. The error terms that are shown
are sometimes calculated as $\sqrt{1 - R^2}$.[3] Then, direct and indirect effects of
the variables are calculated in Table 18.1. *Direct effects* are simply the beta
coefficients of the variables that immediately affect another variable. **Indirect effects** are calculated as the product of beta coefficients of each pathway. Note that the variables "dependents" and "substance abuse" have two
indirect pathways to "employment" (see Table 18.1). The results shown in
the table are interesting because they show that, although interviewing has
a greater direct effect on employment than training, the indirect effects of

Figure 18.3 ─────∿∿── Path Analysis Results

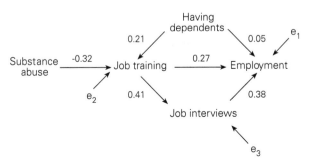

Table 18.1 ————〜〜— Calculating Direct and Indirect Effects on Employment

	Effects		
Variable	**Indirect**	**Direct**	**Total**
Job training	0.41*0.38 = 0.16	0.27	0.43
Job interviews	—	0.38	0.38
Dependents	0.21*0.27 + 0.21*0.41*0.38 = 0.09	0.05	0.14
Substance abuse	−0.32*0.27 + −0.32*0.41*0.38 = −0.14	—	−0.14

training are substantial. The total effect of job training exceeds that of interviewing. If only multiple regression had been used (with "employment" as a dependent variable), this indirect effect would have gone undetected. The results also show that the variables "substance abuse" and "having dependents" have less impact on "employment" than do the other two variables.

Path analysis is a relatively simple extension of multiple regression. The standards for its proper use are as follows:

- The model must be theory based. Although many different models can be constructed from even a modest number of variables, the relationships that they depict must make sense (have face validity). Typically, analysts specify a family of plausible models, and even though only one model might be reported, all models should have similar substantive conclusions.
- There are no feedback loops and all models satisfy standard regression assumptions. Thus, problems of outliers, heteroscedasticity, linearity, autocorrelation, and multicollinearity should be identified and addressed.
- All error terms should be uncorrelated with all exogenous variables. The correlation of an error term with an exogenous variable suggests that that variable has an effect on the endogenous variable associated with the error term. In such a case, another path should be drawn that reflects the impact of the exogenous variable with the endogenous variable. The absence of such correlation does not prove that the model is specified correctly, only that it is not specified incorrectly.

Getting Started

Find examples of the techniques of this chapter in your area of interest.

Beyond Path Analysis

Path analysis is limited to models that have no feedback loops. When feedback loops are present, error term assumptions are violated. Causal models with feedback loops are called *nonrecursive* models. *Two-stage least squares* (known as 2SLS) is an econometric technique (that is, a statistical method used in economic research) for estimating two regression models that have feedback loops, such as the following:

(1) $$x_{10} \leftarrow x_{11}, x_{12}$$
(2) $$x_{11} \leftarrow x_{13}, x_{14}, x_{10}$$

In model 1, x_{11} is endogenous and x_{12} is exogenous. The basic strategy of 2SLS is to use a modified version of x_{11} in model 1 that does not violate error term assumptions. The name *two stage* indicates a two-step process for estimating such systems of models. The purpose of the first step is to estimate the modified variable, here, x_{11}. Typically, x_{11} is predicted by other variables that are, hence, called instrumental variables. The predicted variable x_{11} is denoted $\hat{X}_{11}$. In the second stage, $\hat{X}_{11}$ is used to predict the dependent variable x_{10}, hence, $x_{10} = f(\hat{X}_{11}, x_{12})$.

In recent years, advances in software interfaces have increased the popularity of *structural equation models* (SEMs). These are models that simultaneously estimate (1) the relationship between observed variables and their factor constructs and (2) relationships among variables and constructs that involve feedback loops. Estimation requires specific software such as LISREL or AMOS (now integrated as an add-on module with SPSS). Figure 18.4 shows an example of this approach. In the model, classroom violence is composed of measures of physical contact, weapons, and verbal assaults. GPA is measured through math and verbal test scores. The impact on classroom violence is predicted through the same variables as in the logistic regression example in Chapter 16, namely, gender, grade level, and GPA. However, this model also,

Figure 18.4 ⎯⎯⎯〰️⎯ SEM Model

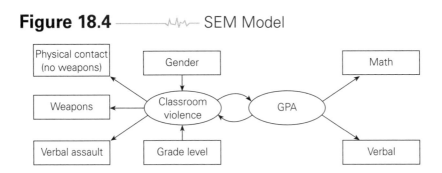

and simultaneously, examines the impact of classroom violence on GPA. The estimation methodology is quite complex, and analysts test for robustness and validity in ways that are dissimilar from those used in multiple regression.

SURVIVAL ANALYSIS

Another limitation of regression is that it assumes that complete information is available about all observations. *Survival analysis* deals with techniques that analyze information about events that is not yet available.[4] Assume that a welfare manager in our earlier example (see discussion of path analysis) takes a snapshot of the status of the welfare clients. Some clients may have obtained employment and others not yet. Clients will also vary as to the amount of time that they have been receiving welfare. Examine the data in Table 18.2. It shows that neither of the two clients, who have yet to complete their first week on welfare, has found employment; one of the three clients who have completed one week of welfare has found employment. *Censored observations* are observations for which the specified outcome has yet to occur. It is assumed that all clients who have not yet found employment are still waiting for this event to occur. Thus, the sample should not include clients who are not seeking employment. Note, however, that a censored observation is very different from one that has missing data, which might occur because the manager does not know whether the client has found employment. As with regression, records with missing data are excluded from analysis. A censored observation is simply an observation for which a specified outcome has not yet occurred.

Assume that data exist from a random sample of 100 clients who are seeking, or have found, employment. *Survival analysis* is the statistical procedure for analyzing these data. The name of this procedure stems from its use in medical research. In clinical trials, researchers want to know the survival (or disease) rate of patients as a function of the duration of their treatment. For patients in the middle of their trial, the specified outcome may not have

Table 18.2 ⎯⎯⎯⎯⎯⎯ Censored Observations

Obs	Week	Emp	Obs	Week	Emp	Obs	Week	Emp
1	0	0	6	2	0	11	4	1
2	0	0	7	2	0	12	4	0
3	1	1	8	3	1	13	5	1
4	1	0	9	3	0	14	5	1
5	1	0	10	4	1	15	5	0

Note: Obs = observations (clients); Emp = employment; 0 = has not yet found employment; 1 = has found employment.

Table 18.3 ⎯⎯⎯⎯⎯⎯~⋀⋀~⎯ Life Table Results

Start time	# Entering interval	# Terminal events	Cumulative proportion surviving until end of interval	Probability density
0.0	100.0	0.0	1.0000	0.0000
1.0	91.0	2.0	0.9762	0.0238
2.0	75.0	5.0	0.9055	0.0707
3.0	58.0	6.0	0.7979	0.1076
4.0	37.0	9.0	0.5867	0.2112
5.0	22.0	14.0	0.1304	0.4563

Note: The median survival time is 5.19.

occurred yet. We obtain the following results (also called a *life table*) from analyzing hypothetical data from welfare records (see Table 18.3). In the context shown in the table, the word *terminal* signifies that the event has occurred. That is, the client has found employment. At start time zero, 100 cases enter the interval. During the first period, there are no terminal cases and nine censored cases. Thus, 91 cases enter the next period. In this second period, 2 clients find employment and 14 do not, resulting in 75 cases that enter the following period. The column labeled "Cumulative proportion surviving until end of interval" is an estimate of probability of surviving (not finding employment) until the end of the stated interval.[5] The column labeled "Probability density" is an estimate of the probability of the terminal event occurring (that is, finding employment) during the time interval. The results also report that "the median survival time is 5.19." That is, half of the clients find employment in 5.19 weeks.

Survival analysis can also examine survival rates for different "treatments" or conditions. Assume that data are available about the number of dependents that each client has. Table 18.3 is readily produced for each subset of this condition. For example, by comparing the survival rates of those with and those without dependents, the probability density figure, which shows the likelihood of an event occurring, can be obtained (Figure 18.5). This figure suggests that having dependents is associated with clients' finding employment somewhat faster.

Beyond Life Tables

Life tables require that the interval (time) variable be measured on a discrete scale. When the time variable is continuous, *Kaplan-Meier survival analysis* is used. This procedure is quite analogous to life tables analysis. *Cox regression*

Figure 18.5 ——— ⌇⌇ ——— Probability Density

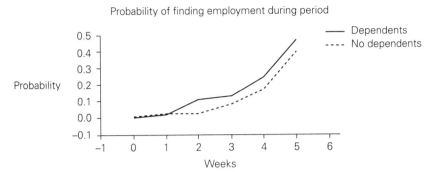

Probability of finding employment during period

is similar to Kaplan-Meier but allows for consideration of a larger number of independent variables (called covariates). In all instances, the purpose is to examine the effect of treatment on the survival of observations, that is, the occurrence of a dichotomous event.

FACTOR ANALYSIS

A variety of statistical techniques help analysts to explore relationships in their data. These exploratory techniques typically aim to create groups of variables (or observations) that are related to each other and distinct from other groups. These techniques usually precede regression and other analyses.

Factor analysis is a well-established technique that often aids in creating index variables. Earlier, Chapter 3 discussed the use of Cronbach alpha to empirically justify the selection of variables that make up an index. However, in that approach analysts must still justify that variables used in different index variables are indeed distinct. By contrast, factor analysis analyzes a large number of variables (often 20 to 30) and classifies them into groups based on empirical similarities and dissimilarities. This empirical assessment can aid analysts' judgments regarding variables that might be grouped together.

Factor analysis uses correlations among variables to identify subgroups. These subgroups (called factors) are characterized by relatively high within-group correlation among variables and low between-group correlation among variables. Most factor analysis consists of roughly four steps: (1) determining that the group of variables has enough correlation to allow for factor analysis, (2) determining how many factors should be used for classifying (or grouping) the variables, (3) improving the interpretation of correlations and factors (through a process called rotation), and (4) naming the factors and, possibly, creating index variables for subsequent analysis. Most factor analysis is used for grouping of variables (R-type factor analysis) rather than observations (Q-type). Often, discriminant analysis is used for grouping of observations, mentioned later in this chapter.

The terminology of factor analysis differs greatly from that used elsewhere in this book, and the discussion that follows is offered as an aid in understanding tables that might be encountered in research that uses this technique. An important task in factor analysis is determining how many common factors should be identified. Theoretically, there are as many factors as variables, but only a few factors account for most of the variance in the data. The percentage of variation explained by each factor is defined as the eigenvalue divided by the number of variables, whereby the eigenvalue of a factor is the sum of correlations (r) of each variable with that factor. This correlation is also called *loading* in factor analysis. Analysts can define (or "extract") how many factors they wish to use, or they can define a statistical criterion (typically requiring each factor to have an eigenvalue of at least 1.0).

The method of identifying factors is called principal component analysis (PCA). The results of PCA often make it difficult to interpret the factors, in which case the analyst will use rotation (a statistical technique that distributes the explained variance across factors). Rotation causes variables to load higher on one factor, and less on others, bringing the pattern of groups better into focus for interpretation. Several different methods of rotation are commonly used (for example, Varimax, Promax), but the purpose of this procedure is always to understand which variables belong together. Typically, for purposes of interpretation, factor loadings are considered only if their values are at least .50, and only these values might be shown in tables.

Table 18.4 shows the result of a factor analysis. The table shows various items related to managerial professionalism, and the factor analysis identifies three distinct groups for these items. Such tables are commonly seen in research articles. The labels for each group (for example, "A. Commitment to performance") are provided by the authors; note that the three groupings are conceptually distinct. The table also shows that, combined, these three factors account for 61.97 percent of the total variance. The table shows only loadings greater than .50; those below this value are not shown.[6] Based on these results, the authors then create index variables for the three groups. Each group has high internal reliability (see Chapter 3); the Cronbach alpha scores are, respectively, 0.87, 0.83, and 0.88. This table shows a fairly typical use of factor analysis, providing statistical support for a grouping scheme.

Beyond Factor Analysis

A variety of exploratory techniques exist. Some seek purely to classify, whereas others seek to create and predict classifications through independent variables.

Table 18.4 ———〰️— Factor Analysis

Factor analysis of items of managerial commitment			
"*In our city, most managers . . .*"	Factor 1	Factor 2	Factor 3
A. Commitment to Performance			
Embrace professional standards	.837		
Are committed to improving effectiveness and efficiency	.826		
Exhibit a lot of energy and personal drive	.752		
Would rather overcome obstacles than accept them	.711		
Set high standards for their programs	.708		
Know nationally recognized best "practices"	.600		
B. Commitment to accountability			
Conduct thorough program evaluations		.767	
Use performance measurement effectively in most programs		.745	
Provide detailed accountability about their programs		.675	
Regularly conduct performance audits		.667	
Receive training in ethics principles and practices		.622	
Ensure that all employees are aware of ethics standards and requirements		.552	
C. Commitment to public participation			
Seek frequent input from community leaders in defining program goals			.826
Solicit feedback from community leaders about our performance			.799
Have regular discussions with community leaders on city problems			.795
Seek citizen input to assess program performance			.787
Encourage public participation processes in decision making			.750
Are effective in building community consensus			.579
SSL (sum of squared loadings)	4.084	3.836	3.236
Variation explained (%)	22.69	21.31	17.98
Total variation explained (%)	22.69	44.00	61.97

Note: Factor analysis with Varimax rotation.

Source: E. Berman and J. West. (2003). "What Is Managerial Mediocrity? Definition, Prevalence and Negative Impact (Part 1)." *Public Performance & Management Review*, 27 (December): 7–27.

Multidimensional scaling and *cluster analysis* aim to identify key dimensions along which observations (rather than variables) differ. These techniques differ from factor analysis in that they allow for a hierarchy of classification dimensions. Some also use graphics to aid in visualizing the extent of differences and to help in identifying the similarity or dissimilarity of observations. *Network analysis* is a descriptive technique used to portray relationships among actors. A graphic representation can be made of the frequency with which actors interact with each other, distinguishing frequent interactions from those that are infrequent.

Discriminant analysis is used when the dependent variable is nominal with two or more categories. For example, we might want to know how parents choose among three types of school vouchers. Discriminant analysis calculates regression lines that distinguish (discriminate) among the nominal groups (the categories of the dependent variable), as well as other regression lines that describe the relationship of the independent variables for each group (called classification functions). The emphasis in discriminant analysis is the ability of the independent variables to correctly predict values of the nominal variable (for example, group membership). Discriminant analysis is one strategy for dealing with dependent variables that are nominal with three or more categories.

Multinomial logistic regression and *ordinal regression* have been developed in recent years to address nominal and ordinal dependent variables in logic regression. Multinomial logistic regression calculates functions that compare the probability of a nominal value occurring relative to a base reference group. The calculation of such probabilities makes this technique an interesting alternative to discriminant analysis. When the nominal dependent variable has three values (say, 1, 2, and 3), one logistic regression predicts the likelihood of 2 versus 1 occurring, and the other logistic regression predicts the likelihood of 3 versus 1 occurring, assuming that "1" is the base reference group.[7]

When the dependent variable is ordinal, ordinal regression can be used. Like multinomial logistic regression, ordinal regression often is used to predict event probability or group membership. Ordinal regression assumes that the slope coefficients are identical for each value of the dependent variable; when this assumption is not met, multinomial logistic regression should be considered. Both multinomial logistic regression and ordinal regression are relatively recent developments and are not yet widely used. Statistics, like other fields of science, continues to push its frontiers forward and thereby develop new techniques for managers and analysts.

> **Key Point**
> Advanced statistical tools are available. Understanding the proper circumstances under which these tools apply is a prerequisite for using them.

SUMMARY

A vast array of additional statistical methods exists. In this concluding chapter, we summarized some of these methods (path analysis, survival analysis, and factor analysis) and briefly mentioned other related techniques. This chapter can help managers and analysts become familiar with these additional techniques and increase their access to research literature in which these techniques are used. Managers and analysts who would like more information about these techniques will likely consult other texts or on-line sources.

In many instances, managers will need only simple approaches to calculate the means of their variables, produce a few good graphs that tell the story, make simple forecasts, and test for significant differences among a few groups. Why, then, bother with these more advanced techniques? They are part of the analytical world in which managers operate. Through research and consulting, managers cannot help but come in contact with them. It is hoped that this chapter whets the appetite and provides a useful reference for managers and students alike.

KEY TERMS

Endogenous variables (p. 311)
Exogenous variables (p. 311)
Factor analysis (p. 316)
Indirect effects (p. 311)

Loading (p. 317)
Path analysis (p. 309)
Recursive models (p. 310)
Survival analysis (p. 314)

Notes

1. Two types of feedback loops are illustrated as follows:

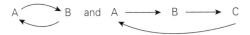

2. When feedback loops are present, error terms for the different models will be correlated with exogenous variables, violating an error term assumption for such models. Then, alternative estimation methodologies are necessary, such as two-stage least squares and others discussed later in this chapter.
3. Some models may show double-headed arrows among error terms. These show the correlation between error terms, which is of no importance in estimating the beta coefficients.
4. In SPSS, survival analysis is available through the add-on module in SPSS Advanced Models.

5. The functions used to estimate probabilities are rather complex. They are so-called Weibull distributions, which are defined as $h(t) = \alpha\lambda(\lambda t)^{a-1}$, where a and 1 are chosen to best fit the data.

6. Hence, the SSL is greater than the squared loadings reported. For example, because the loadings of variables in groups B and C are not shown for factor 1, the SSL of shown loadings is 3.27 rather than the reported 4.084. If one assumes the other loadings are each .25, then the SSL of the not reported loadings is [12*.25² =] .75, bringing the SSL of factor 1 to [3.27 + .75 =] 4.02, which is very close to the 4.084 value reported in the table.

7. Readers who are interested in multinomial logistic regression can consult on-line sources or the SPSS manual, *Regression Models* 10.0 or higher. The statistics of discriminant analysis are very dissimilar from those of logistic regression, and readers are advised to consult a separate text on that topic. Discriminant analysis is not often used in public affairs.

APPENDIXES

Appendix A
Normal Distribution

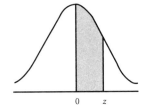

z	.00	.01	.02	.03	.04	.05	.06	.07	.08	.09
0.0	.0000	.0040	.0080	.0120	.0160	.0199	.0239	.0279	.0319	.0359
0.1	.0398	.0438	.0478	.0517	.0557	.0596	.0636	.0675	.0714	.0753
0.2	.0793	.0832	.0871	.0910	.0948	.0987	.1026	.1064	.1103	.1141
0.3	.1179	.1217	.1255	.1293	.1331	.1368	.1406	.1443	.1480	.1517
0.4	.1554	.1591	.1628	.1664	.1700	.1736	.1772	.1808	.1844	.1879
0.5	.1915	.1950	.1985	.2019	.2054	.2088	.2123	.2157	.2190	.2224
0.6	.2257	.2291	.2324	.2357	.2389	.2422	.2454	.2486	.2517	.2549
0.7	.2580	.2611	.2642	.2673	.2704	.2734	.2764	.2794	.2823	.2852
0.8	.2881	.2910	.2939	.2967	.2995	.3023	.3051	.3078	.3106	.3133
0.9	.3159	.3186	.3212	.3238	.3264	.3289	.3315	.3340	.3365	.3389
1.0	.3413	.3438	.3461	.3485	.3508	.3531	.3554	.3577	.3599	.3621
1.1	.3643	.3665	.3686	.3708	.3729	.3749	.3770	.3790	.3810	.3830
1.2	.3849	.3869	.3888	.3907	.3925	.3944	.3962	.3980	.3997	.4015
1.3	.4032	.4049	.4066	.4082	.4099	.4115	.4131	.4147	.4162	.4177
1.4	.4192	.4207	.4222	.4236	.4251	.4265	.4279	.4292	.4306	.4319
1.5	.4332	.4345	.4357	.4370	.4382	.4394	.4406	.4418	.4429	.4441
1.6	.4452	.4463	.4474	.4484	.4495	.4505	.4515	.4525	.4535	.4545
1.7	.4554	.4564	.4573	.4582	.4591	.4599	.4608	.4616	.4625	.4633
1.8	.4641	.4649	.4656	.4664	.4671	.4678	.4686	.4693	.4699	.4706
1.9	.4713	.4719	.4726	.4732	.4738	.4744	.4750	.4756	.4761	.4767
2.0	.4772	.4778	.4783	.4788	.4793	.4798	.4803	.4808	.4812	.4817
2.1	.4821	.4826	.4830	.4834	.4838	.4842	.4846	.4850	.4854	.4857
2.2	.4861	.4864	.4868	.4871	.4875	.4878	.4881	.4884	.4887	.4890
2.3	.4893	.4896	.4898	.4901	.4904	.4906	.4909	.4911	.4913	.4916
2.4	.4918	.4920	.4922	.4925	.4927	.4929	.4931	.4932	.4934	.4936
2.5	.4938	.4940	.4941	.4943	.4945	.4946	.4948	.4949	.4951	.4952
2.6	.4953	.4955	.4956	.4957	.4959	.4960	.4961	.4962	.4963	.4964
2.7	.4965	.4966	.4967	.4968	.4969	.4970	.4971	.4972	.4973	.4974
2.8	.4974	.4975	.4976	.4977	.4977	.4978	.4979	.4979	.4980	.4981
2.9	.4981	.4982	.4982	.4983	.4984	.4984	.4985	.4985	.4986	.4986
3.0	.4987	.4987	.4987	.4988	.4988	.4989	.4989	.4989	.4990	.4990

Source: Adapted from Table II of R. A. Fisher and F. Yates, *Statistical Tables for Biological, Agricultural, and Medical Research,* 6th edition, Longman Group, Ltd., London, 1974. (Previously published by Oliver & Boyle, Ltd., Edinburgh). Used with permission of the authors and publishers.

Appendix B
Chi-Square (χ^2) Distribution

Degree of Freedom (df)	0.10	0.05	0.01	.001
1	2.706	3.841	6.635	10.827
2	4.605	5.991	9.210	13.815
3	6.251	7.815	11.341	16.266
4	7.779	9.488	13.277	18.467
5	9.236	11.070	15.086	20.515
6	10.645	12.592	16.812	22.457
7	12.017	14.067	18.475	24.322
8	13.362	15.507	20.090	26.125
9	14.684	16.919	21.666	27.877
10	15.987	18.307	23.209	29.588
11	17.275	19.675	24.725	31.264
12	18.549	21.026	26.217	32.909
13	19.812	22.362	27.688	34.528
14	21.064	23.685	29.141	36.123
15	22.307	24.996	30.578	37.697
16	23.542	26.296	32.000	39.252
17	24.769	27.587	33.409	40.790
18	25.989	28.869	34.805	42.312
19	27.204	30.144	36.191	43.820
20	28.412	31.410	37.566	45.315
21	29.615	32.671	38.932	46.797
22	30.813	33.924	40.289	48.268
23	32.007	35.172	41.638	49.728
24	33.196	36.415	42.980	51.179
25	34.382	37.652	44.314	52.620
26	35.563	38.885	45.642	54.052
27	36.741	40.113	46.963	55.476
28	37.916	41.337	48.278	56.893
29	39.087	42.557	49.588	58.302
30	40.256	43.773	50.892	59.703

Source: Adapted from Table IV of R. A. Fisher and F. Yates, *Statistical Tables for Biological, Agricultural, and Medical Research*, 6th edition, Longman Group, Ltd., London, 1974. (Previously published by Oliver & Boyd, Ltd., Edinburgh). Used with permission of the authors and publishers.

Appendix C
T-Test Distribution

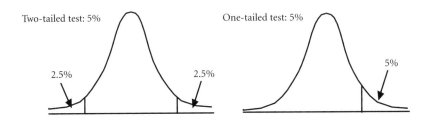

	Alpha Level for One-Tailed Test					
	.10	.05	.025	.01	.005	.0025
Degree of	Alpha Level for Two-Tailed Test					
Freedom (df)	.20	.10	.05	.02	.01	.005
1	3.078	6.314	12.706	31.821	63.657	127.32
2	1.886	2.920	4.303	6.965	9.925	14.089
3	1.638	2.353	3.182	4.541	5.841	7.453
4	1.533	2.132	2.776	3.747	4.604	5.598
5	1.476	2.015	2.571	3.365	4.032	4.773
6	1.440	1.943	2.447	3.143	3.707	4.317
7	1.415	1.895	2.365	2.998	3.499	4.029
8	1.397	1.869	2.306	2.896	3.355	3.833
9	1.383	1.833	2.262	2.821	3.250	3.690
10	1.372	1.812	2.228	2.764	3.169	3.581
11	1.363	1.796	2.201	2.718	3.106	3.497
12	1.356	1.782	2.179	2.681	3.055	3.428
13	1.350	1.771	2.160	2.650	3.012	3.372
14	1.345	1.761	2.145	2.624	2.977	3.326
15	1.341	1.753	2.131	2.602	2.947	3.286
16	1.337	1.746	2.120	2.583	2.921	3.252
17	1.333	1.740	2.110	2.567	2.898	3.222
18	1.330	1.734	2.101	2.552	2.878	3.197
19	1.328	1.729	2.093	2.539	2.861	3.174
20	1.325	1.725	2.086	2.528	2.845	3.153
21	1.323	1.721	2.080	2.518	2.831	3.135
22	1.321	1.717	2.074	2.508	2.819	3.119
23	1.319	1.714	2.069	2.500	2.807	3.104
24	1.318	1.711	2.064	2.492	2.797	3.091
25	1.316	1.708	2.060	2.485	2.787	3.078

(continued)

Degree of Freedom (df)	Alpha Level for One-Tailed Test					
	.10	.05	.025	.01	.005	.0025
	Alpha Level for Two-Tailed Test					
	.20	.10	.05	.02	.01	.005
26	1.315	1.706	2.056	2.479	2.779	3.067
27	1.314	1.703	2.052	2.473	2.771	3.057
28	1.313	1.701	2.048	2.467	2.763	3.047
29	1.311	1.699	2.045	2.462	2.756	3.038
30	1.310	1.697	2.042	2.457	2.750	3.030
40	1.303	1.684	2.021	2.423	2.704	2.971
60	1.296	1.671	2.000	2.390	2.660	2.915
120	1.289	1.658	1.980	2.358	2.617	2.860
∞	1.282	1.645	1.960	2.326	2.576	2.807

Source: Adapted from Table III of R. A. Fisher and F. Yates, *Statistical Tables for Biological, Agricultural, and Medical Research,* 6th edition, Longman Group, Ltd., London, 1974. (Previously published by Oliver & Boyd, Ltd., Edinburgh). Used with permission of the authors and publishers.

Appendix D
Durbin-Watson Distribution
Five percent significance points of d_l and d_u for Durbin-Watson test[†]

N	k = 1		k = 2		k = 3		k = 4		k = 5	
	d_l	d_u	d_l	d_u	d_l	d_u	d_l	d_u	d_l	d_u
15	1.08	1.36	0.95	1.54	0.82	1.75	0.69	1.97	0.56	2.21
16	1.10	1.37	0.98	1.54	0.86	1.73	0.74	1.93	0.62	2.15
17	1.13	1.38	1.02	1.54	0.90	1.71	0.78	1.90	0.67	2.10
18	1.16	1.39	1.05	1.53	0.93	1.69	0.82	1.87	0.71	2.06
19	1.18	1.40	1.08	1.53	0.97	1.68	0.86	1.85	0.75	2.02
20	1.20	1.41	1.10	1.54	1.00	1.68	0.90	1.83	0.79	1.99
21	1.22	1.42	1.13	1.54	1.03	1.67	0.93	1.81	0.83	1.96
22	1.24	1.43	1.15	1.54	1.05	1.66	0.96	1.80	0.86	1.94
23	1.26	1.44	1.17	1.54	1.08	1.66	0.99	1.79	0.90	1.92
24	1.27	1.45	1.19	1.55	1.10	1.66	1.01	1.78	0.93	1.90
25	1.29	1.45	1.21	1.55	1.12	1.66	1.04	1.77	0.95	1.89
26	1.30	1.46	1.22	1.55	1.14	1.65	1.06	1.76	0.98	1.88
27	1.32	1.47	1.24	1.56	1.16	1.65	1.08	1.76	1.01	1.86
28	1.33	1.48	1.26	1.56	1.18	1.65	1.10	1.75	1.03	1.85
29	1.34	1.48	1.27	1.56	1.20	1.65	1.12	1.74	1.05	1.84
30	1.35	1.49	1.28	1.57	1.21	1.65	1.14	1.74	1.07	1.83
31	1.36	1.50	1.30	1.57	1.23	1.65	1.16	1.74	1.09	1.83
32	1.37	1.50	1.31	1.57	1.24	1.65	1.18	1.73	1.11	1.82
33	1.38	1.51	1.32	1.58	1.26	1.65	1.19	1.73	1.13	1.81
34	1.39	1.51	1.33	1.58	1.27	1.65	1.21	1.73	1.15	1.81
35	1.40	1.52	1.34	1.53	1.28	1.65	1.22	1.73	1.16	1.80
36	1.41	1.52	1.35	1.59	1.29	1.65	1.24	1.73	1.18	1.80
37	1.42	1.53	1.36	1.59	1.31	1.66	1.25	1.72	1.19	1.80
38	1.43	1.54	1.37	1.59	1.32	1.66	1.26	1.72	1.21	1.79
39	1.43	1.54	1.38	1.60	1.33	1.66	1.27	1.72	1.22	1.79
40	1.44	1.54	1.39	1.60	1.34	1.66	1.29	1.72	1.23	1.79
45	1.48	1.57	1.43	1.62	1.38	1.67	1.34	1.72	1.29	1.78
50	1.50	1.59	1.46	1.63	1.42	1.67	1.38	1.72	1.34	1.77
55	1.53	1.60	1.49	1.64	1.45	1.68	1.41	1.72	1.38	1.77
60	1.55	1.62	1.51	1.65	1.48	1.69	1.44	1.73	1.41	1.77
65	1.57	1.63	1.54	1.66	1.50	1.70	1.47	1.73	1.44	1.77
70	1.58	1.64	1.55	1.67	1.52	1.70	1.49	1.74	1.46	1.77
75	1.60	1.65	1.57	1.68	1.54	1.71	1.51	1.74	1.49	1.77
80	1.61	1.66	1.59	1.69	1.56	1.72	1.53	1.74	1.51	1.77
85	1.62	1.67	1.60	1.70	1.57	1.72	1.55	1.75	1.52	1.17
90	1.63	1.68	1.61	1.70	1.59	1.73	1.57	1.75	1.54	1.78
95	1.64	1.69	1.62	1.71	1.60	1.73	1.58	1.75	1.56	1.78
100	1.65	1.69	1.63	1.72	1.61	1.74	1.59	1.76	1.57	1.78

[†]N = number of observations; k = number of explanatory variables (excluding the constant term).

Source: Reprinted with permission from J. Durbin and G. S. Watson, "Testing for Serial Correlation in Least Squares Regression," *Biometrika*, vol. 38, 1951, pp. 159–177.

Appendix E
F-Test Distribution ∝ = .05

Degree of freedom (df) between groups [numerator]

Degree of freedom (df) within groups [denominator]	1	2	3	4	5	6	7	8	9	10	12	15	20	24	30	40	60	120	∞
1	161.4	199.5	215.7	224.6	230.2	234.0	236.8	238.9	240.5	241.9	243.9	245.9	248.0	249.1	250.1	251.1	252.2	253.3	254.3
2	18.51	19.00	19.16	19.25	19.30	19.33	19.35	19.37	19.38	19.40	19.41	19.43	19.45	19.45	19.48	19.47	19.48	19.49	19.50
3	10.13	9.55	9.28	9.12	9.01	8.94	8.89	8.85	8.81	8.79	8.74	8.70	8.66	8.64	8.62	8.59	8.57	8.55	8.53
4	7.71	6.94	6.59	6.39	6.26	6.16	6.09	6.04	6.00	5.96	5.91	5.86	5.80	5.77	5.75	5.72	5.69	5.66	5.63
5	6.61	5.79	5.41	5.19	5.05	4.95	4.88	4.82	4.77	4.74	4.68	4.62	4.56	4.53	4.50	4.46	4.43	4.40	4.36
6	5.99	5.14	4.76	4.53	4.39	4.28	4.21	4.15	4.10	4.06	4.00	3.94	3.87	3.84	3.81	3.77	3.74	3.70	3.67
7	5.59	4.74	4.35	4.12	3.97	3.87	3.79	3.73	3.68	3.64	3.57	3.51	3.44	3.41	3.38	3.34	3.30	3.27	3.23
8	5.32	4.46	4.07	3.84	3.69	3.58	3.50	3.44	3.39	3.35	3.28	3.22	3.15	3.12	3.08	3.04	3.01	2.97	2.93
9	5.12	4.26	3.86	3.63	3.48	3.37	3.29	3.23	3.18	3.14	3.07	3.01	2.94	2.90	2.86	2.83	2.79	2.75	2.71
10	4.96	4.10	3.71	3.48	3.33	3.22	3.14	3.07	3.02	2.98	2.91	2.85	2.77	2.74	2.70	2.66	2.62	2.58	2.54
11	4.84	3.98	3.59	3.36	3.20	3.09	3.01	2.95	2.90	2.85	2.79	2.72	2.65	2.61	2.57	2.53	2.49	2.45	2.40
12	4.75	3.89	3.49	3.26	3.11	3.00	2.91	2.85	2.80	2.75	2.69	2.62	2.54	2.51	2.47	2.43	2.38	2.34	2.30
13	4.67	3.81	3.41	3.18	3.03	2.92	2.83	2.77	2.71	2.67	2.60	2.53	2.46	2.42	2.38	2.34	2.30	2.25	2.21
14	4.60	3.74	3.34	3.11	2.96	2.85	2.76	2.70	2.65	2.60	2.53	2.46	2.39	2.35	2.31	2.27	2.22	2.18	2.13
15	4.54	3.68	3.29	3.06	2.90	2.79	2.71	2.64	2.59	2.54	2.48	2.40	2.33	2.29	2.25	2.20	2.16	2.11	2.07
16	4.49	3.63	3.24	3.01	2.85	2.74	2.66	2.59	2.54	2.49	2.42	2.35	2.28	2.24	2.19	2.15	2.11	2.06	2.01
17	4.45	3.59	3.20	2.96	2.81	2.70	2.61	2.55	2.49	2.45	2.38	2.31	2.23	2.19	2.15	2.10	2.06	2.01	1.96

(continued)

Appendix E Continued
F-Test Distribution ∝ = .05

Degree of freedom (df) between groups [numerator]

Degree of freedom (df) within groups [denominator]	1	2	3	4	5	6	7	8	9	10	12	15	20	24	30	40	60	120	∞
18	4.41	3.55	3.16	2.93	2.77	2.66	2.58	2.51	2.46	2.41	2.34	2.27	2.19	2.15	2.11	2.06	2.02	1.97	1.92
19	4.38	3.52	3.13	2.90	2.74	2.63	2.54	2.48	2.42	2.38	2.31	2.23	2.16	2.11	2.07	2.03	1.98	1.93	1.88
20	4.35	3.49	3.10	2.87	2.71	2.60	2.51	2.45	2.39	2.35	2.28	2.20	2.12	2.08	2.04	1.99	1.95	1.90	1.84
21	4.32	3.47	3.07	2.84	2.68	2.57	2.49	2.42	2.37	2.32	2.25	2.18	2.10	2.05	2.01	1.96	1.92	1.87	1.81
22	4.30	3.44	3.05	2.82	2.66	2.55	2.46	2.40	2.34	2.30	2.23	2.15	2.07	2.03	1.98	1.94	1.89	1.84	1.78
23	4.28	3.42	3.03	2.80	2.64	2.53	2.44	2.37	2.32	2.27	2.20	2.13	2.05	2.01	1.96	1.91	1.86	1.81	1.76
24	4.26	3.40	3.01	2.78	2.62	2.51	2.42	2.36	2.30	2.25	2.18	2.11	2.03	1.98	1.94	1.89	1.84	1.79	1.73
25	4.24	3.39	2.99	2.76	2.60	2.49	2.40	2.34	2.28	2.24	2.16	2.09	2.01	1.96	1.92	1.87	1.82	1.77	1.71
26	4.23	3.37	2.98	2.74	2.59	2.47	2.39	2.32	2.27	2.22	2.15	2.07	1.99	1.95	1.90	1.85	1.80	1.75	1.69
27	4.21	3.35	2.96	2.73	2.57	2.46	2.37	2.31	2.25	2.20	2.13	2.06	1.97	1.93	1.88	1.84	1.79	1.73	1.67
28	4.20	3.34	2.95	2.71	2.56	2.45	2.36	2.29	2.24	2.19	2.12	2.04	1.96	1.91	1.87	1.82	1.77	1.71	1.65
29	4.18	3.33	2.93	2.70	2.55	2.43	2.35	2.28	2.22	2.18	2.10	2.03	1.94	1.90	1.85	1.81	1.75	1.70	1.64
30	4.17	3.32	2.92	2.69	2.53	2.42	2.33	2.27	2.21	2.16	2.09	2.01	1.93	1.89	1.84	1.79	1.74	1.68	1.62
40	4.08	3.23	2.84	2.61	2.45	2.34	2.25	2.18	2.12	2.08	2.00	1.92	1.84	1.79	1.74	1.69	1.64	1.58	1.51
60	4.00	3.15	2.76	2.53	2.37	2.25	2.17	2.10	2.04	1.99	1.92	1.84	1.75	1.70	1.65	1.59	1.53	1.47	1.39
120	3.92	3.07	2.68	2.45	2.29	2.17	2.09	2.02	1.96	1.91	1.83	1.75	1.66	1.61	1.55	1.50	1.43	1.35	1.25
∞	3.84	3.00	2.60	2.37	2.21	2.10	2.01	1.94	1.88	1.83	1.75	1.67	1.57	1.52	1.46	1.39	1.32	1.22	1.00

(continued)

Appendix E   Continued
F-Test Distribution ∝ = .01

Degree of freedom (df) within groups [denominator]	\multicolumn{19}{c}{Degree of freedom (df) between groups [numerator]}

nominator]	1	2	3	4	5	6	7	8	9	10	12	15	20	24	30	40	60	120	∞
1	4052	4999.5	5403	5625	5764	5859	5928	5981	6022	6056	6106	6157	6209	6235	6261	6287	6313	6339	6366
2	98.58	99.00	99.17	99.25	99.30	99.33	99.36	99.37	99.39	99.40	99.42	99.43	99.45	99.46	99.47	99.47	99.48	99.49	99.50
3	34.12	30.82	29.46	28.71	28.24	27.91	27.67	27.49	27.35	27.23	27.05	26.87	26.69	26.60	26.50	26.41	26.32	26.22	26.13
4	21.20	18.00	16.69	15.98	15.52	15.21	14.98	14.80	14.66	14.55	14.37	14.20	14.02	13.93	13.64	13.75	13.65	13.56	13.46
5	16.26	13.27	12.06	11.39	10.97	10.67	10.46	10.29	10.16	10.05	9.89	9.72	9.55	9.47	9.38	9.29	9.20	9.11	9.02
6	13.75	10.92	9.78	9.15	8.75	8.47	8.26	8.10	7.98	7.87	7.72	7.56	7.40	7.31	7.23	7.14	7.06	6.97	6.88
7	12.25	9.55	8.45	7.85	7.46	7.19	6.99	6.84	6.72	6.62	6.47	6.31	6.16	6.07	5.99	5.91	5.82	5.74	5.65
8	11.26	8.65	7.59	7.01	6.63	6.37	6.18	6.03	5.91	5.81	5.67	5.52	5.36	5.28	5.20	5.12	5.03	4.95	4.86
9	10.56	8.02	6.99	6.42	6.06	5.80	5.61	5.47	5.35	5.26	5.11	4.96	4.81	4.73	4.65	4.57	4.48	4.40	4.31
10	10.04	7.56	6.55	5.99	5.64	5.39	5.20	5.06	4.94	4.85	4.71	4.56	4.41	4.33	4.25	4.17	4.08	4.00	3.91
11	9.65	7.21	6.22	5.67	5.32	5.07	4.89	4.74	4.63	4.54	4.40	4.25	4.10	4.02	3.94	3.86	3.78	3.69	3.60
12	9.33	6.93	5.95	5.41	5.06	4.82	4.64	4.50	4.39	4.30	4.16	4.01	3.86	3.78	3.70	3.62	3.54	3.45	3.36
13	9.07	6.70	5.74	5.21	4.86	4.62	4.44	4.30	4.19	4.10	3.96	3.82	3.66	3.59	3.51	3.43	3.34	3.25	3.17
14	8.86	6.51	5.56	5.04	4.69	4.46	4.28	4.14	4.03	3.94	3.80	3.66	3.51	3.43	3.35	3.27	3.18	3.09	3.00
15	8.68	6.36	5.42	4.89	4.56	4.32	4.14	4.00	3.89	3.80	3.67	3.52	3.37	3.29	3.21	3.13	3.05	2.96	2.87
16	8.53	6.23	5.29	4.77	4.44	4.20	4.03	3.89	3.78	3.69	3.55	3.41	3.26	3.18	3.10	3.02	2.93	2.84	2.75
17	8.40	6.11	5.18	4.67	4.34	4.10	3.93	3.79	3.68	3.59	3.46	3.31	3.16	3.08	3.00	2.92	2.83	2.75	2.65
18	8.29	6.01	5.09	4.58	4.25	4.01	3.84	3.71	3.60	3.51	3.37	3.23	3.08	3.00	2.92	2.84	2.75	2.66	2.57
19	8.18	5.93	5.01	4.50	4.17	3.94	3.77	3.63	3.52	3.43	3.30	3.15	3.00	2.92	2.84	2.76	2.67	2.58	2.49

(continued)

Appendix E   Continued
F-Test Distribution ∝ = .01

Degree of freedom (df) within groups [denominator]	Degree of freedom (df) between groups [numerator]																		
	1	2	3	4	5	6	7	8	9	10	12	15	20	24	30	40	60	120	∞
20	8.10	5.85	4.94	4.43	4.10	3.87	3.70	3.56	3.46	3.37	3.23	3.09	2.94	2.86	2.78	2.69	2.61	2.52	2.42
21	8.02	5.78	4.87	4.37	4.04	3.81	3.64	3.51	3.40	3.31	3.17	3.03	2.88	2.80	2.72	2.64	2.55	2.46	2.36
22	7.95	5.72	4.82	4.31	3.99	3.76	3.59	3.45	3.35	3.26	3.12	2.98	2.83	2.75	2.67	2.58	2.50	2.40	2.31
23	7.88	5.66	4.76	4.26	3.94	3.71	3.54	3.41	3.30	3.21	3.07	2.93	2.78	2.70	2.62	2.54	2.45	2.35	2.26
24	7.82	5.61	4.72	4.22	3.90	3.67	3.50	3.36	3.26	3.17	3.03	2.89	2.74	2.66	2.58	2.49	2.40	2.31	2.21
25	7.77	5.57	4.68	4.18	3.85	3.63	3.46	3.32	3.22	3.13	2.99	2.85	2.70	2.62	2.54	2.45	2.36	2.27	2.17
26	7.72	5.53	4.64	4.14	3.82	3.59	3.42	3.29	3.18	3.09	2.96	2.81	2.66	2.58	2.50	2.42	2.33	2.23	2.13
27	7.68	5.49	4.60	4.11	3.78	3.56	3.39	3.26	3.15	3.06	2.93	2.78	2.63	2.55	2.47	2.38	2.29	2.20	2.10
28	7.64	5.45	4.57	4.07	3.75	3.53	3.36	3.23	3.12	3.03	2.90	2.75	2.60	2.52	2.44	2.35	2.26	2.17	2.06
29	7.60	5.42	4.54	4.04	3.73	3.50	3.33	3.20	3.09	3.00	2.87	2.73	2.57	2.49	2.41	2.33	2.23	2.14	2.03
30	7.56	5.39	4.51	4.02	3.70	3.47	3.30	3.17	3.07	2.98	2.84	2.70	2.55	2.47	2.39	2.30	2.21	2.11	2.01
40	7.31	5.18	4.31	3.83	3.51	3.29	3.12	2.99	2.89	2.80	2.66	2.52	2.37	2.29	2.20	2.11	2.02	1.92	1.80
60	7.08	4.98	4.13	3.65	3.34	3.12	2.95	2.82	2.72	2.63	2.50	2.35	2.20	2.12	2.03	1.94	1.84	1.73	1.60
120	6.85	4.79	3.95	3.48	3.17	2.96	2.79	2.66	2.56	2.47	2.34	2.19	2.03	1.95	1.86	1.76	1.66	1.53	1.38
∞	6.63	4.61	3.78	3.32	3.02	2.80	2.64	2.51	2.41	2.32	2.18	2.04	1.88	1.79	1.70	1.59	1.47	1.32	1.00

Source: Adapted from Table II of R. A. Fisher and F. Yates, *Statistical Tables for Biological, Agricultural, and Medical Research*, 6th edition, Longman Group, Ltd., London, 1974. (Previously published by Oliver & Boyd, Ltd., Edinburgh). Used with permission of the authors and publishers.

GLOSSARY

Activities: in the logical model, processes, events, technologies, and actions that a program undertakes, with its resources, to produce results. Examples include the number of police patrols, the number of courses offered, the number of permit applications that have been logged in, and the like. (Chapter 4)

Actors: in data collection, observers who are actively involved in what they observe, for example, through role playing as a program client. (Chapter 5)

Adjusted R-square: a measure of R-square used in multiple regression that controls for the number of independent variables in the model. (Chapter 15)

Administrative data: data generated in the course of managing programs and activities. There are many sources of administrative data, such as activity logs and reports, error logs, inspection and repair reports, work orders, and the like. (Chapter 5)

Alternate hypothesis: the logical opposite of the null hypothesis (see also "null hypothesis"). All possibilities must be accounted for between the null hypothesis and the alternate hypothesis. (Chapter 10)

Analysis of variance (ANOVA): a family of statistical techniques, often used in medicine, psychology, education, agriculture, and other settings in which experiments are common. The text discusses one-way ANOVA as an essential extension of the t-test. (Chapter 13)

Analysis of variance (ANOVA) assumptions: (1) the dependent variable is continuous, and the independent variable is ordinal or nominal, (2) the groups have equal variances, (3) observations are independent, and (4) the variable is normally distributed in each of the groups. (Chapter 13)

Applied research: research whose purpose is to solve practical problems. (Section II introduction)

Areas of ethical concern: see "ethics in research." (Chapter 1)

Associations: relationships that do not define or assume any cause-and-effect relationship between variables. (Chapter 2)

Attributes: the characteristics of a variable, that is, the specific ways in which a variable can vary (for example, the attributes of "gender" are "male" and "female"). (Chapters 2 and 6)

Autocorrelation: in multiple regression, the problem that successive observations are correlated with each other; they are not independent. Autocorrelation is common in time series data and is detected using the Durbin-Watson test statistic. (Chapters 15 and 17)

Autoregressive integrated moving average (ARIMA): an advanced forecasting technique often used for financial forecasting (for example, in stock markets). ARIMA models require users to specify the nature of moving averages, autoregression, and seasonality, and may include independent variables, too. (Chapter 17)

Balanced scorecards: a descriptive focus on, for example, an organization's financial state, customer and stakeholder satisfaction, efficiency and effectiveness of delivery processes, and activities to promote learning and improvement within the organization. (Chapter 4)

Bar charts: graphs that show the frequency of occurrences through stacks; used with categorical (nominal or ordinal) data. (Chapter 7)

Basic research: research whose purpose is to develop new knowledge about phenomena such as problems, events, programs, or policies, and their relationships. (Section II introduction)

Benchmarks: standards against which performance is measured, sometimes adapted from other jurisdictions or organizations to which one aspires. (Chapter 4)

Bivariate analysis: analysis of two variables. (Section III introduction)

Boxplot: graphical device that shows various measures of dispersion that is based on the location of values rather than their values; useful for quickly detecting outliers (Appendix to Chapter 7)

Categorical variables: variables with either ordinal- or nominal-level measurement scales (same as discrete variables). (Chapters 3 and 6)

Causal relationships: relationships that specify cause and effect among variables. (Chapter 2)

Census: a canvassing (for example, a survey or count) of an entire group or population. (Chapter 5)

Central limit theorem: a theory that states that an infinite number of relatively large samples will be normally distributed, regardless of the distribution of the population from which they are drawn. (Chapter 12)

Chi-square: a quantitative measure (test statistic) used to determine whether a relationship exists between two categorical variables. (Chapter 10)

Chi-square test assumptions: (1) variables must be categorical, (2) observations are independent, and (3) all cells must have a minimum of five expected observations. (Chapter 10)

Chi-square with the Yates' continuity correction: an alternative to chi-square to be used when samples sizes are small (see also "Fisher exact test"). (Chapter 11)

Classic, randomized experiment: an experimental design method in which participants are randomly assigned to either a control or an experimental (or study) group to ensure that the only difference between the groups is that one gets the treatment and the other does not. This design attempts to make the logical inference that any differences between the two groups are due to the experimental treatment and not to any other factor. (Chapter 2)

Classification table: in logistic regression, the percentage of corrected predicted observations. (Chapter 16)

Coefficient of determination, R^2: in regression, a statistic whose value is interpreted as the percentage of variation in the dependent variable that is explained by the independent variables. R^2 varies from zero to one and is called a goodness-of-fit measure (see also "adjusted R-square"). (Chapter 14)

Column percentages: in a contingency table, these are the values of data cells that are calculated by dividing each frequency by the column total. (Chapter 8)

Competencies for analysis: managers and analysts should (1) be familiar with data sources, (2) be able to gather their own data, (3) be able to analyze data, (4) effectively communicate results, (5) bring to their analysis the theory and practice of management and policy analysis, and (6) have a sound and strong sense of research ethics. (Chapter 1)

Concepts: abstract ideas that are indirectly observed (measured) through variables (for example, "democracy," "trust"). (Chapter 3)

Conceptualization: the process by which a researcher specifies the various dimensions or meanings of a concept, each of which is to be measured (see also "operationalization"). (Chapter 3)

Confidence interval: the range within which a statistic is expected to fall on repeated sampling; also used to estimate population means from samples. (Chapter 7)

Constant: empirical phenomena that do not vary. (Chapter 2)

Construct validity: a justification or argument pertaining to measurement validity in which an index measure is compared against other (internal) study measures (variables) with which it should be correlated, based on theoretical grounds. (Chapter 3)

Content validity: a justification or argument pertaining to measurement validity that states that variables should encompass the (broad) range of aspects of the concept and its dimensions. (Chapter 3)

Contingency table: a table that shows the relationship between two categorical variables; one variable is shown in rows and the other in columns. (Chapter 8)

Continuous variables: variables with either interval- or ratio-level measurement scales. (Chapters 3 and 6)

Control variables: variables used to detect whether relationships between independent and dependent variables hold up under the presence of alternative, rival explanations for the observed pattern of outcomes. (Chapter 2)

Covariates: in ANOVA, a term used to describe continuous independent variables. (Chapter 13)

Criteria for causality: causation requires both (1) empirical (that is, statistical) correlation and (2) a plausible cause-and-effect argument. (Chapter 2)

Criterion validity: a justification or argument pertaining to measurement validity in which an index measure is compared against another external measure (from other research) with which it should be correlated as based on theoretical grounds. (Chapter 3)

Critical value: the minimum value that a test statistic must be in order to reject the null hypothesis (and thus rule out chance as the cause of a relationship). (Chapter 10)

Cronbach alpha: a measure of the internal consistency (or internal reliability) of variables that make up an index variable. When variables are not highly correlated, analysts should consider whether, perhaps, one or more of the variables measure some other concept. Cronbach alpha values range from 0 to 1, and measures above .70 are thought to be acceptable for any index. (Chapter 3)

Curve estimation: a statistical technique of modeling curve lines that is also used to make forecasts. (Chapter 17)

Data cell: in the context of contingency tables, commonly used to refer to table cells that show the counts or percentages based on the values of the two variables. (Chapter 8)

Data cleaning: the process of identifying and removing reporting and recording errors. (Chapter 5)

Data coding: the process of preparing data (from pen-and-paper surveys or from electronic or other sources) for input into statistical software programs, such as identifying variable names on spreadsheets. (Chapter 5)

Data input: the activity of recording these data in statistical software programs. (Chapter 5)

Degrees of freedom: a statistic used to determine the critical value of test statistics. Different test statistics define degrees of freedom differently. (Chapter 10)

Delphi method: a forecasting method that asks experts to respond anonymously through written surveys using several rounds. (Chapter 4)

Dependent samples: samples in which the selection of one subject affects the selection of other subjects. By convention, the following three situations constitute dependent samples: (1) the before-and-after test scores of subjects in (quasi-) experimental situations (including other repeated measures of subjects), (2) subjects who have been matched (or paired, that is, chosen as having similar characteristics), and (3) the ratings of evaluators. Dependent samples are also called "related" samples. (Chapter 11)

Dependent variables: variables that are affected by other variables (hence, they are dependent on them). (Chapter 2)

Descriptive analysis: provides information about the nature or main features of variables—such as the mean or frequency distribution of a variable. (Chapter 2)

Descriptive statistics: statistics that provide summary information about variables, such as their average, frequency distribution, and other measures. They are used widely; for example, knowing how much pollution is occurring, or the percentage of citizens favoring a program, is often meaningful information that affects public decision making. (Section III introduction)

Direction of a relationship: a positive or negative relationship between two variables. (Chapter 11)

Directional measure: bivariate test statistics whose value varies according to which variable is defined as the dependent variable (for example, Somers' d). (Chapter 11)

Discrete variables: variables with either ordinal- or nominal-level measurement scales (same as categorical variables). (Chapter 3)

Dual purposes of analysis: (1) to further programs and policies, such as by making them more efficient or effective, and (2) to establish factual, objective truths that meet standards of scientific evidence and that hold up under scrutiny. A concern of ethics is that these purposes may come into conflict. (Chapter 1)

Dummy variables: variables with values zero and one, only; used in multiple regression as an approach to including nominal variables as independent variables. (Chapter 15)

Durbin–Watson test statistic: a statistic for detecting autocorrelation. Values of the Durbin-Watson test statistic range from 0 to 4. Values close to 2 indicate the lack of serial correlation; values closer to 0 and 4 indicate serial correlation. Values less than 2 indicate positive serial correlation, whereas values greater than 2 indicate negative serial correlation. (Chapter 17)

Effectiveness: the level of results (outcomes) by input of a program. (Chapter 4)

Efficiency: the unit cost (or input) to produce a good or service. It is calculated as the output or outcomes over inputs, or O/I. An example is student learning outcomes per unit cost of instruction (see also "workload ratio"). (Chapter 4)

Efficiency and effectiveness analysis: an analytical effort that focuses on defining, calculating, and displaying efficiency and effectiveness measures from a dataset. (Chapter 9)

Endogenous variables: in path analysis and other modeling techniques, variables that are affected by other variables in the model. (Chapter 18)

Equity: in performance measurement, a comparison of different population groups or jurisdictions with regard to services and outcomes. (Chapter 4)

Equity analysis: an analytical effort that focuses on showing how program resources, efforts, and outcomes vary across groups. (Chapter 9)

Error term: in regression, the difference between the observed and predicted values of the dependent variable. (Chapter 14)

Error term plot: in multiple regression, a plot of the standardized error term (or residual) against the standardized predicted value of the dependent variable; used to identify outliers. (Chapter 15)

Ethics in research: standards of conduct and behavior in research; some main foci of research ethics are (1) the integrity of purpose, (2) the integrity of the process of analysis and communication, and (3) the integrity of dealing with human subjects see also Table 1.1. (Chapter 1)

Exogenous variables: in path analysis and other modeling techniques, variables that are unaffected by other variables in the model. (Chapter 18)

Expected frequencies: the frequencies that would be expected when no relationship exists between two variables. (Chapter 10)

Experimental design: a study design method that assesses rival hypotheses through the use of control groups. (Chapter 2)

Experts: in data collection, people with credible and typically advanced knowledge about a certain matter. (Chapter 5)

Explanation: in contingency table analysis (elaboration paradigm), the result in which, after adding a control variable, the initial results have been explained away for all levels of the control variable (that is, previously statistically significant results now no longer are). (Appendix to Chapter 10)

Exponential smoothing: in forecasting, a technique that estimates the dependent variables based on their level, trend, and seasonality: $y(t) = f($level, trend, seasonality$)$. (Chapter 17)

Face validity: a justification or argument pertaining to measurement validity that states that the measures used are reasonable, common-sense ways of measuring the underlying concept. (Chapter 3)

Factor analysis: a statistical technique that creates groupings of variables; aids in index construction. (Chapter 18)

Factors: in ANOVA, a term used to describe discrete independent variables. (Chapter 13)

Fence: in boxplots, the value beyond which observations are deemed to be outliers. (Appendix to Chapter 7)

First-order differences: differences between successive observations; used in time series analysis as a strategy to reduce autocorrelation. (Chapter 17)

Fisher exact test: an alternative to chi-square to be used for two-by-two tables and small sample sizes (see also "chi-square with the Yates' continuity correction"). (Chapter 11)

Five steps of hypothesis testing: (1) state the null hypothesis (in Greek letters); (2) choose a statistical test; (3) calculate the test statistic (t.s.) and evaluate test assumptions; (4) look up the critical value (c.v.) of the test; and (5) draw a conclusion: If |t.s.| < c.v., do not reject the null hypothesis. If |t.s.| ≥ c.v., reject the null hypothesis. (Chapter 10)

Focus groups: purposive samples used to generate insights about program services and goals. (Chapter 5)

Forecast: the predicted value of a future observation. Sometimes called a projection or prognosis, forecasting is different from planning. Whereas forecasting discusses what the future will look like, planning provides a normative model of what the future should look like, such as a specific vision for a city or school in the future. (Chapters 4 and 17)

Forecast ratios: a non-regression-based approach to forecasting that make forecasts on the basis of known ratios with other variables. (Chapter 17)

Forecasting with leading indicators: a regression-based approach to forecasting that uses independent variables that are lagged (hence, they are leading indicators). (Chapter 17)

Frequency distributions: describe the range and frequency of a variable's values. (Chapter 7)

Friedman test: a test for dependent samples to determine whether evaluators agree in their rankings relative to each other. (Chapter 11)

Full model specification: an approach whereby analysts seek to account for all of the variables that affect the dependent variable. (Chapter 15)

Gamma: a nonparametric test statistic for two categorical variables. (Chapter 11)

Generalization: in sampling, using a finding about one (smaller) group in order to make an inference about a larger group or an entire population. (Chapter 5)

Global F-test: in ANOVA, a test of no differences among any of the group means in the population. (Chapters 13 and 15) also, in regression, a test that all regression coefficients are statistically insignificant. The alternate hypothesis is that, respectively, at least one of the means or one of the regression coefficients is statistically significant. (Chapters 13)

Goals: the ultimate purposes of a program. (Chapter 4)

Goodman and Kruskal's tau: a nonparametric test statistic for the relationship between two nominal-level variables. (Chapter 11)

Goodness-of-fit test: a test to determine whether two distributions are similar, or whether a distribution is consistent with a stated value. (Chapter 11)

Grand total: the total number of observations in a contingency table. (Chapter 8)

Grouped data: data that have already been grouped in different categories, such as already reported in a table. Analysts sometimes need to calculate statistics from grouped data. (Appendix to Chapter 6)

Guiding principles of scientific research: to be honest, objective, accurate, and complete. Analysts should not hide facts, change data, falsify results, or consider only data that support a favored conclusion. (Chapter 1)

Heterogeneity of variances: when variances of two or more distributions are unequal. In both ANOVA and t-tests, this is a violation of test assumptions (see also "Levene's test"). (Chapter 12)

Heteroscedasticity: in multiple regression, the problem of unequal variances of the error term (see also "multiple regression assumptions"). (Chapter 15)

Histogram: a visual graph that shows the number of observations in each stack or category. (Chapter 7)

Homogeneity of variances: when variances of two or more distributions are equal. Both ANOVA and t-tests have this assumption (see also "Levene's test"). (Chapter 12)

Homogeneous subsets: in ANOVA, subsets in which means are not statistically different (Chapter 13).

Hypothesis: a statement about a relationship that has not yet been empirically assessed. (Chapter 2)

Independent samples: when the selection of one group (or sample) of subjects has no effect on the selection or responses of the other group (or sample) of subjects. Generally, samples are assumed to be independent, unless they meet the criteria for being "dependent" samples. (Chapter 11)

Independent-samples t-test: a t-test for independent samples; commonly used unless the samples meet the criteria of being dependent samples. (Chapter 12)

Independent variables: variables that cause an effect on other variables but are not themselves shaped by other variables (hence, they are independent of other variables). (Chapter 2)

Index variable: a variable that combines the values of other variables into a single indicator or score. (Chapter 3)

Indirect effects: in path analysis, an approach using beta coefficients to calculate the indirect effects of variables in a model. (Chapter 18)

Inputs: resources used by a program to produce its goods and services. Programs use financial, human, organizational, and political resources, not all of which are quantifiable. (Chapter 4)

Interaction effect: in n-way AN(C)OVA, the interaction of two or more independent variables on the dependent variable. (Chapter 13)

Internal reliability: the correlation of the measurement variables that are used for an index (see also "Cronbach alpha"). (Chapter 3)

International Association of Schools and Institutes of Administration (IASIA): organization planning for future accreditation of international programs. (Chapter 1)

Interquartile range: in boxplots, the difference between the first quartile and the third quartile values (also called midspread). (Appendix to Chapter 7)

Interval-level scale: a scale that exhibits both order and distance among categories. For example, someone who has an IQ score of 120 has a score of 20 points higher than someone who has an IQ score of 100 (see also "ratio-level scale"). (Chapters 3 and 6)

Kendall's tau-b: a nonparametric test statistic for the relationship between two categorical variables that have an equal number of categories (i.e., square tables). (Chapter 11)

Kendall's tau-c: a nonparametric test statistic that is also an alternative to chi-square. (Chapters 10 and 11)

Kolmogorov-Smirnov test: a test for the normality of a variable that is used for samples with more than 50 observations. The null hypothesis is that the variable is normally distributed. A problem with this test is that it is sensitive to deviations. See text on determining the normality of distributions. (Chapter 12)

Kruskal-Wallis' H test: a nonparametric test that is an alternative to ANOVA and that can also be used to determine whether evaluators agree in their rankings of subjects. (Chapters 11 and 13)

Kurtosis: a measure of the extent to which data are concentrated in the peak versus the tail of a probability distribution (for example, normal distribution). (Chapter 7)

Lagged variable: used in time series analysis, a variable whose impact on the dependent variable is delayed (for example, x_{t-1}). (Chapter 17)

Layer variable: in a contingency table, a variable that defines the subset of data used for subsequent data tables. (Chapter 8)

Level of statistical significance: the level of probability of being wrong about stating that a relationship exists when in fact it does not (see also "statistical significance"). (Chapter 10)

Levels of measurement: the way in which attributes are related to each other. There are four levels of measurement: nominal, ordinal, interval, and ratio. (Chapter 3)

Levene's test: used in t-tests to test for the homogeneity of variances. SPSS and other software programs provide separate t-tests for homogeneity of variances and heterogeneity of variances, and the Levene's test points analysts to which t-test they should use. (Chapter 12)

Likert scale: a common type of ordinal scale named after Rensis Likert. Responses used on Likert scales come in many variations, such as strongly agree, agree, somewhat agree, don't know, somewhat disagree, disagree, and strongly disagree. (Chapter 3)

Line charts: graphs that show the trend of a variable; used with continuous data. (Chapter 7)

Linearity: in multiple regression, the assumption that independent variables are linearly correlated with the dependent variable. Nonlinearity (such as curvilinearity) is detected through visual inspection of (partial) error term plots. (Chapter 15)

Loading: the percentage of variation explained by each factor in factor analysis. (Chapter 18)

Log likelihood value: in logistic regression, a goodness-of-fit statistic that is analogous to the global F-test in regression. (Chapter 16)

Logic model: a model that defines relationships among resources, activities, outputs, outcomes, and goals. (Chapter 4)

Logistic regression: a regression technique that is used when the dependent variable is dichotomous. (Chapter 16)

Logit: in logistic regression, Z is called the logit, and is defined as $Z = a + b_1x_1 + b_2x_2 + \ldots$. Z is used to calculate the probability of an event occurring, $\text{Prob(event)} = 1/(1 + e^{-Z})$. (Chapter 16)

Main effect: in n-way AN(C)OVA, the effects of each independent variable on the dependent variable. (Chapter 13)

Mann–Whitney test: a nonparametric alternative to the independent-samples t-test. (Chapter 12)

Marginal totals: the row or column totals in a contingency table. (Chapter 8)

McNemar test: a test to determine discrimination (or discrepancy) in outcomes of paired cases; used with dependent samples and small sample sizes. (Chapter 11)

Mean: the sum of a series of observations, divided by the number of observations in the series. Also called the arithmetic mean, it is commonly used to describe the central tendency of variables. (Chapter 6)

Measurement error: inaccurate measurement of the underlying study concept. (Chapter 15)

Measurement validity: the extent to which a measurement measures that which it intends or purports to measure. (Chapter 3)

Measures of central tendency: univariate statistics that provide information about the most typical or average value of a variable (for example, mean, median, mode). (Chapter 6)

Measures of dispersion: univariate statistics that provide information about how the values of a variable are distributed (for example, frequency distribution, standard deviation). (Chapter 7)

Median: defined as the middle value in a series (or array) of values. The median is, by definition, unaffected by a few very large or small values, and the median should always be used when a few very large or very small values affect estimates of the mean. (Chapter 6)

Mode: defined as the most frequent (typical) value(s) of a variable. (Chapter 6)

Multicollinearity: in multiple regression, the problem of two independent variables being correlated to such a high degree that their effects on the dependent variable are indistinguishably similar. Multicollinearity in multiple regression can be detected through the variance inflation factor (VIF) statistic (see also "multiple regression assumptions"). (Chapter 15)

Multiple regression assumptions: (1) no outliers, (2) no multicollinearity, (3) linearity, (4) no heteroscedasticity, (5) no autocorrelation, (6) no specification error, and (7) no measurement error. (Chapter 15)

Nagelkerke R^2: in logistic regression, the percent variance of the dependent variable explained by all of the independent variables in the model. Analogous to R-square in multiple regression. (Chapter 16)

National Association of Schools of Public Affairs and Administration (NASPAA): the accrediting organization for graduate programs in public administration and affairs. The accreditation processes includes compliance with generally worded standards regarding the teaching of quantitative techniques in the curriculum. (Chapter 1)

Negative relationship: a statistical relationship whereby large values of one variable are associated with small values of the other variable and small values of one variable are associated with large values of the other variable. (Chapter 8)

Nominal-level scale: a scale that exhibits no ordering among the categories. For example, the variable "gender" has a nominal scale because there is no ordering among the attributes "men" and "women." Nominal-level scales typically provide the least amount of information relative to other types of scales. (Chapters 3 and 6)

Nomothetic mode of explanation: an approach to analysis whereby researchers try to identify the most important factors affecting a dependent variable. This approach is contrasted with idiographic explanations, which identify all factors affecting a dependent variable. Nomothetic explanations are consistent with the philosophy of seeking complete but parsimonious explanations in science, and they are practically useful because they require data about fewer variables. (Chapter 15)

Nonresponse bias: the extent to which views of nonrespondents differ from those of respondents, thus affecting generalizability from the sample to the population. (Chapter 5)

Normal distribution: the distribution of a variable that resembles the familiar bell-shaped curve. (Chapter 7)

Null hypothesis: a statement that no relationship exists between variables (typical). (Chapter 10)

Null hypothesis of normality: variable is normally distributed, thus the null hypothesis is not rejected. (Chapter 12)

Odds ratio: in logistic regression, the ratio of P(event)/P(no event). The odds ratio shows how much more likely it is that an event will occur than it will not occur. (Chapter 16)

One-sample t-test: tests whether the mean of a single variable is different from a prespecified value (norm). (Chapter 12)

One-tailed t-test: a t-test that is used when analysts have prior knowledge about which group has a larger mean. (Chapter 12)

One-way ANOVA: used for testing the means of a continuous variable across more than two groups. (Chapter 13)

Operationalization: the process of identifying variables that are used for measuring each dimension of a concept. (Chapter 3)

Ordinal-level scale: a scale that exhibits order among categories, though without exact distances between successive categories. For example, assume that we measure anger by whether someone feels irritated, aggravated, or raging mad. Although we can say that "raging mad" is more angry than "aggravated," we cannot say how much more angry "raging mad" is than "aggravated. Hence, there is order among the categories, but no exact distance. (Chapters 3 and 6)

Outcomes: behaviors or conditions as measures of different aspects of program goals. (Chapter 4)

Outliers: values that are unusually (or extremely) small or large relative to other values in one's distribution. Outliers can affect statistics and are often removed when they are deemed to be erroneous or highly atypical values. In multiple regression, outliers are often detected by the size of their residual, using visual inspection of the error term plot or residuals calculated by software programs. (Chapters 7 and 15)

Output and outcome analysis: an analytical effort that focuses on defining, calculating, and displaying output and outcome measures from a dataset. (Chapter 9)

Outputs: the immediate, direct results of program activities. (Chapter 4)

Paired cases: method used to distinguish among similar, dissimilar, and tied pairs to determine direction of relationship. (Chapter 11)

Paired–samples t-test: a t-test for paired samples, such as subjects whose before and after scores are compared. (Chapter 12)

Path analysis: a technique for estimating models with complex, causal relationships among variables. (Chapter 18)

Pearson's correlation coefficient, *r*: a measure of association between two continuous variables, providing information about the significance, direction, and strength of the relationship. (Chapter 14)

Performance analysis: the use of statistics to gain understanding of a program's performance and the factors affecting it. (Chapter 4)

Performance management: activities to ensure that goals are consistently being met in an effective and efficient manner. (Chapter 4)

Performance measurement: a measurement effort for assessing progress toward achievement of program goals, outcomes, and outputs. May result in information about efficiency and effectiveness. (Chapter 4)

Periodicity: in forecasting, systematically fluctuating (or modulating) values that are used for making forecasts. (Chapter 17)

Pie charts: visual representations of data that often help focus on matters of equity; used with categorical variables. (Chapter 7)

Pivot tables: contingency tables that analyze continuous variables, in addition to categorical variables. (Chapter 8)

Policy variables: dummy variables that indicate when the policy has caused an effect; used in regression and time series analysis to estimate the impact of a policy. (Chapter 17)

Positive relationship: a statistical relationship whereby large values of one variable are associated with large values of the other variable and small values of one variable are associated with small values of the other variable. (Chapter 8)

Post-hoc test: in one-way ANOVA, the name given to tests that test all possible group differences and yet maintain the true level of significance. Three popular post-hoc tests are the Tukey, Bonferroni, and Scheffe tests. (Chapter 13)

Practical relevance of relationships: whether the relationship of one variable to another results in large enough changes to be of practical significance; sometimes also called "practical significance," as opposed to "statistical significance." (Chapter 8)

Predicted value of the dependent variable, $\hat{y}$: in regression, that which is calculated from $y = a + b_1X_1 + b_2X_2 + \ldots$ for each observation. (Chapter 14)

Prior moving averages: a non-regression-based approach to forecasting that uses the average of the current preceding observations to predict the following period. The problem with this widely used approach is that it underestimates future values by basing forecasts on the average of the recent past (see also "prior moving changes"). Non-regression-based approaches to forecasting are often used when analysts have few data. (Chapter 17)

Prior moving changes: a non-regression-based approach to forecasting that makes forecasts on the basis of changes in preceding periods. Non-regression-based approaches to forecasting are often used when analysts have few data. (Chapter 17)

Program evaluation: the use of social science research methods to determine whether, and in what ways, a program works. (Chapter 2)

Proportional reduction in error (PRE): the improvement, expressed as a fraction, in predicting a dependent variable due to knowledge of the independent variable (see also "strength of a relationship"). (Chapter 11)

Purpose of hypothesis testing: to determine whether a relationship exists (or, to establish the degree of certainty by which we can say that a relationship exists beyond chance alone). (Chapter 10)

Purposive sampling: a nonrandom sampling method that is used to produce further insight, rather than to generalize to another population. (Chapter 5)

Qualitative research methods: research methods that refer to the collection and analysis of words, symbols, or artifacts that are largely nonstatistical in nature. Such data often are collected through interviews, focus groups, and direct observation. Typically, the purpose of qualitative research is to identify and describe new phenomena. Qualitative research provides a detailed, rich understanding of phenomena but may suffer from a lack of generalizability and quantification. (Section II introduction)

Quality-of-life analysis: an analytical effort that focuses on defining, calculating, and displaying quality-of-life measures of a community as based on a dataset. (Chapter 9)

Quantitative research methods: research methods that involve the collection of data that can be analyzed using statistical methods. Such data typically are collected through surveys or compilations of administrative records, and they produce numbers used to describe the extent of societal problems, to monitor program operations, to determine program efficiency and effectiveness and to analyze by how much they can be improved, and to evaluate the impact of programs. Quantitative methods may suffer from a lack detail provided by qualitative methods. (Section II introduction)

Quasi-experimental designs: comparisons between experimental and comparison groups that do not meet the standard of classic research designs. Quasi-experimental design often lack randomization, baseline measurement and/or comparison group. (Chapter 2)

Random sampling: a sampling method whereby each population member has an equal chance of being selected for the study sample. Random samples are thought to result in representative samples. (Chapter 5)

Ratio-level scale: a scale that exhibits both order and distance among categories. Someone who earns $75,000 per year makes exactly three times that of someone making $25,000. The only difference between interval and ratio scales is that the latter have a true "zero" (for example, income can be zero, but IQ cannot) (see also "interval-level scale"). (Chapters 3 and 6)

Recursive models: models without feedback loops. Path analysis assumes recursive models; when feedback loops are present, then two-stage least squares or structural equation models should be used. (Chapter 18)

Regression-based forecasting: a family of approaches for making forecasts that involve forecasting with leading indicators, curve estimation, exponential smoothing, and ARIMA (autoregressive integrated moving average). (Chapter 17)

Regression coefficient: the slope in a regression line, $b_i = \Delta y_i / \Delta x_i$. (Chapter 14)

Regression coefficients in multiple regression (interpretation of): each of the regression coefficients in multiple regression is interpreted as its effect on the dependent variable, controlled for the effects of all of the other independent variables included in the regression. (Chapter 15)

Regression line: a line that is calculated by the equations $y = a + bX$ in simple regression and $y = a + b_1X_1 + b_2X_2\ldots$ in multiple regression. (Chapter 14)

Relationships: specifications of which variables are related to each other, and the ways in which they are related to each other. (Chapter 2)

Replication: in contingency table analysis (elaboration paradigm), the result in which, after adding a control variable, the initial conclusion about the statistical significance is retained (replicated) for all levels of the control variable. (Appendix to Chapter 10)

Representative sample: a sample that has characteristics similar to those of the population as a whole. (Chapter 5)

Research methodology: the science of methods for investigating phenomena. (Section II introduction)

Rival hypotheses: alternative explanations for observed outcomes. (Chapter 2 and Appendix to Chapter 10)

Robust: a statistical term sometimes used to describe the extent to which test conclusions are unaffected by departures from test assumptions; also used to describe the extent to which study conclusions are unaffected by conditions or study assumptions. (Chapter 12)

Sample: a selection, such as of citizens, from a population or sampling frame. (Chapter 5)

Sample size (and hypothesis testing): most statistical tests are also affected by sample size; it is easier to conclude that statistically significant relationships exist in large datasets than in small ones. (Chapter 10)

Sampling error: the range within which one can be 95 percent certain that the population estimate falls as calculated from the sample statistic. Sampling errors reflect the discrepancy that occurs between sample statistics and population parameters because of random sampling. (Chapter 5)

Sampling frame: a list from which a sample is drawn. The sampling frame of a population is usually not exactly identical to a population because the identities and locations of some population members are unknown. (Chapter 5)

Scale: a collection of attributes used to measure a specific variable. For example, the variable "gender" is commonly measured on a scale defined by the specific attributes "male" and "female." (Chapters 3 and 6)

Scatterplot: a plot of the data points of two continuous variables. (Chapter 14)

Scientific misconduct: the violation of norms about scholarly conduct and ethical behavior in scientific research. Although some norms are codified, other norms exist as unwritten but expected practices. (Chapter 1)

Scientific research: the careful, systematic process of inquiry that leads to the discovery or interpretation of facts, behaviors, and theories. (Chapter 1)

Seasonality: see "periodicity." (Chapter 17)

Secondary data: data used in analysis that were collected for some other purpose, usually by another organization. An extraordinary amount of secondary data are available; however, a limitation of secondary data is that they may not be relevant for one's purpose. (Chapter 5)

Serial correlation: see "autocorrelation." (Chapter 17)

Shapiro-Wilk test: a test for the normality of a variable that is used for samples with less than 50 observations. The null hypothesis is that the variable is normally distributed. A problem with this test is that it is sensitive to deviations. (Chapter 12)

Simple regression assumptions: (1) the relationship between continuous variables is linear, (2) the linear relationship is constant over the range of observations, and (3) the variables are continuous. The last assumption is relaxed in more advanced forms of regression. (Chapter 14)

Six steps of program evaluation: (1) define the activity and goals that are to be evaluated, (2) identify which key relationships will be studied, (3) determine the research design that will be used, (4) define and measure study concepts, (5) collect and analyze the data, and (6) present study findings. (Chapter 2)

Skewness: a measure of whether the peak is centered in the middle of the distribution. (Chapter 7)

Somers' d: a nonparametric test statistic for two categorical variables. (Chapter 11)

Spearman's rank correlation coefficient: a nonparametric alternative to the Pearson's correlation coefficient. (Chapter 14)

Specification error: in multiple regression, the omission of relevant variables and the inclusion of irrelevant ones (see also "multiple regression assumptions"). (Chapter 15)

Stages of proficiency: the stages through which students and managers often progress as they improve their statistical proficiency: "know nothing," journeyman, technocrat, and sophisticated expert. (Chapter 1)

Standard deviation: a measure of variability that is calculated based on the distance (or dispersion) of individual observations from their mean. (Chapter 7)

Standard error of the estimate: a measure of the spread of y values around the regression line; used for predicting values of the dependent variable. (Chapter 14)

Standardized coefficient, β: in multiple regression, defined as the change produced in the dependent variable by a unit of change in the independent variable when both variables are measured in terms of standard deviation units. Beta allows analysts to compare the impact of different independent variables on the dependent variable. (Chapter 15)

Standardized variable: a variable that has been transformed such that its mean is 0 and its standard deviation is 1. (Chapter 7)

Statistical control strategy: an approach to accounting for rival hypotheses by (1) identifying plausible rival hypotheses, (2) collecting data about them, and (3) using statistical techniques to examine their impact on the independent variable under study. (Chapter 2)

Statistical forecasting methods: techniques that use data about the present and past for forecasting the future. (Chapter 17)

Statistical modeling: used to forecast phenomena based on variables that significantly explain the phenomena in the present and past. (Chapter 17)

Statistical power: the probability of wrongfully concluding that a relationship does not exist when in fact it does (Type II error). (Chapter 10)

Statistical relationship: as one variable changes, so too does another. (Chapter 8)

Statistical significance: the probability of being wrong about stating that a relationship exists when in fact it does not exist. The "level of statistical significance" refers to the level of that probability. (Chapter 10)

Statistics: the body of systematic knowledge and practice that provides standards and procedures for correctly analyzing one's data. (Chapter 1)

Stratified sampling: a sampling approach that first divides the sampling frame according to each subpopulation to be surveyed, and then samples within each subgroup. (Chapter 5)

Strength of a relationship (PRE): PRE is a measure of the strength of a relationship. PRE fractions range from 0.00 (no association or improvement in prediction) to 1.00 (perfect association or prediction). Many analysts regard scores of less than 0.25 as indicating a weak association, scores between 0.25 and 0.50 as indicating a moderate association, and scores above 0.50 as indicating a strong association. (Chapter 11)

Student's t-distribution: the distribution of critical values for the t-test. (Chapter 12)

Suppressor effect: in contingency table analysis (elaboration paradigm), the (rather rare) result in which, after adding a control variable, initially insignificant results have become significant for all levels of the control variable. (Appendix to Chapter 10)

Survival analysis: a family of techniques that analyze information about events that is not yet available; uses information about censored events, that is, observations for which the specified outcome has yet to occur. (Chapter 18)

Test of significance of the regression coefficient: a test to determine whether each regression coefficient is significant, hence, testing whether a relationship exists between the independent variable and the dependent variable. (Chapter 14)

Threats to external validity: rival hypotheses that jeopardize the generalizability of study conclusions. (Chapter 2)

Threats to internal validity: rival hypotheses stemming from the study design that jeopardize study conclusions about whether an intervention in fact caused a difference in the study population. (Chapter 2)

Transposing: in a contingency table, interchanging the locations of these variables; column variables become row variables, and vice versa. (Chapter 8)

Trend extrapolation: a statistical forecasting method that uses past trends in order to forecast future periods. (Chapter 17)

Trend variable: used in time series analysis, a variable that records the order in which observations appear (for example, year 1, year 2). (Chapter 17)

T-test: a test statistic for testing whether the means of a continuous variable differ across two different groups. The t-test tests whether the difference of the means of the two groups is statistically different from zero. (Chapter 12)

T-test test assumptions: (1) one variable is continuous, and the other variable is dichotomous; (2) the two distributions have equal variances; (3) the observations are independent; and (4) the two distributions are normally distributed. (Chapter 12)

Two-tailed t-test: tests whether the difference of the means of the two groups is statistically different from zero. (Chapter 12)

Two-way ANOVA: an ANOVA technique that examines the effect of two independent variables on (the means of) a dependent variable. (Chapter 13)

Types of surveys: the text discusses four types of surveys: mail, Internet, phone, and in-person surveys. Table 5.1 lists some advantages and disadvantages of each. (Chapter 5)

Univariate analysis: analysis of a single variable. (Section III introduction)

Uses of analysis and data: data and objective analysis often are used to describe and analyze problems, to describe policies and programs, to monitor progress and prevent fraud, to improve program operations, and to evaluate outcomes. (Chapter 1)

Variable transformation: a procedure whereby a variable's original values are transformed in some way. In t-tests, this is commonly done to make a variable become normally distributed. (Chapter 12)

Variables: empirically observable phenomena that vary (for example, gender or income). (Chapters 2 and 6)

Wald chi-square: in logistic regression, the test statistic used to determine the statistical significance of logistic regression coefficients. This statistic is analogous to the t-test, $b/\text{se}(b)$, in multiple regression. (Chapter 16)

Weighted mean: a mean for which the observations have been given variable weights; sometimes used in the analysis of survey data to correct for under- or over-representation of some groups. (Chapter 6)

Well-being of human subjects: some key ethical principles in research involving people are that their participation should be voluntary and based on informed consent, that information about them should be held confidentially, and that risks of harm to subjects should be minimized and reasonable in relationship to anticipated benefits. (Chapter 1)

Wilcoxon signed rank test: a nonparametric alternative to the paired-samples t-test. (Chapter 12)

Wilcoxon test: a nonparametric alternative to the independent-samples t-test. (Chapter 12)

Workload ratio: the ratio of activities over inputs, or A/I. An example is the number of students taught per teacher. (see text for discussion of the difference between workload ratios and efficiency ratios). (Chapter 4)

Writing tips: gather relevant reports, develop an outline, choose the language carefully, and check the grammar and other details. (Chapter 3)

Z-scores: the transformed values of each observation of a variable that has been standardized. (Chapter 7)

INDEX